"Overmyer's plays are an actor's feast...so open these pages and fill up your plate..."
**Jimmy Smits, actor**

"Thanks to writing skills unequalled among American playwrights, brilliant wordsmith Eric Overmyer transforms all this paranoia into a theatrical witch-hunt titled IN PERPETUITY THROUGHOUT THE UNIVERSE...Overmyer speaks from the heart of the 20th Century."
**Richard Stayton, *Los Angeles Herald Examiner*, 14 October 1988**

"...Overmyer is a dazzling verbal acrobat as well as a serious student of pop culture. Both linguist and cultural anthropologist get a workout here...a darker expedition, probing the fears and prejudices of society. Overmyer makes it a wild unnerving ride."
**Michael Kuchwara, *AP*, 21 June 1988**

"With a handful of plays - NATIVE SPEECH, ON THE VERGE, IN PERPETUITY THROUGHOUT THE UNIVERSE, and now IN A PIG'S VALISE - Eric Overmyer has established himself as one of contemporary theater's wittiest playwrights. Language-besotted as any die-hard cruciverbalist and hip to the self-referential existentialism of postmodern performance, he keeps his intellect in balance with a deep need to entertain; he's a clown with a thesaurus, an incorrigible punster, and a 'prisoner of genre, a captive of kitsch,' like the all-singing, all-dancing, trench-coated gumshoe narrator of IN A PIG'S VALISE...off Broadway hasn't had such a dazzling little musical since LITTLE SHIP OF HORRORS... A pop semiotician like Jean Baudrillard could go to town analyzing the junk-culture-eats-itself imagery of PIG'S VALISE, and that's what makes the play more than a hyperclever goof: underneath the puns and wordplay, it is a metaphysical detective story about the origin of pop-kitsch (a theme throughout Overmyer's work) that treads the same territory as sci-fi renegades William Gibson and Philip K Dick . . ."
**Don Shewey, *7 Days*, 22 February, 1989**

"Forget that 'nimble wordsmith' jive. Nobody's doped out how the culture's fooling with you better than this guy, and his take on failure, vast conspiracies and lust cuts to the fetid heart of the American dream. Can't hurt he's got bounce in his outs, though - or some of the snappiest comebacks going."
**Jeffrey M. Jones, playwright**

# Eric Overmyer *collected plays*

Eric Overmyer was born in Boulder, Colorado, grew up in Seattle, was educated at Reed College in Portland, Oregon, where he received a BA in Theatre, and did graduate work at The Asolo Conservatory, Florida State University, and at Brooklyn College and the City University of New York. He was the Literary Manager of Playwrights Horizons from 1982-84, an Associate Artist of Center Stage, Baltimore from 1984-91, Visiting Associate Professor of Playwriting, Yale School of Drama, 1991-92, Associate Artist Yale Repertory Theatre, 1991-92, and Mentor, Mark Taper Forum Playwriting Workshop, 1992. His most produced play, *On The Verge*, has been performed extensively throughout the United Stages, Canada, the UK, and Australia, and has been translated and performed in Paris and Oslo. *In Perpetuity Throughout The Universe* has been translated into Quebecois, and presented at the CEAD in Montreal. He is the recipient of grants and fellowships from McKnight, the NEA, the New York Foundation For The Arts, the Rockefeller Foundation, and the Le Comte Du Nouy Foundation. He has written extensively for film and television, and is the author of a play for radio, *Kafka's Radio*, produced by WNYC. His other plays include *Mi Vida Loca* and *Don Quixote de La Jolla*. He lives in New York and New Orleans, makes a living in Los Angeles, and is married to actress Ellen McElduff.

**Smith and Kraus** *Books For Actors*

## THE MONOLOGUE SERIES
        The Best Men's Stage Monologues of 1992
        The Best Men's Stage Monologues of 1991
        The Best Men's Stage Monologues of 1990
        The Best Women's Stage Monologues of 1992
        The Best Women's Stage Monologues of 1991
        The Best Women's Stage Monologues of 1990
        One Hundred Men's Stage Monologues from the 1980's
        One Hundred Women's Stage Monologues from the 1980's
        Street Talk: Character Monologues for Actors
        Uptown: Character Monologues for Actors
        Monologues from Contemporary Literature: Volume I
        Monologues from Classic Plays
        Kiss and Tell: The Art of the Restoration Monologue
## FESTIVAL MONOLOGUE SERIES
        The Great Monologues from the Humana Festival
        The Great Monologues from the EST Marathon
        The Great Monologues from the Women's Project
        The Great Monologues from the Mark Taper Forum
## YOUNG ACTORS SERIES
        Great Scenes and Monologues for Children
        New Plays from A.C.T.'s Young Conservatory
        Great Scenes for Young Actors from the Stage
        Great Monologues for Young Actors
## SCENE STUDY SERIES
        The Best Stage Scenes of 1992
        The Best Stage Scenes for Women from the 1980's
        The Best Stage Scenes for Men from the 1980's
## PLAYS FOR ACTORS SERIES
        Seventeen Short Plays by Romulus Linney
        Lanford Wilson: 21 Short Plays
        William Mastrosimone: Collected Plays
        Terrence McNally: Collected Plays
## GREAT TRANSLATION FOR ACTORS SERIES
        The Wood Demon by Anton Chekhov
## OTHER BOOKS IN OUR COLLECTION
        The Actor's Chekhov
        Humana Festival '93: The Collected Plays
        Break A Leg! Daily Inspiration for the Actor
        Women Playwrights: The Best Plays of 1992

If you require pre-publication information about upcoming Smith and Kraus mono-logues collections, scene collections, play anthologies, advanced acting books, and books for young actors, you may receive our semi-annual catalogue, free of charge, by sending your name and address to **Smith and Kraus Catalogue, P.O. Box 10, Newbury, VT 05051.**

# Eric Overmyer *collected plays*

*Plays for Actors Series*

## SK
A Smith and Kraus Book

A Smith and Kraus Book
Published by Smith and Kraus, Inc.
Copyright © 1993 by Smith and Kraus, Inc.
All rights reserved

COVER AND TEXT DESIGN BY JULIA HILL
Manufactured in the United States of America

First Edition: March 1993
10 9 8 7 6 5 4 3 2 1

Overmyer, Eric.
    [Plays.]
    Eric Overmyer : collected plays.--1st ed.
        p. cm. -- (Plays for actors series, ISSN 1067-9510)
        Contents: Native Speech -- On the verge -- In a pig's valise -- In perpetuity throughout the universe -- The heliotrope bouquet by Scott Joplin & Louis Chauvin -- Dark rapture.
        ISBN soft cover 1-880399-33-4  hard cover 1-880399-40-7
        I. Title. II. Series: Plays for actors.
        PS3565.V432A19   1993             93-15915
        812'. 54--dc20                    CIP

*Dedicated to George Lane.*

## Acknowledgments

The author would like to thank the following people for their help and encouragement over the years: Stan Wojewodski, Peter Culman, Kip Gould, Steven Dansky, and George Lane. Also, thanks to Roberta Tichenor, Robert Peterson, Larry Oliver, Paul Berman, and Jackson Phippin. A tip of the brim to my colleagues Rick Dresser, Lee Blessing, Jeff Jones, Len Jenkin, and Mac Wellman for their perseverance and brilliance and conversation. Kisses to Melissa Cooper, and Arnold and Madge Cooper, for their love and support. And last and always, to Ellen McElduff, for burning the pecan tree.

# Contents

# Preface

A painting is the revelation of a discovery, not the culmination of a plan.

*Picasso, paraphrased.*

The resistance to cliche is what distinguishes art from life.

*Kundera, paraphrased.*

I don't speak any English, just American, without tears.

*Elvis Costello*

I have tried to make discoveries in these plays, and I have tried to avoid cliche. A play ought to reveal itself slowly, to an audience and to its author. This takes patience, and contemporary audiences and critics are impatient, used to a diet of instantly recognizable cliche conventions. I want to be surprised in the theatre. I want theatricality in the theatre. I want charged, shaped, and heightened language. An authentic American language for the theatre. No more Anglophilia. I want bravura performance. I want ideas as well as feelings. I want ambiguity and complexity and imagination. I don't want literalness, preaching to the choir, sentiment, political correctness or polemic, easily explainable motivations or naturalistic dialogue or cliche characters. I'm not interested in what the dramaturg James Magruder characterizes as "talking about my problems in your living room plays." I don't want TV on stage. The American theatre is in a parlous state. Our best writers remain underproduced in the regional theatre, as well as in New York. Theatres and critics alike have failed to nurture an audience for new (in the best sense of the word) work, and the climate remains reactionary, mired in naturalism.

Theatre cannot compete with film and television as a popular art form. If it is not to go the way of other antique, hand-made arts and become completely esoteric, it must re-discover its authenticity. As Chiaramonte says in *Theatre In Utopia*, theatre is not elitist, but it *is* for those who love it. I hope these plays are authentically theatrical, written in a real and new American, and I hope those who love theatre will find some pleasure here.

*Eric Overmyer*

# Eric Overmyer *collected plays*

# NATIVE SPEECH
*for Melissa Cooper*

"If he was not as dead as the cold lasagna on which the tomato sauce has begun to darken, I was a Dutchman. The gaudy and, in the absence of blood, inappropriate metaphor actually came to mind at the moment, as a willed ruse to lure me away from panic – the fundamental purpose of most caprices of language, hence the American wisecrack."

*Thomas Berger, Who is Teddy Villanova?*

NATIVE SPEECH received its professional premiere at The Los Angeles Actors Theatre, Bill Bushnell Producing/Artistic Director. The production was directed by John Olon, and produced by Diane White and Adam Leipzig.

The revised version of NATIVE SPEECH was first presented February 14, 1985, at Center Stage, Baltimore, with Stan Wojewodski, Artistic Director; Peter Culman, Managing Director, and the following cast:

| | |
|---|---|
| HUNGRY MOTHER | Kario Salem |
| FREE LANCE | Lorey Hayes |
| BELLY UP | SàMi Chester |
| CHARLIE SAMOA | Khin-Kyaw Maung |
| JOHNNIE SUCROSE | Tzi Ma |
| JIMMY SHILLELAGH | Robert Salas |
| JANIS | Caris Corfman |
| THE MOOK | Samuel L. Jackson |
| HOOVER | Jimmy Smits |
| FREDDY NAVAJO/LOUD SPEAKER | Melinda Mallari |
| CRAZY JOE NAVAJO | Adam Gish |

The production was directed by Paul Berman. Set Design was by Hugh Landwehr; Costumes, Jess Goldstein; Lights, Jim Ingalls, and Sound, Janet Kalas.

## CHARACTERS
(in order of appearance)

Hungry Mother
Loud Speaker (a woman's voice)
Free Lance*
Belly-Up
Charlie Samoa
Johnnie Sucrose (a transvestite)
Jimmy Shillelagh
Janis*
The Mook
Hoover
Freddy Navajo*
Crazy Joe Navajo

*women

*Notes:* Hungry Mother and Janis are white. The Mook and Free Lance are black. They are an impressive, attractive couple: a Renaissance prince and princess. Belly Up is black, middle-aged (somewhat older than Hungry Mother), a large man, an ex-sarge; the outline of his chevrons is still visible on his fatigue jacket. Hoover, Freddy Navajo, Crazy Joe Navajo, Charlie Samoa, Johnny and Jimmy should be played by Asian-American, Hispanic or Native American actors.

Freddy Navajo is a woman. Loud Speaker is an unseen, amplified, *live* voice: one of those ubiquitous, bland women's voices heard in airports, shopping malls, or on the time-of-day recordings.
Johnnie Sucrose is a transvestite, a convincing one. The drag should be accomplished.

The following parts can be doubled: Freddy and Loud Speaker; Jimmy and Crazy Joe.

Except where indicated, Hungry Mother's voice is not amplified during his broadcast monologues. We hear his voice as he hears it, not as it is heard over the radio by his listeners.

## SCENE

Hungry Mother's underground radio station, and the devastated neighborhood which surrounds it.

The studio is constructed from the detritus of Western Civ: appliances, neon tubing, 45s, car parts. Junk.

Outside, a darkening world. Dangerous. The light is blue and chill. Always winter.

# NATIVE SPEECH

**ACT ONE**

*The Studio. Hungry Mother. Red lights blinking in the black.*
*A needle scrapes across a record. A low hum. Hum builds: the*
*Konelrad Civil Defense Signal. Hungry Mother bops with the*
*tone, scats with it. The tone builds, breaks off. Silence. Hungry*
*Mother leans over the mike, says in a so-good-it-hurts voice:*

**HUNGRY MOTHER**   O, that's a hit. Hungry Mother plays the hits, only
the hits. I want some seafood, mama. (*Beat.*) This is your Hungry
Mother here – and you know it.
(*Lights. Hungry Mother is a shambly, disheveled man in his late*
*thirties. The Broadcast Indicator – a blue light bulb on the mike – is*
*"on." And so is Hungry Mother.*)
**HUNGRY MOTHER**   (*Cooool.*) Static. Dead air. Can't beat it. With a
stick. Audio entropy. In-creases ever-y-where. Home to roost. Crack a
six-pack of that ambient sound. (*Beat.*) You've been groovin' and
duckin' to the ever-popular sound of "Air Raid" – by Victor
Chinaman. Moan with the tone. A blast from the past. With vocal
variations by yours truly. The Hungry Mother. (*Beat.*) Hard enough for
you? (*A little more up tempo.*) Hungry Mother here, your argot
argonaut. Stick with us. Solid gold and nothing but. Hungry Mother be
playing the hits, playing them hits, for you, jes' for youuuu . . .
(*Full-out manic now.*) Uh-huh! Into the smokey blue! Comin' at you!
Get out de way! Hungry Mother gonna hammer, gonna glide, gonna
slide, gonna bop, gonna drop, gonna dance dem ariel waves, til he get
to you, yes you! Razzle you, dazzle you, blow you a-way! This one
gonna hammer . . . gonna hammer you blue!
(*Dryly.*) Flatten you like a side of beef, sucker.
(*Mellifluous.*) This is WTWI, it's 7:34, the weather is *dark,* dormant
species are stirring, cold and warm bloods both, muck is up, and I'm
the Hungry Mother. The weather outlook is for continued existential
dread under cloudy skies with scattered low-grade distress. Look out
for the Greenhouse Effect . . . We'll be back, but first – a word about
succulents – (*Beat. Flicks switches.*) We're coming to you live, from
our syncopated phonebooth high above the floating bridge in violation
of *several* natural laws, searching, strolling, and trolling, for the
sweetest music this side of Heaven.
(*Beat. Then:*) Back at you! This is the Hungry Mother, just barely

holding on, at WTWI, the cold-water station with the bird's-eye view, on this beautifully indeterminate morning, bringin' you monster after musical monster. Chuckin' 'em down the pike, humpin' 'em up and over the DMZ, in a never-ending effort to make a dent in that purple purple texture. And right now I've got what you've all been waiting for – Hungry Mother's HAMMER OF THE WEEK! And Mother's Hammer for this week, forty seven with a silver bullet – "Fiberglass Felony Shoes" – something slick – by Hoover *and* the Navajos. (*Friendly.*) And, as always, behind every Mother's Hammer of the Week – there's a human being. And a human interest story. You're probably hip to this already, but I'm gonna lay it on you anyway. Hoover – is a full-blooded, red-blooded *Native American.* One of several in the annals of illustrated American Pop.

(*Slight pause.*) Hoover had a monster a few years back: "Fiberglass Rock" – just a giant on the Res. And elsewhere. That, *mais oui,* was before the tragic accident in which Hoover – ah, I don't know if this is public knowledge – but, o why not grovel in gore? (*Bopping.*) With the fallout from his titanium monster, "Fiberglass Rock," Hoover put something down on a preowned dream, a Pontiac Superchief, drive it *away.* A steal. A *machine.* Four on the floor and three on the tree, a herd of horses under the hood! (*Beat. Solemn.*) Four flats. Cracked axle. Hoover – his heart as big and red as the great outdoors – goes down . . . with a wrench. The Superchief slips the jack – and pins Hoover by his . . . pickin' hand.

(*Beat.*) WIPE OUT!

(*Beat.*) Crushed dem bones to milk.

(*Rising frenzy.*) But now he's back. Back where he belongs! With the aid of a prosthetic device! Back on the charts again! PIONEER OF PATHO-ROCK! (*Slight pause. Then: warm, hip.*) Many happy returns of the day, Hoover, for you and yours.

(*Flicks switches. Mellow.*) The sun is up, *officially,* and all good things, according to the laws of thermodynamics, must come to an end. Join us – tomorrow – for something approaching solitude. WTWI now relents and gives up the ghost of its broadcasting day.

(*He flicks switches. The blue light, the Broadcast Indicator, goes "off." Over the loudspeakers, a woman's voice, live.*)

**LOUD SPEAKER**   Aspects of the Hungry Mother.

**HUNGRY MOTHER**   (*Reading from a book of matches.*) Success
   without college. Train at home. Do not mail matches.

**LOUD SPEAKER**   Hungry Mother hits the streets.

**HUNGRY MOTHER**   (*To Loud Speaker.*) I be gone . . . but I lef' my
   name to carry on.

(*Hungry Mother shuffles into the street. Free Lance approaches. They recognize one another, tense, draw closer. They do a street dance, slow, sexy, dangerous. Freeze. They release. Free Lance slides back and out.)*

**LOUD SPEAKER**  Hungry Mother after hours.

*(Hungry Mother slides into the bar where there is a solitary figure drinking.)*

**HUNGRY MOTHER**  Belly Up.

**BELLY UP**  Say what?

**HUNGRY MOTHER**  Belly Up, it's been a coon's age.

**BELLY UP**  I know you?

**HUNGRY MOTHER**  Think it over.

**BELLY UP**  Buy me a drink.

**HUNGRY MOTHER**  City jail.

**BELLY UP**  Hungry Mother. What it is, Mom, what it is. How's it goin', Home? How goes the suppurating sore?

**HUNGRY MOTHER**  It's coming along. Thank you.

**BELLY UP**  Hungry Mother. Whose tones are legion. Hungry Mother, voice of darkness. Impressario of derangement. Tireless promoter of patho-rock. The man who'll air that wax despair.

**HUNGRY MOTHER**  When no one else will dare.

**BELLY UP**  The quintessential Cassandra. The damn Jonah who hacked his way out of the whale. Hungry Mother, the bleating gurgle of those who've had their throats cut.

**HUNGRY MOTHER**  You give me too much, Belly Up, my boy. It's all air time. Air-waves access, that's what it's all about. I just prop 'em up over the mike and let 'em bleed – gurgle gurgle pop short.

**BELLY UP**  Credit where credit is due.

**HUNGRY MOTHER**  Why, thank you, Brother Belly. It's a comfort to know that, a genuine solid comfort. My cup is filled with joy to know that someone's *really* listening. Why, late at night and on into the dawn, I have my doubts, I surely do. Casting my pearls – over the brink –

**BELLY UP**  *(Picking it up.)* Into the trough. On a wing and a prayer. Before the swine of despond. *(Pause.)* Not so, Hungry Mother, not so; not a bit. Your words hang on the barbed wire of evening, glistering in the urban nether vapors like a diamond choke chain on black satin.

**HUNGRY MOTHER**  Belly Up, you have the gift, you surely do. It's a wonder you don't pursue some purely *metaphorical* calling.

**BELLY UP**  My sentiments precisely. Please indulge me as I continue to flesh out my figure . . . Hungry Mother turns tricks quicker than a dockside hooker hustling her habit. He fences insights, pawns epiphanies. And we redeem those tickets in nasty corners. You the laser wizard. The magnetic pulse. The cardiac arrest. The barbarians have smashed the plate glass window of Western Civ and are running amok in the bargain basement. (*Hungry Mother applauds.*) Thank you. Transistor insights. Diode data. Crystal-tube revelations. That why we dial you in, Mothah.

**HUNGRY MOTHER**   You and who else?

**BELLY UP**   You'd be surprised. (*Pause.*) I got a chopper on the roof.

**HUNGRY MOTHER**   What?

**BELLY UP**   (*Winks and laughs.*) I got a chopper on the roof.

**HUNGRY MOTHER**   (*Beat*) Look, I got a question for you. Say the hoodlums, punks, pervos, perps, feral children, coupon clippers, and all the other bargain basement thrift shoppers, say they skip Housewares. Sporting goods. Electronic lingerie. Junior misses. All the lower floor diversions. And go straight for the suites at the top.

**BELLY UP**   (*Laughs.*) I got a chopper on the roof! Got my own sweet chopper to take me outa this! See? I anticipate your question. Like I anticipate the situation. And the answer. An-ti-cipate. Got to have that getaway hatch, Mother. Got to have it. Even a fool can see what's comin'. (*Slight pause.*) You're *sensitive,* Mother. We can read you like a rectal therm. Any little fluctuation. Fuck Dow Jones. we got the good stuff. (*Slight pause.*) We tune you in, we know when to split. Any little fluc. You our miner's canary, Mother. We hang you out there on the hook and hope you smell the gas in time. You croak – we go.

**HUNGRY MOTHER**   I'll try to give you five.

**BELLY UP**   Man, five is all I ask. My ears are glued.

**HUNGRY MOTHER**   Keep those cards and letters coming. So I know you're still glued.

**BELLY UP**   Don't sweat. As long as you still singing, we still listening. When you on the air, we say "Hosannah!"

**HUNGRY MOTHER**   Say "Hungry," sweetheart.
  (*They toast. Darkness. As Hungry Mother walks back into the studio his amplified voice booms over the PA.*)

**HUNGRY MOTHER**   (*On tape.*) Hoover is crawling back from near annihilation, a mighty mean accident for the little red man –
  (*Sound of car crash.*)
  (*Lights. Hungry Mother freezes at the mike.*)

**LOUD SPEAKER**   Further aspects of the Hungry Mother – re*vealed!* For the very first time – the Hungry Mother in jail!
  (*The jail appears in a flash of light: Charlie Samoa and Johnny and Jimmy. They babble in several languages, cursing. Jail vanishes. Lights up on Hungry Mother. He breaks freeze. Flicks switches, blue light "on."*)

**HUNGRY MOTHER**   (*High speed.*) Career-wise, a mighty mean accident, a tough break for the little red man. We'll be back with the

Prick Hit of the Week – ha, ha, oh – Freudian faux pas – Pick Hit of the Week, "Nuking the Chinks," by Dragon Lady and the Flying Paper Tigers, but first – a word about peccaries . . . Friends – like so many vanishing species, these ugly little critters need your help. A tusk or two, a hoof, a stewpot of glue. It's all over for them, but what about their by-products? (*Dramatic.*) Next week – blue whales and dog food. (*Mellifluous.*) This is WTWI, the station with no visible means of support, this is a weekday, this is the Hungry Mother, blistering the dusk to dawn shift, grinding 'em down and pulling 'em out, monster after effervescent monster. Holocaust warnings are up. They continue to machine-gun survivors outside our studio. And the ozone keeps oozing away! And now – Mother's got what you've all been waiting for – nearly an hour of unrelieved agony! Twilight Desperation News! Brought to you by Universal Antipathy – Universal Antipathy, engendering tensions all over the globe – and by Sorghum – a fast food whose time is ripe ripe ripe! Invest in sorghum futures today! And now the hour's top headlines.

(*Newscaster tones, pounding out a teletype rhythm on a tiny plastic typewriter as he speaks.*)

"Killer Bees from Brazil Drop Texas Rangers in Their Tracks" . . . "Starfish Finish Off Great Barrier Reef" . . . quote, The sky's the limit, endquote . . . "Couple Flees Talking Bear" . . . One last note for you nature lovers: fossil fuels now coat 87% of the known universe. Those slicks are tough. No wonder drycleaning costs an arm and two legs . . . On the international beat, expatriate citizens of the island of Malta are demanding restitution from the community of nations. Malta was mugged early yesterday by two large black countries with hydrogen knuckles . . . it sank without a trace. Shades of Krakatoa. The usual measures to contain the radioactive dusk are being implemented with, as one official so succinctly put it, little or no chance of success. We'll have more this hour on the latest in genetic mutation, both here and abroad but first – late, and leg, breaking sports . . .

(*Hungry Mother pick up a pair of mechanical birds, and winds them into motion: they waddle and squawk.*)

**HUNGRY MOTHER**   (*To the birds.*) You're brilliant and you're blue . . . conjugal bijou babies. Doves of love. Beaks of lazuli, warbles of tin. (*The birds wind down and halt.*)

**HUNGRY MOTHER**   (*Intones.*) Wound down.

(*He eats beans from a can.*)

**HUNGRY MOTHER**   Interlude In Which Beans Are Eaten.

**LOUD SPEAKER**   The authorized autobiography of the Hungry Mother. The truth – with a twist!

**HUNGRY MOTHER**   First . . . lemme say . . . unequivocally – and between bites – that the Hungry Mother was made not born. Not of woman born. Heh heh heh. Puts me up there with the all-time greats, right? I want to be most emphatic about this. The Hungry Mother is – my own creation. Nom de wireless! Home-made man! So fine!

**LOUD SPEAKER**     Hungry scat! Mother doo wop! Fonky Mothah! (*Loudspeaker.*)

**HUNGRY MOTHER**     (*To the mike, sings*)
> Put on your felony shoes
> Put on your felony shoes
> Everybody gonna want you to
> Put on your felony shoes ·
> Come on wit' me
> We gonna cut somethin' loose
> We gonna boost
> Something fine
> And shiny and new
> If you'll jes'
> Put on your felony shoes

**LOUD SPEAKER**     And now – number one with a dum-dum – Mother's Hammer Too Hot To Handle!

**HUNGRY MOTHER**     And now, getting tons of extended hot air play in S and M loading zones and up and down the leather docks from coast to disco coast – the newest from Hoover and the Navajos – parvenu of patho-rock – "Fiberglass Creep and the Rotating Tumors!"
(*He begins teletype noise, and speaks gravely.*) Police today busted a waterfront distillery, arresting twenty-seven adults. The distillery produces a wine brewed from the sores of children, which is quite popular locally and in the contiguous states, and easily available without a prescription. The cops said the kids were kept in cages underneath the piers because, quote, the salt water facilitates the festeration process, end quote. The perpetrators will be arraigned tomorrow on tax evasion charges, and the children, several hundred of them, have been released into the custody of leading lending institutions . . .
(*Upbeat.*) The block buster scoop this solid gold weekend – thousands of citizens roaming the streets in states of bliss-out and fat poisoning. Watch out for those psychoparalytic hallucinations. They can be tricky. Speaking of weather, the outlook through the weekend remains bleak. Our five-day forecast calls for continued historical uneasiness mingled with intermittent bouts of apocalyptic epiphany, and occasional oxygen debt – under cloudy skies. So wear your rubbers . . .
(*Jaunty.*) This has been The Agony News Hour, an exclusive twilight feature of WTWI, with your host, the Hungry Mother. Stay tuned for

"Name My Race," the game guaranteed to offend nearly everyone, brought to you by Ethnic Considerations, dedicated to exacerbating racial tensions through violence – Ethnic Considerations, a hallmark of the Twentieth Century, don't leave home without them. And now it's time once again for *Dear Mother.*
*(He holds a stack of letters impaled on a bowie knife. He plucks off the top letter and reads it in a cheery DJ voice.)*

**HUNGRY MOTHER**   "Dear Mother: My boyfriend has a fishhook in the end of his penis. This makes congress difficult. Even painful. What can I do about it? Signed, Afraid to Swallow." *(He crumples it up and tosses it away.)*

**HUNGRY MOTHER**   Eighty-six that. Prick Hit of the Week. Cranks. Who do they think they're kidding. I'm not just fooling around here. *(Next letter.)*
"Dear Mother: My husband is an unreconstructed Stalinist. He refuses to de-Stalinize, knowing that recantation would expose him as an accomplice to the most heinous crimes of this vile century. This ideological rift has been the recrudescent cause of numerous domestic conflicts and, I believe, threatens the dialectic of our marriage. Just yesterday I suggested opening bilateral summit talks on the question of rehabilitating Trotsky for the family shrine of revolutionary heroes, and he broke my jaw. Dear Mother, for the sake of the children, what do you suggest? Signed, Just a Bourgeois Social Fascist At Heart." *(Slight pause.)* Dear Just a Bourgeois: I suggest a fight to the death with needle-nosed pliers. *(He tears it up.)* What's happening to the language? It's scary, Jim. The Great Nuance Crisis is upon us. One last letter for this fiscal year.
*(A cheery DJ voice.)* "Dear Mother: I listen to you every night. You are a great comfort to me. I don't know what I'd do without you. Please help me, Mother. It hurts so bad I can barely talk. Signed, Desperate." *(Slight pause.)* Dear Desperate . . . For once I'm at a loss for words. *(Slight pause.)* Perhaps you've mistaken me for you natural mother. I'm nobody's mama, sweetheart. *(Slight pause.)* Dear Desperate, I can't help you – if you don't give me something more to go on. Who are you, where, and what's troubling you, Bunky. Please try and nail it down a little closer, dear . . . Friends, got an esoteric problem? Send it to Mother and he'll devour it for you. And now it's time once again for – *The Big Dose, A Taste Of Things To Come,* when the Mother lets you in on what it's really gonna be like once the rude boys start playing for keeps. So here it is, tonight, at no extra charge, Hungry Mother brings you more than two hours of – dead air. Enjoy.
*(Flicks switches. Blue light "off." Shrugs into an overcoat and goes into the street. Encounters Free Lance. They do their dance, as before.*

*Freeze. Slight pause.*)

**LOUD SPEAKER**   Hungry Mother – Street Solo!

(*He runs downstage scatting some "theme" music. At the appropriate moment:*)

**LOUD SPEAKER**   And now! Heeeeeeeere's . . . HUNGRY!!

**HUNGRY MOTHER**   (*Bopping.*) Could be Japanese! . . .Genetic . . . engineering! Charnel – numbah— five! *Smoke!* (*Changing gears.*) Friends . . . let's have a chat. Heart to heart. Would Mother hand you a bum steer? . . . As you know, the suggested agenda topic for today's luncheon is . . . Why Do De Gu'mint Be De Boz Ob De Scag Trade, or . . . Methadone – Magic or Madness? . . . But I, uh, I have something of more immediate import to . . . impart. (*Slight pause.*) Friends . . . let's talk about . . . *crude drugs.*

(*Clears throat.*) Brothers and sisters, I was down at the Hotel Abyss the other day, down at that old Hotel Abyss, when I chance to run into an old old friend of mine. A legend in his own time. A man who knows the score. Who never lets the sun get in his eyes. A man with no holes in his cosmic glove . . . I am speakin' of course about . . . Cocaine Ricky. (*Slight pause.*) Your friend and mine. (*Slight pause.*) Brothers and sisters, Cocaine Ricky tell me there be some mighty cold stuff goin' 'round out there, and I just want you to watch it. Very very cold. Ice cold. Dude be pushin', be pushin' it as snow. You know? Snow fall. Snow job. Snow blind. Snow go. (*Slight pause.*) Ain't snow. It's *Lance.* Lance. (*Slight pause.*) Instant death. (*Slight pause.*) Powdered nerve gas. (*Slight pause.*) Government issue. Sooo cooold. Huh!

(*Hungry Mother and Free Lance enter the studio. She is dressed to street-kill.*)

**FREE LANCE**   This place look like a Cargo Cult beach head. You always had a knack for dives, Mother.

**HUNGRY MOTHER**   Thank you very much.

**FREE LANCE**   I don't truck with the radio much. It doesn't occur to me. It's not one of my . . . habits. I don't have time for media. What I'm saying is – I haven't caught your show.

**HUNGRY MOTHER**   Fuck you very much.

**FREE LANCE**   Don't be bitter.

**HUNGRY MOTHER**   Where you live dese days, honey chile?

**FREE LANCE**   On the docks.

**HUNGRY MOTHER**   Couldn't cotch me down dere, anyways.

**FREE LANCE**   Armegeddon Arms. Condos de rigueur. Sing Sing singles. Know them?

**HUNGRY MOTHER**   No, but I know the neighborhood. Intimately. Whatchew dew down dere, woman? You ain't involved with dem child distellers, is you?

**FREE LANCE**   I don't believe so. Not to my knowledge. It hasn't come to my attention. You ought to come visit me, Mother.

**HUNGRY MOTHER**   I should, it's true.

**FREE LANCE**   It's much nicer than this, really. Chrome furniture. It'd be a change.

**HUNGRY MOTHER**   I don't get out much. Don't leave the 'hood. I'm cooped.

**FREE LANCE**   Cooped.

**HUNGRY MOTHER**   Up.

**FREE LANCE**   It's very outre, you know. Swank and chic in the nastier neighborhoods. I just crave the danger. It's narcotic. And there's really nothing to worry about. The building itself is just the best. Impregnable. White boys from Missoura.

**HUNGRY MOTHER**   I can appreciate that.

**FREE LANCE**   Eliminates the Fifth Column spectre. My parents *never* hired black servants. No mammies for me. Don't tell me about race loyalty. When push comes to shove, I mean. Save on silver, too. And being near the water gives me a warm warm feeling.

**HUNGRY MOTHER**   For a quick and hasty exit.

**FREE LANCE**   When the time comes. We've made the arrangements. There won't be any trouble. When the time comes.

**HUNGRY MOTHER**   You'll take some casualties, of course.

**FREE LANCE**   When the time comes. Probably. Of course. One learns to live with one's losses.

**HUNGRY MOTHER**   Don't one? That reminds me.

(*He flicks switches: blue light "on."* )

**HUNGRY MOTHER**   (*Red hot.*) Back at you, sports, this is *the* Hungry Momma, the one and only, the original Hungry Momma, accept no substitutes, coming at you out of the blue-black on this elusive weekday ay-em in a possibly transitional stage in the floodtide of human affairs. Let the historians decide. You've been listening – to more than two hours *of – dead air*. C'est frommage. The time just got away from me there, mon cher. We'll be phasing out our broadcasting day with vanishing species animal noises, what a hoot. And we'll finish off with a new one, got it in the mail today, from the purveyors of patho-rock, Hoover and the Navajos, their latest – "Fiberglass Repairman"! (*Sings a slow blues, keeping the beat with handslams.*)

**HUNGRY MOTHER**   (*Sings.*)

> I'll insulate yo' home
> I'll fibreglass yo' phone
> An' I'll Navajogate
> The little woman
> Befo' yo'

Back is turned.

(*Low key.*) Just breaks my goddamn heart. Sayonara, kids. I'll be back later in the week at my regularly unscheduled time. So – keep dialing and keep *hoping*. This is the Hungry Mother, the man who put the *hun* back in hungry, reminding you to stay cool, take it light, and *say* – *Hungry!* (*Slight pause, then cool and bureaucratic.*) WTWI has now pissed away/Its broadcasting day. (*Hungry Mother switches the blue light "off."*)

**FREE LANCE**   I'm surprised you don't lose your license.

**HUNGRY MOTHER**   Tell you the secret of my success. Nobody hears me. This tube gear eats it. Raw. I got a radius range of under a mile. Barely covers one police precinct. I'm very proud of my precinct. It ain't much, but it's home. I pledge allegiance to my precinct . . . Nobody lives up here. 'S all bomb-outs. Gutted projects. Arsonated rubble.

**FREE LANCE**   Listener response?

**HUNGRY MOTHER**   Rubble don't write a lot of post cards. The junkies call me sometimes. *Hit* Line requests. Sugar Bear and Oz. They call on their anniversary. Four years, a mutual monkey. Many happy returns of the day. Born to junk. Scrapin' along and strung far-out on meth-a-done. Sugar Bear and Oz, this is the hit, this is the one, to which you first shot each other up and fell in love, oh so long ago. Sugar Bear and Oz, up on the roof, this one's for you. So slick.

**FREE LANCE**   (*Laughs.*) One hears stories.

**HUNGRY MOTHER**   It's been known to happen.

**FREE LANCE**   About you, dear. One hears them. In the air. Snatches. All over. Faceless celeb. You ought to take precautions. You have more listeners than you think. Than you might imagine.

**HUNGRY MOTHER**   Funny you should say that. I have been getting more letters. Got one today, it was a mistake. She mistook me. It's a serious letter.

**FREE LANCE**   Aren't they all?

**HUNGRY MOTHER**   Just crazy. This one was crazy, too. But serious.

**FREE LANCE**   What are you going to do about it?

**HUNGRY MOTHER**   What can you do about it?

**FREE LANCE**   Respond.

(*Pause.*)

**HUNGRY MOTHER**   She wants help.

**FREE LANCE**   Then help her.

**HUNGRY MOTHER**   How?

(*Pause.*)

**FREE LANCE**   I've changed my name.

**HUNGRY MOTHER**   Ah.

**FREE LANCE**   I've *altered* it.

**HUNGRY MOTHER**   I remember. You were into brand names. Rumor had it.

**FREE LANCE**   Generic. Not brand, generic.

**HUNGRY MOTHER**   "Polish Vodka."

**FREE LANCE**   Very tasty. I was all over the society pages. But I gave it up when I left the Agency. It's Free Lance now.

**HUNGRY MOTHER:** Oooo. Evocative. (*Slight pause.*) I prefer Polish Vodka.

(*Pause.*)

**FREE LANCE**   If wishes were horses,

(*Pause.*)

**HUNGRY MOTHER**   If the river was whiskey,

**FREE LANCE**   You've always been the Hungry Mother. Ever since I've known you. (*Pause.*) I work for the Mook now.

**HUNGRY MOTHER**   The Mook. Oh my.

**FREE LANCE**   Again. That's how I heard about you. That's how I tracked you down.

**HUNGRY MOTHER**   The Mook? Listens to me?

**FREE LANCE**   Faithfully.

**HUNGRY MOTHER**   It's almost an honor. In a patho-spastic sort of way.

**FREE LANCE**   He told me you were back on the air.

**HUNGRY MOTHER**   I'll have to upgrade my shit. Can't have no cut-rate shit if the Mook's tuned in.

**FREE LANCE**   You ought to be more careful. The Mook's worried about your license.

(*Slight pause.*)

**HUNGRY MOTHER**   I don't have no license. And I'd bet my momma he knows that. His momma, too. How's his reception? Where's he based?

**FREE LANCE**   He *floats.*

(*Pause.*)

**HUNGRY MOTHER**   Why'd you go back?

**FREE LANCE**   Oh, honey. (*Laughs.*) Oh honey. I'd drink his bathwater. (*Beat.*) I did super at the Agency. It was dull, darling. Dull as crushed rock. For them. On my own, it's a breeze. *Free Lance.* Don't you just dig the shit out of it? (*Pause. Cool smile; sardonic.*) I *love* the way he beats me, Mother. Swell hands. Something of a setback for personal liberation, right Mother? (*Pause.*) I tried to cut him loose.

**HUNGRY MOTHER**   You sure you're not involved with those kids? Ask Mook.

**FREE LANCE**   Mook doesn't do kids. You're very tender, Mother, but I could never count on you. Maybe after the revolution.

**HUNGRY MOTHER**   Right. The coup d'etat will make us straight . . . Thanks for stopping by, uh, Free Lance. Always nice to see you.

**FREE LANCE**   You, too, Mother. Like old times. Good, yes?

**HUNGRY MOTHER**   Absolutely golden. Better than a poke in the eye with a sharp stick. The best of them.

**FREE LANCE**   Don't become a stranger, Mother. *(She drifts into the street.)*

*(Hungry Mother switches blue light "on.")*

**HUNGRY MOTHER**   And now a word from one of our sponsors. The Bantustan Shooting Gallery's One Hundred and Sixth Street Branch will be open twenty-four hours a day throughout the holiday weekend for your intravenous entertainment. They're stocking up on your favorite brands of smack, so get your shit together and get on over to One Hundred and Sixth Street now. They're running a special on Spearchucker, got a brand new batch of Black on Black, the ever-popular Pussy Whipped is always on hand, and, fresh off the boat, while it lasts, that perennial Bantustan favorite, White Flight. And the one thousandth customer this holiday weekend will receive, free of extenuating circumstances, a red-hot two-tone maroon Jew Canoe with fresh plates, plenty of mirror surface, and brand new Cuban credit card with sanitary nozzle. That's this weekend at the Bantustan One Hundred and Sixth Street Shooting Gallery – *rush* on over.

*(He turns the blue light off. Shrugs into his coat.)*

**LOUD SPEAKER**   A walk – on the wild side.

*(Hungry Mother hits the street, and slides into the bar. Belly Up is drinking alone. He's wearing his old sergeant's fatigue jacket, the shadow of the chevrons still visible on the sleeve.)*

**BELLY UP**   You're taking off like a target-seeking, heat-sensitive, laser-directed, anti-personnel device. Stuffed with shrapnel. *Plastic* shrapnel. *(Laughs.)* Cluster bomb, Mom. Cluster bomb! *(Slight pause.)* Plastic shrap don't X-ray. That's the holy beauty of it. X-rays can't cope. Can't lo-cate it. Can't dig it out. *(Slight pause.)* Cluster fuck. *(Slight pause.)* Hungry Mother, the voice of the voiceless, the articulator of the ineffable, the thing that goes bump in the night. I never miss a show.

**HUNGRY MOTHER**   I wish I could say the same.

**BELLY UP**   You're getting better. More conscientious. Know what I saw? In a window? A record. By Hoover and the Navajos.

*(Long pause.)*

**HUNGRY MOTHER**   Outstanding. *(Pause.)* Was there a picture? What'd they look like?

**BELLY UP**   No picture. Crazy thing. It came in a fiberglass dust jacket. I got that shit up my ass. It burns like hell. Gets into every nook and cranny. Fibers. They're far out. They're a far-out group. Insulation. Navajogation. Kills me. This – ?

**HUNGRY MOTHER**   Patho-rock.

**BELLY UP**   Knocks my socks off. I love it. Better than mime for the blind. Heaps better. "Fiberglass Finger Fuck!" "Fiberglass Felony Shoes!" "Carcinogenic Concierge!" Can you dig it? Blows me away. You ought to have them on the show.

**HUNGRY MOTHER**   Don't bug me, Belly Up. I just get this stuff in the mail.

**BELLY UP**   From the record company.

**HUNGRY MOTHER**   From *nobody*. It just floats in on the tide.

**BELLY UP**   You're gonna break 'em, Mother. You're gonna break 'em big. When I saw them in a store I was *fiberglassted*. Heh heh. I had no idea they were for real. I thought you . . . created them, you know? The holy power of PR.

**HUNGRY MOTHER**   So did I. In a way, I mean. As far as I know, I don't know if there really is a "Hoover and."

**BELLY UP**   I purchased it.

**HUNGRY MOTHER**   LP or single?

**BELLY UP**   LP. A botanica. Voodoo boutique. Haitian herb shop. I was on the prowl for a pack of mojo and a slice of John the Conqueroo. Saw it in amongst the loas and the gris-gris.

**HUNGRY MOTHER**   That's a good sign. That's encouraging. Those places are more underground than I am. Maybe we can nip this in the bud. I'd hate for it to get out of hand. I never intended to inflict Hoover and the Navajos on general public. Something like this. A trend.

**BELLY UP**   Maybe they're ready for it. Look at it this way – Hungry Mother, hit maker!

**HUNGRY MOTHER**   Right. Just another top-forty jock. Sounds good. I want it. I need it. I want to have impact . . . I'm a fucking artist, man. I want to be taken seriously.

**BELLY UP**   To which end?

**HUNGRY MOTHER**   The bitter end, natch. Tell me, Belly, to what do you attribute my sudden surge of popularity?

**BELLY UP**   To the fact you're coming in loud and clear. Everywhere I go, Hungry Mother, that's who folks be talkin' bout.

**HUNGRY MOTHER**   Where do you go?

**BELLY UP**   Dark places. Places that slide. Places that glide. Places that aren't quite solid underfoot. You're becoming very big on the fringes. Amongst the rubble. Don't be downcast. You're articulating a definite need.

**HUNGRY MOTHER**   Don't think I'm not grateful. I like it. I love it.

Here I thought I was only reaching my local rubble, and now you tell me I'm a smash in the rubble all over town.

**BELLY UP**   An idea whose time has come.

**HUNGRY MOTHER**   It's a heavy responsibility. Walk me home, Belly Up.

**BELLY UP**   Sorry. Not at this hour. I don't leave the bar.

**HUNGRY MOTHER**   What are you afraid of?

(*Pause.*)

**BELLY UP**   Get your hungry ass over here on time, I'll give you a lift. (*Beat*) Back to the World.

**HUNGRY MOTHER**   I hear you. (*Beat.*) I hear you (*Beat.*) Belly Up, I keep getting these letters.

(*The bar fades. Hungry Mother on the streets.*)

**LOUD SPEAKER**   Aspects of the Hungry Mother. The Hungry Mother in Jail.

(*The jail scene appears: Charlie Samoa, and Johnnie and Jimmy in silhouette, cursing in polyglot.*)

**HUNGRY MOTHER**   This is a flashback. A reprise. I don't think I care for this right now.

**LOUD SPEAKER**   Manana, manana. You're just postponing the inevitable. It's on the playlist, baby. This is a very *tight* playlist.

**HUNGRY MOTHER**   Maybe later. How about? I want a reprieve from this reprise.

**LOUD SPEAKER**   (*Miffed.*) You're just postponing the sooner or later, babe.

**HUNGRY MOTHER**   Fuck off.

(*Jail fades. Hungry Mother runs into the studio. He flicks the blue light "on."*)

**HUNGRY MOTHER**   Dead air redux! Those acid flashbacks are murder! Hey! This be your happy, hopping and high-speed Hungry Mother – doin' it to you before you can do it to yourself. Our special this hour, Hungry Mother's Horoscope – a penetrating peek at the Big Zee. So stick around and watch the Mother scope it and dope it – just for you. Also on the bill this o-bliterated amorphous morn – broken glass . . . and Hungry Mother's Consumer Guide to Junk, where to score and what to pay, where to shoot and what to say, all the places and all the pushers, why not have the best possible habit in this, the Best, of all possible worlds? But first – this hour's top headlines. (*Teletype sound and newscaster voice.*) That illegal cordial made from kid pus is still circulating. Several deaths have been reported . . . More mastodon sightings in the North Cascades . . . Wolves in the outlying districts – if you're walking in the suburbs this morning, remember – Wolf Warnings are up. Pedestrians are advised to travel in packs and exercise the usual precautions . . . We'll be back after something brief. This is WTWI, and this is the Hungry Mother, live – if you call this living, from our Twilight Studios. Remember to say, "Hungry!" And now, another interminable episode of "Sexual Shadow Land," the show that's sweeping the station.

*(Rod Serling:* ) His was an ordinary fetish – with a difference – *(Phone rings.)* I'll get it. *(Flicks switches.)* You're on the air! Hey there!

**JANIS** *(Live, over PA)* Hello? *(Hello? hello?)*

**HUNGRY MOTHER** Turn down your radio! Please! Turn it down!

**JANIS** What? *(What? what?)*

**HUNGRY MOTHER** Turn that radio down! Turn it down! You're on the air! Trust me!

**JANIS** Okay! *(Okay! Okay!)*

*( When Janis next speaks, the echo and feedback are gone.)*

**JANIS** Better?

**HUNGRY MOTHER** Much! I'd starve on feedback. What can Mother do for you? What can you do for Mother?

**JANIS** Oh, Mother, I know. I listen to you all the time. I sit by the radio. I wait. I don't want to miss you. I hardly go out anymore. I don't.

**HUNGRY MOTHER** You sound like a fan.

**JANIS** Believe me, I am . . . I am. I don't go out anyway. But – I am. A fan. It's a comfort.

*(Pause.)*

**HUNGRY MOTHER** Yes? Was there something else? You're killing my air.

**JANIS** My name is Janis, Mother. I'd like to see you. You don't know me. I'm a stranger. We've never met.

**HUNGRY MOTHER** Sure. C'mon up.

*(Slight pause.)*

**JANIS** This is serious. I want to meet you. *(Slight pause.)* Mother. I really need to see you. Please . . . Can you tell me how to get there?

**HUNGRY MOTHER** Sure. Ah, it's One Marauder Avenue, just past Faghag Park. Always hungry to have visitors in the studio, little lady. *(He hangs up. Looks pointedly at the "on" blue light.)*

**HUNGRY MOTHER** Whatever happens. Hang loose. Go with the flow. Lean with the scene. Strive with the jive. Fuck it.

*(The Jail scene appears. Hungry Mother walks into it. The trio regards him ravenously.)*

**CHARLIE SAMOA** My name is Charlie Samoa.

**HUNGRY MOTHER** Right away.

**CHARLIE SAMOA** And these are . . . the Samoans. *(Indicating the transvestites.)* Johnnie Sucrose – take a bow, sweetie – and Jimmy

Shillelagh.
**HUNGRY MOTHER**   Charmed, I'm sure. My name is . . . uh, professionally I'm known as, uh, a.k.a. –
**CHARLIE SAMOA**   We know who you are –
**JOHNNIE SUCROSE**   There's no need to shit us –
**JIMMY SHELLELAGH**   We never miss a show –
**JOHNNIE SUCROSE**   We'd know the golden tones anywhere. We're big big fans of yours.
**CHARLIE SAMOA**   But we got a question. The question is – what are you doing here?
**JOHNNIE SUCROSE**   Not that we mind, you understand –
**JIMMY SHILLELAGH**   Not that we're not thrilled –
**CHARLIE SAMOA**   Even honored –
**JOHNNIE SUCROSE**   But it comes as something of a shock –
**JIMMY SHILLELAGH**   To say the least.
**CHARLIE SAMOA**   We hope it does not have to do with your superb radio show –
**JOHNNIE SUCROSE**   Of which we never miss a single segment –
**JIMMY SHELLELAGH**   At considerable risk to ourselves in view of the multiple restrictions pertaining to the use of, access to, and ownership of tube gear and ghetto blasters in this, ah, ah –
**JOHNNIE SUCROSE**   *Penal* institution.
**CHARLIE and JIMMY**   Yeah.
**HUNGRY MOTHER**   You guys are desatively bonnaroo. A matched set. Siamese triplets, joined at the mouth. I predict a great future for you, should you consider it. Give me a call when you get out.
(*Pause.*)
**CHARLIE SAMOA**   Answer the question.
**JOHNNIE SUCROSE**   It behooves me.
**JIMMY SHILLELAGH**   Believe me.
**CHARLIE SAMOA**   Believe him.
(*Pause.*)
**HUNGRY MOTHER**   Criminal mischief . . . I . . . mmm . . . I shattered a subway window. (*Slight pause.*) With a golf club.
(*Pause.*)
**CHARLIE SAMOA**   *Why?*
**HUNGRY MOTHER**   I was . . . *sore.*
(*Pause.*)
**JOHNNIE SUCROSE**   How many strokes?
**HUNGRY MOTHER**   Just one. (*Slight pause.*) Nine iron.
**JIMMY SHILLELAGH**   Good choice.
(*Pause.*)
**CHARLIE SAMOA**   Penny ante, Mother, strictly penny ante.

**JOHNNIE SUCROSE**   We are very disappointed.

**JIMMY SHILLELAGH**   Although at the same time greatly relieved that this does not have to do with your illegal yet highly entertaining radio program.

**HUNGRY MOTHER**   Oh, no. Not on your sweet. It's not illegal, anyway. *Para-legal.* I've never had any trouble. Nobody listens.

**CHARLIE SAMOA**   We do.

**JOHNNIE SUCROSE**   We're interested –

**JIMMY SHELLELAGH**   We're concerned –

**CHARLIE SAMOA**   We're anxiety ridden.

**JOHNNIE SUCROSE**   You don't have a license.

**HUNGRY MOTHER**   What a bitch. They license every goddamn thing in this goddamn city. You need a license to change a light bulb and a permit to take a piss.

**CHARLIE SAMOA**   Good thing, too. Where would we be without social order? You got to maintain it.

**JOHNNIE SUCROSE**   Very impor-*tant.*

**JIMMY SHILLELAGH**   Somebody's got to do it. Gotta have that social scheme.

**CHARLIE SAMOA**   A modicum of status quo.

**JIMMY SHILLELAGH**   To go along with a lot of expensive tube gear and no visible means of support.

**JOHNNIE SUCROSE**   And no license.

**HUNGRY MOTHER**   Very acute. Ah . . . where do you get your dope on me?

**CHARLIE SAMOA**   We asked around.

**JIMMY SHILLELAGH**   We checked the score.

**JOHNNIE SUCROSE**   We heard it through the grapevine.

*(The Samoans laugh raucously, then subside.)*

**HUNGRY MOTHER**   And that's how you come to be such . . . fans.

**CHARLIE SAMOA**   Thereby hangs a tale. It begins with a grudge. As most tales do. I was freelancin'. That's my thing. A little liaison. A middle-man shuffle 'tween U.S. Guv Intelligence cats and a certain Kuomingtang warlord. Local scag baron . . . Am I boring you? Got a minute?

**HUNGRY MOTHER**   Not at all. I mean certainly, yes, most certainly, I do.

**CHARLIE SAMOA**   Where am I?

**JOHNNIE SUCROSE**   *(Suggestively.)* The Golden Triangle.

**JIMMY SHILLELAGH**   Enmeshed in webs. High intrigue.

**JOHNNIE SUCROSE**   Boo-Coo bucks.

**JIMMY SHILLELAGH**   So fine.

**JOHNNIE SUCROSE**   *Sweet.*

**CHARLIE SAMOA**  Put a lid on it. Oh, by the way, Mother, your junk reports are . . . very helpful – somewhat fanciful – but very informational in a metaphorical sort of way. We're grateful, Mother. Say thank you, boys and girls.

**JOHNNIE** and **JIMMY**  Thank you, Mother.

(*Long pause.*)

**HUNGRY MOTHER**  You're not supposed to take that . . . (*Pause.*) Sure. Sure.

**CHARLIE SAMOA**  We think you got your finger on something. Some sort of . . . *pulse*. But I digress. (*Sniffs.*) In the course of negotiating these delicate, er, negotiations, I happened to run into certain disagreements with, that is to say, run afoul of an associate, more of a colleague actually, concerning in connection with distribution rights . . . very complex. This gentleman . . . in order to press me, in order to, I suppose, exert a primitive kind of leverage – kidnapped my daughter. (*Pause.*) When this rather crude ploy failed to have the desired effect, he did something very unpleasant to her. (*Pause.*) Nobody pushes me around. I want you to understand, Mother, that she'll be all right. I'm convinced of that. My daughter means everything to me. You know that, don't you, Mother? *Her* mother was a *slut*, but she means everything to me. (*Pause.*) I went to his apartment house. I walk past the doorman. He didn't even see me. I'm a ghost. I walk up the back stair. Two at a time. No hurry, I was in no hurry. I rang the bell. Bang bang. I put the muzzle up, the muzzle of my magnum up – against the eyehole, the glass peephole. I rang the hell. He came to the door, I could hear his footsteps. He slid the cover back. Ffffffffftt. The cover of the peephole back. Click. Who could this be? His stomach's falling out. He couldn't see nothing, you understand. To him it just looked dark. But it was *steel*. (*Slight pause.*) He put his eye up to the glass. I make a clicking sound in the back of my throat. Click. Click. I shot him through the eye. Through the glass. That's how it was. I blew his fucking head apart.

(*Pause.*)

**HUNGRY MOTHER**  Why are they in here?

**CHARLIE SAMOA**  Ask 'em.

**HUNGRY MOTHER**  Her. How can she be here?

**JOHNNIE SUCROSE**  I'm his conjugular visitor.

(*Slight pause. They laugh.*)

**CHARLIE SAMOA**  Pull the strings, Mom, you got to pull the strings.

(*They are laughing, shouting, pushing and shoving Hungry Mother – a mock mugging. At last, Hungry Mother breaks away. A moment, then:*)

**HUNGRY MOTHER**  I have to be going now.

**CHARLIE SAMOA**  Take it light –

**JOHNNIE SUCROSE**   Everything'll be all right –
**JIMMY SHILLELAGH**   Uptight and out of sight!
   (*They are laughing again.*)
**JOHNNIE SUCROSE**   Out of state! Out of state!
**CHARLIE SAMOA**   That's good! Out of state! Johnnie, you kill me
   babe!
**JOHNNIE SUCROSE**   Don't become a stranger!
**JIMMY SHILLELAGH**   Right!Right! Right!
   (*Raucous laughter. They fade. Hungry Mother walks out and into the
   studio, up to the mike; blue light is still "on."*)
**HUNGRY MOTHER**   And while we're waiting for our mystery girl
   guest, here's Hungry Mother's Horo-scope. (*Mellifluous, honeyed.*)
   Virgo: your stars are black dwarves, be advised. But don't take it too
   hard, my dear. Thermodynamic entropy comes to us all. Libra: proceed
   with caution. A romantic entanglement may lead to a social disease.
   Sagittarius: your moon is in eclipse and your spouse in the house of
   your best friend. Taurus: your moon is in Uranus. Success is light-
   years away. Capricorn: copasetic! Aries: if you open your mouth, I
   wanna see some teeth. Leo: you were so ugly when you were born, the
   doctor slapped your mother. Gemini: once black, they never come
   back. Cancer: you've got it, what can I say? Tough nuggies. Moloch:
   take the first-born boy-child of every *house* – (*Phone rings.*)
   Hang on! The lines are burning up[ (*Switch flicking.*) Hello? Maybe I'll
   turn this mother into a *talk* show! Hello! You're *radio*-active!
**THE MOOK**   (*Live, over P.A.*) The planets are propitious. Hello, Mother.
**HUNGRY MOTHER**   Hey.
**THE MOOK**   How's by you?
**HUNGRY MOTHER**   Passable.
**THE MOOK**   Long time no you know.
**HUNGRY MOTHER**   Not long enough. You know?
**THE MOOK**   I'm looking for Free Lance.
   (*Slight pause.*)
**HUNGRY MOTHER**   So'm I.
**THE MOOK**   I'll be right up.
   (*Click. Hungry Mother stares at the blue light, still '"on." He spears
   beans with a fork.*)
**HUNGRY MOTHER**   How long can he keep this up? Three beans, three
   prongs. One bean per prong, it's only fair. How long, ladies and
   gentlemen? Stick with me, friends, the suspense is killing.
   (*Janis enters.*)
**HUNGRY MOTHER**   Like beans?
   (*Flings one.*) What's your opinion? (*Flings another.*) On-the-spot
   woman-in-the-street interview how do you like your beans?

**JANIS**  Boiled.

**HUNGRY MOTHER**  Very good. You're right in step with the rest of America. Just another pedestrian. (*Flings a forkful of beans, striking Janis.*) Hey! Bull's eye! Well, maybe not a direct hit, maybe not *ground zero*, but certainly *close enough for jazz*, wouldn't you say? Yes, once again, *that's – close enough for jazz!* . . . You ought to do something about that bean stain, little lady. Isn't she pathetic, ladies and gentlemen?

(*Janis, wary, backs off. Pause.*)

**HUNGRY MOTHER**  Oh . . . yeah. Don't be alarmed. Just part of my standard improvisation avec beans. Nothing to be ashamed of.

**JANIS**  Are you, Hungry Mother? That's a stupid question. Of course you are.

**HUNGRY MOTHER**  The first.

**JANIS**  I'm Janis.

**HUNGRY MOTHER**  I figured.

**JANIS**  I called ahead.

**HUNGRY MOTHER**  Right.

**JANIS**  You said I could come up.

**HUNGRY MOTHER**  I thought you were another Janis. Different Janis. Janis I used to know.

**JANIS**  Oh. It's a common name. Not like Hungry Mother.

**HUNGRY MOTHER**  Aw shucks, that's just my nom de ozone . . . Give it time. The wave of the future. (*Pause.*) Something I can do for you?

**JANIS**  I wanted to see you.

**HUNGRY MOTHER**  You're the first, the very first! Hey! Reaching that wider audience! Hungry Mother has impact! It pays to listen! Kudos. Kudos are in order. My first fan. How's it feel, little lady? How do you like the studio?

**JANIS**  It's nice.

**HUNGRY MOTHER**  But small. Nice but small. But who knows, if this keeps up, this wild adulation, in twenty or thirty years I'll be able to (*Used Car salesman:*) trade it in on something nicer, yes, friends, why wait, empty those ashtrays and come on down . . . Beans?

**JANIS**  No. Thanks.

**HUNGRY MOTHER**  Something Japanese, perhaps. They do very well with that little shit. Transistors, crap like that. Minutia. A definitive talent for the diminutive, don't you think? Tell me, as my numero uno fano, do you find I have a sexy voice?

**JANIS**  No.

**HUNGRY MOTHER**  Robust. Virile. Vaguely Mediterranean. Like a swollen sack of coffee beans.

**JANIS**  No. (*Slight pause.*) Soothing. Possible.

**HUNGRY MOTHER**  I see.

**JANIS**  There's pain. In your voice . . . I came to talk to you. I need to talk to you. Don't be cruel.

**HUNGRY MOTHER**  Rings a bell. I have a famous sinking feeling.

**JANIS**  I recognize the pain.

**HUNGRY MOTHER**  Do you?

**JANIS**  It's like my own. Familiar. Similar. Like what I feel at night. In my chest. Your voice sounds like that. That pain.

(*Pause.*)

**HUNGRY MOTHER**  You're Desperate, aren't you?

**JANIS**  (*Flushing.*) No, no, I would never that, would be over –

**HUNGRY MOTHER**  No no no no no. That's how you sign your letters. "Desperate."

**JANIS**  Yes.

**HUNGRY MOTHER**  Janis Desperate. Jesus.

(*Pause.*)

**JANIS**  I want you to help me.

**HUNGRY MOTHER**  People in hell want ice water.

**JANIS**  What? What does that mean? What is that supposed to mean? I want you to help me. Please.

**HUNGRY MOTHER**  It's a joke, Janis Desperate. A joke.

**JANIS**  I don't get it. I don't see anything funny.

**HUNGRY MOTHER**  You're not concentrating. Is all. Now pay attention. This is Pop Analogy Number One. Rock n' roll Metaphor. You might just cop on to what I'm laying down – dig? You can't always get what you want. But if you try sometime. You get what you need. (*Pause.*) Biggest buncha bullshit I ever heard. I hate to be the one to break it to you sister, but people in hell don't *want* ice water, they *need* it. And – guess what? They *don't* get it . . . Do you get it?

**JANIS**  I don't feel good, Mother. I know you know what I'm – I know you feel the same.

**HUNGRY MOTHER**  I'm asking do you get it. Your asking me to help is the joke. I'm laughing. I'm larfing. You'd better larf too.

**JANIS**  I know you know how I feel.

**HUNGRY MOTHER**  Not a glimmer.

(*Pause.*)

**JANNIS**  I don't have furniture in my place. Nothing. A radio. I play the radio. Full blast. Keep the junkies away. They run through the building at night. Up and down the stairs. Fire escape. Rip the copper out of the walls. The wiring. There's no water. No light. They steal the stoves. The gas crawls up the wall. (*Slight pause.*) I turn it up. Way up. Radio. Play it all night. Afraid to sleep. They run through the building all night. Scratch the walls. (*Slight pause.*) I said that. (*Slight pause.*)

That's how I found you, Mother. One night. Down at the end of the dial. Before dawn. Strange voice. Cracked. Had a crack in it. Down at the end of the dial. Pain in it. (*Slight pause.*) Thanks for turning up. You were so faint at first. When I first found you. Just a crackle. Clearer in winter than summer or spring . . . No, that's silly, but – my place is right across the park. I think the leaves must interfere? Anyway, lately – you're coming in as clear as a bell.

**HUNGRY MOTHER**  A lucky bounce offa the clouds. It's all in the angle, sweetheart. I'm 26,000 light-years off center.

**JANIS**  Incredibly clear. What I am telling you. What I am trying to say. For more than a year now your voice has really made a difference to me, Mother.

(*Pause.*)

**HUNGRY MOTHER**  Why don't you buy some furniture? Beanbag chairs. Shag rug. Plexiglass coffee tables. Big glossy books. Galopagos this and that. Austerity is salubrious but poverty can be painful. Cheer yourself up. Hanging plants, that's the ticket. Junkies don't truck with hanging plants.

**JANIS**  (*Trying again, in a rush.*) I felt you were lonely, you said you wanted letters, I could tell, I could tell you were, by your jokes, you were worried no one was listening, no one cared, no one was hearing you, so I wrote, I wrote you. I never dreamed, you know, of writing to a, a public person, a stranger, I wouldn't you know, infringe on someone's privacy . . . so I was really distressed when you read my letters over the air . . . but in a way that was all right, it was okay, it was like you were listening, like you were answering. I never expected you to – that's why I signed my letters Desperate, I thought –

**HUNGRY MOTHER**  That's the way God planned it.

**JANIS**  Mother, I didn't mean to write you about me, my problems. I was going to cheer you up, believe me –

**HUNGRY MOTHER**  Believe me.

**JANIS**  Oh, I do.

(*Pause.*)

**HUNGRY MOTHER**  Look, uh . . . what's on your mind?

**JANIS**  I just – want you to be my friend. A friend. Is that so much to ask?

**HUNGRY MOTHER**  Depends. Come here. (*Janis moves to him.*)

**JANIS**  Okay.

**HUNGRY MOTHER**  Tight squeeze.

**JANIS**  That's okay. Cozier.

(*She sits. Hungry Mother puts an arm around her. She smiles, slightly. She relaxes, just a bit.*)

**HUNGRY MOTHER**  'S nice, huh?

**JANIS**  Yeah. Yeah.

**HUNGRY MOTHER**  I . . . can't do it.

**JANIS**  What?

**HUNGRY MOTHER**  Janis, there's something I should tell you.

**JANIS**  (*Touching his face.*) Sssshhh, don't talk. You don't have to talk.

**HUNGRY MOTHER**  Yeah, there's something I should have mentioned earlier. (*Slight pause.*) You're lonely, right?

**JANIS**  Yes.

**HUNGRY MOTHER**  Well, I'm lonely too.

**JANIS**  Oh, Mother, I know you are. I know you are.

**HUNGRY MOTHER**  Well, darling – as one lonely person to another – (*Pause.*) – we're on the air!

(*Janis jumps to her feet, looks at the blue light.*)

**JANIS**  Oh. Oh.

**HUNGRY MOTHER**  (*Goes to mike.*) Wasn't that touching, friends? You heard it here, first. Hang in there, there's more to come from Janis Desperate, much more.

**JANIS**  Bastard.

**HUNGRY MOTHER**  Sorry.

**JANIS**  Yes.

**HUNGRY MOTHER**  That's my style, sweets. Free-form freefall. Wing it over the edge and see how long it takes to hit bottom.

**JANIS**  Jesus.

(*The Mook enters. A large man. Elegant. Terrifying. A black Renaissance Prince of the Underground.*)

**HUNGRY MOTHER**  Ah, Mook! Mook! I'm honored. Long time no you know. I believe you two, you know, too.

**THE MOOK**  You're off the beam. I haven't had the pleasure. Seen Free Lance?

**HUNGRY MOTHER**  How about her?

**THE MOOK**  I doubt it. You lookin' to get out of show business, Mother, and into an honest line of work? Why for you cute, Mom? She's nice, but the Free Lance I have in mind is nicer by far.

**HUNGRY MOTHER**  Right. Sorry. Mook. Janis. Janis. Mook.

**THE MOOK**  Enchante.

**JANIS**  Fine! (*She stalks out.*)

**THE MOOK**  Whatsa matta for her? The rabbit died?

**HUNGRY MOTHER**  Naw . . . We just met.

**THE MOOK**  Mark my words, Mother. The price of fame is a paternity suit.

**HUNGRY MOTHER**  I'll watch my step.

**THE MOOK**  You'll know you're in the big time when you find you have a couple of café au lait kids who bear not the slightest resemblance to anyone you ever knew. (*Pause.*) Where's Free Lance?

**HUNGRY MOTHER**   Changed her name.

**THE MOOK**   You said she'd be here.

**HUNGRY MOTHER**   I said I was expecting her. I am. I still am.

**THE MOOK**   You ought to get out more, Mother. Away from the mike. Clear your head.

(*Pause.*)

**HUNGRY MOTHER**   Free Lance.

(*Pause.*)

**THE MOOK**   She didn't tell me. She was going to change her name. She just changed it.

(*Pause.*)

**HUNGRY MOTHER**   I could use more air.

**THE MOOK**   I liked Polish Vodka better.

**HUNGRY MOTHER**   To drink or on her?

**THE MOOK**   Both . . . *Simultaneous.*

**HUNGRY MOTHER**   I thought she was working for you.

**THE MOOK**   In this assumption our thoughts concur. (*They dap.*) Coincide. (*Dap.*) Collide. (*Dap.*) She's not treating me well, Mother. Or herself. She's going out on the limb of principles. I want her to come down. If you snag the drift of my metaphor.

**HUNGRY MOTHER**   I think I follow it. (*They begin a complicated dap, a handjive.*)

**THE MOOK**   Free Lance. That's rich.

**HUNGRY MOTHER**   Snap!

**THE MOOK**   It's a question of precedents. She needs her insurance, Mother, like a child needs her vitamins. And this is a world, Mother, as you well know, in which a child cannot hope to survive without a little luck and some kind of insurance.

**HUNGRY MOTHER**   Crack!

**THE MOOK**   She knows I cannot allow this. Not just my livelihood is threatened by her rash and precipitous action. What if my other ladies take it into their heads. I wouldn't want to see them get hurt.

**HUNGRY MOTHER**   Pow!

(*They finish dap.*)

**THE MOOK**   Exactly. Thank you, Mother, for extending my metaphor.

**HUNGRY MOTHER**   Not at all. Any time. (*Pause.*) Maybe she's lucky.

**THE MOOK**   I'm her luck. (*Pause.*) The thing that really gets my goat, Mother, that really galls the living shit out of me – is that she's setting this whole thing up like some kind of walking 3-D cliche. Right offa the silver screen. Ruthless pimp with the cold-as-stone heart. Prosty with the tits of gold. They get down – to brass tacks. Small-time indy versus rapacious multinational. Victory for free enterprise. Yea. Sheep farmer whips cattle baron. Score one for the free fucking market and laissez-faire capital-ism. Creeping socialism crawl under de rock. Music up and out. (*Pause.*) The record's scratchy, Mother. A bad print. I seen it before. I heard it before.

**HUNGRY MOTHER**   Why'd she do it? She said she missed you.

**THE MOOK**   She saw it in the movies.

**HUNGRY MOTHER**   Oh.

**THE MOOK**   For Christ sake, I'll give you ten to one. She took it into her head . . . Mother, Mother. I'm chiding you, Mother. Tsk, tsk. In America – life – (*Strikes pose.*) – imitates – media. (*Slight pause. Drops pose.*) Who should know better than you?

**HUNGRY MOTHER**   I hang my head.

**THE MOOK**   I resent being put in this position. I resent being made to play some kind of classic American morality schtik. I resent being made archetypal. You know? It gives me a black *burning* sensation behind my eyes.

**HUNGRY MOTHER**   What are you going to do to her? (*Long pause.*)

**THE MOOK**   Ask her to come in. (*Slight pause.*) Nicely. (*Beat.*) *You* were close.

**HUNGRY MOTHER**   (*Brusquely.*) Old days. Stone Age. Before I became the Hungry Mother.

**THE MOOK**   Don't kid me. You always been the Hungry Mother. From time immemorial . . . You comin' in loud and clear dese days.

**HUNGRY MOTHER**   Yeah?

**THE MOOK**   Right. Somebody's monkeyed with your volume.

**HUNGRY MOTHER**   Atmospheric turbulence. Sunspots. Geothermal radiation.

**THE MOOK**   You ought to watch your ass.

**HUNGRY MOTHER**   So everybody tells me. Christ, it's enough to make a corpse paranoid.

**THE MOOK**   Especially those Junk Reports.

**HUNGRY MOTHER**   Mook, they aren't for real.

**THE MOOK**   Oh, yes they are. Now they are. Every junkie in town, Mom. Every junkie, every narc, every pusher, every pimp. You the *source*, man, the Wall Street fuckin' Journal of Junk . . . Everybody knows you're illegal, Mother. It's no secret. Folks concerned. Highly concerned. There are rumors. Grand jury activity. They might get together. They might *convene*. This whole gig just might go titties up.

**HUNGRY MOTHER**   I can't explain it, Mook. This tube gear is shot. It's cream of shit. It's a miracle it gets off the block.

**THE MOOK**   (*Leans forward, very black, very deep.*) Tell it to the judge. (*Laughs, booming crackle.*) They taping you 'round the clock, little man.

**HUNGRY MOTHER**   (*Yelling.*) I don't broadcast around the clock!

**THE MOOK**   If only you'd keep a schedule, Mother. They don't want to miss a single spasm. A single spurt. Right now, they trying to ascertain just who listening. Besides themselves, I mean. A demographic sample. To determine your threat extent. It's proving elusive.

**HUNGRY MOTHER**   I'll bet it is.

**THE MOOK**   Just a friendly gesture. If you see Free Lance, tell her to come on in. Just like the movies. It'll go easier. Plea bargain. One week only. Tell her that.

(*The Mook heads for the door.*)

**HUNGRY MOTHER**   Hey, Mook.

**THE MOOK**   Yes dear?

**HUNGRY MOTHER**   You're on the air!

(*The Mook looks at the blue light a long moment. Then grins.*)

**THE MOOK**   Motha fucka!

(*He exits. Hungry Mother races to the mike.*)

**HUNGRY MOTHER**   Well, there you have it, gas fans, the heat is on. You heard it all, *live,* from the life of Hungry Mother, a true story. Cross my heart. If you'd like to participate in the life of Hungry Mother, just drop me a card – indicate your primary field of interest – philosophical, sexual, athletic, dinner, dress, or aperitif – and mail it to . . . Hungry Mother, Got To Get You Into My Life, Hubba Hubba Hubba Hubba, WTWI, Frantz Fanon Memorial Tenement, Number One Marauder Avenue, just past Faghag Park. All entries will remain on file for use at my personal discretion.

(*Weatherman.*) The long-range outcast for this weekend – *diphtheria!* Followed by bubonic plague and intermittent spotted fever. Enjoy. Right now outside our studio – continued existential dread dappled with parapsychological phenomena, and streaked with low-grade anxiety. Speaking of weather, we'll have the latest prices for bone marrow and rendering in a moment, but first . . .

(*He slumps on stool. Silence. He returns to mike: teletype and newscaster.*)

Flash news update. That acute distress has gone – *terminal.* Closed with a rush. Check it out. Other tidbits about our town . . . That dog rapist remains at large. Pet owners – do you know where your pets are tonight? Coming up in the near future – if there is one – heh heh, always the optimist, Mother, check it out! Always the optimist. *Lycanthropy in the Home!* Always a hairy subject, we'll have some tips on just how to deal with it. We'll be talking to a bonafide cat burglar, and you'll find out *exactly* what they do with our furry friends . . . the fiends. We'll also have our Prick Hit of the Week, when you

ladies can line up the sexual puerco of your choice and sock it to him –
right here in our soundproof booth.

(*Mellifluous.*) That just about puts a merciful end to our broadcasting
day here at WTWI, the twilight station with the demeanor that only a
Mother could love. We'll top it off with our ever-popular Slumlord of
the Day Award, we'll be back after somebody's briefs, but first – a
word about *mange* . . . This is the Hungry Mother, wrapping it up here,
boss, with a mouthful of joy buzzers and a handful of static, telling you
to have a hopeful day, spelled with two ells.

(*Three swarthy individuals enter the studio: two men and a woman.*)

**HUNGRY MOTHER**   Has to *be* – (*Long pause; then a whisper.*) *Hoover
and the Navajos.*

(*Freeze. Tableau. Lights fade. Blue light still "on," in the black.
Long moment. Snaps off. Blackout.*)


END OF ACT ONE

## ACT TWO

*Black*

**LOUD SPEAKER**   The Rising *Popularity* of Hungry Mother . . .
Beginning with – (*Blue light pops "on," silhouetting four figure freeze:*) Tableaux Vivants! Avecs peaux rouges!
(*Lights up slowly on Hoover and The Navajos, and Hungry Mother. They remain still, as Hoover speaks simply, in the classic mode:*)

**HOOVER**   In the moon of grass withering . . . or perhaps in the moon of vanishing animals . . . I surrendered my people to General Howard. My heart was . . . *broke.* I said to him – the chiefs are dead. Looking Glass is dead. All the young men are dead. Or scattered like dry leaves. Or drowning in whiskey. My children chew bark. Their feet are frozen. The old women gobble dead grass and devil's brush. We are starving. My lungs are full of clotted blood. As I said before – from where the sun now sets, I will fight no more, forever. This is what I said to General Howard. (*Pause.*) So he gave me a job.
(*Pause. Hoover holds up a brightly colored plastic package in one hand, and points to it with his other hand, on which he is wearing a black leather glove.*)
Selling these . . . The snack that never grows old . . . Fiddle Faddle . . . That's how I became Chief Fiddle Faddle. (*Hoover flips down his shades. Pause. Grins.*) Just kidding.
(*The Navajos begin poking around in the studio. Hungry Mother takes over from Hoover at the mike.*)

**HUNGRY MOTHER**   Hey, hey! Hoover, fella, you really had me going there. I was brewing up some really fierce Apache crocodile tears. Isn't he something, ladies and gentlemen? We're here today with our special guests, Hoover and the Navajos –

**HOOVER**   Just kidding.

**HUNGRY MOTHER**   Yes, yes, just fooling around. Tell us, Hoov – a lot of us – the listening and yearning audience would like to know something more about Hoover and the Navajos. All they know is what I tell 'em, what I, you know, make up off the top. On the spur.

**HOOVER**   You got it right. You got it right, Mother. You got it so right. Except in smallest details. No way you could miss. The light comes down on you . . . Smallest things. Our names. My friends. Mother, my companions . . . Crazy Joe Navajo.
(*Crazy Joe burps delicately by way of greeting.*)
Freddy Navajo.
(*Freddy nods coldly. Hoover smiles.*)

The light comes down on you, Mother. (*Long pause.*) Indians are always silent. Having nothing to say. Ask your stupid questions.

**HUNGRY MOTHER**  (*After a slight hesitation.*) In the fawning fanmag manner, then – when did you write your first song? When did you first start playing the guitar? When did you decide to devote your lifestyle to music?

**HOOVER**  In the moon of rising expectations.

**HUNGRY MOTHER**  In the little magazine manner then – when did you first concieve, and begin to develop as a distinct genre of popular music, *patho-rock?* What sets *patho-rock* apart from other strands, such as goat-bucket blues or coon-cajun cakewalks? Compare and contrast. Trace its evolution in a sociohistorical context. How do you account for your obsession with fiberglass? Is it worthwhile speculating along psychosexual dysfunction lines?

**HOOVER**  In the moon of historical necessity . . . Out of the blue . . . Unrelenting bitterness, as long as the waters shall flow and the grass shall grow – you know the phrase? . . . An environmentally generated malignancy contracted as an immediate consequence of contact through deliberate exposure to the carcinogenic substance. In that order.

**HUNGRY MOTHER**  (*Brightly.*) I see. That's too bad!

**HOOVER**  In the moon of bowing to the inevitable. In the charnel moon of abject capitulation. In the blue moon of genocide. In the quarter moon of going completely off the wall . . . In the moon *of forced labor* . . .

**HUNGRY MOTHER**  Right. Got it. That's what gives your songs that grit, that nit, that *sliced life.* Tell me – and I'm sure your fans at home would be more than super interested too – where do you get those boffo bonnaroo titles like *Fiberglass God?*

**HOOVER**  I got drunk and fell on the floor. (*Pause. Then Freddy stands.*)

**FREDDY**  Freddy Navajo here. Earth to Freddy. I hear voices. Indian voices. Mescalito. Coyote. Charlie Chan. Joan of Navajo speaks in my ear. It ain't easy to hear myself think – with all those voices going. All the old voices. Covered here today. Hoover did his Poetic Indian to his usual turn. (*Freddy and Crazy Joe applaud.*) Aplomb. Aplomb. And Crazy Joe's taciturn Drunken Injun is, as always, subtle and tragic. Impeccable. Correct.

(*Freddy and Hoover applaud. Slight pause.*)

**CRAZY JOE**  (*Ever so slightly slurred.*) Thanks.

**FREDDY**  A classic of its kind. You see my predicament? So many voices. A welter. A goulash. So hard to find a point of view. Which piece of history to vocalette.

**HUNGRY MOTHER**  (*Cheerily.*) How about TB? You know,

tuberculosis, Easter Seals for brown babes? Famine? Smallpox
sleeping bags?

**FREDDY**     Hostility is always in good taste.

**HUNGRY MOTHER**     Uh . . . Freddy, what's the – why don't you do the
new single?

**FREDDY**     Right . . . This is a song I wrote one night while breaking glass
on the reservation . . . I calls it – Fucking on Fiberglass!

**HOOVER**     Give me a ball 'n a beer, anyday.

**FREDDY**     Right. Sheer shock value. No other redemptions. Oh,
incidental alliteration. A simple tune. Our only aim is sensation.

**HOOVER**     I wasn't always a poet. I used to work for a living.

**HUNGRY MOTHER**     That's great. Swell, and heartwarming. Here it is,
fans, what you've all been waiting for! If this single don't send you,
you got no place to go! Hoover and the Navajos – *Fucking – On
Fiberglass!*

(*Hungry Mother puts on the 45, flick switches. It blasts out over the
PA: primitive guitar chording, hand drums, yowling and chanting,
screaming, glass shattering. After three minutes of earsplitting sound,
a blues-fragment snarls its way out of the maelstrom:*)

**HOOVER**     (*Singing, on the 45.*)

Fuckin'
On fiberglass . . .
Got that shit
Up my . . . aaaaaaaaasssss!

(*This is followed, on the 45, by a scream from Freddy that's like a
baby's howl. During the playing of the single, The Navajos rock out, a
violent and erotic frenzy. Fucking on Fiberglass ends with a crescendo
of drumming and breaking glass. Silence.*)

**HUNGRY MOTHER**     (*Softly.*) So visceral . . . I *can feel* it. Uch. Where
do you guys get this stuff? Monstrous. Colossal. Curdled blood, see?
Destroys me. Primal.

**FREDDY**     (*Snickering.*) Primordial.

(*Crazy Jo gets up off the refrigerator. A hush. He goes to the turn-
table, takes off the 45, drops it on the floor. Pours whiskey on it. Takes
a drink. Smiles. Smacks his lips.*)

**CRAZY JOE**     Primitive.

(*The Navajos laugh wildly. They seize piles of 45s, and begin flinging
them through the air, slowly at first, then faster, to crescendo – a
blizzard of black plastic. It stops. The studio floor is covered in 45s.
Pause. Hoover smiles cool behind his shades and says softly:*)

**HOOVER**     *Aborigine.*

(*Hoover and The Navajos exit. Hungry Mother stands in the debris.
Studio light out as streetlight snaps on. Hungry Mother walks into the*

*light. Janis is in a shadow. He stops and stares at her. Finally:*)

**HUNGRY MOTHER** Wha'choo doin' out here?

**JANIS** Lurking.

**HUNGRY MOTHER** Lurking. Huh. (*Slight pause.*) Hell of a place to lurk. (*Slight pause.*) Lurking long?

**JANIS** Hours.

**HUNGRY MOTHER** And lived to tell the tale. A-mazing. I shake my head. (*He does.*)

**JANIS** So. What's the word?

**HUNGRY MOTHER** *Hungry.*

**JANIS** Listen, I thought maybe – you busy? I thought maybe we could get a bite.

**HUNGRY MOTHER** In this neighborhood? A bite is a breeze. But will they quit after just one? (*They both laugh.*)

**JANIS** Listen. I know a place.

**HUNGRY MOTHER** Yeah? Well. Okay. All right.

**JANIS** It's near here. You'll like it. Under Marauder Avenue. It floats.

**HUNGRY MOTHER** A floating dive. Abso-fucking-lutely. Lezgo.
(*The streetlight flickers. The light is blue and wintery: a cold evening. Mook and Free Lance enter. Hungry Mother and Janis stop. Draw back. Unseen.*)

**THE MOOK** Ho Chi Minh Trail runs through the park now.

**FREE LANCE** Uptown to down.

**THE MOOK** Natch. Built that way. They brought it over after the war. Reconstituted it. As it were.

**FREE LANCE** What you run on it?

**THE MOOK** Scag. Just like the war. Like it never ended. Them good old days. They got a replica of the war goin' on in there. Minature. Jes' a few blocks away . . . Business as usual, babe. (*He turns his gaze on her.*) Back on the street.

**FREE LANCE** Back on the streets again.

**THE MOOK** I stand corrected. Back on the streets. The phrase that pays . . . I thought you were sick of the street. I been to see Mother, looking for you.

**FREE LANCE** I've missed the street.

**THE MOOK** I know you have. I wasn't surprised.

**FREE LANCE** And the street missed me.

**THE MOOK** No, no, I wasn't surprised you weren't there. I know you done with him. I wanted to check out Mother's crib. Wanted to get some kinda line on just what we boosting, here. We had a nice chat. (*Slight pause.*) Mother said you missed me.

**FREE LANCE** I miss the street. Mook. Same difference . . . I miss you. What kind of chat you say you had?

**THE MOOK**   Minimal. I dropped him a hint. Dammit, Free Lance, whachoo doin' out here?

**FREE LANCE**   Looking for you.

**THE MOOK**   On the street? Come on, baby. I been all over town, I come home find you *walking* my block.

**FREE LANCE**   (*Laughs.*) You my main squeeze, sugah. Mama want Papa-san be her first trick. Numbah one, dig?
(*Pause.*)

**THE MOOK**   You set me up, Free Lance. Like a damn tar baby. Some kind of story. You fictionalizing my position. Dig? People talk. A legend in my own time. Shit. Legend in my own mind. They talkin' now. Hear 'em?

**FREE LANCE**   No.

**THE MOOK**   Erodes my credibility. People don't think I'm real. Think I'm the damn Baron Samedi or some voodoo shit. Gets tough to keep the muscle up when they put you in the same bag with Mickey the Mouse and Agent Orange. (*Hisses.*) Know what I talk, bitch?
(*She is about to respond when she hears something in the distance. They both listen.*)

**FREE LANCE**   Guns.

**THE MOOK**   *Gunners.* (*He smiles. She shivers.*)

**FREE LANCE**   I love The Street. I go wandering on The Street. In the back of my head. Stay there forever. Stay there for good. Disappear behind my eyes. You understand?

**THE MOOK**   Free Lance.

**FREE LANCE**   I'm not going upstairs with you, Mook.

**THE MOOK**   Free Lance. (*Slight pause.*) I promised Mother.

**FREE LANCE**   No, not upstairs. I like it here. (*Slight pause.*) Leaving Mother's, I get a screamer. A rag ghost. I see him all the way down at the end of the block. He sees me. He turns. Gunfight at the Okay. I freeze. He takes a step. Takes two. Now he's running. Right at me. His mouth is open like a siren and he's screaming. He's getting closer. Closer. I can smell rot. He's got a bottle in his hand. A mickey. Like a knife. He's right on top of me. I step aside. and he goes right on by. Still screaming. Disappears into the park. Screams stop. Siren stops. *Chop.*

**THE MOOK**   Fags got him. Gorilla fags. They drop out of the trees like fruit.

**FREE LANCE**   Nothing like that happens upstairs.

**THE MOOK**   Damn straight. I ain't no punk. You have any other adventures since I saw you last?

**FREE LANCE**   Run of the mill rubble walk. Trash fire circle jerks. Rubble rabble. They try'n come on you as you walk past.

**THE MOOK**  It's an art. That'll teach you to run away from home. Come on in, Free Lance. Come on in, baby. Come on in with me.

**FREE LANCE**  Of course.

**THE MOOK**  Mother's worried about you. You ought to give Mother a call.

**FREE LANCE**  I will.

**THE MOOK**  I know you were close. Just tell him you okay. Set his mind. The kid's all right.

**FREE LANCE**  Mook. Mother's on the rag about some kids. You have anything to do with that? You boosting, hustling some kids?

**THE MOOK**  'S an idea, baby. Get all my best notions from Mother.

**FREE LANCE**  Pimp.

*(Slight pause.)*

**THE MOOK**  *(Mildly.)* Don't call me that. Don't rub The Mook the wrong way. Call me monger instead.

**FREE LANCE**  Monger?

*(Free Lance begins to laugh, undertones of hysteria. The Mook smiles.)*

**THE MOOK**  Yeah. Flesh monger.

*(She stops laughing. Slight pause.)*

**THE MOOK**  Come on up. Come on in. *(She is listening in the distance, again.)*

**FREE LANCE**  Fire fight.

**THE MOOK**  See? Got to come with me, baby. Can't go 'way down there.

*(Pause.)*

**FREE LANCE**  For now. It's chilly.

*(He puts his arm around her. They start to leave.)*

**FREE LANCE**  *(Black.)* Whatchoo tell Mothah?

**THE MOOK**  Heh heh heh. I tell Mothah to watch his *ass*. You blackisms gettin' bettah, baby.

**FREE LANCE**  *(Laughs.)* Ah, Mook, Mook. *(Strokes his face.)* You're a dizzy cunt. You know that?

*(He stares. Then laughs. Roars. Mook and Free Lance exit. Streetlight flickers. Hungry Mother steps out and stares after them. Charlie Samoa appears behind them. He's dressed as a derelict.)*

**DERELICT (CHARLIE SAMOA)**  'Member the cat.

*(They start. Hungry Mother doesn't recognize him.)*

**HUNGRY MOTHER**  Cat.

**DERELICT (CHARLIE SAMOA)**  'Member the cat. Curiosity and the cat. *(He starts off. Turns back.)*

**DERELICT (CHARLIE SAMOA)**  Jesus was not a white racist – as some people suppose. He was the only son of the living god.

*(Derelict (Charlie Samoa) exits.)*
**JANIS**   You know them.
**HUNGRY MOTHER**   Who?
**JANIS**   The . . . couple.
**HUNGRY MOTHER**   Oh yes.
**JANIS**   What was that? That scene.
**HUNGRY MOTHER**   He wants her.
**JANIS**   What does she want?
**HUNGRY MOTHER**   Out.
**JANIS**   What are you going to do?
**HUNGRY MOTHER**   What can I do?
**JANIS**   She wants help?
**HUNGRY MOTHER**   No. No. She doesn't *want* it.
*(Silence. Streetlight out.)*
**LOUD SPEAKER**   Oooeeeooo, baby, baby. Oh, oh, oh, Miss Ann.
   Dime-a-dance romance. No-tell motel. *Skank. Tryst. Tropics. Tristes*
   *tropiques.* Photo Opportunity. . . The House of Blue Light (*Beat.*)
   Hungry *and* . . . Friend!
   *(Studio illuminated. Hungry Mother and Janis on the refrigerator cot.*
   *The studio is still a wreck from the Navajos' visit. Janis lights a*
   *cigarette.)*
**JANIS**   At least we weren't on the air.
**HUNGRY MOTHER**   Community standards. I think I'll torch these
   platters. Do the whole dump in hot wax.
**JANIS**   I don't think it's right, quite.
*(Silence.)*
**HUNGRY MOTHER**   Well.
**JANIS**   Well.
**HUNGRY MOTHER**   Hope you feelin' better . . .
**JANIS**   Bye 'n bye.
*(He's pleased she finished the phrase.)*
**HUNGRY MOTHER**   Yes.
**JANIS**   You too?
**HUNGRY MOTHER**   Mmmm. Bye 'n bye. 'S been a long time.
**JANIS**   Why? Why not?
**HUNGRY MOTHER**   Out Of fashion. *Intimacy.* A blast from the past.
**JANIS**   I should talk. I haven't been, mmm, with anyone for ages. Long
   long time . . . Good for the blues.
**HUNGRY MOTHER**   Curin' or causin'?
*(Silence.)*
**HUNGRY MOTHER**   Walkin' blues. Talkin' blues. Stalkin' blues . . .
   *(He lets it go.)*
**JANIS**   Mother.

**HUNGRY MOTHER**   Yes'm.

**JANIS**   Mother, would you put me on the air?

(*Slight pause.*)

**HUNGRY MOTHER**   Sure.

(*He gets up and goes to the console. Flicks switches. Blue light goes "on." She goes to the mike. Now they are both standing nearly naked in the twilight debris.*)

(*Silence. She lights a cigarette. Drags. Long moment. She returns to the cot and picks up the rest of her clothes. Puts them on. They look at each other.*)

**HUNGRY MOTHER**   Minimal. In fact, minimal to the max. I dug it. I especially dug it when you put on your clothes. Getting dressed on the radio. It's hot. No commercial possibilities of course. Could be cognescenti.

**JANIS**   I don't know what I wanted to say. I just wanted to put my voice out there. On the radio. . . What a strange phrase. Strange thing to say. On the air. I wanted to put it out there. On the air. Air waves. Radio waves go on forever. To other stars.

**HUNGRY MOTHER**   Pulsars, baby. Will the Hungry Mother Radio Hour be a hit on Betelgeuse six million light-years from today? Stay tuned.

(*Silence.*)

**HUNGRY MOTHER**   Let's do it again sometime.

**JANIS**   Let's. (*She moves to the door.*)

**HUNGRY MOTHER**   Absofuckinglutely.

**JANIS**   See you.

**HUNGRY MOTHER**   Abyssinia, Janis.

**JANIS**   Right.

(*She exits. Hungry Mother retrieves his tennis shoes.*)

**LOUD SPEAKER**   The White Man's moccasins.

**HUNGRY MOTHER**   Shaddup.

**LOUD SPEAKER**   Hungry Mother, the Vandal of the Vernacular. HUNGRY JAM! Mega Hertz! Kinky reggae. Rising tide. The ratings surge! He bends their ears! Wild in the streets! Hungry funk! Damp all over! Hard nipples! HUNGRY MOTHER MANIA!

(*He bounds to the mike. Blue light "on."*)

**HUNGRY MOTHER**   You're right, you're right, you got good taste. Hey hey hey. All systems go! This will be the Hungriest Mother alive, this be WTWI, the twilight station with the terminal blues and the twilight debris, this be a blight and bleary predawn radio debauch with the only Mother that'll *ever* love you! Coming up this hour, Agony News Headlines, something spicy about the Pope, and the evermore popular Prick Hit of the Week. Plus – a bonus. A fab new soap op:

MULATTO SPLENDOR! Yes, Antebellum blues! Miscegenation, America's favorite preoccupation! Intricate intra-ethnic color schemes! Ancestor worship and the Daughters of the Confederacy! Something for everyone! Impossibly overwritten! Here! On WTWI! Don't miss *Mulatto Splendor*, the soap that's guaranteed to become a *class* struggle. In this week's episode, Rhett discovers that Scarlett's been 'passing' – and the annual debutantes' ball is crashed by the field hands. And now – *Moan Along With Mother!*

*(He sings a blues moan, minor key. First note's melodic, it quickly becomes harsh, going out of control into sobbing and retching. Subsides. Slight pause.)*

There. Doesn't that feel better? *(Attacks the typewriter furiously Newscaster:)*

And now this hour's top short stories . . . Dengue Fever raging out of control across Sub-Saharan Africa . . . absolutely terminal, no, I repeat, no antidote . . . Green Monkey Virus spreads from Germany to Georgia! If you gush black blood you've got it! And you're a goner! Isn't that something?! . . . And . . . the Pope is engaged! We'll be back later in the week with more on the Forty-Second Street sniper. These are this hour's top tales, brought to you by Ominous Acronyms – Ominous Acronyms, dedicated to raising the ante no matter the pot. And now a spiritual word of advice from the pastor of the First . . . Chinese Baptist . . . Church of the Deaf!

*("Chinee":)* Leveland Bluce Ree here. Lememble! Don't wait for the hearse to take you to church!

*(Cheery.)* Thank you, Leveland Bluce. Next hour, my impression of a JAP. And I don't mean Japanese. Don't miss it. But first – *(Slight pause.)*

Trying to get over. *(Slight pause.)* Hauling ass.

*(Slight pause. Then, shakes himself, full-speed:)* I seem to be wandering today, fans, please forgive me, bouncing off the boards like a rabid hockey puck, coming up hungry, coming up short, coming up the up and coming group destined to dethrone the once-mythical Hoover and The Navajos: Jumpin Lumpen and the Juke Savages and the new blockbuster, *Idi Amin Is My Doorman!* Don't you dare miss it. But first, it's time once again for – Our Prick Hit of the Week! Yes, every week the Mother invites you and your nominee into the studio for a little *slug-fest*. With the aid of our superbly trained staff of Swiss guerillas, we hold him down, and you let him have it! So ladies – ah, *women*, keep those nominations coming. And now – here we go again with *Mother's Prick Hit of the Week!*

*(Flicks switches. A tape goes on over the PA: it's a tape of Mother's moaning just previous. As the moaning plays, Hungry Mother rocks*

*out, finger snaps and vocal bops. When the tape finishes he grins into the mike:)*

HUNGRY MOTHER    So good. I *really* identify. The weather outlook is for unparalleled nausea – followed by protracted internal bleeding. A million-dollar weekend.

*(Newscaster, á la Paul Harvey.)* Top headline . . . This . . . or any other . . . hour . . . slavery . . . on the rise . . . once again . . . in most . . . of the civilized . . . world. *(Slight pause. Low, intense.)* Consider, if you will, the following felicitous phrases . . . Jones. Slud. Double dog dare. Going down slow. Walking wounded. Hunger artist. Bane. *(Weatherman.) Thick as slick out there, you better watch your step. (Screaming.)* Mexican standoff! Yes! Yes! No motherfucker can touch me now! I full of the Night Train! Hear the Midnight Special call my name! I be full, so full of that damn Night Train! Nothin' I ever seen can equal the color of my i-ma-gin-ation! I am the Midnight Prerogative!

*(Slight pause. Frenzied but quiet, under control, just barely: this is the emotional high of his set:)*

Speaking of *jones* – I got it – for what you've been waiting for – for those with the baddest jones of all – for those with the cold at the core of their *soul – Mother's Junk Report!* Needles are *up*. Ditto fits and kits. Rubber tubing's down. Likewise brown dreck. Something cleaner cost you more . . . here we go! Black Magic go for a dime, if you can find it, and so will Foolish Pleasure. Fifteen for Light 'n Lively, and they be gettin' a quarter for 200 Years of Jive. Hard to believe, isn't it? Topping out at a flat thirty, Death Wish! . . . Sorry, brothers and sisters, you know that's the way it goes, whiter is brighter, and less is more. Now, getting away from dreamtime and down to the street, your Mother's gonna tell you straight. All that's out there is Brown Bomber and Death Boy. A quarter, that is, seven little spoons goes for fifty, and a rip-down, half of that, jack, will cost you twenty-five. That's what's on that open market! The shit is stepped on, Jack, stepped on! Worth your life to stick that shit! Cut with fucking Drano, Jack! Drano! *(Cooler.)* Active trading in fluff stuff around town: quarter scoops of coke scored easily on the approaches to the park, and it's snowing all over town. Storms of angel dust, methadone in ice buckets, on the rocks or with a crystal cranq chaser, and horse tranqs galore. On the sunny side up, the use of personal weapons in lethal transactions is riding a slight cooling trend – and that's *got* to be good news. This has been another edition of *Mother's Junk*.

*(Slight pause. Upbeat.)* Ah, once that's over, I'm back on the tracks, I really am. Works like a charm. Tomorrow: *Pantheon of Scum:* a grisly scavenge through the deserted cities of the heart. You've been listening

to more of the same this last half-century – brought to you by *Sayanora Thermonukes* – check us if your megatonnage droops! *Sayanora Thermonukes* – say goodbye and mean it! And now let's join, already in progress, Sugar Bear and Oz – cutting up in the Cuban Room.

(*He grabs his coat and walks out, leaving the blue light "on."*)

**LOUD SPEAKER** The *Casa – Cubana!*

(*Hungry Mother walks into the bar.*)

**BELLY UP** Mother! Salud! How hangs it, Ma?

**HUNGRY MOTHER** Somewhere else. Give me a drink. Something for the inner city man. (*He downs it and burps.*)

**BELLY UP** You bet. (*He follows suit.*) Feel better?

**HUNGRY MOTHER** Some.

**BELLY UP** Since you're a star, have another.

**HUNGRY MOTHER** Catch Hoover's act?

**BELLY UP** Indelible. Crushed my head. Had to be Hoover and the Navajos. You're getting very big, Mother. There's already a movement to save your ass.

**HUNGRY MOTHER** I haven't lost it.

**BELLY UP** You will. Committee to Save Hungry Mother's Ass. The Mook is getting it all together. The DA's hot and heavy on your case. He dug up a diva, and she's shrieking an aria about you to the Grand Jury right now.

**HUNGRY MOTHER** What's her name?

**BELLY UP** La Mook. (*He snickers. Slight pause.*)

**HUNGRY MOTHER** Pays to play both ends of the street.

**BELLY UP** 'S a good deal. Immunity from prosecution, all counts 'cept murder one, lifetime guarantee. He tags up – spray paints it on the DA's door: you The Man.

**HUNGRY MOTHER** He's The Man.

**BELLY UP** You The Man, Mom. Your Junk Report peddles his junk.

**HUNGRY MOTHER** That's absurd.

**BELLY UP** Huh huh. Scag pimps snortin' up a storm on your say so, Ma.

(*Slight pause.*)

**HUNGRY MOTHER** Belly Up . . . you think they should sell smack over the counter – like aspirin?

**BELLY UP** (*Laughs softly.*) C'mon, Mom. Why spoil a good thing? I'm checking on those kids for you.

**HUNGRY MOTHER** Mmmmmmmmm.

**BELLY UP** Interesting scenario. After they go into custody of the lending institutions, poof – they disappear. I dig deeper. The big runaround. I run it down. It's easy. . . The banks sold 'em. Mook's the middle man. Commission on every kid.

**HUNGRY MOTHER**   Sold them.

**BELLY UP**   Into slavery . . . Big deal. Every two-bit banana tyrant keeps a couple of Indians around the house. Right here in town I know where you can buy, no questions asked, retarded kids. Cash on the barrelhead. Watch the tube?

**HUNGRY MOTHER**   Never.

**BELLY UP**   White slavery's license to print money. (*Slight pause.*)

**HUNGRY MOTHER**   I made it happen. Made it all happen. Make it up – make it happen. I kept . . . talking about it . . . reporting it, you know? Fictional fact, a metaphor . . . sort of true, you know? . . . and . . . and it comes back at me. It all comes back. Drifting up from downtown . . . humming . . . the wires have picked it up . . . 'fore you know it, it's *news,* it's . . . happened . . . Honest, officer, it was only a fucking metaphor . . . The junk report! The junk report! Belly Up, from junk I knew from nothing! The Mook is trying to set me up . . . Last broadcast I did a slavery newsbit. Just a comedy sketch. Somebody must have picked up on it.

(*Slight pause.*)

**BELLY UP**   Paranoid schizophrenia. Classic case. Delusions of grandeur. Unholy power to make manifest The Word. Unable to distinguish between cause and effect. Egocentric cosmology . . . Pull yourself together. You just water, Mother, Glass. You just show it back. Artists count for nothing, Mom. Don't take it so tough.

**HUNGRY MOTHER**   (*Mumbles.*) Bui doi.

**BELLY UP**   You don't say.

**HUNGRY MOTHER**   Bui doi.

**BELLY UP**   Dust of life. Street urchins. Half-breed Honda banditos. (*Slight pause.*) Shit. I had you lamped, Mom. I knew you been there. The 'Nam. Moo goo gai pan, my ass. (*Slight pause. Softer:*) Whadjoo take the fall for? Over *there.*

**HUNGRY MOTHER**   (*Winks, smiles wanly.*) Fragged the fucker. Fragged him.

(*He gets up and leaves the bar. After he's gone:*)

**BELLY UP**   See you 'round, Mom.

(*On the street, Hungry Mother turns his collar up against the cold. A Prostitute (Johnnie Sucrose) and a Pimp (Jimmy Shellelagh) loiter on the edges of the light. A Derelict (Charlie Samoa) stutter dances up to Hungry Mother.*)

**DERELICT (CHARLIE SAMOA)**   Ladies and gentlemen! For your listening entertainment – the Latin from Manhattan! Hey! Hey, man, it's cold! Cold! Thirty cents for some apricot brandy, man. That's it. That's all we need.

**HUNGRY MOTHER**  Sorry.

**DERELICT (CHARLIE SAMOA)**  It's cold, man. Anything. Come on, we just shot some junk, man, we need that brandy, come *on!*

**HUNGRY MOTHER**  I don't have anything.

**DERELICT (CHARLIE SAMOA)**  Man, your heart's so hard you wouldn't give God a break. Shit. Hey, brothers, c'mon . . .

*(They fade. Hungry Mother enters the studio; the blue light is "on.")*

**HUNGRY MOTHER**  Hungry Mother here, it's a fine fine super fine predawn funk – smoke blankets the greater metropolitan area, they continue to machine-gun survivors outside our studio rap rap rap rap rap and the *hits* just keep on comin' – and all told it looks like another fine fine super fine day in this fine fine city of ours! Before we descend into a welter of obscure pronouns, here's the plot –

*(Lickety-split lung-screech.)* SUNDAY! Beautiful Sunday at U.S. Dragstrip Thirty just south of the tarpits! Thrill to the unholy smells and sounds and sight-gags as Captain O-blivion two-time cracked vertebrae champion heading for a head-on collision in his plutonium-charged heavy water under glass thresher goes against Free Bubba Free B. in his multinational banana consortium funny car! PLUS! Demolition Derby! You'll want to be there when the lights go out! PLUS! Hundreds of prize doors! PLUS! Chapped lips! PLUS! Blood-mad brahma bulls released every few seconds in the seating areas to stampede crazily through the stands! DON'T YOU DARE BE THERE! MISS IT! MISS IT! SUNDAY! SUNDAY! SUNDAY!

*(Pause. Cool, calm, very liberal underground FM.)* And now, this week's interview with a Woman in the streets . . . Screaming Annie, dressed in ribbons.

*(Phone rings, rings again. Flicks switches. Hungry Mother jumps at it.)* Free Lance?

*(Janis voice live over PA – thick and drowsy.)*

**JANIS**  Mother, this is me.

**HUNGRY MOTHER**  How are you?

**JANIS**  All right . . . I wanted to say thank you . . .

**HUNGRY MOTHER**  For what? You sound sort of –

**JANIS**  . . . ah . . . I just . . . just wanted, just want you – I just, Mother – we on the air?

**HUNGRY MOTHER**  Yeah, you want me to take us off?

**JANIS**  Won't be necessary . . . Mother, I'm sorry.

*(There is a sound, something falling, a hard surface. We no longer hear Janis' drowsy breathing over the PA, but the line is still open.)*

**HUNGRY MOTHER**  For what? *(He freezes. Blackout.)*

**LOUD SPEAKER**  Live Flashback! Live! From the Hotel Abyss! The Flophouse of Stalinism! The Very First Broadcast! Hungry Mother –

In the Beginning!

(*Studio illuminated. A tres haute couture Free Lance strikes a pose. Hungry Mother's taped voice comes over the PA:*)

**HUNGRY MOTHER**  (*On tape.*) A warm warm welcome to WTWI call letters, and to the station for which they stand.

(*Hungry Mother breaks freeze and goes to mike. They are both younger, fresher.*)

**HUNGRY MOTHER**  Dressed to kill. To a T. To the teeth. As she parades up and down in front of our microphone – (*She does, flashing a barracuda grin on every turn.*) isn't she lovely? Isn't she wonderful, ladies and gentlemen? Wrapped from head to toe in delicious apricot leather.

**FREE LANCE**  (*Laughs.*) Bitch.

**HUNGRY MOTHER**  Yes, just a vision of fruit loveliness. This is the Hungry Mother, at WTWI, a nouveau station with a nouveau view, on what we hope to be the first of many many twilight broadcasts with you. And on our maiden broadcast we have a maiden broad –

**FREE LANCE**  Vaudeville's dead, sweetie.

**HUNGRY MOTHER**  Here in our fruit lovely studios. With us today – Polish Vodka! One of the highest paid, uh, what exactly is it you do, dear?

**FREE LANCE**  Make it up, baby.

**HUNGRY MOTHER**  Right. And for our inaugural broadcast we're going to feature something that's uniquely suited to the very special medium of radio: a fashion show. That's right. Ought to give you some idea of what you're up against here at WTWI. So, let's shove off. The First Annual WTWI Twilight Fashions Show. Isn't she lovely? A vision. Simply a vision. Pol Vod is so – well, slender – no, thin . . . cadaverous, really . . . poking ribs, hollow cheeks . . . a dream, really – slight potbelly, haunted eyes, leather boots, and all the rest of it. Wearing a lovely barbed wire pendant, and modelling for us that sensational new black lip glass. So positively sado-masch, wouldn't you say? Deco-deco, innit? If I were to coin it, I'd call it – *Dachau Chic*. How's that strike you, darling?

**FREE LANCE**  Perf, Mother. Just perf. (*She is still moving up and down in front of the mike, hitting high-fashion poses.*)

**HUNGRY MOTHER**  Dachau Chic, indeed. Absolutely stunning. And now Polish Vodka is going to do something very *kinetic*, demonstrating the amazing glide and flow, warp and woof woof of apricot leather, aren't you darling? Yes, she's sweeping up and down in front of our microphone – (*In fact, she is standing very still now, watching him.*) whew. What a woman. Sheer Poetry, pretty as a picture. What a woman, lovely, lovely. What? What's she doing now?

Ladies and gentle –

(*Hushed.*) Oh, I wish you could see this. She's – dare I describe it? Who dat who say who dat? She's taking *off* that scrumptious apricot leather – *strip* by scrumptious *strip*. She's – *peeling off!* Oh, my, oh God, oh gracious! Oh so fine! Backfield in motion! Peel me, baby, peel me off! Oh, my, oh . . . what . . . breasts, what – what dugs! . . . and – and now . . . she's doing something perfectly . . . *indescribable* . . . with a silk handkerchief . . . oh . . . my . . . I ONLY WISH I COULD DESCRIBE IT TO YOU FULLY! WORDS FAIL ME! OH! OH! OH! . . . oh. (*Pause.*) Whew. Oh my. Thank you, ducks. Worked me into a veritable lather. Thanks so much.

**FREE LANCE**   (*Dryly.*) Not at all.

**HUNGRY MOTHER**   Really . . . stunning. No other word will do. State of the art striptease.

**FREE LANCE**   My pleasure. Avec plaisir.

**HUNGRY MOTHER**   No, no mine. How d'you feel?

**FREE LANCE**   A bit chilly.

**HUNGRY MOTHER**   I don't wonder. Feel free to cover up. I hope that was as good for you as it was for me. Do you have something beautiful for us? Song and dance? A bit of the old soft foot? Why don't you just *whip* something up?

**FREE LANCE**   Oh, yes, I've got something for you. I've come prepared. I'd like to do for you now at this time – my impression of a JAP. (*Slight pause.*)

**HUNGRY MOTHER**   I beg your pardon.

**FREE LANCE**   Jewish-American Princess.

**HUNGRY MOTHER**   Oh . . . sounds *fun.*

**FREE LANCE**   Well . . . here goes.

(*As she speaks – nasal Long Island accent – she sinuously removes her clothes. Her speech, harsh and sharp, absolutely counterpoint to her sexy elegant movement. Hungry Mother watches the strip, amazed.*)
I just you know been hanging out, you know? You know what I mean? I got these like you know *problems* on my head, you know – I mean it's so off-putting. And if I could just iron 'em out you know, don't you know, it would be *smooth sailing,* no problem, I'm telling you. But it's anything but easy. It has to do with this relationship, and it's so heavy. It's like, you know, such a *hassle.* Who am I to know where it's going? I swear to God I just don't understand men for the rest of my natural life. I mean, it is so *shitty.* It's shitty being with him. It's shitty being without him. I mean, he is such a fuck. You know? I tell him, I say to him, you are such a fuck. I mean, it is trauma time again . . . Am I making sense? (*She finishes the strip perfectly timed on the last word.*)

**HUNGRY MOTHER**   Very convincing.

**FREE LANCE**   Felt good.

**HUNGRY MOTHER**   I'm not a Jewish-American Princess, but I found it as offensive as the next person.

**FREE LANCE**   I thought you'd like it. (*Slight pause.*) Kiss my vagina. (*Slight pause.*)

**HUNGRY MOTHER**   Meshuga. I don't think I can do that on the air.

**FREE LANCE**   Why not? You're such a fuck. Oh Mother, kiss my vagina.

(*Slight pause.*)

**HUNGRY MOTHER**   Extend my *metaphor* . . . Kiss my vagina, extend my metaphor . . . Listening audience, the next sound you will hear – will be – me and Pol Vod – playing chess.

(*Blackout.*)

(*In blackout.*)

**LOUD SPEAKER**   We'll be back . . . we'll be back . . . we'll be back . . . we'll be back . . .

(*Studio illuminated. Hungry Mother stares at the phone in his hand. A loud, empty drone . . . He drops it. Grabs his coat, walks into the street. It's dark and cold. The Derelict approaches.*)

**DERELICT (CHARLIE SAMOA)**   Hey, man. I almost made my trap. Just about got it, just about got it made. Just four cents short. I know you got a nickle. It's cold. Come on, man, I ast you before. *Nice.*

**HUNGRY MOTHER**   Okay. (*Hungry Mother hands The Derelict a coin; he gives Hungry Mother one in return.*)

**DERELICT (CHARLIE SAMOA)**   Here, man. Change.

**HUNGRY MOTHER**   Honest man.

**DERELICT (CHARLIE SAMOA)**   Apricot brandy. Jesus in a bottle. (*The Derelict scuttles off into the dark. The Pimp and The Prostitute appear on the edges of the light.*)

**PROSTITUTE (JOHNNIE SUCROSE)**   Hey, John. Looking for something?

**HUNGRY MOTHER**   Pay phone.

**PIMP (JIMMY SHILLELAGH)**   Not on this block.

**PROSTITUTE (JOHNNIE SUCROSE)**   Lonely, honey? Party? (*The Derelict (Charlie Samoa) comes back around the corner, a bottle in a paper bag.*)

**DERELICT (CHARLIE SAMOA)**   Care for a choke?

**HUNGRY MOTHER**   No thanks.

(*The Derelict hits Hungry Mother across the face with the bottle. He falls to his knees. Blood.*)

**DERELICT (CHARLIE SAMOA)**   How 'bout now?

**HUNGRY MOTHER**   Stuff it.

*(The Derelict walks around Hungry Mother, stops, sighs.)*

**DERELICT (CHARLIE SAMOA)**   Hungry Momma. Hungry Momma. The real item.

**HUNGRY MOTHER**   Charlie Samoa.

*(Slight pause.)*

**CHARLIE SAMOA**   Acute.

**HUNGRY MOTHER**   Cholly. Whatchoo doin' on the street, Cholly?

**CHARLIE SAMOA**   I beat the rap, Mom.

**HUNGRY MOTHER**   Congratulations.

**CHARLIE SAMOA**   I knew you'd be happy for me.

**HUNGRY MOTHER**   Nobody loves you like your Mother, Cholly. Where's your pals. Johnnie Suc. Jimmy Shill.

**CHARLIE SAMOA**   At home.

*(Jimmy Shillelagh strikes a match, illuminating the darkness. Charlie laughs.)*

Tuning up their fingers.

*(Hungry Mother glances at Johnnie and Jimmy.)*

**HUNGRY MOTHER**   Okay, Cholly Sam, I'm mugged. Consider me mugged. Take it all. Spectacles, testicles, wallet, and wings.

**CHARLIE SAMOA**   *(Half grins.)* Sssssssssss.

**HUNGRY MOTHER**   C'mon, Cholly Sam! Do your number! Run it down! Dissemble!

*(Slight pause.)*

**CHARLIE SAMOA**   Dissemble. Shit . . . Big Ma-moo, ain't you somethin'? Talk about barbarians, shit like that. You sound just like a boo-jwa-zee. You know that?

**HUNGRY MOTHER**   Where'd you learn that word?

**CHARLIE SAMOA**   What word? Bar-barian?

**HUNGRY MOTHER**   Bourgeoisie.

**CHARLIE SAMOA**   CC. C'mon, Mom, lighten up. Get rid of that boojwa snide. I been to CC. We all been to CC. All God's chillun been to City College . . . *(Laughs.)* Which accounts for dem rising expectations. *(He begins to stalk Hungry Mother.)* Expectations which can in no way be satisfied. Now or ever.

*(Hungry Mother begins speaking very rapidly, as if to fend him off with words.)*

**HUNGRY MOTHER**   Tell me, as a member of the affected class, do you believe there is a deliberate, that is to say conscious, effort on the part of the authorities, if you will, the powers that be, or, if you prefer, the money men, the movers and shakers, the high-rolling, high-rise boys, the fat cats, the leopard-coat ladies –

*(Jimmy and Johnnie join the stalk, snarling; Hungry Mother falters, but goes on:)* – to, uh, uh, cut back, uh, basic social services, restrict

access to education, lower the already abysmal standard of living and further degrade the quality of life for the poor, in a cynical calculated attempt to discourage democratic tendencies, stifle aspirations, slay rising expectations, and narcoticize anger, in order to escape culpability and social conflagration?

**CHARLIE SAMOA**   Yeah. In a word.

**HUNGRY MOTHER**   Fat lot of good it did you, learning that word.

**CHARLIE SAMOA**   (*Laughs.*) Barbarian? No, Mother. it did not do me no good at all. I shoulda known better. Waste a time. Coulda been out on the street. Fulfilling my destiny as a social predator. My folks, you know?

**HUNGRY MOTHER**   Is there a pay phone around here?

**CHARLIE SAMOA**   Old folks, you know? They get sappy. All the resins harden up. They didn't cop to the dead end.

**HUNGRY MOTHER**   (*Cheery radio.*) They never apprehended the dynamics of racial interaction.

**CHARLIE SAMOA**   Yeah. They never apprehended the *dynamic*. Anybody can talk like you, Mother. You know that? Anybody. Who you wanna call this hour?

**HUNGRY MOTHER**   Emergency. 911.

**CHARLIE SAMOA**   Number's been changed. Unlisted. That l'il girl snuffed herself on your show tonight. That your idea?

**HUNGRY MOTHER**   Fuck off.

**CHARLIE SAMOA**   Way too late for the SOS. Is that a first?

**HUNGRY MOTHER**   What do you think?

**CHARLIE SAMOA**   I think so . . . I think it is. Now, *that's a* record. Mother. Your best show. So far.

**HUNGRY MOTHER**   My fan club. You guys must be the new bulge in my demographics.

**JOHNIE SUCROSE**   I told you. We never miss a show.

**JIMMY SHILLELAGH**   Bastard.

**JOHNNY SUCROSE**   I be all over you. Like ugly on a gorilla.

**CHARLIE SAMOA**   Like *white* on rice.

(*They laugh. Charlie Samoa is winding a chain around his fist.*)

**HUNGRY MOTHER**   Is this any way for a fan club to act?

**JOHNNIE SUCROSE**   I wouldn't give you the sweat off my balls.

**JIMMY SHILLELAGH**   Mistah Kurtz, Mothah, he dead.

(*They mug him, ferociously. As they do, studio lights up: Hoover and The Navajos enter, in their dark glasses, and trash the studio; blue broadcast light in studio goes out; mugging ends; Charlie, Johnnie and Jimmy exit, exhilarated; trashing stops, Crazy Joe and Freddy exit; Hoover, with great ceremony and delicacy, pulls a white feather from his vest and floats it down upon the wreckage; Hoover smiles*

*cooly and strolls out.)*
*(Bloodied and shaken, Hungry Mother staggers into the ruined studio.)*
**HUNGRY MOTHER**   Oh, sweet Christ. *(He picks up the feather.)*
Got to be – Hoover and the – *(He pulls the dead blue bulb out of the socket and smashes it on the floor.)* Navajos! *(Roots around, finds another blue bulb.)* All right.
*(Carefully replaces it. Nothing. He starts to laugh. Flicks switches. Strikes the console, tearing his hands. Laughter becomes sobs, then screams on each blow. Stops, exhausted. The Mook enters. Hungry Mother turns to The Mook and raises his bloody hands.)*
**HUNGRY MOTHER**   My impersonation of Screaming Annie.
**THE MOOK**   With ribbons.
**HUNGRY MOTHER**   Agaga.
**THE MOOK**   I come to get you out, Mother.
**HUNGRY MOTHER**   Can't.
**THE MOOK**   Why?
**HUNGRY MOTHER**   I'm . . . *estranged.*
**THE MOOK**   Anomie?
*(Hungry Mother looks up at him.)*
**HUNGRY MOTHER**   You been to CC too. Cholly Sam's right. Anybody can talk like me. Yeah. Anomie. It's *rude* out there.
**THE MOOK**   Rude.
**HUNGRY MOTHER**   The weather today, Mook, very rude with streaks of mean. Never underestimate the effects of rudeness on the disintegrating personality.
**THE MOOK**   A little rude, maybe. Somewhat abrupt. Always a little rude this time of year. Gulf stream. Me, I call it brisk. Crisp collars, sharp lapels.
**HUNGRY MOTHER**   I lead a life of rudeness.
**THE MOOK**   Genteel. Always.
**HUNGRY MOTHER**   Rudeness. Covered with dogshit. Tell you something. Shit doesn't increase arithmetically. It increases geometrically. So, instead of twice as much shit, you got shit squared and shit cubed.
**THE MOOK**   *(Laughs softly.)* I can dig it. Come on, Mother. Come with me.
**HUNGRY MOTHER**   Why?
**THE MOOK**   They gonna bust you.
**HUNGRY MOTHER**   How you know that?
**THE MOOK**   I set you up.
*(Pause. Hungry Mother gets to his feet, stumbles, finds the bean can.)*
**HUNGRY MOTHER**   Bean?
**THE MOOK**   Le's go.

**HUNGRY MOTHER**  Lemme alone. It's been a tough day.

**THE MOOK**  Le's go baby! I can . . . *finesse* it for you.

**HUNGRY MOTHER**  Forget it. No big deal. Been busted before.

**THE MOOK**  But whatchoo gonna do with yo' mouthpiece shut down? Whatchoo gonna do when you can't run yo' mouth?

**HUNGRY MOTHER**  Tell you what you can do for me, Mook. Tell you what. (*Formally.*) Why don't you loan me a dollar or two . . .

**THE MOOK**  So the dogs won't piss on you? (*They both laugh.*)

**HUNGRY MOTHER**  Outstanding. You know the phrase.

**THE MOOK**  (*Doing a little dance of inspiration.*) C'mon, big Mom. Snap back, baby, snap back! You my second string. The Mook lookin' for you to follow in his steps. Bounce back, Mom. You can do it. Bounce back!

(*Hungry Mother lies down.*)

Charp. (*He flips a coin on Hungry Mother's chest.*) There you go, boy. Knock yo'se'f out.

(*Hungry Mother leaps up and grabs the bowie knife.*)

**HUNGRY MOTHER**  (*Very quietly.*) What do you say we engage in a little internecine behavior?

**THE MOOK**  Stay cool, baby. You can hack it.

**HUNGRY MOTHER**  Let's go to the mat. Just you and me.

**THE MOOK**  Don't act the honkey. I found Free Lance.

(*This stops Hungry Mother cold. He stares at The Mook for a moment, then throws the knife into the floor.*)

**HUNGRY MOTHER**  Where?

**THE MOOK**  She came in. I took her back.

**HUNGRY MOTHER**  That's *white* of you.

**THE MOOK**  Easy. Easy. Don't press your luck.

**HUNGRY MOTHER**  Sorry . . . She all right?

**THE MOOK**  Well, you know, Mother, excess sentiment has always been my tragic flaw. My tragic flaw. She had made a monkey out of me, Mother. Set a deadly precedent. She had burned the goddamn church. To see the church burn, Mother, is to realize you *can* burn the church. Powerful realization. It was incumbent upon me – as a businessman – to provide a metaphor. An antidote. Powerful one. I cannot abide no more fires . . . Of course, I realize I was in danger – danger of fulfilling the cliché Free Lance had constructed for me. So I struggled. I love Free Lance. You know that. But what could I do? There was just no way home. She had put herself in the box. Deep. So I said to my pretty little self – piss on it. Ever cut yourself on a piece of paper? (*The Mook draws a hand across his throat.*) Linen stationery. Slit. Gush. *Sharp.* Bled blue, bled blue. Black gash. Mouth to mouth. My hands were cold. What bothered me most was fulfilling the cliché.

Predestination jive. 'Course, she could have been rescued. By you. Violins up, violins out. Perfect. And let me off the hook. Muffed it, Mother.

**HUNGRY MOTHER**   I could call you names.

**THE MOOK**   Charlie Samoa works for me.

*(Slight pause.)*

**HUNGRY MOTHER**   Why'd they mug me? Give me a plot point. Something to hang on to.

**THE MOOK**   Reason? Let go, baby. *(Laughs.)* What if I told you that l'il slit who checked out over your air – that was Charlie's sister. I had to let him have you.

**HUNGRY MOTHER**   No relation.

**THE MOOK**   No *reason. No reason at all.* 'Cause *he felt* like it ... I made you, Mother. Don't you dare forget it. Was The Mook who turned yo' volume up, and nobody else. So's you could be *heard.* So's you could run yo' mouth. Put it out there. On de air. You done good by me. I 'preciate that. Made me a lot of scratch. The bust be here soon. I got to bust my Mother now – but I sure as shit can still save yo' ass.

**HUNGRY MOTHER**   Pimp. Scag sum. Smack ghoul.

**THE MOOK**   Tsk. Tsk. Tsk. Feeble. Mighty lame. You shoulda held on to that knife, boy. You ignorant, Mama. Got to teach you all the rules to you own game. *(Tenderly.)* Come with me, Mother. Don't be bitter. Be my, be my minion. My one and only minion.

**HUNGRY MOTHER**   *(Shaking his head.)* The exigencies change.

*(A beat, and then The Mook roars, raucous falsetto laughter.)*

**THE MOOK**   Keep after them blackisms, boy! You keep after them blackisms, boy! You get there yet! ... You know, you right, Mom. I be feelin' pimpish to-day! Be feeling pimpish. *(At the door, he turns back.)* Momma – I thought you'd like to know – I got a terrific price for them kids. *(Roars again. Stops.)* Keep after it, boy. You get to be a nigger yet. *(Roars again. Exits.)*

*(Hungry Mother makes his way to the mike. Flicks switches. The blue light stays "off." He doesn't seem to notice.)*

**HUNGRY MOTHER**   *(Into the mike.)* Test if it dead ... Give me a try before you pass me by ... Close enough for ground zero ... I've got some good phrases from romantic literature in my head. It's too bad ... This is the Hungry Mother. The Universal Disc Jockey. God's own deejay. Goin' down slow. *(Black.)* Cat's pajamas ... This is your Hungry Mother talkin' to you! I cannot be slow – that why I'm so fast! *(Sings an offhand blues.)* Goin' down slow – oh goin' down slow – but at least I am – going down – on yoouuu. *(Laid back Top 40.)* One of our very very large numbers, I just know you're gonna love this one – an old old stand-bye, a super-monster in its time – an antediluvian smash – *Sweet Gash!* Oh so sweet! Play it for me just one more time! (*Frenzied Top 40.*) Get down! As your audio agitator I strongly advise you to get down! Get Down! Work yourselves into a frenzy with – Screaming Annie! (*A series of gagging screams. Then in the grand manner.*) When men were men and rock and roll was king. Never the twain shall meet. Send a salami to you boy in the army. (*Slight pause.*) Human freedom diminishing, even vanishing. Ruination. (*Mellifluous.*) We'll have the latest up-to-date quotations on – human wreckage futures in a moment. (*Beat.*) This is you favorite Hungry Mother, illuminating the dark contours of native speech. (*Pause. From this point on, the various radio voices drop away.*) Fuck. Fuck it. Fucked up. Hit you across your fucking mouth. Fuck with me and I'll really fuck you up . . . I try to watch my language, but I'm a victim of history. Or is it eschatology? Verbal inflation is at an all-time high. (*Slight pause.*) First Chinese Baptist Church of the Deaf. (*Slight pause.*) Social engineering. Upward mobility. *Stiletto.* (*Slight pause. A travel agent.*) Vacation in – *steamy* – South Africa! (*Slight pause.*) Say *hungry.* (*Slight pause. Cheery salesman.*) Death Boy, Brown Bomber, White Death, Stallion Stick, Casa Boom, Snow Storm. Allah Supreme, White Noise, Sweet Surrender, Death Wish, Turkish Delight! Any size lot, any cut ratio, buy in bulk and saaaave! If we don't have it, it ain't worth having! If our sauce don't send you, you got no place to go! (*Laughs, then screaming.*) That junk is shit! Shit! Stay 'way. Mother advises you to stay a-way – lay off it all 'cept for Death Wish Smoking Mixture Number 3. After all – why stick when you can blow? (*Slight pause.*) Stick with us. (*Laughs.*) Stick *with* us. Stick with us. Stick it. (*Slight pause.*) Twenty-four hour shooting galleries. (*Slight pause.*) The American Meat Institute presents. Our Lady Of The Cage. A new barbed-wire ballet. With automatic weapons. (*Slight pause.*) Say hungry . . . I'm interested in abused forms. (*Black.*) She not only willing, she *able.* (*Sportscaster.*) Playing hurt. Photo finish. Cut to ribbons . . . That goes without saying. (*Slight pause.*) Dead on my feet. (*Slight pause.*) I pay lip service every chance I get. Flophouse of Stalinism. Two mules and a colored boy. Better a cocksucker than a Communist. (*Pause.*) Down avenues of blue exhaust. (*Pause.*) Voodoo kit. Razor ribbon. Front me 'til Friday. A day late a and dollar short. Tryin' to get over. (*Pause.*) Spike that beautiful black vein! Spike it! (*Pause.*) Say *hungry!* . . . Born to shoot junk. Strafe me, baby. Strafe me. Up against it. *Aphasia.* All the rage. Hungry. Riff. On the rag. In the name of the father, and of the son, and of the holocaust. World without end. Shit from shortcake. Estatic suffering. (*He falters.*) I disremember. (*Slight pause. Trembling:*) Brush fire wars. Bane of my existence. Blue sky *ventures!* (*Top 40 outburst.*) The watchword for today – *hydrogenize slumism!* Bear that in mind. (*Pause.*) Under the gun. (*Pause.*) Under the gun. (*Pause.*) Under the gun. (*Pause.*) Free-fire zone. (*Pause.*) When I get back . . . When I get back to The World – (*Lightly.*) I ain't gonna do nothin' . . . but stay black – an' *die.* (*Slight pause.*) *I'm serious.* (*Laughs. Freezes.*)

(*The blue broadcast light pops "on." After a moment the lights dim and slowly fade. Out. The blue light glows a moment, then extinguishes. Blackout.*)

## END OF PLAY

**ON THE VERGE or The Geography of Yearning**
*is dedicated to Arnold Cooper on the occasion of his sixtieth birthday*


Perhaps the imagination is on the verge of recovering its rights.
*Andre Breton*
(paraphrased by E.O.)


ON THE VERGE (or THE GEOGRAPHY OF YEARNING) received its professional premiere on January 5, 1985, at Center Stage, Baltimore, Stan Wojewodski, Artistic Director, Peter Culman, Managing Director. The production was directed by Jackson Phippin, with the following cast:

| | |
|---|---|
| MARY | Mary Layne |
| FANNY | Brenda Wehle |
| ALEX | Marek Johnson |
| GROVER et al. | James McDonnell |

The sets were by Tony Straiges, lights by James F. Ingalls, costumes by Del Risberg, sound and music by Paul Sullivan and Janet Kalas, and props by Susan Andrews and Barbara Robinson.


**SCENE**

The play begins in 1888. In Terra Incognita.


**CHARACTERS**

Fanny
Mary
Alexandra
Grover, Alphonse, The Gorge Troll, The Yeti, Gus, Madame Nhu, Mr. Coffee, and Nicky Paradise

All three ladies are *adventurers*.

Alphonse, Grover, et al., are played by a single actor.

The ladies are American, and speak a good 19th-century American speech – not British, nor mid-Atlantic.

The ladies are in full Victorian trekking dress, plus practical accessories – pith helmets, etc.

The titles and journal entries separate each scene. The titles of each scene should be conveyed visually, or aurally, by slide, sign, or recording. The titles are essential, and *must* be used.

The Journal Entries are done to the audience as direct address. They are not written in the moment, but have been composed previously, and are now presented to the audience.

# ON THE VERGE

## ACT ONE

### (1) On the Verge

*The ladies are in a hot, white light.*

**MARY**   Day One. Landfall.
**FANNY**   Beach.
**MARY**   Island or continent?
**ALEX**   Isthmus or archipelago?
**FANNY**   Beach. Narrow ribbon. Cliff face. Sheer. Beyond – ?
**ALEX**   Up and over – ?
**FANNY**   Unbearable anticipation.
**MARY**   Mysterious interior.
　　　*(They sigh.)*
**MARY**   We have reached our embarcadero.
**ALEX**   Into the unknown.
**MARY**   1888. The last undiscovered, unexplored – bit.
**ALEX**   Of globe.
**FANNY**   The sudden force of circumstance.
**ALEX**   An inheritance.
**MARY**   Money and time. Time and money.
**FANNY**   Grover said –
**MARY**   A mandate from the Boston Geo –
**FANNY**   "Go!"
**ALEX**   We find ourselves –
**FANNY**   Up against it – in the Antipodes –
**MARY**   Latitude 15 degrees south –
**FANNY**   Of the Equator.
**MARY**   Longitude 125 degrees west –
**FANNY**   Of Greenwich.
**ALEX**   Somewhere east of Australia, and west of Peru.
**MARY**   Tropics.
**FANNY**   Should be good anchovy fishing.
**MARY**   Poised.
**FANNY**   On the brink.
**ALEX**   On the beach.
**MARY**   On the verge.

**ALEX**  Set to trek.

**MARY**  Trekking in *Terra Incognita!*

*(They clasp hands.)*

**MARY, ALEX,** and **FANNY**  Terra Incognita!

*(Mary comes down to do her journal entry.)*

**MARY**  Before I began my travels in the uncharted reaches of the world, an avuncular colleague took me aside. "I have heard your peregrinations are impelled, in part, by scientific curiosity," he said. "Allow me to offer you some sage counsel. Always take measurements, young lady. And always take them from the adult male." *(Beat.)* Sound advice.


### (2) Taking Stock – or – on Sartorial Custom, Civil and Savage

**MARY**  I have always traveled solo hitherto.

**FANNY**  As have I.

**ALEX**  As have I.

**MARY**  Occasionally encountering a sister sojourner on a trek –

**FANNY**  Pausing briefly for the pro forma cuppa –

**ALEX**  And then going our separate ways, alone.

**MARY**  By "alone" you mean of course in the company of dozens of native bearers, beaters, porters, sherpas, and guides.

**FANNY**  We agreed. No porters.

**ALEX**  *(Sighs)* No sherpas.

**FANNY**  You carry what you collect.

*(They begin to do inventory.)*

**MARY**  Machetes. Three.

**FANNY**  Umbrellas. A brace.

**ALEX**  Rope. Some yards.

**FANNY**  A gross of hand-tinted picture postcards.

**MARY**  By your own hand, Fanny?

**FANNY**  I had them fabricated. I anticipate they will not be readily available en route.

**ALEX**  Imaginative preconceptions of Terra Incognita, Fanny?

**FANNY**  Preconceptions? Precisely.

**ALEX**  Are you clairvoyant, Fanny?

**FANNY**  Look. Generic scenes of general interest. Generic fauna. Generic jungle. Generic bush.

**MARY**  They will complement our cartography, which is highly speculative and totally fanciful. Ink pens. Journals, hand-sewn and leather-bound.

**FANNY** Hand me my toothbrush, won't you?

**MARY** Peacock feathers. Beads. Colored glass. Patent medicines. Specimen bags. Lanterns. Butterfly nets. Cello. Ocarina. Mandolin. Rock-climbing apparatus. *Sherry.* A Persian carpet of modest dimension. Parasols. Mosquito netting. Mineral water. Canteens. Water colors. Sketching canvas. Canopy clips. Bamboo staves. Quartz knives. Iodine. Shepherd's pie. Barley sugar. Lemon drops.

**FANNY** Pith helmets.

*(She distributes them. They don them ceremoniously, and in unison.)*

**MARY** We're not short of pith – that's sure.

*(Fanny pulls out a rhinestoned tiara and blonde wig.)*

**FANNY** Whenever I must palaver with pasha or poobah, I don this tonsorial getup. And lay out a formal tea. It never fails to impress.

**MARY** I don't wonder.

**FANNY** It stands to reason. Savages are naked. For the most part.

**ALEX** I for one am impressed. I've a Kodak! *(She rummages.)*

**MARY** No, really?

**FANNY** Where did you get it?

**ALEX** Friends in high places.

**FANNY** Show.

*(Alex shows.)*

**FANNY** Is that it? That little box?

**ALEX** The film, it's called, captures the image.

**FANNY** Oh?

**ALEX** Like honey. Insects in amber. Silver nitrate. I have no way of printing the images. That requires a laboratory. Which would have meant porters.

**FANNY** We agreed.

**ALEX** We did. Fanny –

*(Fanny models tiara and wig. Alex Kodaks her.)*

**FANNY** You won't see what you've Kodaked?

**ALEX** Not until we return home.

**FANNY** How do you know that it works?

**ALEX** You just trust. You "click." You store. You protect. You wait.

**FANNY** You hope and pray.

**ALEX** You trust. Transport. Guard with your very life. Years of deserts, mountains, pagan tribesmen, and inclement weather. Back in civilization, you hand over your nascent images. Have they survived the travails of the trek? Breathless, you await the results of the chemical revelation. With a little luck – voilá! Kodaks! Lovely mementos. And, best of all, incontrovertible proof for posterity. Documentation.

**MARY** I wouldn't trust 'em. Misleading. The natives say they steal your spirit.

**ALEX**  Funny word, native.

**MARY**  A Kodak is no more the thing itself than an etching. Flat. A shadow. Physical specimens are what count. Hides, horns, and bobtails.

**FANNY**  We agreed. No porters.

**ALEX**  Your natives are mistaken. An unseen moment that would have vanished without a trace is brought to light. The spirit is not stolen. It is illuminated.

**MARY**  Mysticism.

**ALEX**  Science.

**MARY**  That's not science, dear. That's engineering. No, Alexandra, we must have something the Boston Geo can lay hands on.

**FANNY**  You carry what you collect.

**MARY**  Physical evidence. Not impressions. Not imagery. Not emotion. Objectivity. Not poetry, m'dears. Not romance. You know what I'm saying.

**ALEX** and **FANNY**  Mmmmmmmmmmmmmmmm.

**MARY**  Shall we saddle up?

(*Something in the sand catches Alex's eye. She uncovers it.*)

**ALEX**  A glint in the sand.

**FANNY**  Hooper do!

**MARY**  An artifact! So soon! This is lucky!

**ALEX**  Qu'est ce que c'est?

(*She picks up a metal button and hands it to Mary.*)

**ALEX**  Gloss this.

**MARY**  Metallic button. Writing. Oh, this is lucky. Latin letters. What a surprise. I'd have thought runes.

**FANNY**  I'd have thought glyphs. Can you make it out?

**MARY**  Not English.

**FANNY**  Phonetically.

**MARY**  ( *Puzzles it out.* ) "Hec – kwhod – ont."

**FANNY**  There's a question mark after it. It's a question.

(*They try various pronunciations and inquisitive inflections.*)

**ALL**  "Hec – kwhod – ont?" "Hec – kwhod – ont?" "Hec – kwhod – ont?"

**FANNY**  Pity it's not English.

**ALEX**  You didn't expect English, did you, Fanny?

**MARY**  It would not have surprised me. English is everywhere.

**FANNY**  A good thing, too.

**MARY**  Is it? English is the vehicle, and its engine is Empire.

**FANNY**  Stuff.

**ALEX**  Perhaps we'll find a translator.

**MARY**   The first of many mysteries!

*(Alex does her journal entry.)*
**ALEX**   I have seen wonders in the Himalayas. Magic. Mystery.
In Ladakh, it was a quotidian trick for the lamas to raise their body
temperatures by mere mental exertion. Sheer dint of will. They
would sleep all night in snowbanks. At dawn, they would douse
themselves in freezing streams. Then, ice-blue and on the verge of
extinction, they would sit lotus and meditate ferociously. Instantly,
steam would sizzle off them in clouds, rising past their furrowed
brows. In an hour, their robes would be dry as toast – and neatly
pressed. *(Beat.)*
In the blue shadow of Crystal Mountain, I watched a Bon shaman
wrap himself in his black cape, fold himself thrice, become a giant
origami crow, flap flap flap his wings, rise into the sky, and fly
across the saffron moon. *(Beat.)*
In Lhasa, on the bone-white hill of the Potala, before the lunar
congregation of Buddhist alchemists, I saw the Dalai Lama
himself transmute great buckets of gold coins. *(Beat.)* Into yak
butter.

### (3) Up and Over

*The ladies saddle up.*

**MARY**   Let us trek.
**FANNY**   Mary! Alexandra!
**ALEX**   Ladies! To the wall!
   *(They trek. )*
**FANNY**   Look behind us.
**MARY**   Is something gaining?
**FANNY**   In the sand.
**ALEX**   Ooooo!
**MARY**   Our footprints.
**FANNY**   Making our mark. *(They continue trekking. )*
**MARY**   *(A deep inhalation)* Salt air always brings out the metaphysician
   in me.
**FANNY**   I always leave Grover in Terre Haute. The Antipodes are not the
   sort of place one should bring a man.
   *(They reach the cliff face. Fanny eyeballs it.)*
**FANNY**   Steep.
**MARY**   Daunting.

**FANNY** Truculent.

**MARY** Vertiginous.

**ALEX** Child's cake.

(*They prepare their ropes.*)

**ALEX** Surely you will both agree trousers would be far more practical for scaling this promontory.

**MARY** Alexandra, the civilizing mission of Woman is to reduce the amount of masculinity in the world. Not add to it by wearing trousers. The wearing of trousers – by women – leads inexorably to riding astride a horse. Instead of the modest sidesaddle.

**FANNY** And encourages the use of the bicycle. Which for women can never be proper.

**ALEX** I happen to be a "wheel enthusiast." And I have often worn trousers – out of sight of civilized settlement, to be sure – whilst wheeling. Or riding horseback. *Astride.* Far more comfortable and sensible than sidesaddle.

**FANNY** What can one say?

**ALEX** Out of sight of sedentary eyes, I whip off my skirt, under which I have worn sturdy trousers, and am set for practical traveling.

**FANNY** Alexandra, are you wearing trousers at this, moment?

**ALEX** Trousers, ladies, are the future!

**MARY** Yes, I am constantly told by armchair travelers that I must wear trousers in the jungle, and leave my skirt at home.

**FANNY** Men can be soooo trying.

**MARY** I pay no heed, and have often had cause to celebrate my independence. One evening in Malaya near dusk, I fell ten feet into a man-eating tiger trap. Found myself nestled on a cathedral of punji sticks. If I had been wearing trousers, I would have been pierced to the core, and done for. Instead, I found myself sitting on a dozen razor-sharp spikes, in comparative comfort.

**FANNY** A petticoat is the only thing for punji sticks. A good stiff petticoat is worth its weight in gold.

(*Snorts.*) Trousers in the tropics!

**ALEX** Oh, jungles. In the Himalayas, trousers are de rigueur. Allons!

(*Alex leads the way. They scale the cliff. Jungle light. Jungle sounds. Dazzled, they survey the surround.*)

**ALEX** A jeweled jungle!

(*Fanny comes down to do her journal entry.*)

**FANNY** I introduced croquet to the headhunters of the headwaters of the Putamayo. The sport of kings. They loved it. Simply adored the game. Of course, I insisted they use only regulation wooden balls. I would accept no substitutes. The rascals were always batting their latest trophies about. I was strict. They respected me for that.


## (4) The Mysterious Interior

**ALEX**  Terra Incognita!
**FANNY**  Ooooo. Hooper Do!
**MARY**  The mysterious interior.
**ALEX**  Fantastic! A jeweled jungle! I am extruded! I mean ecstatic. Not extruded.
**MARY**  Ladies, shall we bushwhack?
*(They step forward and bushwack.)*
**FANNY**  Some years back, while on assignment in the Amazon River Basin, for my favorite tabloid, *True Trek,* my arch nemesis on *The Globetrotteress* reported I had got myself up in male haberdashery.
**MARY**  Did you sue?
**FANNY**  Grover sued. I would have had the wretch horsewhipped.
**MARY**  I would sooner saunter across the Sahara sans sandals than don trousers.
**ALEX**  Ladies, I am not advocating trousers for general usage. Or polite society. But there are times one simply must – bite the bullet!
**MARY**  An umbrella comes in handy. In the jungle.
**ALEX**  Jungle is not my metier.
**MARY**  We know. Fanny, what thousand and one uses do you find for your umbrella?
**FANNY**  Prodding the suddenly faint of heart. Marine soundings. Poking hippopotamii. And whacking the recalcitrant croc. Thwack! The Mighty Silurian!
**ALEX**  What is a Mighty Silurian?
**MARY**  So Fanny's lurid tabloids call the crocodile.
**ALEX**  *(Working out a lyric.)* Umbrella. Hmmm. Chum. Fella. Drum. Fun. Swa – swa – swa – swa – Swoon! Ta – ta – ta – Typhoon! La la – tropical fever has got me in its mighty thrall.
*(A sudden downpour. The ladies blossom their umbrellas.)*
**FANNY**  No, dear. There's no protection from a tropical downpour.
**ALEX**  None?
**FANNY**  It must be endured.
**ALEX**  Jungle jungle, what a foreboding –
*(The rain stops.)*
**ALEX**  – what a mystery. A jeweled jungle!
**FANNY**  It'll do. Puts one in mind of the great cloud forest of the Orinoco.

**MARY** Not annoying! Not annoying at all! ( *With great resolve.*) Ladies – shall we whack the bush?

(*They start forward, whacking the bush.* )

**FANNY** Ah, the familiar chop chop swack swack. Takes me back. The cloud forest of the Orinoco. Now there is a jungle, ladies. Spiders the size of flapjacks! They flop on you out of the trees! You have to get 'em on the fly! Cut 'em in half in mid-air! Thwack! Spider blood splatters! – hello, what's this ? Mysteries underfoot.

(*Fanny finds something: An old-fashioned egg beater, slightly rusty. She holds it various ways, rotors it, giggles.*)

**FANNY** What do you think it could be?

**MARY** A fan..For this glaze of tropical heat.

**FANNY** (*Rotors.*) Does not generate the slightest breeze.

**MARY** A talisman.

**FANNY** Totem.

**MARY** Amulet.

**FANNY** Taboo. Alexandra?

(*She hands it to Alex, who turns it beaters-down, and rotors it with resolve.*)

**ALEX** Marsupial's unicycle.

(*Hands it to Fanny, who puts it in her belt, like a six-shooter.*)

**JOURNAL ENTRY:**

**MARY** The bane of my many travels in the tropics is a bland, mucilagenous paste called manioc, made from the forlorn and despicable cassava, a tuber of dubious provenance. A vile concoction, manioc tastes, in the best of recipes, like the bottom of a budgie's cage – and is more suited for masonry than human consumption. Manioc is the quintessential native chop, occurring circumglobularly in the tropics. For those with a taste for prussic acid, manioc may be just your cup of tea.

### (5) Native Chop

*The ladies are bushwhacking. Jungle noises all about.*

**ALEX** I am delicious! I mean delirious. Not delicious.

**MARY** Ladies! Shall we whack the bush?

(*They start off. Alex pricks herself on a thorn.*)

**ALEX** Ow! Ligament, juicy Nordic, quiz!

**FANNY** Marvelous strange oaths, Alexandra.

**ALEX** These spikey stickers are a bother. Itch! Lasso pork liquor!

**MARY**  The bush has its logic.

**ALEX**  Fine. The glacier is my milieu. Give me an ice face, a mountain of howling wind and stone, or an impassable crevasse. Below zero, I'm in my element. Why can't a jungle be more like a park?

**FANNY**  Regulated undergrowth?

**ALEX**  Why not? A little order.

**MARY**  A jungle has its order, of course.

**ALEX**  Tips for lady travelers? Or just brushing up on your next address to the Boston Geo?

**MARY**  Don't snip, or snipe. Dear.

**FANNY**  When I was last at the Explorer's Club, I had the most extraordinary meal. It was written up in *True Trek*.

**ALEX**  Please, Fanny, not one of those stories.

**MARY**  This jungle is not so awful. As jungles go, this jungle is not annoying.

**ALEX**  It is nothing but. It is one annoyance after another.

**MARY**  It is dry. A dry jungle is a mercy.

**ALEX**  Mary, it is soggy. It is saturated. I have fungi growing on my corset stays.

**MARY**  Comparatively dry. As jungles go, this one is almost arid. Oh, I have waded through swamps for hours on end, emerging at last with a frill of leeches around my neck like an astrakhan collar.

**ALEX**  There are no astrakhan leeches in the Himalayas. No spikey swamp stickers, no mighty silurians –

**MARY**  But there are abominable snowmen. I've read Fanny's tabloids.

**FANNY**  Abominable snowman was on the menu when I was last at the Explorers' Club. But I suspect it was yak. They pride themselves on their Native Chop. I always have something outlandish. Thinking about the Explorers' Club whets my appetite. We must stop for refreshment. (*She puts down her pack and rummages, preparing a snack.*) On my last visit, we had bear chops, buffalo hump, glacé bees' knees, and armadillo knuckles. Which I for one never suspected armadillos had. Followed by muckleshoots, sweet and sour zebra, wolverine surprise, porcupine quills á la Louis quatorze, locust liqueur, and the celebrated moose mousse. I hear not a good year for gnu, I said. I'd skip the snake salad, if I were you, my companion replied, and the candied cats' eyes aren't worth a penny postcard home. We both agreed to eschew the jellied viscera.

**ALEX**  Fanny, you make the gorge rise.

**FANNY**  The Explorers are famous for their grubs. Their motto: Grubs from around the globe! And there are always the usual boyish sallies about mighty good grub. Ho ho. Sheer bravado. The Explorers are always throwing up in their top hats at the end of an evening

**MARY**  I regret I have never had the pleasure.

**FANNY**  The grand art of Native Chop is quite impossible to recreate in the effete precincts of civilization.

**MARY**  Native Chop, in my experience, is inevitably manioc.

**FANNY**  Always and forever, world without end. Have you ever had manioc fritters?

**MARY**  No.

**FANNY**  Not bad. Not good – but not bad.

**ALEX**  I am famous.

**FANNY**  Date bread?

**MARY**  Please.

**ALEX**  I mean famished. Not famous.

**MARY**  (*Takes date bread.*) Thank you. This is scrumptious, Fanny.

**FANNY**  Alex –

**ALEX**  Thank you. Mmmm, lovely.

**MARY**  Super, Fanny. Puts manioc to shame.

**FANNY**  High praise.

**MARY**  Ubiquitous manioc. We won't escape it. Mark my words. (*Shudders.*) Native Chop.

**FANNY**  This is not Africa, Mary. This is Terra Incognita. Cream cheese?

**ALEX**  I don't believe I've ever. What is it?

**FANNY**  Not cream and not cheese, but it's thick and rich and comes in tins.

**ALEX**  Thick and rich? Like Mrs. Butterworth!

**MARY**  Who is Mrs. Butterworth?
(*Pause.*)

**ALEX**  Oh. (*Beat.*) I don't know.

**MARY**  I'll hazard some. Looks harmless. Spread it on my date bread. Thank you. Has the same consistency as manioc.

**FANNY**  Mary!

**ALEX**  What a treat! Is it new?

**FANNY**  Invented in Chicago, I believe. Well, everything is. Take the ice cream sandwich.

**ALEX**  I've never had one. This is rather nice. Where did you get it? Friends in high places? Will it keep?

**FANNY**  We must devour it immediately. You know, I don't remember packing it. Or buying it for that matter. I didn't make it. I made the date bread.
(*Pause.*)

**MARY**  Another slice, Fanny.

**FANNY**  You know, only a few days on, and I am desperate for a bath.

**MARY**  I concur. What is life without a loofah? Look!
(*They peer ahead.*)

ALEX   He's wearing a uniform.

FANNY   What power? Whose sphere of influence is this plateau?

MARY   This is Terra Incognita! A New World. Sans spheres.

FANNY   Manifest Destiny and the American Way are not spheres.

ALEX   (*To herself.*) Rhomboids of influence, trapezoids. of destiny.

FANNY   We are emissaries, Alexandra, of the good will and benignity of President McKinley. Cleveland. Taft. Whoever is president now. You know. One of those Ohio politicians. Muttonchops.

ALEX   Can you name the vice-president?

FANNY   Not if my life depended on it.

ALEX   Nor I.

MARY   Perhaps he traded for it.

FANNY   The vice-presidency? Of course he traded for it. He's a Democrat. Well? Isn't he?

MARY   No, the native. Perhaps he traded for the uniform.

ALEX   Shall we palaver? He sees us. (*She waves.*)

MARY   I once traded twelve calico blouses to the Masai. Empress sleeves.

ALEX   What did you trade them for?

MARY   My life. White knuckles and chewed nails, dear.

ALEX   (*Dreamily.*) The Masai. Sigh.

MARY   When worn by a brawny warrior with noth ing – but red paint – and a necklace of leopard tails (*Beat.*) a calico blouse – (*Beat.*) is really quite – (*Beat.*) fetching.

ALEX   I should think so.

FANNY   I once encountered the Masai. I said: Wow! Wow! Wow!

ALEX   And how did they reply?

MARY   He's approaching.

FANNY   They seemed to like that. Let's set tea. I'll change.
   (*Fanny goes off to change. Mary and Alex watch the native's approach, as they prepare for tea.*)

ALEX   Funny word, native. Assuming he is a native. Everyone is a native of somewhere, when you think about it. So I guess he must be a native at that. Where are you a native, Mary?

MARY   I haven't a thing to wear. I wish I could wash. Oh, what is life without a loofah!

**JOURNAL ENTRY:**

MARY   In Kuala Lumpur, the seraglio of the Sultan was – a honeycomb. It was as many chambered as the heart of a tribe. I recall the cavernous steam rooms on cold evenings, full of echoing voices and escarpments of mist. The inlaid geometric gold-leaf calligraphy. The rattan sofas. The acres of tile the color of sky.

And a sponge conjured from the exoskeleton of an indigenous fruit. The loofah. Loofah –

## (6) High Tea – or, Many Parts Are Edible

*The ladies have set tea. Fanny has donned not only her wig and tiara, but an elaborate rhinestoned gown. Their guest, Alphonse, wears an impeccable German airman's uniform, and speaks with an extravagant German accent.*

**ALEX**   Loofah. Loofah. Now there's a word to conjure with! Powerful juju.

**FANNY**   More date bread?

**ALPHONSE**   Oh zank you zo much.

**FANNY**   Another cup of tea?

**ALPHONSE**   No, zank you. Mein kidneys are floatink. Heh heh.

**ALEX**   Are you a native?

**ALPHONSE**   Zorry?

**ALEX**   You don't mind my asking.

**ALPHONSE**   Nein.

**MARY**   If you don't mind my saying so, Mr. Bismark –

**ALPHONSE**   Please. Call me Alphonse.

**MARY**   Alphonse. If you don't mind my saying so, you sound a trifle German.

**ALPHONSE**   Alsace-Lorraine.

**ALEX**   Fascinating.

**FANNY**   How do you happen to find yourself here?

**MARY**   Is Alsace-Lorraine French or German these days?

**ALPHONSE**   Gut qvestion. Geography iz deztiny, ladies!

**ALEX**   Oh, that's good! I'll make a note of it.

**MARY**   Alphonse, sprechen sie Deutsch, s'il vous plait?

**ALPHONSE**   Nein. I never haf been dere.

**FANNY**   How do you happen to find yourself in this country, did you say?

**ALPHONSE**   I am a native.

**ALEX**   This is not Alsace-Lorraine – am I wrong?

**ALPHONSE**   I never haf been dere. I haf not der foggiest notion vich vay Alsace-Lorraine iz. Schtraight up in der air, vy not, eh?

**MARY**   Forgive me, but I don't follow.

**ALPHONSE**   He vas! Him. Not me. No! No! No! No eat! No eat! No eat Alphonse! No eat Alphonse! I am varningk you! I am schtringy! No eat Alphonse! Aaaaaiiiieeeeeeeeeeeee!

(*A stricken pause.*)

**FANNY**  I no savvy, as they say out west in Indian Territory. What is this fellow's problem?

**MARY**  He is not Alphonse from Alsace-Lorraine.

**ALPHONSE**  No vay, José. I'm from right here at home. Dat vas him. Alphonse. Der von I ate. His uniform, his accent. His syntax. Zide effects. Occupational hazard. Hoppens everytime I eat schomevon.

**FANNY**  Oh, goodness.

**ALPHONSE**  I should schtick to date bread. Delicious.

(*He has another slice.*)

**ALEX**  He's a cannibal.

**FANNY**  Now that's really native chop.

**MARY**  Nothing to be alarmed about. Cannibals are perfectly rational human beings.

**FANNY**  You are a liberal, Mary.

**MARY**  I am an anthropologist. I traveled extensively amongst the Indigos. Cannibals – but lively. Anthropophagii tend to be sluggish, you know. I found them no bother to me at all. Of course, you had to keep them from eating your porters. Frequent head counts were the order of the day. There are two sorts of folks in the world. The sort you drink with, and the sort you eat with. Cannibals you drink with.

**ALPHONSE**  Ja! I am a Free Mason! (*Pause.*) Or, radder, that little rascal Alphonse vas a Free Mason. Egxcuze me, ladies, I am, at der moment, a little confuzed. Too zoon after zupper.

**MARY**  A Free Mason. What else do you know about your – about Alphonse?

**ALPHONSE**  He vas a pilot.

**FANNY**  A riverboat?

**ALPHONSE**  Nein, nein, nein. He flew. May I have some more of zis date bread, pliz? Und cream cheese? Good schtuff, zis cream cheese.

**MARY**  You were saying, Alphonse?

**ALPHONSE**  I vas sayingk, I vas sayingk, ja, um, I vas, he vas, ve vas, whoever ve vas now, ve vere a pilot. Of a flyingk machine.

**FANNY**  Nonsense.

**ALPHONSE**  Ja, you betcha. Heavier dan der air. A dirigible.

**MARY**  A dirigible.

**ALPHONSE**  Ja. Dirigible.

**FANNY**  A dirigible.

**ALEX**  Dirigible.

**ALPHONSE**  Dirigible, ja, dirigible.

**MARY**  What is a dirigible? Alphonse?

**ALEX**  What a succulent word! Dirigible, dirigible, dirigible. Dirigible. Dirigible.

**MARY**  Alex!

**ALEX**  Up your old dirigible. Give us your huddled dirigibles, yearning to breathe free. Have a dirigible on me, big fella. One mint dirigible to go.

(*A pause. Alphonse regards Alex askance.*)

**ALPHONSE**  Vell, it's a balloon.

**MARY**  Hot air?

**ALPHONSE**  Inert gazz.

**ALEX**  Inelegible dirigible. Illegible dirigible. Incorrigible dirigible. Gerbil in a dirigible! I'll wager it's one of those words which has no true rhyme in English. Of course, it's not an English word, is it?

**FANNY**  You must explain your obsession with rhyme. It borders on the unhealthy. I've read that preoccupation with rhyme is one of the symptoms of incipient hysteria.

**ALEX**  Knackwurst!

**MARY**  What happened to the dirigible, Alphonse?

**ALPHONSE**  Schtill dere, as far as I know. You vant a look, cuties?

**FANNY**  You, sir, are growing impertinent.

**ALPHONSE**  Zay, dat's a nice vig you got dere. Mein zizter haz a vig like dat.

**FANNY**  Does she enjoy it?

**ALPHONSE**  She lofs it! A lot!

**MARY**  How do we locate your dirigible?

**ALPHONSE**  Follow der yellow brick road, shveeties.

**MARY**  Sorry?

**ALPHONSE**  Take der segund egxit. Vatch for der Burma Shave signs. Oh, buoy. I should never had taken dat exxtra schlice of date bread. Never eat on a full schtomach.

**MARY**  Alphonse –

**ALPHONSE**  Egxcuze me, ladies. Zank you for der chow. You must come to eat viz me shomeday. I make a mean manioc strudel.

**ALEX**  Manioc, my favorite.

**FANNY**  Have you ever had manioc fritters?

**ALPHONSE**  Ve vill haf to trade recipes.

**MARY**  Alphonse, couldn't you see your way clear to guide us to the dirigible? We'll pay wages.

**ALPHONSE**  Zorry. I am not vell. I haf to get zis Alphonse out of mein zyztem. Perhops ve meet again, mein blue angels. Vaya con Dios!

**MARY**  Auf wiedersehn.

**ALPHONSE**  (*He hands Fanny a bundle.*) A token of mein steam. Big juju. Lof dat vig. (*He exits.*)

**FANNY**  His steam, indeed.

(*She unwraps it. It's another egg beater, a rather different model.*

*Fanny hands it to Alex.*)
**FANNY**   I've already got one.
**ALEX**   Thank you so much. I'll keep it with me always.
(*They rotor at one another and laugh.*)
**MARY**   A cannibal from Alsace-Lorraine. Will wonders never cease?
**FANNY**   Yes, Mary, there are two sorts of people in the world. There are
cannibals – and there are lunch.
**MARY**   Fanny, you are a Social Darwinist.
**ALEX**   What do you suppose he meant by Burma Shave?
**FANNY**   I've been to Burma.
**MARY**   As have I.
**ALEX**   (*With sudden fierce conviction.*) There are no cannibals in Tibet!
No matter what the Red Chinese claim!
(*Pause.*)
**MARY and FANNY**   What on Earth is a Red Chinese?

**JOURNAL ENTRY:**
**MARY**   By and large the company has been charming. As a
confirmed-since-childhood solo sojourner, I am astonished.
Perhaps I have overvalued the pleasures of solitude heretofore.
(*Takes a deep breath.*) I feel the rare air of Terra Incognita
working its way upon me like acid on an old coin, the tarnish of
the past dissolving in a solvent of iridescent light. I tingle. Objects
shimmer on the horizon. At sunset, a tantalizing mist, a web, a
membrane envelopes us.

## (7) Ember Tales

*Twilight descends. A campfire. The ladies are telling tales.*

**MARY**   There is nothing so fascinating as fire.
**FANNY**   When I was sleeping in a rice paddy under a blood moon, near
the Irriwaddy River Delta, I awoke to find myself surrounded. By a
band of cut-throat dacoits. Thuggees. Brigands. Buccaneers. They
wore turbans with rubies set in the brow, and bejeweled daggers. And
they were led by a woman – a Bandit Queen! She was a devotee of
Kali, the Goddess of Death!
**ALEX**   I am often asked about Tibetan cuisine. In Lamdo, I apprenticed
myself to a sorcerer. My mentor had quarrelled with a rival shaman. A
blood feud. One morning, Master Dzo baked two great cakes of ground
millet. He baked them flat as platters and hard as wheels. When the
cakes were cool, he spun them into the sky. Hurled them, as though

they were discuses. They spun and spun, rising in the sky, sailing over the city until they searched out the stone hut of the second sorcerer. The cakes whirled like saw blades, swooped down, and sliced the hut in half. Battered it to crumbs. (*Beat.*) I think that sums up Tibetan cuisine. It is not haute.

**FANNY** While travelling in the Rocky Mountains some years back, I repelled a rabid drooling grizzly bear with a series of piercing yodels. (*She demonstrates: three bloodcurdling yodels.*)

**MARY** That reminds me of my father, who was a famous pharmacist.

**ALEX** Did your father yodel, Mary?

**MARY** No. He invented a tonic for catarrh.

**ALEX** After an hour, their robes would be dry as toast. And neatly pressed. Extraordinary visages. They would *concentrate*.

**FANNY** I once encountered the Masai. I said – "Wow!"

**MARY** Talking drums always bring out the Neolithic Man in me.
(*Pause.*)
(*Fanny, reflecting on the Masai, silently mouths a "Wow!" The ladies settle in for the night.*)


(*Fanny does her journal entry.*)
**FANNY** Dear Grover. We had lunch today – or was it yesterday – with the most amicable cannibal. He admired my wig. The tabloids will feast. I can hear *The Globetrotteress* licking her chops now. "Fanny's Cannibal – Discovers Maneating Balloonist in Darkest Antipodes-Boston Geo Views Claim Warily." The jaundice of yellow journalism. One more card in the catalogue my critics are fond of calling Fanny's Follies. (*Beat.*) Terra Incognita exhilarates. Intoxicates. There is an hallucinatory spiciness to the air. We are in the grip of a communal fever dream. Alex mutters continually about the "Red Chinese," and Mary makes reference to an anthropological penny-dreadful entitled *The Naked and the Dead.* Myself, I dream about mysterious machinery, discover strange objects in my baggage, and strange phrases in my mouth: "Air-mail." "Blue-sky ventures." "So long."


### (8) An Apparition

*The ladies are sleeping around the fire. Fanny snores, a ferocious sound. A figure appears on the edge of the light: Grover, Fanny's husband, a prosperous Mid-West broker. He is wearing a large black oval carved African mask. He listens to Fanny snore. Scratches his eyebrow. Growls softly. Fanny awakes with a start.*

**FANNY** What? Who? (*Looks closer. Mouths a silent "Wow!" She gets up and approaches him.*) I have no calico blouses, but I will trade you cream cheese. It is not bad. Not manioc, but not bad.
(*Grover chuckles. Fanny examines Grover's suit and shoes.*)
**FANNY** Are you or are you not Masai?
**GROVER** I'm just your grizz-a-ly bear, Fanny. (*Taking off mask.*) What a snore, Fanny. You'll keep the leopards away.
**FANNY** Grover!
**GROVER** Don't be cross.
**FANNY** Why shouldn't I be? Bother a body in the middle of the night. In the middle of the jungle.
**GROVER** I came to give you a message.
**FANNY** I'm all ears.
**GROVER** Don't speculate on the future.
(*Pause.*)
**FANNY** Your mother warned me you were hermetic.
**GROVER** I also wanted to say goodbye.
**FANNY** Grover, we said goodbye. In Terre Haute. Some months ago. Are you staying dry?
**GROVER** Dry as toast. Well, Fanny. I had something up my sleeve for Arbor Day next. It was – sorta special. Yikes. Well, Fanny. Goodnight.
**FANNY** Goodnight, Grover. Are those new shoes?
**GROVER** Don't forget to write.
**FANNY** Do I ever?
**GROVER** You are a faithful correspondent, Fanny. Goodbye.
(*He disappears. Fanny stares after him. Shivers a little. Alex wakes, gets up, goes to Fanny, and taps her on the shoulder. She starts.*)
**FANNY** Oh!
**ALEX** Fanny – are you a somnambulist?
**FANNY** What? Oh, I must be. Fancy that.
**ALEX** Come back to the fire.
(*Alex returns to the fire.*)
**FANNY** I have had the most vivid dream.

(*Mary arises and does her journal entry.*)
**MARY** At dawn and dusk, the essence of the jungle increases a hundredfold. The air becomes heavy with perfume. It throbs with unseen presence. A savage tapestry of squawks, cries, and caws presses upon one with an almost palpable pressure. A cacophonous echolalia – snarling, sinister menace – as though the sound of the jungle itself could tear one limb from limb.

### (9) Fort Apache

*Dawn breaks. Jungle noises. The ladies break camp. The ladies*
*travel. Jungle noises all about. The ladies are alert, cautious.*
*Suspenseful.*
*The jungle noises increase in ferocity. They become menacing.*
*The ladies draw and open their umbrellas. They form a defensive*
*triangle, shoulder to shoulder.*
*The jungle noises attack, snarl, and snap.*
*The ladies fend off the jungle noises with their umbrellas, fencing*
*and jabbing sharply.*
*The umbrellas blossom.*
*The ladies rotate across the stage, a vanquishing star, scattering*
*the jungle noises, which howl and flee.*
*The ladies lower their umbrellas. They celebrate quietly.*

**JOURNAL ENTRY:**

**ALEX**   Funny word, native. Native. Native. (*She Kodaks an*
*imaginary native.*) Image. Native. Image-native. Imaginative. I am
a native of the image. An indigine of the imagination. Gone
native. Renegade. Commanchero.


### (10) In the Jungle – The Mighty Jungle

*The ladies bushwhack through a swamp.*

**ALEX**   Ooo, ow, natterblast! Savage sour lichtenstein! Lactating minuet!
This jungle exhausts me! Surely you must agree trousers would be far
and away more practical for this primeval muck.

**MARY**   On the contrary, Alexandra. One evening near dusk, as we were
negotiating the treacherous Black Quicksands of Baluchistan, I slipped
off solid ground, and found myself sinking into infinite bog. Fortu-
nately, my sturdy skirt ballooned around me, held its shape, and kept
me buoyant until assistance arrived. A few moments later, I lost half a
dozen porters in the blink of an eye. Sucked under the sands, like that!
Fooop! Poor men weren't wearing skirts.

**ALEX**   Ah! Look!

(*Sound of a croc. Fanny vanquishes it.*)

**FANNY**   The Mighty Silurian! Thwack!

(*The ladies reach solid ground.*)

**MARY**   Time for a nose powder.

**FANNY**   I could do with a bit of a primp.

**ALEX**   I'll follow suit.

*(They pull beaded handbags from their packs, move some distance through the jungle, and freshen up.)*

**MARY**   In the Congo, I was known as Only Me.

**ALEX**   Only Me?

**MARY**   I would enter a village or burst into a clearing or emerge from the bush shouting, "It's only me, it's only me!"

**FANNY**   Immediately disarming the hostile natives, who naturally enough spoke English.

**MARY**   Dear Fanny. Tone of voice is everything.

**FANNY**   I was known as Bebe Bwana.

**ALEX**   Bebe?

**FANNY**   It's difficult to explain. Out of context.

**MARY**   I never got over being called "Sir."

**ALEX**   Nor I.

**FANNY**   Nor I.

**MARY**   Human once more.

**FANNY**   I am revivified.

**ALEX**   I am refurbished. I mean refreshed. Not refurbished. Ah! Feel that breeze, ladies!

*(The wind comes up. The ladies prepare for cold weather, donning scarves, goggles, etc.)*

**JOURNAL ENTRY:**

**FANNY**   I felt as though I were a prisoner in a kaleidescope.


### (11) A Prisoner in a Kaleidescope

*The wind comes up. They move across the stage. The wind whistles. They stop.*

**FANNY**   Alexandra. Here's your howling ice field.

**ALEXANDRA**   My forte. Allons!

*(They cross the ice field in slow motion. The invisible rope between them breaks, and they begin twirling slowly over the ice, in different directions, away from one another, toward the edges, in silence. At the brink, they stop. Teeter. Freeze. Relax. They catch their breath.)*

**MARY**   A narrow one –

**ALEX**   Whoo whistle lug –

**FANNY**   A scrape –

*(Relieved laughter. They make their way carefully to the center and one another.)*

**MARY**  What happened, did the rope –

**ALEX**  The rope –

**FANNY**  It snapped, I felt it go –

**ALEX**  Broke –

**MARY**  Spinning like a gyro –

**ALEX**  Spinning –

**MARY**  Graceful, I was so –

**FANNY**  So –

**MARY**  Calm –

**FANNY**  Calm, yes –

**FANNY and MARY**  Calm –

**FANNY**  Eeerily calm –

**ALEX**  Spinning toward the lip of the void –

**MARY**  My mind clear –

**ALEX**  Into the infinite cerulean –

**MARY**  I thought of my father, the famous pharmacist –

**ALEX**  Did your life, you know, flash before you?

**MARY**  Too dizzy, my dear –

**ALEX**  They say drowning sailors –

**MARY**  No, just him.

**FANNY**  I felt as though I were a prisoner in a kaleidescope.

**ALEX**  Oh, Fanny, that's good.

**MARY**  A book title. I'd make a note of it.

*(Fanny does. They sigh.)*

**ALEX**  Whew, lacerated fingerbowl!

**MARY**  Fingerbowl, indeed! Well said, Alex.

**FANNY**  A scrape. A palpable scrape.

**MARY**  Sheer luck, running into that ice wall.

**FANNY**  Fortuitous.

**ALEX**  I'm all over bruises in the morning.

*(Fanny is hit by a snowball.)*

**FANNY**  Alexandra!

**ALEX**  Yes?

**FANNY**  High spirits need not always be accompanied by hi-jinks.

**ALEX**  You always cast your eye upon me because I'm the youngest. But that missile came from over there.

*(They all look. A barrage of snowballs. They dodge.)*

**MARY**  Oh, dear!

**FANNY**  Watch yourselves! Oh, Alexandra!

*(Dodging, Alex slips and pratfalls. The breath flies out of her.)*

**ALEX**  Whomp!

**MARY**  Are you all right?

*(A yeti appears at the stage edge – a silky mane from head-to-foot.)*

**YETI**  (*Growls beast language.*) ARRGGGGRRRACKAAACK!

**MARY**  A silkie.

**ALEX**  (*Picking herself up.*) Silkies are seals, silly. That's a yeti.

**YETI**  (*Growls beast language.*) LLLLLLLLUUUUUUUURRRRRAA
AAAAAEEECCCCCKOOO!

**ALEX**  Oh, yes you are!

**YETI**  (*Growls beast language*) RASSRASSRASS!

**ALEX**  Tibet teems with 'em, m'dears. Yes, Fanny's tabloids call them
abominable snowmen.

**FANNY**  He's not so abominable.

**MARY**  He's rather adorable.

**ALEX**  He's smallish, for a yeti.

**MARY**  He's a baby yeti.

**FANNY** and **MARY**  He's sweet.

(*The ladies chick and coo and gush, luring the yeti closer. He retreats,
terrified.*)

**YETI**  (*Growls beast language.*)
WHHHUUUWHHAAAASNARP!

(*He vanishes.*)

**MARY**  Oh, dear. Frightened him off.

**ALEX**  The yeti is shy and elusive. Although his cry is often human, and
tuneful.

(*From offstage:*)

**YETI**  (*Growls beast language.*) AIIIIIYIIIIIIIYAIIIAIWHA!

**FANNY**  The little sasquatch has gone for more snowballs, no doubt.
(*She is hit by a snowball.*) AHHHH!

**MARY**  Baby yeti may have yeti cronies. I think prudence dictates we
move on.

(*They hike downstage. Peer into a deep gorge.*)

**ALEX**  Ooo!

**FANNY**  Precipice.

**MARY**  Chilling.

**ALEX**  This gorge is so like the Himalayas!

**MARY**  There's a bridge. Vines and planks. Shall we risk it?

**FANNY**  By all means.

(*Alex takes three Andean breaths.*)

**ALEX**  Now – this (*Breath.*) is (*Breath.*) air (*Breath.*) ladies!

**JOURNAL ENTRY:**

**FANNY**  An awful yawning chasm. An antediluvian suspension.

## (12) Not Quite Robert Lowell

*The ladies are crossing a high gorge on a swaying, single-plank, vine-rope bridge.*

**MARY** "Mysticism and Mesmerism in Madagascar" was a paper I delivered to the Ladies Fetish and Taboo Society of Annapolis. It was a sensation. I followed that with "Tribadism in the Tropics" – which caused quite a stir. Rubbed several spectators the wrong way.

**ALEX** What is "tribadism"?

**FANNY** *(Knowing exactly what it is.)* I'm sure I haven't the least notion.

**ALEX** This gorge is so like the Himalayas.

**FANNY** I am convinced that the modern craze for anthropology is actually a subterranean sexual inflammation, flimsily got up as scientific curiosity.

**ALEX** I am hypnotized.

**FANNY** An unhealthy obsession with rites –

**ALEX** I mean homesick. Not hypnotized.

**FANNY** Mating rites, puberty rites, rites of sacrifice, rites of passage, poly this and poly that and poly the other –

**ALEX** Nacho frazzle asterisk! It is so delicious to be out of that leech-infested swelter. Look! *(They turn in the direction Alex points.)* Oh! Dirigible!

**MARY** Pilotless. Caroming off the canyon walls.

**FANNY** The Flying Dutchman dirigible! What a story for *True Trek!* *(They have nearly completed their crossing. Their way is blocked by the Gorge Troll, a young man in a leather jacket, blue jeans, t-shirt, and sideburns and greased-back hair.)*

**TROLL**
> What have we here but travelers three
> Comin' cross the bridge to rap with me
> In Xanadu said Ka-u-ba-la Khan
> Hey there sweet things what's goin' on?

*(Pause)*

**FANNY** Alex, I believe verse is your province.

**ALEX** You speak English!

**TROLL**
> This ain't Swahili, I gotta confess
> You hearin' more if you talkin' less

**FANNY** Swahili seems mathematically more probable than English, my good man. Although I welcome its appearance in this obscure corner of the globe – even in your ghastly patois.

**TROLL** Castigate the way I talk –

I'll agitate the way you walk!

(*He sways the bridge.*)

**ALL**   Whoooooooo!

**MARY**   English is the language of Empire, Fanny.

**FANNY**   I do not wish to embroil us in a political discussion on *the lip of the void*, Mary. Don't you think we ought to seek Terra Firma?

**TROLL**
> You may not dig my lingo but I'll settle your hash
> You wanna get by me gotta have some cash

**FANNY**   I don't believe I savvy.

**TROLL**
> This is my bridge, baby, and I'm the Troll
> To step on over you gotta pay the toll.

**ALEX**   A troll's toll. How droll. He's good. But not quite Robert Lowell.

**FANNY**   Alex.

**ALEX**   Whoever he is. Robert Lowell, I mean.

**FANNY**   This is extortion!

**TROLL**
> You want sun sometimes you get rain instead
> If you can't hack it you shoulda stood in bed

**MARY**   When in Rome.

(*She pays. They cross off.*)

**MARY**   Baksheesh! In Terra Incognita!

**TROLL**   Baksheesh-kabob, baby.

**ALEX**   What's it like, being a troll?

**TROLL**   Like?

**ALEX**   How do you find it?

**TROLL**   This is just my day job.

**FANNY**   You're not a born-to-the-bridge troll?

**TROLL**   I'm an actor. I study.

**FANNY**   Where do you study?

**TROLL**   At the Studio.

**FANNY**   That seems reasonable. Have you done Congreve?

**TROLL**   I don't think so.

**FANNY**   What have you done?

**TROLL**   C'mon, I've done it all. "Sense memory," "emotional recall," "private moment" –

**MARY**   These must be new plays from Terra Incognita. Indigenous drama. How would you characterize "Private Moment"?

**TROLL**   Intense.

**FANNY**   You aren't, by any chance, Mr. Coffee?

**TROLL**   Not the last time I looked. Hey, ladies.
Costume drama – get over it.

(*To Alex.*) You I like. What about a spin on my chopper?

**ALEX**   Some other time.

**TROLL**

>   Your loss, angel food.
>   Ladies, take it light
>   And everything will be all right.

(*He exits.*)

**ALEX**   Vaya con Dios!

(*Sound of an enormous unmufflered motorcycle roaring off into the sunset.*)

**MARY**   I think we must presume English to be the Lingua Franca of Terra Incognita.

**FANNY**   (*Snorts*) None dare call it English.

**MARY**   Did you fancy his lyrics, Alexandra?

**ALEX**   No. But I admired his dedication to his art:

**MARY**   Irony is not one of your strong suits, is it?

**ALEX**   What do you mean? I understand that troll! Despite outward appearances, I am an artist, not an intrepid polytopian.

**FANNY**   Oh, Alex, for goodness sakes, yes you are. You're one of the original polytopians, don't dissemble.

**ALEX**   Well, yes, I am. High adventure and stupefying risk are my metier. But, ladies – all this rigor and unimaginable hardship, all this uninsurable danger, all this adrenal giddiness, all this oxygen debt and spartan discipline and rude hygiene – all this is mere prelude. A prologue to my brilliant career. I'm not making a life out of all this tramping about, you know. I shall shed my wanderlust like a damp poncho. And become a lyricist. Of popular songs.

**FANNY**   Victor Herbert quakes.

**MARY**   I wonder what that conveyance was?

**ALEX**   He called it a chopper.

**FANNY**   Loud.

**ALEX**   (*With sudden conviction*) The future is loud!

**JOURNAL ENTRY:**

**MARY**   I feel a sea change coming over me. A disturbance of my very molecules. As though the chemical composition of my blood has been altered by breathing the rare air of Terra Incognita. I have begun to dream in a new language. My imagination seems to sculpt the landscape. Images flow between the inner and outer worlds, and I can no longer determine their point of origin. I have a growing premonition we are about to pierce the membrane.

## (13) Plot Thickener

*The ladies have moved some distance from the bridge.*

**FANNY**  I rather think that Troll is one of the elusive Mole People. The speculative literature on the Antipodes postulates the existence of a subterranean race. Oh, look – (*She has spied a bit of paper caught in a branch. She plucks it.*)

**ALEX**  Share, Fanny.

**FANNY**  A clipping. Folded thrice. From *The New York Times*.

**MARY**  Reputable. Trustworthy.

**FANNY**  The *Herald-Tribune*, pour moi. This sheds new light. Terra Incognita cannot be utterly benighted if one can get *The New York Times*. (*Studies clipping.*) A Kodak of a man. Never heard of this fellow. Behind him an impressive array of snow mountains. His arms are spread – so: (*Imitates a man gesturing about the size of a large fish.*) The caption reads: President Nixon. Grand Tetons. June, 1972. Quote: "I had trout from the lake for dinner last night. They were so good I had them again for breakfast. I haven't had anything but cereal for breakfast since 1953." Endquote.

(*Pause.*)

**MARY**  1953? 1972?

**ALEX**  Printer's errors?

**MARY**  Two such errors in one tiny *Times'* item? Not credible.

**FANNY**  Dickensian character. Looks like something off the bottom of the sea bed. (*Pause.*) President. President Nixon. President of what?

**ALEX**  Some eating club or other. Where men have breakfast, and compare their trophies.

**MARY**  No. The United States.

**FANNY**  How do you know?

**MARY**  I just know. Don't ask me how.

**FANNY**  I thought McKinley was President.

**MARY**  Garfield.

**ALEX**  Taft, you daft duo.

**FANNY**  Alexandra, the interjection of song lyrics into otherwise civilized conversation is strictly prohibited.

**ALEX**  Surely not president of the United States. How could a man who hasn't had an egg for breakfast in twenty years be president of the United States?

**FANNY**  You know, he rather resembles an orangutan in a dinner jacket.

**MARY**  I could do with some trout.

**ALEX**  The Grand Tetons are a lovely little range.

**FANNY**  Someday they will be preserved as a national park by Teddy

Roosevelt.

**MARY**  Teddy Roosevelt?

**ALEX**  I've never heard of him.

**FANNY**  Oh, yes you have. Bully bear and San Juan Hill, and all that.

**ALEX**  No.

**FANNY**  His statue is in front of the Museum of Natural History.

**MARY**  In New York? No. It is not. Not when I was there last.

**FANNY**  Certainly not. That statue will not be erected until 1936.

(*Pause.*)

**ALEX**  Do you know why there is evil in the world?

**FANNY**  Metaphysical speculation, Alexandra?

**MARY**  I don't think so. Do you?

**ALEX**  Yes, I do.

**FANNY**  You are so young.

**MARY**  Why is there evil in the world, Alexandra?

**ALEX**  To thicken the plot.

(*Pause.*)

**FANNY**  I believe you are exactly right.

(*Alex seizes the clipping.*)

**ALEX**  (*Happily.*) This is plot thickener!

**MARY**  Yes!

**FANNY**  Yes! Ladies, we are in a strange new world.

**MARY**  Terra Incognita, by definition, could not be otherwise. I have a
theory. One that explains the unknown objects. The strange words in
our mouths. The references to persons unknown that spring to mind.
Spring to mind. It is spring in our minds, ladies. A New World.
Blossoming! Within and without! I believe, with each step, each chop
of the machete, we are advancing through the wilderness of time as
well as space. Chronology as well as geography. Not – as we usually
do in savage lands, moving backward into the past, into pre-history –
but forward, into the future! A New World, within and without!
Beckoning!

(*Pause.*)

**FANNY**  A new world! Within and without!

**ALEX**  It would explain the dirigible.

**FANNY**  The clipping from 1972.

**ALEX**  The Nixon.

**MARY**  Mrs. Butterworth. Burma Shave. Cream cheese.

**ALEX**  Robert Lowell. The troll.

**FANNY**  It would explain why, now, burning in my forebrain like a
Mosaic tablet, is the copyright date for a novel entitled *Herzog*.

**MARY**  Something else is happening, obviously. Something even more
astonishing. Not only are we advancing in time, not only are we

encountering the future with every step – (*Beat.*) Ladies, we are beginning to know the future! (*Beat.*) It is entering into our consciousness. Like mustard gas. Whatever that is. Wait a moment. I'll tell you. (*She osmoses.*) Oh. Oh. Oh. Unfortunate simile. I withdraw it.

**ALEX**   We are absorbing the future! Through osmosis!

**FANNY**   As long as you're at it, osmos Red Chinese for us.

**ALEX**   Let me try. (*She osmoses.*) Something's coming in, yes, like a radio transmission. (*She holds up a hand.*) Don't ask. (*She osmoses.*) Hmmmm.

**FANNY**   Yes?

**ALEX**   Little Red Book. Great Leap Forward. Swimming the Yang-tze River. Tractor Operas.

**FANNY**   Operas about tractors?

**ALEX**   Running dogs. And – (*Osmoses.*) They're friends of Nixon! (*The ladies leap about excitedly.*)

**MARY**   Ladies, this is fantastic. I presume you are feeling – with me – slightly tremulous – a bit fluttery around the gills. Ladies, I don't know about you, but I am experiencing a definite, a palpable – yearning for the future!

**ALEX**   Oh, Mary! Yes! (*Osmoses a moment.*) Radio. Radio is. Oh. I can't believe that! Voices on the air, ladies! Sounds voodoo. You'll just have to osmose your own description.
(*Pause.*)

**MARY**   We are imbued with the future. (*Pause.*)

**FANNY**   One doesn't have to like it. (*Pause.*)

**MARY**   Nostalgia for the future.
(*Pause.*)

**ALEX**   I shall make my fortune in radio. (*Pause.*)

**MARY**   We shall go from year to year, as if we were going from tribe to tribe.

**ALEX**   Big fun!
(*Mary finds a button in the grass.*)

**MARY**   Look. Another button. Similar to the one we found our first day on the beach.

**FANNY**   "Hec – kwhod – ont"?

**MARY**   Once could be a fluke. Twice is a trend.

**ALEX**   What what what does the button read, Mary?

**MARY**   "I – Like – Ike."
(*Pause. Simultaneously:*)

**MARY, ALEX** and **FANNY**   Who's Ike?
(*They laugh. Pause.*)

**FANNY**   I don't know about all of you, but I do have a sudden craving. A burning desire. Intense, painful longing. (*Beat.*) For "*Cool*" Whip."

(*Pause.*)

**ALEX** and **MARY**   Hmmmmmmm.

(*The ladies come downstage, grasp hands, and survey their prospects.*)

**MARY**   Ladies! Let us segue!

(*They disappear in a blaze of light.*)


END OF ACT ONE

# ACT TWO

## (14) Fanmail from the Future

*The ladies are fording a stream, their skirts hiked up.*

**FANNY**   Ladies, we are in a strange new world. Where life as we know it is, well, not as we know it.

**MARY**   Treacherous underfoot. Careful on the bank.

**ALEX**   You will agree that trousers are eminently more sensible for situations like these.

**MARY**   Not at all.

**FANNY**   They'd be drenched. Damp for days at this altitude.

**ALEX**   You roll them up! You roll them up! You roll them up! You roll them up!

**FANNY**   Alexandra, collect yourself!

**MARY**   For all our sakes.
  *(They have reached the other side and unhike their skirts.)*

**ALEX**   You cannot resist the future! It is futile! You must embrace it with all your heart!

**FANNY**   Alexandra. One has to accept the future. One doesn't have to embrace it.

**ALEX**   Pendejo!

**MARY**   Ladies, we are on the frontier of the future.

**FANNY**   I have always been a pioneer.

**MARY**   We have been encountering residue from the future. Flotsam from many different moments.

**FANNY**   "Fanmail" from the future.

**MARY**   What is "fanmail," Fanny?

**FANNY**   *(Osmosing.)* Mash notes. Autographed glossies. Secret decoder rings.

**MARY**   Multiple mysteries!
  *(A pathway of light. Objects appear in the air before them: a dazzling array of toys and junk and gadgets and souvenirs and appliances and electronic wonders, everything from an acid-pink hula hoop to a silver laser video disc.)*
  *(The ladies gasp, delighted.)*

**FANNY**   "Fallout" from the future!
  *(They begin to examine the objects, oooing and murmuring and clucking.)*
  *(Fanny tries to osmose an odd toy.)*

**FANNY**   "Tweezer!" No. "Yo-yo!" No. "Mr. Coffee!" No. My osmos is not quite right.

(*Alex follows suit.*)

**ALEX**  "Slot machine." "Juke box." "Squirt gun." "Brass knuckles."

(*Fanny finds a magazine.*)

**FANNY**  A tabloid *"The National Review."* (*She puts it in her pack.*)

**ALEX**  "Ovaltine." "Bosco." "Double Bubble." "Velvee-eeta."

**MARY**  A rain forest of fossils from the future.

**ALEX**  Oh, look! A mini-dirigible! (*She reads the fine print on an inflatable banana.*) "Not to be used as a life preserver." Hmmmm.

(*Fanny peers into a side-view mirror from an automobile.*)

**FANNY**  "Objects in mirror may be closer than they appear?" Hmmmm. Well, Mary, here is your physical evidence. What do you make of it?

**MARY**  Ladies. We have the artifacts –

(*They hold up their artifacts, including egg beaters and buttons.*
*Fanny and Alex have been wearing their egg beaters like pistols.*)

**MARY**  – we must find their historical moment. Let us camp tonight in this – orchard of the future. Tomorrow we shall enter fully the era that awaits us.

**FANNY**  I hope with all my heart I shall be able to have a bath. And find a post office.

(*Alex points at Mary's Ike button.*)

**ALEX**  Ladies, let us not forget. "Ike" is waiting.

(*Fanny and Alice rotor at one another.*)

**JOURNAL ENTRY:**

**MARY**  We spent the night in the future. Around us swirled a silent storm of images, a star shower of light from a new world.

### (15) The Starry Deep

*A starry night falls. The ladies pitch a gossamer canopy. They
light lanterns. They write in their journals, each by her own light.*

**ALEX**  Under a calliope of stars. Below the firmament. The glittering empyrean. The night above the dingle starry. (*Beat*) That's not mine. Damn this interference. (*Beat*) The vasty deep. The starry deep. (*Beat*) Under welkin.

**MARY**  Difficult to hack one's way through this thicket of voices from the future.

**FANNY**  Grover, my tender parsnip – shall I ever see you again?

**MARY**  Notes for a paper for the Boston Geo. I have tentatively dubbed this phenomenon we are experiencing – chronokinesis. (*Beat*) Fanny's tabloids will call it "time travel."

**FANNY**  Time travel is a tricky business, dear Grover. Beyond our ken.

**MARY**  Chronokinesis! Life membership in the Boston Geo. The Academy of Arts and Sciences. Honorary membership in the Royal Geo and Academie Francaise. Director of the Smithsonian. The first woman. The Nobel Prize in physics –

**ALEX**  My fellow polytopians are splendid and intrepid. Mary is excessively anecdotal, and Fanny scorns my lyrics.

**FANNY**  Mary and Alexandra are quite sweet, really. Appalling politics. Appalling. If we are detained in this country, I shall order them both a subscription to *The National Review*. I am quite certain you would adore *The National Review*, Grover. I do. It is the sole thing I've so far discovered in the future which reminds me of the nineteenth century.

**ALEX**  I foresee the day – it is exceedingly easy to foresee the day here – I foresee the day Fanny will eat her words. I shall secure an exclusive recording contract with a multinational conglomerate, and make consecutive gold records. (*Beat.*) Note: meditate and osmose what those things are, exactly.

**FANNY**  The possibility exists that we shall not return, dear Grover. Certainly – in the northern hemisphere – one cannot simply go back and forth in time as one pleases. Time is not a revolving door. We have access to the future here. Do we have egress as well?

**ALEX**  We are beseiged by a barrage of fact. From here the future looks –

**MARY**  The future looks –

**ALEX**  The future looks positively – AMERICAN.

**FANNY**  Loud –

**MARY**  – invigorating. Quite promising, except, perhaps, for the theatre – which threatens to degenerate into imitations of anthropological kinship studies.

**FANNY**  We ought to be approaching a post office. Of course, it is a verity that the tropical post will forever be a sink of inefficiency, world without end.

**ALEX**  I expect to publish these memoirs with an insert of Kodak reproductions. I adore Kodaking.

**FANNY**  Can the post office deliver to you, in 1889, a letter from me – some decades later? I know they can do it the other way 'round. That's commonplace.

**MARY**  I for one am looking forward to meeting this "Ike." "Ike" "Ike" "Ike." "Iko Iko." "Willy and the Hand Jive."

**FANNY**  Beyond our ken, dear Grover. Trust you are staying dry. All my love. From Terra Incognita to Terre Haute. Fanny.

(*As Mary and Fanny sleep, Alex comes down and does her journal entry.*)

**ALEX** (*Taking a deep breath*) The rare air of the future. Breathe. Aspirate. Aspire. A – spire. (*She takes another deep breath.*) One of the ecstacies of hiking in the Himalayas was to crest a ridge, and suddenly confront the infinite surround. Mountains and rivers without end. Untouched. Glistening with possibility. We are climbing a spire of time. The topography of the future is coming into view. Unmapped and unnamed. Distant vistas shining. You must not shrink. You must embrace it with all your heart.

### (16) Manna from Heaven—or, Among the Jesuits

*Dawn. The ladies stir, take down the gossamer canopy.*

**FANNY** I slept not a wink.
**MARY** Nor I.
**ALEX** Nor I.
**MARY** Fascinating as fire imagery. I long to learn more about "Willy and the Hand Jive."
**FANNY** From what little I could fathom, the future seems a dubious prospect.
**ALEX** (*A sudden transmission.*) Beep!
**FANNY** I beg your pardon.
**ALEX** Wrong!
**FANNY** Are you contradicting me, young lady?
**ALEX** College bowl! State for twenty! The future is not a dubious prospect! The future is – just a bowl of cherries!
**FANNY** Mary, we must locate a translator. Alexandra will soon be totally incomprehensible.
**ALEX** Fanny, the future is now!
**FANNY** Alexandra. (*Sighs.*) I would elude the future, if I could.
**ALEX** Fanny, you must embrace it with all your heart.
**FANNY** Why? Why why why why why?
**ALEX** Fanny, you sound like a broken record, a busy signal, a car alarm –
**FANNY** Alexandra! (*Beat.*) I must accept the future, Alexandra, as I accept the existence of cyclones and pit vipers and bad grammar. But you would have me embrace them?
**ALEX** Yes!
**FANNY** You would. Cyclones? Pit vipers? Bad grammar?
**ALEX** In a way. Yes.
**FANNY** You are a reckless child.

**ALEX**   And you, Fanny, you – are – so – so – so – SQUARE!
   (*Pause.*)
**FANNY**   I have seen the future. And it is slang.
   (*Pause.*)
**MARY**   It is uncommonly close this morning. I must put on a new face.
**ALEX**   I'll follow suit.
   (*Mary and Alex exit.*)
   (*Fanny takes out her letter to Grover, which has grown into a small
   volume. She calms herself by writing.*)
**FANNY**   Dearest Grover. Another addendum. As we home in on the
   future, I begin to feel curiously at ease, and happy. Content. We have
   been cantering along at a terrific clip. The future looms. (*Pause. She
   opens a music box. It plays.*) The future looms as steady and stable as a
   table top. I anticipate we shall find a year which suits me perfectly, and
   settle in for a long refreshment. I shall have a bath. There will be a post
   office. Oh, dear Grover – I feel we are on the verge of something
   grand.
   (*An elegant gentleman in a beautiful white suit – Mr. Coffee  – appears
   at the end of the path. Fanny is quite taken with him.*)
**MR. COFFEE**   Good afternoon, Madame.
**FANNY**   Sir.
   (*He moves to her. He takes two cigarettes from a silver case, lights
   them, and gives one to her.*)
**FANNY**   Thank you. (*A little giddy.*) And I don't even smoke. (*A sultry
   dual inhalation.*) Oooo. In my day, Sir, a lady did not smoke tobacco.
**MR. COFFEE**   Modern times, Fanny, modern times.
**FANNY**   Too true.
**MR. COFFEE**   How are you finding your travels?
**FANNY**   Trying.
**MR. COFFEE**   Worth the candle?
**FANNY**   Without question. (*Beat.*) Are you Mr. Coffee?
**MR. COFFEE**   I've been called worse.
**FANNY**   I've had a premonition about meeting you.
**MR. COFFEE**   I'm sure you have.
**FANNY**   You are not of this era.
**MR. COFFEE**   No. Not exclusively.
**FANNY**   Much too well spoken. Let me tell you, Mr. Coffee – language
   takes a beating in the future.
**MR. COFFEE**   And that goes double for diction. These things are
   cyclical, my dear. Do not despair. What goes around, comes around.
**FANNY**   Is that a local proverb?
**MR. COFFEE**   One of my favorites. An airmail letter?
**FANNY**   "Air-mail?" How funny. If you say so.

**MR. COFFEE** (*Without looking.*) Terre Haute, 1889. Air-mail part of the way. Then Pony Express.

**FANNY** (*Laughs.*) Terre Haute is not Indian Territory, Mr. Coffee. This letter is a long-running serialization by now. I must mail it before the cost of postage becomes absolutely prohibitive.

**MR. COFFEE** Preserve it for posterity. A fascinating memoir. You wouldn't want people to forget.

**FANNY** Oh, no, it's much too long to copy. I suppose I could edit out the personal parts.

**MR. COFFEE** If you venture on into the future, you'll eventually come across something called a Xerox.

**FANNY** Oh, zeeroxen, I've seen those in Greenland.

(*Pause.*)

**MR. COFFEE** There is no hope of Grover ever receiving your letter, Fanny.

**FANNY** The postal system is worrisome, Mr. Coffee, but not yet hopeless.

(*Pause.*)

(*Fanny understands.*)

**FANNY** Do you know Grover?

**MR. COFFEE** We've met.

**FANNY** Recently?

**MR. COFFEE** Seems like only yesterday. But I have no sense of time.

**FANNY** How was he? Was he dry?

**MR. COFFEE** Dry as toast. Frankly, he's been better. Bit of a cough. His wife was not unduly concerned.

**FANNY** I'm his wife.

**MR. COFFEE** His second wife. He had you declared legally dead, dear. Terre Haute Superior Court, 1910.

**FANNY** That man.

**MR. COFFEE** Remarried a few years later.

**FANNY** He never minded being alone when we were married.

**MR. COFFEE** The Great War made him anxious. And wealthy.

**FANNY** I thought those were new shoes. He came to me, Mr. Coffee. In a dream. (*Beat.*) He told me not to speculate on the future.

**MR. COFFEE** In his own brokerish fashion, Grover was trying to say – so long.

**FANNY** So long. So long.

(*Beat.*)

When did you last see Grover, Mr. Coffee?

**MR. COFFEE** Our one and only meeting. October, 1929.

(*Pause.*)

**FANNY** How – ?

**MR. COFFEE**  He hurled himself off the top of a grain silo.

**FANNY**  Oh, dear.

**MR. COFFEE**  Part of a gentle rain of brokers who fell from heaven that autumn all over the country.

**FANNY**  I've been out of touch.

**MR. COFFEE**  Grover was speculating on the commodities market. Blue sky ventures. You know. Futures.

**FANNY**  Blue sky ventures. Did he miss me?

**MR. COFFEE**  Very much, once he realized you were never coming home from Terra Incognita. Less and less, over the years. He'd get a little misty on the seminal holidays. Christmas. Easter. Arbor Day. Each and every Arbor Day he'd have three or four peppermint schnapps, in your memory, and plant a bush in the back yard. (*Beat.*) At heart, he wasn't surprised you never returned from Terra Incognita. He'd always suspected you'd disappear one day. Vanish without a trace.

**FANNY**  Yes. He was always rather taken aback whenever I walked through the front door. Well. Thank you, Mr. Coffee.

**MR. COFFEE**  My pleasure.

**FANNY**  Tell me, Mr. Coffee. Do you find it easy to foresee the future?

**MR. COFFEE**  I've never had any trouble.

**FANNY**  No. I don't suppose you would.

**MR. COFFEE**  But I confine myself to the basics.

**FANNY**  We will meet again, I trust.

**MR. COFFEE**  I feel certain of it.

**FANNY**  But not for many years.

**MR. COFFEE**  You never know. (*He takes her hand.*)

**FANNY**  I have been wanting to speak to you.

**MR. COFFEE**  Yes. Here I am, after all. (*Kisses her hand.*) A bien tot.

**FANNY**  Vaya con Dios, Mr. Coffee.

**MR. COFFEE**  Charming. See you later. Alligator.
   (*He exits. Passing Mary and Alex.*)

**MR. COFFEE**  Ladies.
   (*He disappears.*)

**MARY**  Who on earth was that?

**ALEX**  (*Osmosing.*) That was "Bebe Rebozo"!

**FANNY**  That was Mr. Coffee.

**ALEX**  Oh. Really. Sometimes this osmosing is wildly inaccurate.

**MARY**  The multiple possibilities of the future, dear. A man might be Mr. Coffee, or he might be Bebe Rebozo. What's his line?

**FANNY**  Prognostication. He had news. We're on the right track.

**MARY**  Splendid. Saddle up.
   (*Alex and Mary pick up their stuff and start off.*)

**JOURNAL ENTRY:**

**FANNY**   (*Fanny, after a moment, silently folds the letter, tucks it away, and closes the music box.*)

### (17) Vintage Crystal

*Moonlight. A beautiful unearthly snow begins to fall.*

**ALEX**   What is that?
**FANNY**   Snow. Unless I miss my guess.
**ALEX**   Cold and wet on the tongue. Melts right off.
**FANNY**   Snow it is.
**ALEX**   Like no snow I've known before.
**FANNY**   A new snow. A strange snow. An unknown snow.
**MARY**   Lambent. Luminous.
**ALEX**   Snow from the moon, ladies!
**FANNY**   Yes!
**MARY**   Yes! Lunar snow is not annoying!
   (*Alex catches snow and tastes.*)

**JOURNAL ENTRY:**

**ALEX**   Lunar snow is, despite its apparent immaturity, a vintage precipitate. Coarser and sweeter than Himalayan, it stands up to all but the most robust Karakoram. Fruitier than Rocky Mountain powder, and a touch more acidic than Vermont sludge, it is altogether full-bodied and elusive. This is a young snow but not a callow snow, and should be confronted early – like the finest Hindu Kush – before the blush is off the slush, and the bloom is gone.

### (18) Woody's Esso

*Music: "Rock Around the Clock" playing on a radio. A gas pump and an Esso sign appear. Music fades out.*

**ALEX**   Civilization.
**MARY**   The outskirts.
**FANNY**   How far our standards have fallen.
**ALEX**   If I were wearing trousers at this moment, I would change.
**FANNY**   (*An outburst.*) You needn't suck up to me, Alexandra!
**MARY**   Fanny! Is that a vulgarity?

(*A pause.*)

**FANNY**  I am sorry, Alexandra. I plead the future.

**ALEX**  I understand.

**FANNY**  You needn't mollify me, is what I meant. It seems to me that you were right.

**ALEX**  How nice. About what, dear Fanny?

**FANNY**  Trousers. Trousers trousers trousers. It seems clear to me that everyone in the future wears 'em. I am so glad I shan't live to see it. Of course, I am seeing it. I am so flummoxed. I wonder if we will remember all this when we return home.

**MARY**  If we return home.

(*A palanquin, with its shades drawn, rolls on. On it, a sign: The Dragon Lady, Fortunes Told, Palms Read, Charts, Crystal Ball, Tarot Cards, Etc.*)

**MARY**  I know what that is –

**ALEX**  A "hot rod."

**MARY**  A palanquin.

**FANNY**  Honestly, Alexandra, how quickly you've forgotten our own era.

**MARY**  Do you realize that palanquin is now an antique?

**FANNY**  So are we, my dear, so are we.

**MARY**  But what is it doing here? (*Indicates gas pump.*) And what is that? And who is The Dragon Lady?

**FANNY**  Warrants investigation.

(*They start forward. A hand with long painted fingernails pulls back the shade suddenly, startling the ladies. It is Madame Nhu, who is wearing a beautiful if slightly ferocious half-mask. The eyes of the mask are Asian, the cheekbones high, and she wears a wig of long, jet-black hair. The effect is at once feminine and frightening. She looks them over. Her voice is low (not falsetto), and she speaks with a slight accent, both French and Asian.*)

**MME. NHU**  Come closer, Let me scrutinize you.

(*They approach cautiously. Mme. Nhu holds up a hand. They stop. After a moment, she begins to speak.*)

**MME. NHU**  Serious trouble will pass you by. Your mind is filled with new ideas – make use of them. He who does not accept cash when offered is no businessman. You are worrying about something that will never happen. Your talents will be recognized and suitably rewarded. You will never need to worry about a steady income. Soon you will be sitting on top of the world. The night life is for you. Praise your wife, even if it frightens her. You have an unusual equipment for success, be sure to use it properly. Be as soft as you can be and as hard as you have to be. Someone is speaking well of you. A new diet or exercise program can be unusually beneficial for you now. An unpleasant situation will soon be cleared to your satisfaction. Read more fine books and better magazines. Avoid fried foods, which angry up the blood. Let them eat barbecue!

(*A pause.*)

(*The ladies look at one another.*)

(*Mme. Nhu thrusts out a plate with three fortune cookies on it. They each take a cookie.*)

**MME. NHU**    Let me tell you secret. The future is now.

(*She pulls the shade and disappears.*)

**ALEX**    That was an image.

**MARY**    An oracle.

**FANNY**    An inscrutable pancake.

**ALEX**    What are these? (*Osmoses.*) "Fortune cookies!"

**MARY**    No smell.

**FANNY**    No taste.

**ALEX**    Edible?

**FANNY**    Definitely not.

**MARY**    (*Breaks hers open.*) Inside – a scrap of paper.

**ALEX**    (*Likewise.*) A message.

**FANNY**    (*Likewise.*) Fanmail from some flounder.

(*They read their messages.*)

**ALEX**    You will become rich and famous.

**FANNY**    You will meet a tall dark stranger.

**MARY**    You will go on a long journey.

**ALEX**    This is exhilarating!

(*She approaches the palanquin, steps on an invisible rubber-tube gas station bell. It chimes: ding-dong, ding dong.* )

(*A sign flies in: Woody's Esso.*)

(*Gus, a fresh-faced American teenager, appears, wearing a baseball cap and chewing gum. Boundless energy.*)

**GUS**    Hi! What'll it be? Hey! Wow! Gosh! Hello!

**FANNY**    Greetings, young man, from President McTaft.

**GUS**    Swell feathers and fancy duds! You ladies look kinda like Kitty! Golly! You goin' to the prom or what! Gosh!

**ALEX**    Kitty?

**GUS**    Didja watch *Gunsmoke* last night? Or *Cimarron City?*

**ALEX**    Kitty?

**GUS**    Kitty see she runs the saloon and she's in love with Marshal Dillon who's the sheriff but he'll never marry her 'cause he's a bachelor – see *Bachelor Father?*

**FANNY**    My dear boy, a bachelor father is a paradox. An oxymoron. A contradiction in terms.

**ALEX**   Ladies – the future.

**FANNY**   (*Snorts.*) Bachelor father. Mary, you have found your niche. Your prurient interest in anthropological smut should stand you in good stead. Bachelor father.

**MARY**   Oh, Fanny. Let us introduce ourselves.

**ALEX**   I'm Alexandra. This is Mary –

**MARY**   Hello, young man.

**ALEX**   And this is Fanny.

**GUS**   Hi! Hi! Hi! I'm Gus!

**ALEX**   Good afternoon, Gus.

**GUS**   Great! Wow, you ladies are kooky, no offense.

**ALEX**   How nice of you to say so.

**FANNY**   Gus, we are so very pleased to meet you. You are the first person we have encountered in our travels with a reasonable accent and an acceptable demeanor.

**GUS**   Lucky for me, huh? You ladies broke down somewhere? I don't see your eggbeater. Say, who do you like in the Series? The Dodgers or the Yanks?

(*Pause. Finally, Alex smiles sweetly and says judiciously:*)

**ALEX**   Whom do you like?

**GUS**   I like the Dodgers.

**ALEX**   Then so do I.

**GUS**   Great!

**MARY**   Gus, dear, tell us about the palanquin.

**ALEX**   About the Dragon Lady.

**MARY**   A lady of ferocious aspect.

**GUS**   Madame Nhu.

**ALEX**   Madame Who?

**GUS**   Madame Nhu. She rents a parking space from Woody.

**MARY**   How did Madame Nhu and her palanquin happen to land here?

**GUS**   Just showed up one day. Out of the blue.

**FANNY**   Gus, dear, what year is it?

**GUS**   You don't know?! Come off it.

**ALEX**   We do not know. Honestly. It's hard to explain.

**GUS**   1955. Everybody knows that.

**ALEX**   We don't.

**GUS**   Gee, I'm sorry. I'd give you a calendar (*Blushes.*) but they're not for girls. (*Beat.*) Hey, you guys are kidding me. Huh? Huh? Come on, lay off. Just 'cause I'm a teenager.

**MARY**   What's a teenager?

**FANNY**   What's an Esso?

**GUS**   Esso is service, parts and dependability. So you're tourists, huh? I thought you had to be, I woulda remembered *you*.

**MARY**   Travelers, not tourists.

**ALEX**   Polytopians. Travelers to many lands.

**FANNY**   Charting the unknown.

**MARY**   Geography, cartography, ethnology, and the natural sciences.

**GUS**   Great. I could use a vacation myself. You need anything? Soda, gum, roadmaps, oil? Chiclets?

**ALEX**   I would like a "Chiclet," please.

**GUS**   Take two, they're small.

*(Gus gives Alex some Chiclets. She examines them, pops them into her mouth, and chews.)*

**GUS**   Where you ladies from?

**MARY**   We are traveling through time, Gus.

**GUS**   You dames are some kidders. No? You mean it? You're on the level? Wow! Like you're from another time?! Another dimension?! PARALLEL UNIVERSE?! Wait'll I tell my Dad! I saw this *show* – *(Beat as he looks them over.)* Wow, so this is how they dress in history! Gee! Do you wanna come to my social studies class? So, do you believe in UFOs?

**ALEX**   Chiclets are sweet and tough, like dried manioc.

**FANNY**   Ah, Gus. We are looking for someone. Perhaps you know him.

**ALEX**   Ike.

**MARY**   Perhaps you've heard of him.

**GUS**   Ike who?

**ALEX**   We do not know his surname.

**MARY**   We found his name on this button.

**GUS**   Nicky might know. He knows everybody.

*(Mary hands Gus the button.)*

**GUS**   Ho ho.

**FANNY**   You know this Ike.

**GUS**   Yeah, sure I know this Ike. Hangs out at the station. Wants to be a grease monkey in his spare time. I'm showing him the ropes. You guys. Whatta buncha kidders.

**ALEX**   You don't know him?

**GUS**   My dad voted for him. Come on. What are ya, gonna vote for that other clown, the Chicago egghead? "I Like Ike." Great.

**ALEX**   Do you like Ike, Gus?

**GUS**   My dad likes him! I betcha Nicky knows this Ike. 'Sides, you wanna stay there while you're in Peligrosa, doncha? Hold on, let me draw you a map. *(He disappears.)*

**ALEX**   Mary! Fanny! Facts!

**FANNY**   Chronological and geographical. We are in Peligrosa!

**MARY**   In the vicinity of 1955!

**ALEX**   Perhaps 1955 is the apotheosis of the future!

**FANNY**  This Ike must be a local Poobah!

**ALEX**  We shall palaver.

*(Gus reappears, with a map.)*

**GUS**  Okay, dokey, here's directions to Nicky's.

**MARY**  Is it far?

**GUS**  Just a hop skip and a jump. We're giving these away with a full
tank. But for you guys – it's on the house.

*(Gus hands Mary an egg beater of yet a third design.)*

**MARY**  Marvelous! A matched set!

**ALEX**  Ladies! Whip them out!

*(Fanny and Alex whip out their egg beaters. They all rotor and laugh.
From this point on, the Ladies always wear their eggbeaters.)*

**GUS**  You collect 'em?!? I'd give you green stamps, but Woody'd kill me
if –

**FANNY**  Gus, dear, does this Nicky fellow have a bath?

**GUS**  Nicky's – are you kidding? Does he have a bath? Are you kidding?
He's got everything! He'll probably put you up. Wait'll you see the
set-up at Nicky's. You are gonna flip!

**FANNY**  Hooper Do! *(She grabs the map.)* Gus, my undying devotion.
Ladies – dog my heels.

**ALEX**  Adieu, Gus.

**GUS**  See you later, alligator.

**MARY**  Thank you, Gus. Perhaps we'll pass this way again.

**GUS**  After awhile, crocodile.

**MARY**  Ah, Gus! The Mighty Silurian!

**GUS**  Whatever you say, lady. Give Nicky some skin for me.

**MARY**  Whatever you say, Gus.

*(Gus exits.)*

*(Traveling music throbs: The theme from Peter Gunn. The ladies
travel. They reach a spot, and huddle around a map.)*

**MARY**  X marks the spot.

*(Peter Gunn fades away.)*

**ALEX**  Have we misread it?

**FANNY**  Impossible. But perhaps we've passed it.

**ALEX**  My eyes were peeled.

**FANNY**  In time. Perhaps we've passed it in time. Perhaps it was here
once. But now it's gone.

**MARY**  I think not. I have an unshakable conviction we have come to the
center of 1955.

**ALEX**  Smack dab in the middle.

**MARY**  Well said, Alex.

**FANNY**  If the map's right, and the time's right, where the devil is this
Nicky fellow? I'll horsewhip anyone who stands between me and a hot

bath.

**ALEX**  I broke up a knife fight with a whip once. Oh, yes I did. Two
sherpas were vying for a place by the fire.

(*Strains of Big Band music.*)

**MARY**  Do you hear that music?

**FANNY**  A mynah bird escaped from a cocktail lounge.

**ALEX**  Fanny, you redefine pessimism. What is a "cocktail lounge"?

**FANNY**  Osmose it yourself.

**ALEX**  (*Osmosing.*) "Happy Hour!"

(*A loud burst of Big Band music.*)

**MARY**  Ladies – I believe we're on the verge!

(*All three ladies do journal entry in unison.*)

**ALEX, MARY** and **FANNY**  We arrive in '55!

### (19) Paradise '55

*Lights! A flashy sign, neon: Nicky's. Some palm trees and
streamers: A gaudy, prerevolutionary Havana-style night club.
Nicky rolls on with a piano and live mike. Does a splashy finish.*

**NICKY**  Vaya! Vaya! Vaya! Con! Dios! Wo Wo Wo Wo Wo –
yeaaaaaah! Pow!

(*The ladies applaud.*)

**NICKY**  You're too kind.

(*Checks them out.*)

**NICKY**  My my my my my my my. Holy cow. What have we here. Our
humble joint. Nicky's Peligrosa Paradise Bar and Grill. Graced by
style, beauty, pulchritude and wit. Hi, I'm Nicky Paradise. Welcome to
paradise – where hospitality still means something.

**ALEX**  (*Instantly smitten.*) O brave new world, that has such creatures in
it!

**FANNY**  Alex, you are a terrible plagiarist.

**MARY**  Instantly smitten.

**NICKY**  Make yourselves at home. (*His best smile.*) Mi casa es su casa!
(*Reprise – best smile.*) My house is your house. Toss back a coupla
stiff ones, grab a bite, cool out in the casino, catch a show, let your hair
down, loosen your corsets –

**MARY, FANNY** and **ALEX**  Mr. Nicky!

**NICKY**  Please. Nicky.

**ALEXANDRA**  Alexandra Cafuffle.

**FANNY**  Mrs. Cranberry. You may call me Fanny.

**NICKY**  It would break my heart if I couldn't.

**MARY**  Mary Baltimore. From Boston.

**NICKY**  Such tropicana, such feminality. Overwhelmed, truly.

*(He dashes to the piano and plays and sings a phrase of "Bad Boy.")*

**NICKY**  "I'm just a bad boy-oy-oy-oy-oy-oy-oy-oy-oy-oy-oy –
All dressed up in fancy clothes
I am takin' the trouble
To blow all my bubbles away."

**ALEX**  Mr. Paradise!

**NICKY**  Nicky.

**FANNY**  Mr. Paradise –

**NICKY**  Nicky, Nicky, Nicky!

**FANNY**  Nicky, Nicky, Nicky. I hope you won't think me indelicate –

**NICKY**  Never.

**FANNY**  – but I simply must have a scrub immediately. Post haste. It's been eons. Can you arrange for me to have a bath?

**NICKY**  For you, Fanny – a whirlpool. *(He snaps his fingers and plays the piano. A light appears.)* Follow that light, Fanny. Don't be stingy with the bubbles. That's what they're there for.

**FANNY**  Bubbles. I won't ask. I'll just hold my nose and dive in. Ladies.
*(She exits.)*
*(Nicky sings and plays after her: "Vaya Con Dios My Darling/Vaya Con Dios My Love.")*

**MARY**  Nicky's Peligrosa Paradise Bar and Grill?

**NICKY**  Be there or – *(Smiles his best smile.)* be square.
*(Mary holds out her button.)*

**MARY**  Perhaps you can shed some light.

**NICKY**  Oh yeah. I like Ike. Who doesn't?

**MARY**  Who don't?

**NICKY**  Have it your way, Mary. I'm easy.

**MARY**  I like Ike. Heck, who don't?

**NICKY**  Hardly anybody.
*(Mary pulls out the original button she found on the beach.)*

**MARY**  Indeed. "Heckwhodon't?" Heck – who – don't. It's a companion button. I like Ike. Heck, who don't?

**NICKY**  You're sharp. Need a job?

**ALEX**  Brava, Mary! I love a good mystery, don't you?
*(Mary pins the buttons on Alex.)*

**MARY**  Do you know him? Gus said you might.

**ALEX**  We would very much like to meet him.

**MARY**  He has become a point of some interest with us.

**ALEX**  Do you know this Ike?

**NICKY**  We're like this. Never vacations anywhere but Nicky's. He and

Mamie are nuts about the joint. He's gonna make Nicky's a national monument.

**ALEX**  Is he in residence at present?

**NICKY**  Yeah, he's in back, smoking a cigar. I'll take you around.

**ALEX**  Oh, goody. I'll Kodak him for posterity!

**NICKY**  You'll like Ike. Everybody does. He's a likeable guy. Plays a fair round of golf. No duffer, Ike. You play?

**MARY**  The Scottish game? No. Speaking of games, am I correct in understanding that there is a gambling emporium on the premises?

**NICKY**  The casino. First rate. Slap a little blackjack, shoot some craps, spin the wheel, pull some slots, float a check. Whatever.

**MARY**  Gambling provides a fascinating study in cross-cultural comparisons. For instance, did you know that the Ute Indians of the American West are avid gamblers, and will wager their life's possessions on a single throw of the dice?

**NICKY**  No, I did not know that. Did you know that the Nevada looney bins are full of catatonic bluehaired ladies going like this? (*He demonstrates: catatonic slot-machine addicts plus sound effects.*)

**MARY**  No, I did not. Fascinating. I do not indulge, personally, of course, but with your permission, I should like to take notes.
(*Nicky hands her some chips.*)

**NICKY**  Have a ball, Mar' – knock yourself out.
(*He snaps his fingers, plays the piano. A light appears.*)

**MARY**  Not annoying! (*She follows the light. As she is about to exit, she turns;*) Ah, Nicky. Gus said to give you some of his skin.

**NICKY**  Thanks, doll.
(*She exits. Nicky plays, sings after her: "There Goes My Baby/Movin' On Down the Line."*)
(*He turns his attentions to Alex.*)

**NICKY**  Great kid, Gus.

**ALEX**  He drew us a map. That is how we located you.

**NICKY**  No, it's not.

**ALEX**  I beg your pardon.

**NICKY**  I said, that's not how you came to Nicky's, Al.

**ALEX**  Are you contradicting me?

**NICKY**  It wasn't a map that brought you to me, Al It was – (*Best smile.*) Kismet.

**ALEX**  I don't understand.

**NICKY**  You were destined to come to Nicky's.

**ALEX**  Perhaps you're right. I do have a positive feeling about 1955. It's – it's – it's – keen!

**NICKY**  I'm having a great year. So you stopped at Woody's. See the Dragon Lady?

**ALEX** Madame Nhu?

**NICKY** Madame Nhu. She's usually parked out front, filing her foot-long nails.

**ALEX** Lovely palanquin.

**NICKY** Isat what it is? I thought it was a chopped Chevy. Ike should be done with his cigar now. Want to meet him?

**ALEX** Desperately.

(*Nicky snaps his fingers plays the piano. A light.*)

**NICKY** Second door on the fight. Knock three times. If Mamie answers, come back. We'll do it later.

**ALEX** At long last, Ike! I'm off to meet the Ike! Ta! Ike get a kick out of you! Ike, can't get you out of my mind!

**NICKY** Hold your hula hoops! Al, you aren't, by any chance, a lyricist?

**ALEX** How did you guess?

**NICKY** I can spot talent! I could use a good word jockey. Meet me in the lounge later. We'll pen some tunes. I have a lucrative new contract to script some billboards for Burma Shave.

**ALEX** Fantastic! I've been dying to know what Burma Shave is.

**NICKY** Al, I told you. Kismet.

**ALEX** Ike can't get no satisfaction!

(*She exits. As Nicky styles on the piano Fanny enters, resplendent and transformed in 50's cocktail dress and blonde wig, still wearing eggbeater.*)

**NICKY** Holy smokes! I have not seen duds like that since *High-School Confidential.*

(*He sweeps Fanny off her feet.* )

**NICKY** What do you say we trip the light fantastic?

(*They do a slow romantic dance to Duke Ellington's Dual Highway, Nicky showing Fanny some sharp moves. Fanny grows more confident with every step. By the end of the dance, they are falling in love. They finish the dance and go to the table.*)

**NICKY** Fred and Ginger have nothing on us – nothing! (*Gets intimate.*) Say, do you remember those little Danny Boone hats with the wacky raccoon tails?

**FANNY** I'm afraid not.

**NICKY** They were a gas. How was the whirlpool?

(*After a sensuous pause, Fanny says:*)

**FANNY** Wow – wow – wow! Captivating. All those little jets of water were – quite – mesmerizing. I feel light-headed. Swoozy all over. (*Beat.*) Jacuzzi all over.

**NICKY** I don't follow you.

**FANNY** Your whirlpool is called a jacuzzi. Or will be.

**NICKY** I like the sound of that. Jacuzz'.

**FANNY**  Your establishment is uncanny. A veritable pleasure dome.

**NICKY**  I like to think of it that way.

*(She pulls out one of her postcards.)*

**FANNY**  It's just like my postcard.

**NICKY**  Hey! Where did you get this? These are sharp!

**FANNY**  I brought it with me. It's a postcard from the future. Of Nicky's. The view come true! Generic nightspot.

**NICKY**  Like I always say, Fanny – the future is now. I'm gonna put 'em in all the rooms with the Gideon Bibles.

**FANNY**  Mister Paradise –

**NICKY**  Hey, I'm gonna get cross wit' you –

**FANNY**  Nicky. Since we've been in the vicinity of 1955, there's something I've had a craving for –

**NICKY**  Please. Say no more.

*(He prestidigitates a huge glass goblet and two spoons. As Fanny closes her eyes –)*

**FANNY**  I am agog with anticipation.

*(He holds the goblet under her nose. She inhales deeply, with ecstasy, and slowly opens her eyes.)*

**FANNY**  Cool Whip!

**NICKY**  The Real McCoy.

*(He hands her a spoon. They each dish out a spoonful of Cool Whip. They lock eyes. They lock arms, as though drinking champagne. They raise the spoons to their lips.)*

**NICKY**  Here's to you – Fanny.

*(They clink spoons. They take a bite. A dazzled pause.)*

**FANNY**  Oh! good!

*(Freeze. Music swells. Nicky and Fanny exit.)*


*(Alex enters and does journal entry. )*

**ALEX**  *(Formally, still, a bit out of rhythm, and trying to snap her fingers, perhaps using Nicky's mike.)*

On the go or at the beach
After hours or safe at home
For a cheek as smooth as a Georgia peach
You need the shave that's like a poem –
Burma Shave!


### (20) Later That Same Evening

*Alex moves to the table and examines Cool Whip.*

**ALEX** (*Osmoses.*) "Mo-hair." No. "Jello mold." No. (*Tastes.*) Noxzema! Yes! Heaven!

(*Mary enters, to a swirl of music, tipsy and exhilarated.*)

**MARY** I have experienced an epiphany in the casino. I beat the one-armed bandit, kid! As they say here in 1955. Look!

(*She pours a cascade of nickles out of her helmet onto the table.*)

**ALEX** Fantastic! I love the future!

**MARY** And how did you do, Alexandra? Did you run the elusive Ike to ground? Tree him? Beard him in his lair?

**ALEX** Mamie answered.

**MARY** You'll collar him tomorrow. Quite a card, Ike. Una tarjeta, en espanol. Not many people know that.

**ALEX** And how do you know that?

**MARY** A bulletin from the future.

**ALEX** What else does your bulletin tell you about Ike?

(*Mary osmoses.*)

**MARY** He is a poobah of the first water. Golf clubs. Cardigan sweaters. (*Rubs her head.*) Cue ball.

**ALEX** Cue ball?

**MARY** (*With great dignity.*)
"He has got a cue ball head that is hard as lead –
But he is all right with me.
Wo wo."

**ALEX** Mary.

**MARY** It is extraordinary what blossoms in one's brain in this country. That is from something called (*Osmoses.*) "Rock and roll."

**ALEX** "Rock and roll." . . . Whomp bop a lula a wombat too!

(*She then scats the guitar part to the Surfari's WIPEOUT! doing 50's rock moves, and ending with a big finish. Mary beats out the drum part on the piano.*)

**ALEX** Wombat!

**MARY** My. Osmosing the future is far more strenuous than navigating the upper reaches of the Congo.

**ALEX** The January 1955 *Variety* magazine says rock and roll will be gone by June. Oh! What month are we?

**MARY** I've no idea.

**ALEX** I hope it's not June. I am dieting to rock and roll. I mean determined. Not dieting.

**MARY** Hello, what's this? Manioc? (*She takes a spoonful of Cool Whip.*)

**ALEX** Noxzema.

**MARY** Have you tried it? (*She smears some on her face.*)

**ALEX** Mmm. The texture is indescribable.

**MARY** (*Takes a big bite – savors.*) Why, this is sheer heaven,

Alexandra.

*(Fanny floats on, now in a tight evening dress, looking blowzy and wonderful, still wearing her eggbeater.)*

**FANNY**   More than sheer heaven, Mary. Paradise.

**ALEX**   You look the cat that swallowed the canary.

**FANNY**   We were dancing!

**ALEX**   Really.

**FANNY**   Nicky is a divine dancer.

**ALEX**   Have some Noxzema.

**FANNY**   Cool Whip!

**ALEX**   Oh!

**MARY**   So this is Fanny's Cool Whip!

**FANNY**   Luscious, isn't it? I had the most extraordinary experience earlier this evening in a celestial contraption called a jacuzzi.

**MARY**   You should have seen the ecdysiastical "floor show" in the casino. The natives call it *Girls A Poppin'!* As fascinating as fire. From an anthropological point of view. Reminiscent of the vernal fertility rites in Sumatra, which always culminated in a riot of gymnastic –

**FANNY**   Mary, spare us your salacious anthropological details.

**MARY**   Remarkably supple. A cornucopia of concupiscence.

**ALEX**   Ladies – get a load of this! I am osmosing jingles like crazy! *(She licks a finger, presses it to her hip, makes a sizzling sound, and uses Nicky's mike.)*

Okay, tiger, striped and brave
A close clean scrape is what you crave
To fashion's whim you are no slave
You take it off – with Burma Shave!

**FANNY**   Wow! Wow! Wow!

**ALEX**   Jingles are the art form of the future!

**FANNY**   Why do they call it Burma Shave? What's it got to do with Burma?

**MARY**   I've been to Burma.

**FANNY**   As have I.

**ALEX**   The future is not dull!

**FANNY**   This is not the future, Alexandra. This is 1955.

**MARY**   Not annoying!

**FANNY**   Not bad! And that jacuzzi is really something.

*(Alex dishes out a spoonful of Cool Whip. The others follow suit.)*

**ALEX**   To the future!

**MARY**   To us!

**ALEX**   To yetis and dirigibles –

**FANNY**   Jacuzzis –

**MARY**   To our adventures, many more!

**ALEX**   And here's to the elusive Ike!
  (*They all clink spoons.*)
**ALL**   Cheers! Ike!
  (*They all take a bite. A dazzled pause.*)
**ALL**   Oh, good!

  (*Lights change. Fanny and Alex exit. Mary comes downstage and does her journal entry.*)
**MARY**   The pleasures of Nicky's Peligrosa Paradise Bar and Grill were – philharmonic. I blossomed into – I almost blush to recall it – a bonafide voluptuary, sampling an assortment of what were called, in the native parlance, "leisure-time activities." Recreation. The casino was an anthropologist's field day, an anthology of human mis-demeanor. Its fascinating as fire floorshow, *Girls-A-Poppin'!*, held, I felt, the key to the culture, and was worth years of intense scrutiny. Television proved an addictive, if ultimately incomprehensible, hypnotic. And I thought the jacuzzi the greatest piece of engineering since the wheel. In short, I went, as the topical lingo had it, on a "bender." (*Beat.*) The Byzantine pleasures of Nicky's intoxicate – but do not satiate. I flash and yearn for adventures beyond the jacuzzi.

### (21) Go-Go Boots – or, Rock and Roll Is Here To Stay

  *Fanny and Alex enter. It is some months later: Fanny is wearing a sensible 50's sun dress and Alex is dressed in pedal pushers, carrying a surfboard. Fanny has a picnic basket and cooler. Both wear eggbeaters.*

**ALEX**   (*To Fanny.*) I've yet to catch a glimpse of him. That Mamie guards him like a gryphon.
**FANNY**   Perhaps Ike is a yeti.
**ALEX**   Mary – look what I found! Surfboard!
**MARY**   What is the cultural application of a surfboard, Alexandra?
**ALEX**   Hang ten. Shoot the pipeline. Curl the Big Kahuna.
**MARY**   Whatever you say, Alex.
  (*Fanny pulls out a pair of white boots.*)
**FANNY**   Alexandra may have her surfboard, but I have my "go-go boots." A white ceremonial shoe. Worn while mashing potatoes, riding ponies, and palavering with the Watusi.
**MARY**   I've found a tile. (*She holds up a green tile.*)
**FANNY**   Terra cotta?
**MARY**   Congoleum.

**FANNY**  Congoleum. What's it got to do with the Congo?

**MARY**  I know not.

**FANNY**  I've been to the Congo.

**MARY**  As have I.

**ALEX**  Mary, you are the ginchiest. Hang in there.

**MARY**  I shall. I shall hang in there. I owe you a great debt, Alexandra.

**ALEX**  No prob, Mar'. No sweat. No skin off my nose.

**FANNY**  Alexandra. Only a moment in 1955, and already your language is beyond redemption.

**ALEX**  Loosen your living girdle, Fanny.

**MARY**  Ah, Alexandra, how are your jingles?

**ALEX**  I've given them up for rock and roll.

**FANNY**  A fleeting fad.

**ALEX**  Fanny, rock 'n roll is here to stay. So, when's the shindig?

**MARY**  Shindig?

**FANNY**  I believe she means the authentic suburban charred meat festival you promised us.

**MARY**  Ah, yes. The bar-be-cue.

**ALEX**  Yes, what are we having – barbecued manioc?

**FANNY**  I am so excited. I haven't set foot outside the Paradise since our arrival.

*(Mary picks up her pack, which is fully rigged out for trekking. )*

**FANNY**  Mary! Where on Earth is this picnic? You have enough gear for a trek.

**MARY**  I have discovered within myself a new world. A voluptuousness which astounds me with its magenta sunsets, its incarnadine passions, its indigo fevers, tropical storms, and throbbing scarlet heart. Having discovered my voluptuous inclination, I have no intention of leaving it unexplored. Ladies – the future beckons! Don't you see? What we all need is further adventures!

**ALEX**  Oh, Mary, yes!

**FANNY**  Might be nice. A few days' trek. See something of the hinterlands.

**MARY**  I had in mind going on.

**ALEX**  Oh, I don't want to go back.

**MARY**  Not back. On.

**FANNY**  I adore 1955. It would break my heart to leave. *(Beat.)* I love this. The occasional barbecue. *(Beat.)* Entre nous – we're engaged!

**MARY and ALEX**  Oh, Fanny!

**FANNY**  Thank you. We are very happy. The night Nicky popped the question, I was agog with anticipation. Yes I said yes yes oh yes I will my mountain flower as well you as another my flower of Andalusia and the pink and blue and yellow houses – *(Stops herself.)* Goodness.

**ALEX** What will Grover say?

**FANNY** Ah, Grover, dear Grover, my tender parsnip. Grover will have apoplexy. You know, I can scarcely recall what Grover looks like. His face is fading from my memory like a hand-tinted picture postcard. I never told you. Grover passed on in 1929. Did away with himself, poor dear. Despondent over pork belly futures.

**MARY** Poor Fanny. How do you know?

**FANNY** Mr. Coffee told me. That man. Did you know he had me declared legally dead?

**ALEX** No!

**MARY** Well, three cheers for you, Fanny.

(*Turns to Alex.*)

Alex? There are new worlds out there. Where the air is rare.

**ALEX** I have a date. I'm writing tunes with the Gorge Troll. We've got an offer from the House O' Hits. They want to buy our new number, *Mind Your Own Beeswax*. Then we're going for a spin on his chopper. Now that I know what a chopper is.

(*Pause.*)

**MARY** It seems a shame to break up the team.

**ALEX** You don't have to.

(*Pause.*)

**MARY** Perhaps we are meant to be solo sojourners after all.

(*Pause.*)

**FANNY** I'll go scout out a spot to fire up the briquets.

**ALEX** I'll follow suit.

(*As they leave:*)

**FANNY** Are you reading your subscription to *The National Review?*

**ALEX** Troll and I are writing tunes. I haven't time for arcane political journals.

**FANNY** Not arcane. Germane.

**ALEX** That's not a true rhyme. But it's not bad.

**FANNY** High praise.

(*They're gone.*)


(*Nicky's Peligrosa disappears as Mary comes downstage and does her journal entry.*)

**MARY** My brain is full of exhilirating bulletins. On the horizon, a transcendent light flashes off the spires of the future. This New World is a garden. Splendors and wonders, marvels and mysteries. Miracles which top even Cool Whip.

## (22) The Geography of Yearning

*Alex enters, in motorcycle leathers.*

**ALEX** Nothing shall ever replace Cool Whip in my affections. So. You're really going?

**MARY** Yes.

**ALEX** Seems a shame.

**MARY** I'm restless. Wanderlust. You know.

**ALEX** I have a faint recollection. (*Beat.*) I do feel a tug. But I belong here.

**MARY** This is what you wanted. The Show Business.

**ALEX** It's Kismet. Here in 1955 is my brilliant career. I am part of the entertainment industry.

**MARY** Good for you.

**ALEX** I am wanton.

**MARY** Alex.

**ALEX** I mean weepy. Not wanton.
    (*They embrace. Fanny enters, dressed for bowling.*)

**FANNY** You're still here. Thank goodness. Alexandra, what a get up.
    (*Alex shoots a look at Fanny's own get-up.*)

**MARY** Dear Fanny.

**FANNY** I do have a bit of a hankering to hit the trail with you, old friend. But 1955 suits me. To a T-Bird. Nicky is such a – dancer.

**MARY** Will you invite Ike to the wedding?

**FANNY** Entre nous, he's Nicky's best man.

**ALEX** Goody! I'll Polaroid him for posterity.
    (*Nicky enters, also ready to bowl a few frames.*)

**NICKY** Fan, you look sensational, doll. Al, I ran your latest lyric up the flagpole, and I saluted, sweetheart, Mar'.

**MARY** Nick'.

**NICKY** And I used to think you had no sense of humor.

**MARY** Live and learn.

**NICKY** I sure will. So, what's the word, thunderbird?

**MARY** Mr. Nicky, your emporium is most enticing. The sirens seduce.

**NICKY** They really wail, don't they?

**MARY** But I have strapped myself to the mast, and must sail on.

**NICKY** When you gotta go, you gotta go. (*He hands her a container of Cool Whip.*) A little pick-me-up for the open road. You're not gonna find a lot of St. Bernards with Cool Whip in their kegs. Happy trails.

**MARY** Oh, Nicky. Congratulations.

**NICKY** Fanny spilled the beans, huh?

**MARY** I think so.

**NICKY**   Sorry you won't be here for the big day.

**MARY**   I shall be here in spirit.

**NICKY**   So long. Just remember the immortal words of Satchel Paige. Don't look back – something might be gaining on you.

**MARY**   Ah, the sage Satchel Paige. He also said, to keep the juices flowing, jangle around gently as you move.

**NICKY**   I'll keep it in mind.

**MARY**   Sound advice. I intend to follow it to the letter.

**ALEX**   Mary. Before you go. You must give us the lowdown on the future.

**MARY**   I've only had glimpses, mind you. Flashes. Bits of light.

*(She osmoses, uttering each new word as if it were being spoken for the very first time. Coining place names for a map of the New World:)*

**MARY**   Electric eyes. Automatic tellers. TV dinners. And that's just the beginning.

Trailer parks. Mobile homes. Home economics.

O! Revolving credit! Spinoffs. Tax shelters, subsidiary rights. Offshore banking. Venture capital. Residuals.

Non-dairy creamer. Non-profit foundations. No-fault insurance.

Pot stickers. Nehru jackets. Lava lamps. Day glo. Black light. The Peace Corps. Soul music. The Fab Four. Fern bars. Fondue. Free love. Romanian Cabernet Sauvignon.

Disposable income. Significant others. Mood elevators.

Mood rings. Mud wrestling. Super stars. Floating anchors. Guest hosts. Low riders.

Slam dancing. Soft ware. Prime time. Time sharing. Word processors. Double speak. Hyper space. Holograms.

Aura cleansing. Angelic intervention. Pace makers. Walk mans. Synthesizers. Ghetto blasters. 45's. Saturday night specials.

Pulsars. Fiber optics. Remote control. Double think. Think tanks. The Domino Theory. The Third World. Boat people. Heavy water.

Enhanced radiation. Silly Putty. Patty melts. Melt down. Ground zero. Fellow travelers.

Windows of vulnerability.

*(Pause.)*

**FANNY**   Fellow travelers, yes, yes, yes, yes, yes we are, yes!

**ALEX**   And vulnerable windows! Marvelous!

**MARY**   Ladies, what do you say we have one last rotor? Just – one for the road, as it were?

**FANNY**   Splendid idea.

*(Egg beaters appear.)*

**FANNY**   Ready?

**ALEX**   Set?

**MARY**   Rotor!

(*They rotor vigorously. A good long rotor and a good long laugh.*)

(*Finished, Mary steps downstage, whips off her long Victorian skirt –*)

**ALEX**   Mary!

**FANNY**   Nicky, don't look!

( *– With a flourish. Underneath, she is wearing trousers.*)

**ALEX**   Brava, Mary!

**MARY**   I told you, Alexandra, I owe you a great debt.

**ALEX**   Intrepid trekking. Perhaps our paths will cross again, at some caravanserai of the future.

**MARY**   I feel certain of it. Our parabolas will intersect once more.

(*Sound of an enormous unmuffled motorcycle puffing up outside.*)

**ALEX**   That's Troll. Gotta go. Ciao.

**FANNY**   Dig you on the flip side.

(*She exits. Motorcycle roars off.*)

**MARY**   Mr. Nicky, thank you for everything.

(*She shakes his hand, and turns it into a hip handshake.*)

**NICKY**   Hey, hey, hey –

**MARY**   (*Gives him a wink.*) Willy and the Hand Jive.

**NICKY**   You're hip, Mar'.

**MARY**   You, Nick', are impertinent. Give Gus some skin for me.

**NICKY**   So long.

**FANNY**   See you later, alligator. Au revoir, bon voyage. Stay dry. Try to write. And look out for zeeroxen.

**MARY**   Goodbye, Fanny.

**FANNY**   Vaya con Dios.

(*Nicky and Fanny exit.*)

(*Mary saddles up and comes downstage.*)

**MARY**   The splash of galaxies across the night sky always brings out the phenomenologist in me.

(*The stars come out.*)

**MARY**   Billions of new worlds, waiting to be discovered. Explored and illuminated. Within and without. The nautilus shell mimics the shape of the Milky Way. Quarks and quasars. My face is bathed in light from a vanished star. (*Beat.*) I stand on the precipice. The air is rare. Bracing. Before me stretch dark distances. Clusters of light. What next? I have no idea. Many mysteries to come. I am on the verge.

(*She surveys the horizon and her prospects.*)

**MARY**   I have such a yearning for the future! It is boundless! (*She takes a deep breath.*) Not annoying. Not annoying at all!

(*She disappears in a blaze of light –*)

### END OF PLAY

# IN A PIG'S VALISE
*For Mark Herrier & Becky Gonzalez*

"Don't kid me. My nerves are frayed," I said. "Who's the junky?"
"Come along, Alfred," the big man said to his companion. "And stop acting girlish."
"In a pig's valise," Alfred told him.
The big man turned to me placidly. "Why do all these punks keep saying that?"

*Raymond Chandler, THE LITTLE SISTER*

IN A PIG'S VALISE was presented as part of the PLAYWRIGHTS 86 series at Center Stage, Baltimore, MD. Stan Wojewodski, Artistic Director; Peter Culman, Managing Director.

It was then produced in New York at the Second Stage Theatre, Robyn Goodman and Carole Rothman, Artistic Directors, with a new score by August Darnell. The first performance was on 11 January 1989, with the following cast and production team:

JAMES TAXI ............................................................Nathan Lane
DOLORES CON LECHE ..............................................Ada Maris
ZOOT ALORS ...................................................Jonathan Freeman
ROOT CHOYCE........................................................Thom Sesma
THE BOP OP ...............................................................Reg E Cathey
BLIND SAX..............................................................Charlie Lagond
SHRIMP BUCKET......................................Michael McCormick
GUT BUCKET...................................................Jonathan Freeman
MUSTANG SALLY.......................................................Lauren Tom
DIZZY MISS LIZZY ....................................................Dian Sorel

*Bass* ........................................................................Carol Colman
*Guitar* ......................................................................Eugene Grey
*Saxophone*...............................................................Charlie Lagond
*Keyboard*...................................................................Peter Schott
*Drums* ........................................................................David Span

*Direction and Choreography* ..............................Graciela Daniele
*Set Design* ....................................................................Bob Shaw

| Lighting Design | .................................................. | Peggy Eisenhauer |
| Costume Design | .................................................. | Jeanne Button |
| Musical Direction | .................................................. | Peter Schott |
| Sound Design | .................................................. | Gary and Timmy Harris |

## CHARACTERS

James Taxi, *a private eye*
Dolores Con Leche, *a thrush*

*Denizens of The Heartbreak Hotel:*
Zoot Alors*
Root Choyce
The Bop Op
Blind Sax

*The notorious Bucket Brothers:*
Shrimp Bucket
Gut Bucket

*The Balkanettes, back-up singers:*
Mustang Sally
Dizzy Miss Lizzy

*The actor who plays Zoot plays Gut Bucket (in a fat suit).

## SCENE

The action takes place in and around The Heartbreak Hotel, at the corner of Neon and Lonely.

## MUSICAL NUMBERS

### ACT ONE
   Neon Heart
   Kiss Me Deadly
   The Skulk

Three-Fingered Glove
Balkan Jam
Mango Culo
Talent Scout
Nuevo Huevo
Shrimp Louie
Vegetable Medley (Caffeine)
Echelon of Scum
Ethnic Jokes Broke My Baby's Heart
Put Your Legs on My Shoulders
Put Your Legs on My Shoulders, reprise
Never Judge a Thriller
Shrimp Louie, reprise

## ACT TWO

Prisoner of Genre
Three-Fingered Glove, reprise
If I Was a Fool to Dream
No More Magic Kingdoms
Doin' the Denouement
If I Was a Fool to Dream, reprise
Never Judge a Thriller, reprise

# IN A PIG'S VALISE

## ACT ONE

*Lots of fog.*
*A streetlight. A couple of neon signs. Pale pink 'n blue neon fluid script.*
*Heartbreak Hotel. Bar.*
*Music: Opening Titles, a smoky instrumental, sax solo, something slow sultry sweet sexy sad and blue.*
*The music starts and swells. The fog drifts and swirls. The sign flashes: Ba Ba Ba Ba Ba Ba Ba*
*A car approaches. Headlights. Fades away. Brakes screech on rain-slick streets.*
*A match is struck. With panache.*
*A man steps out of the fog. You know what he looks like: slouch hat, thread-bare suit, five o'clock shadow, no tie. Under his suit jacket he's wearing a pajama top instead of a shirt.*
*And he's very very short.*
*His voice is cool and tired.*

**TAXI**  Chaka chaka chaka cha. (*Pause.*) Listen, baby.
(*He sings NEON HEART, a hot and cool ballad about the life.*)

### NEON HEART

**TAXI**  It was a foggy night
I heard a sax on the soundtrack
Somewhere a neon light
Flashed me right back to you
I walk the lonely streets
Cruisin' clues on bar stools
My heart's got a private beat
So cool it's neon blue

You know it's lonely out there
Streets are rainy and bare
And the whisky is starting to pour
I know what you're longing for
Goin' to the Neon Heart
You know that's where the records start

You know that's where they keep on keeping the score

I ease the Chevy slow
Ridin' around with the top down
I pay the tab and go
And I drive home alone

Money slick changes hands
Honeyed licks from the trombones
She makes you understand
Going to the Neon Zone

(*Sax Solo*)

You know the neon's so fine
All the saxophones shine
And the dancers are dreaming in bars
Tell me that it's time to part
Goin' to the Neon Heart
You know that's where the records start
You know that's where you'll find the mysteries are

You say "No Vacancy"
But I'm gonna make you love me
It'll be yours to take
Turn me off watch me fade
Watch my Neon Heart break . . .
(*Sweet finish. He sizes up audience.*)

**TAXI**   As long as we're here. Let's smash the bubbly.
(*He lights up. The smoke from the cigarette curls up in the blue
streetlights, and his cool pose is the essence of a classic forties album
cover.*)

**TAXI**   It was two-fifty-two in the fretful A.M. I'd been ensconced in the
back of my Chevy Bel-Air, dreaming I was a fresh-pressed Sinatra
seventy-eight, with classic forties water-color cover art. Pastels. I
could've spun that particular platter all night long, until the grooves
screamed for mercy. Instead, I found myself shivering in my shoes –
scratch that – my gumshoes, on one of the worst corners in this
quadrant of Western Civ. There were a lot of corners reserved for the
criminally insane in this behind-the-eight-ball burg, but this one was
special. Neon and Lonely.
(*He drags on his cigarette.*)

**TAXI**  Neon and Lonely. The co-ordinates of desire. Sax solos. Neon longing. Convertibles. Stolen convertibles.

(*An acid belch.*)

**TAXI**  I'd come in from the valley. Forty-suck-your-heart-out miles of fast food and singed ozone. Avec shot brakes and smoldering upholstery. I was risking a loitering rap in front of a beanbag hotel. The kind of dive where checkout time sometimes comes when you least expect it. Loitering with intent: to meet some mysterioso-ette. Here. In the shadow of The Heartbreak.

(*The neon Heartbreak Hotel sign pops on. Taxi regards the classic pink and blue sign sourly.*)

**TAXI**  Fleabag, beanbag, paperbag, scumbag, douchebag, bodybag hotel. Bagatelle. The Heartburn. This place is a case.

(*He sneezes.*)

**TAXI**  It was another damp one. The latest in a series. It seemed like a lifetime ago that I'd gotten her call. The call that had me sucking up bronchial smog and the kiss-me-deadly night air on the corner of Neon and Lonely with red eyes and flat fleet.

(*Beat.*)

**TAXI**  Feet.

(*Beat.*)

**TAXI**  The air was like Liquid Paper. Whoo. My chronic hypothermia was coming on like a hit of purple haze. Cold cojones, pal. I was shaking like a maracas player on the Feast Day of St. Zenophobe of the Green Card. I played a round of pocket pool and kept hanging in. The fog continued to ladle itself on. Like pea soup in a Merchant Marine mess hall. Like interest on an easy-payment credit plan. Like suffering similies in exhausted sub-genres of pop-tic and modern lit. You couldn't hack through it with an M-16. Not that I had one. On me.

(*Beat. Drags.*)

**TAXI**  All in all, a sweet, sweet set-up for a sap like me.

(*Beat. Drags.*)

**TAXI**  But I couldn't leave. They'd towed my car. The kiss-me-Wednesday night air was putting a chill on my bones like jelly on a gefilte fish. I took a moment to strike a match on my eyebrow and set fire to another coffin nail.

(*He strikes a match on his eyebrow, lights a second cigarette, smokes both.*)

**TAXI**  One more thing. When I face front and talk to you this way – this way! This is the Voice Over voice. The Big VO. When you earn your PI license, they issue you your own VO. Don't let it slow you down. Just pretend that my lips don't move and you can hear my voice surple out over the PA all muffled and crunkly. I'm supposed to be thinking, see.

(*He snuffs one cigarette.*)

**TAXI**  But what I'm really doing is passing on vital exposition as we make an incomplete transition from pulp to performance. In other words, if I didn't tell you, you'd never know.

(*Beat.*)

**TAXI**  It's gotta be how it's gotta be. We're all prisoners of genre.

(*Music.*)

**TAXI**  Warning! If your own personal VO sounds pre-recorded, odds on it's a head cold. Maybe sinus. (*Beat.*)

**TAXI**  The name is Taxi. James Taxi. Mother calls me – when she calls me – Nancy James.

(*He snuffs second coffin nail.*)

**TAXI**  The voice at the other end of the line had had an Hispanic accent that was sweet as sucre and resonated like dollar signs in my ears. I won't perjure myself and tell you that the prospect of meeting that voice in person wasn't better than a poke in the eye with a sharp forty-five. I needed the job.

(*The phone rings. Taxi answers it. Flashback Music.*)

**TAXI**  Give it to me straight.

(*The Flashback Music segues into KISS ME DEADLY, sung by Dolores, who emerges from a phone booth.*)

### KISS ME DEADLY

**DOLORES**  I'm looking for someone to help me out
No cop no doctor just a private eye
Oh, listen to me Taxi hear me out
I'm looking for a stand-up guy

I need help give me a hand
I need help I'm in a helluva jam
If you heard my tale you wouldn't believe your ears
You could not conceive it in a million years
A conspiracy and such a deadly plot
These people are out to get me whether I'm ready or not
They want to, they want to, they want to, they want to . . .

Kiss me deadly
Make me quiver and quake
Kiss me deadly
Keep me wide awake
Kiss me deadly, deadly, deadly

They want to mesmerize me

Are you the man to crack this case or not
There's plenty danger standing in the way
Are you tough enough to be my ace or what
Can you take a chance this is your lucky day

I need help give me a hand,
I need help I'm in a helluva jam
It's muy crazy but come to my aid
I need a Philip Marlowe or a Sammy Spade
He'll have to, he'll have to, he'll have to, he'll have to . . .

Kiss me deadly
Make me shiver and shake
Kiss me deadly
Keep me wide awake
Kiss me deadly, deadly, deadly
He'll have to mesmerize me . . .
(*Music vamps.*)

**TAXI** Nice pair of lungs, Miss . . .
**DOLORES** Con Leche.
**TAXI** Con Leche. What you've told me so far is close enough for Cliff
Notes. Why don't we get together? You can fill in the fine print.
**DOLORES** Your place or mine?
**TAXI** I only face off at center ice.
**DOLORES** Know the Heartbreak?
**TAXI** Hotel for Mutants?
**DOLORES** That's the one. Meet me tonight at the Heartbreak, Mr. Taxi.
After midnight. You can catch my act.
**TAXI** I'm running a fever already.
**DOLORES** It's an eye-opener.
(*Music up: She sings.*)

**DOLORES** If you could be the one to ease my grief
You'd trade your forty-four and your sore eye-teeth
For a chance to hang around with a girl like me
I got a voice like a frozen daiquiri

I need help give me a hand
I need help I'm in a helluva jam
If you take this caper

I'll make it worth your while
You may lose your life
But man you'll go with a smile
Aren't you tough enough
Aren't you tough enough
Aren't you tough enough to

Kiss me deadly
Make me quiver and quake
Kiss me deadly
Keep me wide awake
Kiss me deadly
Honey don't be shy
Kiss me deadly, be my personal private eye
Kiss me deadly, deadly, deadly
Come on and mesmerize me
(*Big finish.*)

(*She hangs up and disappears as lights and music dissolve. Taxi hangs up. He burps delicately.*)

**TAXI**  Those dissolves always make me motion sick. Whoever she was, she gave great phone. After I hung up the horn, I closed the office for the afternoon. I gave my faithful amanuensis, "Legs" Lichtenstein, the rest of the week off. She'd earned it. I hadn't paid her since fiscal '57. Legs. What a word jockey. But that's another story. I sauntered over to my local gin joint and tossed down a couple of muscles. For you rookies out there, a muscle is standard-issue detective drink: Kahlua and Maalox. Then I grabbed some shut-eye in the back of my Chevy. (*Beat.*) Con Leche's voice haunted my dreams like guava jelly. Spread sweet and smooth. I was stuck on that voice. Like enamel on a molar. (*Sneezes.*) If I come down with something. Neon and Lonely. The Heartbreak Hotel at Neon and Lonely. Love it.
(*A throbbing base line is heard. Taxi snuffs his cigarette and turns up his collar.*)

**TAXI**  Something funky this way comes.
(*Taxi slides into the shadows. Root, Zoot, The Bop Op, Sally, Lizzy, Blind Sax and Shrimp juke in. Root and Zoot are carrying what looks to be a body, wrapped in plastic and frozen solid.*)
(*The others are loaded down with funky tube gear and strange devices. All are heavily and obviously disguised. They do THE SKULK, an instrumental dance number. The music is threatening and insidious, and the dancing slinky. Eventually they all skulk on into the Heartbreak.*)

*(Root and Zoot have a little trouble negotiating the stiff through the doorway. One of the Heartbreakers – The Bop Op – drops something.)*
*(Taxi steps out of the shadows and picks it up. It's a white, plump, three-fingered glove, the kind Disney characters wear.)*
*(The music segues into THREE-FINGERED GLOVE.)*

## THREE-FINGERED GLOVE

**TAXI**    Is this a clue
Maybe not
A piece of the puzzle
A part of the plot
Or just an accident
A meaningless event
Not worth caring about

Well you can never tell
I guess I'll have to put it away
And save it for a rainy day
I'll just wait and see

Three-fingered glove
What is it good for
Three-fingered glove
Who's it belong to
I guess that he would have to be
A digital amputee
A sawmill worker or such
Not much to go on

Oh what the hell
You can never ever really tell
I guess I'll have to put it away
And save it for a rainy day
I'll just wait and see . . .

*(Dolores steps out of the shadows.)*
**DOLORES**    Nice pair of – lungs, Mr. Taxi.
*(Taxi hastily stuffs the three-fingered glove in his pocket.)*
**TAXI**    *(In the VO.)* I had egg roll all over my kisser. An Hispanic hallucination was hovering in the vicinity like heat on a desert highway.
**DOLORES**    You talking to me? And why the past tense, pal?

**TAXI**  It's a convention, sweetheart. You ain't supposed to hear, dig? It's for them. (*Indicates audience.*) The Big VO. Keeps 'em au courant.

**DOLORES**  Is a VO anything like an MO?

**TAXI**  (*Warily.*) Maybe. Who wants to know? Let's just say I'm cogitating a capella.

**DOLORES**  It's a free country.

**TAXI**  Don't kid yourself. Say, you got a Dramamine, sister? I got a case of dissolve sickness. I feel like a side o' slaw strewn across a soggy paper plate.

**DOLORES**  Those hard-boiled similies get pretty thin. As thin as the skin on a cup of hot cocoa.

**TAXI**  As thin as the crust on an East Coast pizza pie.

**DOLORES**  Neon and Lonely. Great spot for a rendezvous.

**TAXI**  This corner is seedier than a strawberry.

**DOLORES**  And darker than a landlord's heart. Thanks for showing up, Mr. Taxi.

**TAXI**  My pleasure, Miss Con Leche. Sleep is out of style this season. Let's get down to the storyline. What's the drumbeat, baby?

**DOLORES**  I want you to locate something for me.

**TAXI**  Is it yours?

**DOLORES**  Yeah.

**TAXI**  Sounds legal. Maybe we can do business. I have irresistible charm. Once you meet me, you never want to let me go.

**DOLORES**  I find that difficult to swallow. Although I can believe the vice squad feels that way.

**TAXI**  They refer you?

**DOLORES**  As a matter of fact, Mr. Taxi, I picked you at random from the yellow pages. I was trying to call a cab.

**TAXI**  I've heard that one. If I had a thousand bucks for every time I've heard that one, I wouldn't be here now.

**DOLORES**  I just assumed that all private dicks were alike –

**TAXI and DOLORES**  (*In unison, more or less.*) In the dark.

**TAXI**  Let's eighty-six the bright banter, shall we? And enough with the dick jokes. I hear enough dick jokes in the course of a day –

**TAXI and DOLORES**  (*Unison, more or less.*) To choke a horse.

**TAXI**  Okay, Con Leche. Lay it on me with a trowel. This missing something – stolen?

**DOLORES**  Repeatedly.

**TAXI**  Once rabid, twice shy. Valuable?

**DOLORES**  Priceless.

**TAXI**  Sure, sure, they all say that. I'm not your insurance company, lady.

**DOLORES**  Uninsurable.

**TAXI**  No kidding. Description.

**DOLORES**  Dreams.

**TAXI**  (*Sighs.*) Could we be specific, Miss Con Leche? What are we talking about here?

**DOLORES**  Dreams. Someone is stealing my dreams.

**TAXI**  Dreams.

**DOLORES**  Stolen. Lifted. Light-fingered. Long gone.

**TAXI**  Let's get literal, Miss Con Leche.

**DOLORES**  (*Touching herself.*) This is as literal as I get, Mr. Taxi.

**TAXI**  Metaphor is for poets, kid. We hard-boiled guys go for palpable factology. We like simile. Like or as. Like a dream. As if in a dream. Except the kind that exist out there in the zeitgeist. You can put your meathooks on 'em.

**DOLORES**  Zeitgeist?

**TAXI**  Like, my dream is a pair of center-court season tickets. My dream is a condo in the clouds. My dream is a garnet-colored Jag with custom plates.

**DOLORES**  You're slow, Taxi. I'm hablando-ing straight. Someone is stealing my dreams. My brain's being boosted. Look.
(*Flashback Music.*)

**DOLORES**  It all began a month ago. I answered an ad –

**TAXI**  (*Detecting ferociously.*) What ad? Where?

**DOLORES**  Cool your jets. This ad for folk singers. Ethnic folk dancers. That's my profession. They were hiring ethnic folk dancers down at the Heartbreak Hotel.

**TAXI**  Flashback me back, baby, and don't skip the slow parts. Sure you don't have a Dramamine?

**DOLORES**  Watch my tracks, hard guy.
(*Music. The front of the Heartbreak opens up.*)
(*Seedy. Pathetic palms and pink flamingos.*)

**TAXI**  Wow. Spiff City. Turn down the ambience.

**DOLORES**  It grows on you.

**TAXI**  I'll bet.

**DOLORES**  The ad said ask for a Mr. Bucket. So I did.
(*She walks in. Taxi remains outside, watching the flashback. Zoot is at the desk. Root, Bop and Blind Sax enter. Dolores hesitates in the doorway.*)

**ROOT**  Yo, Bop.

**BOP**  Yo, Root.

**ROOT**  Yo, Zoot.

**ZOOT**  Yo, Root.

**ROOT**  Yo, Sax.
(*Blind Sax plays a riff. Phone rings. Root and Bop pull gats, and aim at phone, as Zoot answers.*)

**ZOOT**  Heartbreak Hotel – no vacancies.

(*He slams down phone. Offstage gunshots, screams, shattering glass.*)

**ZOOT**  Maybe I spoke too soon.

**TAXI**  (*Waves Dolores in.*) Don't stop now. It's just getting interesting.

(*Dolores walks in.*)

**ZOOT**  Yez? Mai ah elp yew? Dew yew rechoir un rheum?

**DOLORES**  Pardon you?

**ZOOT**  Dew yew ave un reservasion?

**DOLORES**  No habla whatever language that is.

**BOP**  Reservations, ya need 'em?

**DOLORES**  No, thanks, I got plenty already. I'm looking for Mr. Bucket.

**ZOOT**  Wheech Monsieur Boockette? Oui ave deux Monsieurs Boockettes.

**DOLORES**  I want to speak to the Mr. Bucket who's looking for ethnic folk dancers.

**BOP**  She wants the Fat Man, Zoot. Give him a ring.

**ZOOT**  Honkey dorey.

(*He rings. Bop cruises Dolores.*)

**BOP**  What kinda ethnic dancing you do, Miss –

**ZOOT**  Allo, Monsieur Shreemp ou Monsieur Le Fat Man?

**DOLORES**  Con Leche. Call me Dolores.

**ZOOT**  Zere ees une dancair ethnique en zuh 1owbie, Monsieur Shreemp.

**BOP**  Okay, Dolores, call me Bop. Everybody does.

**ZOOT**  Oui. Oui. Bon temps roulez, Monsieur.

**DOLORES**  Okay, Bop. I do all kinds.

**BOP**  No wheezing.

**DOLORES**  You name it.

**BOP**  Slavic?

**DOLORES**  Slavic, Serbian, South Philly –

**ZOOT**  Monsieur Boockette ees on iz whey.

**DOLORES**  Que?

**BOP**  Hang ten, the boss is on the lam.

**DOLORES**  The ad didn't say I'd need simultaneous translation.

(*Shrimp enters. Very bad taste: polyester and velvet.*)

**SHRIMP**  May I help you?

**DOLORES**  I hope so. I'm here about the ethnic dancing ad.

**SHRIMP**  (*Sizing her up.*) Yes, yes, you look the part. Of course, I don't hire the dancers, I just run the audition.

**DOLORES**  (*Alarmed.*) Mr. Bucket?

**SHRIMP**  I'm Mr. Shrimp Bucket. My brother, Dr. Gut Bucket –

(*Ominous underscoring from Blind Sax whenever Gut's name is mentioned.*)

(*Taxi watching the flashback, pricks up his ears.*)

**TAXI**  Hmm. Ominous underscoring.

**SHRIMP**  – has final say-so on the ethnics. I do the local talent. Yo-yo artists. Geeks. Talking dogs. My brother, Dr. Gut –

(*Ominous Underscoring.*)

**SHRIMP**  – is tied up in the Ice Bucket at the moment. If you'd care to wait, Miss–

**DOLORES**  Con Leche.

**SHRIMP**  Con Leche. Zoot, ring Root. Been dancing long?

**DOLORES**  Yeah.

**SHRIMP**  Good. Good. That's swell.

**ZOOT**  (*Into phone.*) Root? Zoot. Toot Sweet.

**DOLORES**  (*Overly casual.*) You feature ethnic dancing? Or is this a new thing?

**SHRIMP**  Ethnic dancing? Are you kidding? We're famous for it. The Clam Room: Tops in Ethnic Dancing. The best Ethnic Dancing in Town. Wow. We just lost our lead ethnic dancer. She'd been with us for quite some time.

**DOLORES**  Why'd she leave? Didn't she like it here?

**SHRIMP**  She loved it. But she had to get out of the business.

**DOLORES**  Have I heard of her?

**SHRIMP**  You ask a lot of questions. For a dancer. Mitzi Montenegro. Know her?

**DOLORES**  No.

**SHRIMP**  I find that hard to believe, Miss Con Leche. Small world, ethnic dancing. In fact, you look a little bit like her, the more I think about it. Kind of a smudgy carbon copy, you might say. Let me intro the leftover staff. That's Zoot Alors. He's – the night man.

**DOLORES**  We met.

**ZOOT**  Yew bet. Enchante. Pairhops Ah could interest yew in un course of stoody a L'Ecole Maurice Chevalier?

**SHRIMP**  God I love the way you say that. This is the Bop Op. The Bop Op is wearing a brown pin-stripe suit, a brown button-down shirt from Brooks Brothers, brown socks, brown tie, brown Florsheim shoes, and chocolate brown Bill Blass boxer shorts. He's a very conservative dresser, but that's okay, we love him. And don't mess with him. He's a brown belt.

**BOP**  Hotel Security. How ya doin'?

(*Root enters.*)

**SHRIMP**  This is Root Choyce, Third World piano bar piano player and part-time ponce. Root tickles the ivories in the Clam Room.

**ROOT**  I don't take requests, Mi Chinita.

(*Blind Sax plays a riff.*)

**SHRIMP**  Oh, yeah. Out of sight, out of mind. This is Blind Sax.

**DOLORES**  Nice to meet you, Mr. Sax.

**SHRIMP**  We here at the Heartbreak like to say Blind Sax is "visually challenged."

**DOLORES**  Okay, I can relate to that.

**SHRIMP**  I thought you could. Zoot, cherchez les femmes?

**ZOOT**  Les gals are in rehearsal, mon boss.

**SHRIMP**  A real duo, know what I mean? Well, now that you've met the suspects –

(*Everyone laughs, "heh, heh."*)

**SHRIMP**  – why don't you cool your heels? Your audition's tonight, right here in the lobby. Root, show Miss Con Leche to her room. My brother, Doctor Gut –

(*Ominous Underscoring.*)

**SHRIMP**  – will be with you shortly. I do hope it works out.

**DOLORES**  So do I. Gracias so much, Mr. Bucket.

**SHRIMP**  Don't mention it. In fact, don't ever mention it again. To anyone. Blind Sax, a little traveling music, please.

(*Zoot rings bell.*)

**ZOOT**  Root.

**ROOT**  Zoot. (*To Dolores.*) Walk this way.

(*Blind Sax plays ominous underscoring as Dolores tries gamely to walk like Root as he wends his way to her room.*)

**DOLORES**  (*To Taxi.*) That was easier said than done. This weird music was following me and I had a creepy feeling about the whole set-up.

**TAXI**  Could be the ominous underscoring. Hard-boiled tip number one: Trust your underscoring. Did you know Mitzi Montenegro?

**DOLORES**  (*Suspiciously evasive.*) Why?

**TAXI**  I thought we might ring her bell. Check her pulse. Scan her polygraph.

**DOLORES**  Never heard of her.

(*Dolores returns to the flashback and walks into a pool of light. Root hands her a key.*)

**ROOT**  Enjoy.

(*He exits.*)

**DOLORES**  This isn't the Holiday Inn, Toto.

(*She unwraps a hotel drinking glass and pours water into it from a pitcher; it foams madly.*)

**DOLORES**  I'd have to be stupid to drink this.

(*She drinks. Lights and music as she swoons dead away. The room crackles and glows. She gets up, and dances in her sleep, talking to herself.*)

**DOLORES**  Estaba sonando que tenia mi propio programa en television, "Siempre Con Dolores en Domingo" starring Dolores Con Leche!

*(She stutter-dances back to the bed.)*
*(Dolores re-appears in a pin spot.)*

**TAXI**  You blacked out.

**DOLORES**  Like there was no tomorrow. I knew the tap water in this town was muy malo agua, but oh man! When I came to, I staggered over to my audition. I had the strangest feeling I'd been dancing in my sleep. I was so tired my legs felt like Spandex.
*(She meets Shrimp in the lobby.)*

**SHRIMP**  Miss Con Leche. Have a nice nap? You look so fresh.

**DOLORES**  Is it safe to drink the water?

**SHRIMP**  Don't be ridiculous.
*(Mustang Sally and Dizzy Miss Lizzy saunter in. They wear Balkan folk dancing outfits: full skirts, peasant blouses, beaded vests, braided hair, the works.)*

**SHRIMP**  Meet the Balkanettes.

**SALLY**  This is the last time I wear these duds, mollusc meat.

**SHRIMP**  Mustang Sally and Dizzy Miss Lizzy. Ladies, this is Miss Con Leche. She's here to audition for lead ethnic dancer.

**SALLY**  Shrimp, you etouffee. You promised to bag this ethnic dancing bull when Mitzi bit the bullet.

**DOLORES**  Mitzi Montenegro?

**SALLY**  She a friend of yours, softball?

**DOLORES**  Never heard of her.

**SHRIMP**  Clam down, Sal. Let's do this audition.

**SALLY**  Crustacean face.

**SHRIMP**  *(Counting off)* Bupke, kasha, babushka, latke.
*(The Balkanettes do the BALKAN JAM. Shrimp "choreographs.")*

## BALKAN JAM

**SHRIMP**  All right, sell it, girls. 1 2 3 4 and down, up, down, up.

**LIZZY**  Down up, down up. Hey, that's fresh!

**SALLY**  Bite mine.
*(Shrimp joins them. They sing and dance.)*

**SHRIMP and THE BALKANETTES**
>Hey na a Bucharesti
>O perestroika
>O Stoli twist,
>Hava nagila baba au rhum,
>Pasha
>Panama, panama, panama

**SHRIMP**  HOY!
*(Big ethnic finish.)*

**DOLORES**  You call that ethnic?

**SHRIMP**  I do.

**LIZZY**  He's the choreographer.

**DOLORES**  Oh, it's good, but try this.
   (*She signals the Band. The music changes to Liquid Latino. She does the sinuous steps of MANGO CULO.*)

**DOLORES**  Machito. Barretto. Ventura. Espresso!
   (*Dolores, the Band, and offstage voices sing MANGO CULO.*)

## MANGO CULO

   Mango, mango culo
   Mango, mango culo

**SHRIMP**  (*Spoken.*) Look at that cake action, girls!

   Mango, mango culo mango, mango culo

**SHRIMP**  (*Spoken.*) Boogie me back to Bogota, baby!

   Mango, mango culo mango, mango culo
   (*Jungle noises*)

**OFFSTAGE VOICES**  Shaka Zulu! Shaka Zulu!

   Mango, mango culo mango, mango culo
   Oh oh oh oooo
   (*Flamboyant finish.*)


**SHRIMP**  Say, that was extra extra special. I'm impressed. What do you call that?

**DOLORES**  Mango Culo.

**SHRIMP**  Catchy. I have to check with my brother, Doctor Gut –
   (*Ominous Underscoring.*)

**SHRIMP**  – but I think we might have a relationship here.

**DOLORES**  Oh, Mr. Shrimp, gracias so much.

**SHRIMP**  Don't mention nada, I told you.

**SALLY**  Not too shabby.

**LIZZY**  I liked it.

**SALLY**  Hey, Mex.

**DOLORES**  Qué hey, Tex.

**SALLY**  You're good. Let me give you some unsolicited advice.

**SHRIMP**  Sally –

**SALLY**  Clam up, bivalve. I've seen your type before, Ceviche –

**DOLORES**  Con Leche.

**SALLY**  At least once. Take it from me. Watch your steps.

**LIZZY**  See you at show time. It's going to be great working with you.
   Can't wait. Bye.
   (*They exit, cake-walking.*)

**DOLORES**  What did she mean? Watch your steps?

**SHRIMP**  Isn't that something you dancers say to one another? Maybe she's afraid she can't cut the con carne.

**DOLORES**  Oh no, she's good. Well, not that good.

*(A phone rings. Shrimp answers, listens a moment.)*

**SHRIMP**  I couldn't agree more.

*(Hangs up.)*

**SHRIMP**  Miss Con Leche, you start tonight. My brother, Doctor Gut –

*(Ominous Underscoring.)*

**SHRIMP**  – was most impressed by your audition.

**DOLORES**  But he didn't see it.

**SHRIMP**  My brother sees everything. He ate up your act with a spoon. Beautiful superb and I loved it. His exact words.

**DOLORES**  Oh, that's bueno, Mr. Bucket.

**SHRIMP**  Keep it under your fruit bowl, kid.

**DOLORES**  I'm no little sister from Mar Vista, Mr. Bucket. Carmen Miranda couldn't carry my maracas!

**SHRIMP**  I'm sure she couldn't. See you tonight in the Clam Room. And, Miss Con Leche –

**DOLORES**  Yes, Mr. Bucket?

**SHRIMP**  Try and get some rest. Heh heh.

*(Shrimp cackles and exits. Lights and music dissolve. Dolores rejoins Taxi.)*

**TAXI**  *(In the VO.)* It looked like a cut-and-blow-dried case of Mickey One, pure and simplex. I didn't put much stock in her yarn about sleep dancing and dream stealing. It was my job to soothe her fevered brow. Taxi, the human tranq.

**DOLORES**  Don't do that. It makes me nervous.

**TAXI**  Sorry. I didn't make the mysterious Doctor's mug in the flashback lineup.

**DOLORES**  I've been here for months, and I still haven't seen him. He's elusive. You gotta help me, Taxi. I need. my dreams.

**TAXI**  Why? Why you? Why dreams?

**DOLORES**  That's why I called you, Mr. Taxi. That's your bag.

**TAXI**  That's my racket, and I'm gonna bag it. Lookee, Miss Con Leche, dreams aren't my limo. Hot merch, that's my feedbag. Your basic electronic tube gear that's taken a stroll in felony shoes. The spouse that's a louse, fun on the run. Dreams? I wouldn't know where to begin. I'd be standing there in my flat feet with this big black cartoon question mark balloon coming out of my mouth – and eggnog all over my mugshot.

**DOLORES**  I'll give you a hand. How hard can it be?

**TAXI**  I told you, knock off the dick jokes.

**DOLORES**  Really, you're too sensitive.

**TAXI**  It's my tragic flaw.

**DOLORES**  Mr. Taxi, someone is running a number on me. I wanna know who, and I wanna know why. Somebody's trying to cash my ticket. You think I'm meshuga, Mr. Taxi?

**TAXI**  Meshuga? No. Exotic, but not meshuga. They say, Miss Con Leche, that if you don't dream you eventually book yourself a cruise on the Big Banana Boat. Somebody trying to flip your hotcakes. Now that's an old-fashioned celluloid motive I can get next to. Let's say somebody decides to interfere with your sleep. They convince you your dreams are being stolen. Try telling the cops somebody's stealing your sleep. You'd be a wasp-waist cinch for certification as a solid-gold paranoid.

**DOLORES**  You're not such a slouch after all.

**TAXI**  It's a pretty-out scenario, Miss Con Leche. Who'd buy a set-up like that?

**DOLORES**  You would.

**TAXI**  You're right. I would. Look, before I dip my wick any further, let's get something straight between us. I get fifty clams a day. Plus plenty of sauce for expenses. Boil or steam, no fly. Doctor's orders. A hundred in front, before I even start breathing.

**DOLORES**  No dinero. No habla B-movie lingo.

**TAXI**  Look, sis, you're cute and Hispanic as hell, and when I look up into the depths of those luscious dark eyes I get vertigo and calico and Monaco and like that, but your good looks won't pay my bar bill. (*She bats her eyes. A lot.*)

**TAXI**  I'm a sucker for a pretty face. Miss Con Leche, I didn't catch your moniker.

**DOLORES**  Not Monica. Dolores.

**TAXI**  Dolores. Dolores Con Leche. Sorrows with milk.

**DOLORES**  I didn't know you were quite the linguist, Mr. Taxi.

**TAXI**  Hang around. I may surprise you. Since I'm on the payroll – may I call you Dolores?

**DOLORES**  Not a chance.

**TAXI**  You're on. So, who wants to scramble your sweetbreads, sweetheart? Why such a screwy way of driving you batshit? I got a million questions, Miss Con Leche, and no answers. And in my book, that just doesn't add up. We're going to have to go back in.

**DOLORES**  Walk this way.

(*She starts off. What a walk.*)

**TAXI**  (*In the VO.*) But there was no way I could walk that way. She had a walk that made my circumlocutions look like straight talk. And a pair of gams that could raise gooseflesh on a tossed salad. And they went all the way up to the top of her legs. I didn't exactly put a down payment on her story – but her walk had me more than a little intrigued.

**DOLORES**   Will you stop talking like that?

**TAXI**   Sorry. Bad habit. Too many years living alone.

(*Dolores, mock sultry, puts her arms around Taxi.*)

**DOLORES**   Taxi, tell me. What's so private about a dick?

**TAXI**   It's not fair, you know. I'm an innocent victim of slang warp.

**DOLORES**   I've been dying to know, why do they call them gumshoes, pal?

**TAXI**   Can the snappy patter with syrup, sister. I don't even understand it. Let's make waves. We'll look into this . . . Dream Snatch.

(*Pause.*)

**DOLORES**   Okay. Truce.

(*As they start into the Heartbreak, Taxi checks his gun.*)

**TAXI**   Rod. Roscoe. Gat. Heater.

(*Root, Blind Sax, Zoot, and The Bop Op appear. Taxi sniffs.*)

**TAXI**   (*In the VO.*) The Heartbreak was a definite sushi bar, crawling with once-and-future co-defendants.

(*Hostile stares from the Heartbreakers.*)

**BOP**   House rules. No private moments. Talk to yourself again, buddy, you're history. You're a silent flick that's been sliced into guitar picks. Got me?

**TAXI**   Yeah. Yeah. I got ya.

**DOLORES**   Chill out, you guys.

(*Shrimp enters.*)

**SHRIMP**   Dolores. Looking forward to the show tonight, sweetheart. Those new steps are – what's the word? Crepuscular.

**DOLORES**   Crepuscular?

**SHRIMP**   Why not? Who's your little friend?

**DOLORES**   Mr. Shrimp, this is James Taxi. He's here for the show. James Taxi, Shrimp Bucket.

**SHRIMP**   What's your racket, Mr. Taxi?

**TAXI**   Talent scout. Really. How about you, Mr. Bucket?

**SHRIMP**   This joint is chez moi.

**TAXI**   My condolences to the chef.

**SHRIMP**   You write your own stuff. I like that in a man. Let me intro the leftover staff. This is the Bop Op.

**BOP**   Hotel security. Got any valuables?

**TAXI**   Yeah.

**BOP**   Hand 'em over.

(*The Bop Op gives Taxi a claim check, and pockets his wallet and watch. Sally and Lizzy enter.*)

**SHRIMP**  A real duo, Mr. Taxi. Mustang Sally and Dizzy Miss Lizzy.

**LIZZY**  Hi.

**SALLY**  Bite mine.

**SHRIMP**  Root Choyce palpitates the eighty-eights in the Clam Room.

**ROOT**  I don't take –

**TAXI**  Requests. But I got a request right now. Fast forward through the intro, pal. I caught 'em in the flashback.

**SHRIMP**  Miss Con Leche's been filling you in?

**TAXI**  In a manner of speaking.

**SHRIMP**  Good things I hope.

**TAXI**  Nothing but the best. The highlights of the low lifes.

**SHRIMP**  Well then, you already know that Professor Alors runs L'Ecole Maurice Chevalier.

**ZOOT**  Yew mai call moi Zoot. Pairhops Ah can interest yew in a course of stoody a L'Ecole Maurice Chevalier?

**SHRIMP**  God, I love the way you say that.

**TAXI**  You don't get French lessons at the better hotels. I find that comforting.

**SHRIMP**  We aim to be a full-service hotel. Professor Alors does not teach French, he teaches French accent.

**ZOOT**  Yew nevair know when an accent ague mai sev yewour life.

**TAXI**  (*In the VO.*) Professor Alors' accent smelled like brie, and the whole joint gave off an over-ripe odor like a bistro on a bad day.

**BOP**  I warned you about that, fella. Don't make me have to get litigious with you.

**ZOOT**  Why yew talk lak zat? Lisson, yew should talk lak zees. Lak Moi. An yew can. Zo easy. Zhust enroll at L'Ecole Maurice Chevalier, ze worl will be your camembaert.

**TAXI**  Trés bibliotheque, pal, but I'll pass.

**ZOOT**  Zoot yourself.

**SHRIMP**  He also slings slang. You oughta take from him, Taxi. Be good for business.

**TAXI**  I don't follow you.

**SHRIMP**  You could use some work on your lingo noir, Mr. Taxi.

**TAXI**  Lingo noir? I'm a talent scout, Mr. Bucket, I told you.

**SHRIMP**  I know you did.

**SALLY** and **LIZZY**  A talent scout? A talent scout? Really?

**TAXI**  Everybody wants to be in show business.

**SHRIMP**  Talent scout, eh?

**TAXI**  Really. Trust me.

(*Taxi sings TALENT SCOUT.*)

# TALENT SCOUT

**TAXI**    If you doff your duds or don a drag
I'll break a leg to catch your act
Got a kinky twist or a twisted gag
I'll do anything and that's a fact

'Cause I'm a Talent Scout

**SALLY** and **LIZZY**    Talent Scout!

**TAXI**    Hear me out and I'll tell you what
It's all about
I'm a Talent Scout

**SALLY** and **LIZZY**    Talent Scout!

**TAXI**    Without a doubt I'm the one for sure
who's got the clout

If you do your gig in dry ice fog
You call my number I'll be there
I get the chills for a talking dog
You can trust my guts I'm on the square

'Cause I'm a Talent Scout

**SALLY** and **LIZZY**    Talent Scout!

**TAXI**    Without a doubt, I'm the one for sure
Who's got the clout
I'm a Talent Scout

**SALLY** and **LIZZY**    Talent Scout!

**TAXI**    Let's do lunch! I got something we can talk about Ohhh Ohhh

All the rappers and the tappers and the fakirs and the breakers
and the strippers with their zippers say
Get a load of this you Talent Scout

All the scribblers and the dribblers, all the smugglers and the
jugglers,

all the wheelers and the dealers, all the squealers and the stealers, all the coppers and the boppers, all the talkers and the rockers say take a look at me you Talent Scout

Everybody wants to be in show business

I'm a Talent Scout

**SALLY** and **LIZZY**   Talent Scout

**TAXI**   Twist and shout, come on baby, what we talk about I'm a Talent Scout

**SALLY** and **LIZZY**   Talent Scout!

**TAXI**   Without a doubt, I'm the one for sure who's got the clout

**ALL**   I'm a TALENT SCOUT
(*Big finish.*)

**SHRIMP**   I'm impressed, Mr. Taxi. That was extra extra special. You oughta drop by the Clam Room on Amateur Night, take your chances.
**TAXI**   No thanks, Mr. Bucket, I'm strictly a non-combatant. (*To Sally and Lizzy.*) Nice job, girls, really.
**LIZZY**   Stay for the show, Mr. Taxi.
**TAXI**   Wouldn't miss it. What do you do? In the show, I mean.
**SHRIMP**   The Balkanettes sing back-up for Dolores.
**SALLY**   Temporarily. That is strictly a temporary arrangement.
**SHRIMP**   We'll talk about it later.
**SALLY**   You bet we will, prawn prick.
**SHRIMP**   Ladies, meet me upstairs in my office. If you'll excuse us, Mr. Taxi.
(*Shrimp and The Heartbreakers turn to go.*)
**TAXI**   Is Mitzi Montenegro still on the bill?
(*They all wheel around and stare at Taxi.*)
**SHRIMP**   You know Mitzi like I know Mitzi?
**TAXI**   It's my business to know, Mr. Bucket. Every aficionado of ethnic dancing knows Mitzi Montenegro, the Balkan Bombshell.
**SHRIMP**   Miss Con Leche said she'd never heard of her. Which led me to believe that Mitzi was – obscure.
**TAXI**   Oh. Well. Dancers. What do they know? Where's Mitzi boiling her bulgar these days? I'd like to catch her act.
**SHRIMP**   You're out of luck, Mr. Taxi. The Balkan Blockbuster said so

long to the ever-sweaty world of ethnic dancing some time ago. In fact, Mitzi's in – home appliances now. She's cool. Heh heh.

**HEARTBREAKERS**  Heh heh.

(*They all exit.*)

**TAXI**  I guess Mitzi wasn't, you know – well-liked.

**DOLORES**  Take it light, Tax. Cool the monologues.

**TAXI**  Don't tell me my business.

**DOLORES**  I gotta go warm up.

**TAXI**  I'll take a quick snoop see. Glom some loose threads.

**DOLORES**  Check out my room. Maybe you'll pick up something.

**TAXI**  That's what I'm afraid of. Just kidding. Don't hit me.

**DOLORES**  Meet me in the Clam Room.

**TAXI**  Right.

(*Dolores exits. Taxi alone.*)

**TAXI**  (*In the VO.*) Something Shrimp said had me sweating like a bad paint job. That crack about lingo noir. Were the flats of my feet showing? And Dolores. Who was she really? Femme fatale, fait accompli? The name meant sadness in Español. And I had a hunch this case was gonna bring me more than my share of grief. Why didn't she bag this gig? Something was keeping Con Leche tied to this clip joint. Was it Mitzi? What is Mitzi Montenegro to her, or she to Mitzi Montenegro?

(*The Bop Op has entered quietly behind Taxi.*)

**BOP**  That is the question.

**TAXI**  (*Screams.*) Hah!

(*He turns around, hands in the air. Looks at Bop, looks at his own hands up, covers by pointing with both index fingers still above his head.*)

**TAXI**  What's your racket?

**BOP**  What's yours?

(*Bop frisks Taxi, who still has his hands in the air. Bop removes Taxi's rod.*)

**BOP**  Talent scout, huh?

**TAXI**  Show business is the toughest business there is, Mr. Op.

**BOP**  Don't get cute. I'll just keep this for you. Until you check out.

**TAXI**  Where do I find Doctor Gut?

(*Ominous underscoring. Taxi starts.*)

**TAXI**  Geez, do you ever get used to the soundtrack shadowing you all over the set?

**BOP**  It's like traffic. I don't even hear it anymore.

(*Taxi ostentatiously picks his teeth with a dollar bill.*)

**TAXI**  What's your alias?

**BOP**  What's yours, big boy?

**TAXI**  I'm just another eggbeater, Mr. Op – hanging around for some answers.

(*Taxi picks his teeth with a second bill.*)

**BOP**  You couldn't pry it out of me with a crowbar –

(*Taxi adds a third bill.*)

**BOP**  – that Doctor Gut –

(*Ominous Underscoring.*)

**BOP**  – is tied up in the Ice Bucket.

(*Taxi hands Bop the bills. He shakes them dry.*)

**TAXI**  How do I get to the Ice Bucket?

**BOP**  You don't. Off limits.

(*Taxi pulls out a checkbook and writes him a check.*)

**BOP**  Got two pieces of I.D.?

**TAXI**  My wallet's in your pocket.

**BOP**  And it's gonna stay there. Make an isosceles triangle and follow your nose. (*Looks at check.*) Add a zero to this, I might get careless with my pass key.

(*Taxi changes check. Bop tosses the key. Taxi catches it.*)

**BOP**  Have it back in an hour.

**TAXI**  Beat it, thumbprint. I gotta talk to myself.

**BOP**  Whatever gets you off.

(*Bop exits.*)

**TAXI**  (*In the VO.*) Now that I had the keys to the kingdom, I decided to take the grand tour.

(*Lights and music. Taxi in a spot.*)

**TAXI**  (*In the VO.*) My first stop was the Ice Bucket. It didn't take a detective to find it. I just followed the dry ice to the front door.

(*He travels. Clouds of dry ice.*)

**TAXI**  (*In the VO.*) The stairs were slicker than sea urchin roe.

(*He arrives at the Ice Bucket just as Dolores appears and knocks on door. Shrimp answers. Dry ice and sax music seep out of the Ice Bucket.*)

**SHRIMP**  Dolores. What a treat.

**DOLORES**  (*Checking out dry ice.*) Hey! Muy hielo seco!

**SHRIMP**  I thought dry ice en Español was hielo carbonico.

**DOLORES**  Could be. Is Doctor Gut here?

(*Ominous Underscoring.*)

**SHRIMP**  No. But he left these for you.

(*Hands her a vial.*)

**DOLORES**  Gracias so much.

**SHRIMP**  How's your insomnia?

**DOLORES**  I'm syncopated. I think I've got anemia, too. I'm beat.

**SHRIMP**  You do look run-down. I'll have –

(*Ominous underscoring starts. Shrimp cuts it off.*)
**SHRIMP**  You know who – prescribe some animal vitamins.
**DOLORES**  Well. Okay.
**SHRIMP**  Trust me. They'll do you a world of good. Ciao.
**DOLORES**  Later.
(*He ushers her out. As she leaves, Bop joins Shrimp.*)
**BOP**  Dolores. What a dream, huh?
(*He laughs uproariously.*)
**SHRIMP**  Don't wear it out. Who's her friend?
**BOP**  Half-baked hawkshaw. Bargain-basement shamus. (*Takes out gun.*)
I relieved him of this antiquated armament.
**SHRIMP**  I knew it. I've got an instinct for these things. Why would our
milky senorita bring a hawkshaw into the Heartbreak?
**BOP**  Maybe she's got wise. (*Smiles.*) Mitzi got wise, too.
(*They share an unpleasant laugh.*)
**SHRIMP**  Take care of him after the show. He mustn't muck up our
meeting with the big noise from Nauru.
**BOP**  In my mind, he's already relegated to the dustbin of history.
**SHRIMP**  See how they're doing downstairs.
**BOP**  You're the boss.
**SHRIMP**  Yes. Yes, I am.
(*Lights and music. Shrimp fades. Taxi follows Bop.*)
**TAXI**  (*In the VO.*) I followed Bop to the laundry. Zoot was doing a quick
starch and steam. He didn't seem too happy about it.
(*Bop enters laundry. Zoot holds up a three-fingered glove.*)
**ZOOT**  Cherchez eets mate? Zere ees anozer one of zees. Ahve yew seen
eet?
**BOP**  Uh-oh. Check his coat pockets?
**ZOOT**  Oui. Oui. Bon idear. Oh, eef Ah don't find zat gloove, zee boz
weel be furryous.
**BOP**  More than furious. Livid, positively. Shrimp wants him to look his
best for the Big Noise from Nauru. That means both gloves, babe.
**ZOOT**  Ah! I am un dead man! Monsieur Croque!
**BOP**  Relax. You don't want to hyperventilate down here in all this
humidity. I'll take a look around outside.
**ZOOT**  Merci, merci. Yew are un lumberjacques of un prince.
**BOP**  For you, Frenchie.
(*Bop blows him a kiss, and fades.*)
**ZOOT**  (*Drops accent.*) Three-fingered glove. Where is the other?
(*Lights and music. Zoot exits.*)
**TAXI**  (*In the VO.*) Bop's passkey was solid gold. It was making things
easy. Maybe too easy. My next port of call was a bug on the pay
phone.

(*Lights and music. Taxi puts a transistor in his ear, as Root appears in a pool of light talking on the phone.*)

**ROOT**  (*On phone.*) Hey, this is a sophisticated device. State of the art.

**TAXI**  (*In the VO.*) Bingo.

**ROOT**  He's gonna get a look at their extra extra special stuff. They're gonna pull out the stops, kick out the jams, and boogie their sneakers away for this hombre. Mr. Batsumashball, micro chip czar, the Mitsubishi of Nauru. Where is Nauru, anyway? I heard bird guano. The whole lousy island, nothing but bird guano. Bird guano is what I heard, chucko.

(*Lights and music. Root out.*)

**TAXI**  (*In the VO.*) Suddenly there was more thickener in the plot than corn starch in a coffee shop cherry pie. The meter was still running on Bop's passkey. On my way to the Clam Room, I stopped off to chat up the Balkanettes.

(*Sally and Lizzy, in a backstage dressing room, wearing robes.*)

**SHRIMP**  (*Over PA.*) Five minutes, girls. Showtime.

**SALLY**  Invertebrate.

**SHRIMP**  (*Over PA.*) Remember the new steps.

**SALLY**  They suck gazpacho, lobster breath.

**SHRIMP**  (*Over PA.*) You oughta be nicer to me. Remember, ladies – Mitzi Montenegro.

**SALLY**  That etouffee'll rue the day he messed with Mustang Sally.

**LIZZY**  We better be careful. Remember what happened to Mitzi Montenegro.

**SALLY**  You just remember, two men on a raft and wreck 'em.

(*Taxi appears.*)

**TAXI**  Just what did happen to Mitzi Montenegro?

**SALLY**  Her career didn't work out –

**LIZZY**  The way she'd planned.

**TAXI**  What do you hear from Mitzi? Is she happy in home appliances?

**SALLY**  Why are you so interested in Mitzi, Mr. Talent Scout? She was a lousy dancer.

**TAXI**  Mitzi was my client. I was her agent. That's a sacred relationship.

**SALLY**  We don't know where she is.

**LIZZY**  Honest. Hope you like the show, Mr. Taxi.

**TAXI**  I have my doubts. Eastern European Ethnic Dancing. Unless the Bucket Brothers are in for a surprise.

**SALLY**  What do you mean?

**TAXI**  Two men on a raft and wreck 'em.

**SALLY**  Means scrambled eggs on toast.

**LIZZY**  Nuevo Huevo's gonna be the next big thing.

**TAXI**  Nuevo Huevo? New Egg?

**SALLY**  The Balkanettes are as passé as Raisinettes. From now on we're the Omelettes.

(*They shuck their robes.*)

**SALLY**  And Nuevo Huevo's our jam.

(*They sing NUEVO HUEVO.*)

### NEUVO HUEVO

**SALLY and LIZZY**

> Two men on a raft and wreck 'em
> Means scrambled eggs on toast
> You can boil or poach or breck 'em
> You can coddle fry or roast
>
> Stretch one burn one whisky down
> Nuevo Huevo's back in town
>
> Two men on a raft and wreck 'em
> Means scrambled eggs on toast
> You can boil or poach or breck 'em
> You can coddle fry or roast
>
> Stretch one burn one whisky down
> Nuevo Huevo's back in town

(*Lizzy scats through instrumental.*)

> Stretch one burn one whisky down
> Nuevo Huevo's back in town
> Stretch one burn one whisky down
> Nuevo Huevo's back in town
>
> Oooh oooh back in town
> Oooh oooh back in town
> Oooh oooh back in town

(*Sexy finish.*)

**TAXI**  I can definitely say I'm not altogether uninterested. We'll talk.

**SALLY and LIZZY**  (*Exit singing.*) Oooh oooh back in town

**TAXI**  The questions were mounting up like a stack of unpaid utility bills, and I had to find the answers before somebody turned off the lights. I had a feeling this case wouldn't be brief . . . brief . . . this case . . . wouldn't be brief . . .

*(Rescued by the Band: music.)*
**TAXI**  Showtime?
**BAND**  Showtime!
**TAXI**  *(In the VO.)* That was my cue to cut to the chase.
*(The lights come up full on The Clam Room. A couple of tables. Chase lights. The Bop Op is the maitre d'.)*
**BOP**  This way, Mr. Taxi.
*(He seats Taxi at one of the onstage tables. Taxi is the only customer.)*
**TAXI**  Is it always this slow?
**BOP**  It's been better. What'll you have?
**TAXI**  Ramos fizz. Do I have to be this close? I'll get sequin burn on my retinas.
**BOP**  You're a talent scout, aren't ya?
**TAXI**  Right. Right.
*(Bop exits. Music! Chase lights! Spots!)*
*(THE CLAM ROOM.)*
*(A gaudy sign. Shrimp bounds on, mike in hand, big fanfare, his theme music: SHRIMP LOUIE.)*
*(The Band shouts the refrain from offstage:)*

### SHRIMP LOUIE

**SHRIMP**  I'm a burnin' burnin' hunk of shrimp
      Shrimp Louie
      (O Shrimp Louie)
      I'm a burnin' burnin' hunk of shrimp
      Shrimp Louie
      (O Shrimp Louie)
      Don't fuss with the dressin'
      'Cause you know you ain't messin' with Louie
      (Shrimp Louie to go)
      Shrimp Louie
      (Eat it every day)
      Shrimp Louie
      (Shrimp Louie to go)
      Shrimp Louie
      (Eat it every day)
      Shrimp Louie
      (Shrimp Louie to go)
      Shrimp Louie Louie Louie Louie..
      YEAAHHH

*(Big resolving chord from Band.)*

**SHRIMP**   Thank you. Thank you. Thank you. So sweet so sweet so really nice 'n neat. Hi. I'm your host, Shrimp Bucket. Welcome to the always nectarious Clam Room and our show, Crack of Dawn, I know you're gonna just cream all over it – (*Waves to Taxi.*) Our special guest tonight, ladies and gentlemen, Mr. James Taxi, a bi-time talent scout. Thanks for joining us, Jimmy, here in the ever-humid Clam Room. You're gonna get an eyeful of local talent tonight, I guarantee it. You slay me, Jimmy, right off the old drugstore rack – saaaaaaaaaaaaaaaaaaaaaaaaaaaay –

**SHRIMP**   (*Pointing to lights out front.*) Those mixed fruit gels are really something. Talk about your saturated color! Wow! What is that? Vacation pink! And lavender surprise! And over there a hot rod cherry red! All the way from Vegas, these guys do a super job, ladies and gentlemen, big hands! Big hands! Aren't they beautiful superb and extra extra special? Say, welcome to the ever-livid Clam Room! The temperature's rising, we're getting hot hot hot! While we're waiting for our opening number here in the ever-hepatatic Clam Room – (*Sings á la Johnny Mathis*) Let me entertain you. Let me conk your hair - (*Toothy smile.*) That's just a teaser, folks. More of me anon. And speaking of digits – direct from their record-breaking engagement in the attic of the Heartbreak, where they've been going at it hammer and tong – here to smash some of their very own platters, and spread sunshine and broken petro-chemical plastic all over the place – let's give a hot chowder Clam Room wilkommen to – the Four Freshpersons! Doing their latest – look out it's hot – Vegetable Medley! Vegetable Medley! Ladies and gentlemen, the Four Freshpersons!

(*Root, Zoot, Bop, and Blind Sax, in matching jackets, do an all-purpose soul medley: wonderful harmonies, dramatic shifts in rhythms, great synchronized dance steps.*)

### VEGETABLE MEDLEY (CAFFEINE)

**ROOT**   Early in the morning and all through the night
**QUARTET**   Mainline mainline straight to my heart
**ROOT**   Caffeine caffeine Caffeine
**QUARTET**   Mainline mainline straight to my heart
**ROOT**   Put the spike to my heart and shoot it right in
(*Whoosh.*)
      Put the spike to my brain and shoot it again (*Uhh*)
      Give it to me baby make it hot and black
**QUARTET**   Mainline mainline
**ROOT**   Give it to me baby now don't hold back

**QUARTET**  Mainline mainline straight to my heart
**ROOT**  The pain the pain grab an available vein
**QUARTET**  To ease the pain you
**ROOT**  Grab an available vein
**QUARTET**  Free refill free refill
        Free refill free refill
        Free refill free refill
        Free free free
        Free free
   *(Into)*

## THE ECHELON OF SCUM

**BOP**  I'm going up and down
        On the carousel of crum
        Floating to the top
        Of the echelon of scum
        I'm a bad bad guy
        Don't need no alibi
        I'm the cream of the crop
        And I'm floating to the top
        Of the echelon . . .
**QUARTET**  Ohhh echelon of scum
**BOP**  I'm a nasty man
        And I know that's what I am
        I got crime in my bones
        I put slime on my scones
        I'm the crown prince of quease
        And I do just as I please
        I'm the creme de la crum
**QUARTET**  I'm the sultan of scum
**BOP**  I'm the cream of the crop
**QUARTET**  And I'm floating to the top
**BOP**  Of the echelon . . .
**QUARTET**  Ohhhhhh echelon of scum
   *(The Quartet whistles a chorus.)*

   *(Into)*

## ETHNIC JOKES BROKE MY BABY'S HEART

**TRIO**  *(Root, Bop and Blind Sax)* Didja hear the one?
**ZOOT**  That's what they say
**TRIO**  Didja hear the one

**ZOOT**   Every single day
**TRIO**   Those ethnic jokes
**ZOOT**   About my baby
**TRIO**   Those ethnic jokes
**ZOOT**   They drove her crazy
**QUARTET**   Those ethnic jokes that broke my baby's heart
**TAXI**   I heard that one
**ZOOT**   It ain't funny
**TAXI**   I heard that one
**ZOOT**   You bet your money
**TRIO**   They'd tell those jokes
**ZOOT**   About her brother
**TRIO**   They'd tell those jokes
**ZOOT**   About her mother
**QUARTET**   Those ethnic jokes that broke my baby's heart
**BLIND SAX**   (*Spoken.*)
        She's gone away now, I don't know where
        To a place where they don't tell those kinds of jokes
        To a better world . . . somewhere
**BOP**   (*Spoken.*)
        I say . . . the melting pot ain't so hot!
**ZOOT**   Ethnic jokes about my baby
        Ethnic jokes they drove her crazy
        Ethnic jokes about my baby
        Ethnic jokes they drove her crazy
**QUARTET**   Ethnic jokes they broke my baby's heart
    (*Into*)

## PUT YOUR LEGS ON MY SHOULDERS

**QUARTET**   Put your legs on my shoulders
        Put my head in your lap
        Wrap your kneecaps 'round my earlobes
        And we'll do it just like that

        Put your legs on my shoulders
        Honey drive me 'round the bend
        Let me dive right up on in you
        Wake the neighbors up again
        Hum Hum Hum Hum

**ROOT** and **ZOOT**
        Honey your legs are ba-rooom, ba-rooom

Honey your legs are ba-rooom, ba-rooom

**ZOOT**   Oh my darling when you kiss me
And we get so moist and slick
Just remember when you miss me
Let me give you one last lick

**QUARTET**   Put your legs on my shoulders
Don't tell me I just ate
You know that I always told her
Grab my ears and aim me straight

Put your legs on my shoulders
Put my head in your lap
Wrap your kneecaps round my earlobes
And we'll do it just like that
Hum, Hum, Hum, Hum


**ROOT** and **ZOOT**
Honey your legs are ba-rooom, ba-rooom
Honey your legs are ba-rooom, ba-rooom
**ZOOT**   O my darling when I meet you
And we go to bed in haste
Oh my darling when I eat you
I just long for one more taste

**QUARTET**   Put your legs on my shoulders ooh, ooh, ooh
Put your legs on my shoulders ooh, ooh, ooh
Put your legs on my shoulders ooh, ooh, ooh
Put your legs on my shoulders ooh, ooh, ooh
OH OH OH OH OH OH OH OH AHHHHHHH STOP!

(*Big finish. The Four Freshpersons exit. The Band picks up the groove, as Shrimp comes back on, clapping his hands in rhythm. The Four Freshpersons dance back on for an encore.*)

### PUT YOUR LEGS ON MY SHOULDERS, reprise

**SHRIMP**   All right everybody I want you to put your hands together and when I point to you I want to hear you say "Put Your Legs." Got it? "Put Your Legs" One two three
**QUARTET**   Put your legs on my shoulders

And I'll drive you round the bend
I know that you're feeling bolder
Wake the neighbors up again

**SHRIMP**   And should you be feeling colder
Put your legs

**QUARTET**   Put your legs

| **SHRIMP** | **QUARTET** |
| --- | --- |
| Put your legs | Put your legs |
| Put your legs | Put your legs |
| Put your legs | Put your legs |
| Put your legs | Put your legs |
| Put your legs | Put your legs |

**QUARTET**   On my shoulders YEAH!!

*(The Quartet boogies off.)*

**SHRIMP**   The Four Freshpersons! The Four Freshpersons! Aren't they beautiful superb and extra extra special? They don't call 'em The Four Horsemen of the A capella Lips for nothing. Heh heh heh. We'll continue with "Calamity in the Clam Room" in just a few days but first . . . I want to speak to you directly. Mano a mano as it were. That's the great thing about live theatre. That communication . . . Can I have the house lights, please?

*(House lights come up. Shrimp surveys audience.)*

**SHRIMP**   Great. That communication between us – and you. That living, breathing, okay mistakes can happen kind of communication. The theater is the last bastion of live entertainment. As you may not know – or even believe – the price of a ticket doesn't begin to cover costs. Not even close. There's what you see – lights, costumes, sets, actors. The band. And there's what you don't see. Hidden costs. Limos, lunches, lingerie. Ludes. Union kickbacks. Just kidding, fellas. Don't turn off the lights. But seriously, there are hidden expenses. And sometimes we just can't hide them any longer. I don't think I have to tell you folks – *(To audience member.)* – try to work with the drug. With it. *(Back to audience.)* – *I* don't have to tell you about inflation. A show like this one, expenses have just gone through the roof over the last season. You know, if we were to cover costs through ticket sales alone, we'd have to sell each seat five times. Five times. And that would be mighty uncomfortable. Think about it. Hey! We're having some fun now! And now – accompanied by the ever-lactating Balkanettes – the star of our show – the filibrating thrush herself – the Hispanic Hyperventilator – Dolores Con Leche.

*(Dolores, with Sally and Lizzy. Splashy entrance, gorgeous gowns, wigs. Motown heaven. They sing NEVER JUDGE A THRILLER.)*

# NEVER JUDGE A THRILLER

**DOLORES** with **SALLY** and **LIZZY**
>Never judge a thriller by its cover NO
>Never judge a thriller by its cover NO
>I'm a thriller at large
>A paperback broad
>A killer babe
>I need to be read out loud
>
>Turn my pages sweetheart
>And follow my plot
>Don't skip a single chapter
>'Cause I'm hot hot hot
>
>Never judge a thriller by its cover (Never, never, never)
>Never judge a thriller by its cover (Thriller)
>
>I'm a chiller babe a drugstore dame
>A femme fatale
>That's my claim to fame
>Don't you quit till we're done
>Till we get to the end
>Then we can start me all over again

(*Refrain.*)
(*During an instrumental break, Blind Sax wailing, Dolores transforms herself into the classic image of a pulp covergirl: strap down over one shoulder, cigarette, smoking derringer. Thus transformed, she sings: "I'M A SPINE-TINGLER, BABY" – but the lights suddenly go out, and the sound grinds down, like a record player whose plug has just been pulled. Then, just as suddenly, the lights come back on, and music whirls back up to speed. In the blackout, Taxi has gotten up and is standing in the middle of the stage. He attempts to speak to Dolores, but she ignores him as the Balkanettes finish their set:*)
(*NEVER JUDGE . . .cont.*)

**DOLORES** with **SALLY** and **LIZZY**
>I'm a spine-tingler-baby
>A pulp coquette
>Be a hard guy with me baby
>You will not regret
>Got a ruby forty-four
>Got a cherry new Corvette
>Better buy my cover baby

What you see is what you get

Never judge a thriller by its cover (Never judge a thriller)
Never judge a thriller by its cover (Thriller)
Never, never, never, never, never
Never, never, nooo
Never, never, never, never, never
Never, never, noo
Never judge a thriller by its cover (NO)
Never judge a thriller by its cover (NO)
NO, NO, NO O O ohhhh
*(Big finish. They exit.)*

*(Shrimp bounds back on.)*
**SHRIMP**   Dolores! Dolores! And the Balkanettes! They'll be back later
with some authentic ethnic folk dancing! I guarantee it! Dolores and
the Balkanettes! What a warbler! Now that's ornithology! And the
dance steps! Don't you just love them? Better than synchronized
swimming! They don't call them Balkanettes for nothing! Okay! Kung
Fu fighting next! *(To Taxi.)* Take your seat, fella. Hey! We're having
some fun now! *(To audience member.)* I spoke to you earlier about
that. Work with the drug. The band does.
**TAXI**   I got a coupla plot points I'd like cleared up.
**SHRIMP**   You came in late, fella.
**TAXI**   That's where you're wrong. I've been over my neck in this from
the very beginning.
**SHRIMP**   Come back tomorrow night. I'll flush the rust out of my pipes.
**TAXI**   I'll pass. I wanna know the whereabouts and general prognosis of
Mitzi Montenegro.
**SHRIMP**   What's it to you?
**TAXI**   Mitzi was my client.
**SHRIMP**   Tell me another one, shamus.
*(Taxi grabs Shrimp by the lapels, and being so short, lifts himself off
the ground.)*
**TAXI**   Why don't you buy my cover? What's your trick bag, sleazeball?
Sing.
**SHRIMP**   Calm down, fella.
**TAXI**   And what was that little blackout about? Sounded like somebody
pulled the plug.
**SHRIMP**   You wanna know a lot for the price of admission. Okay, I'll
tell you. Yes, what you suspect is all too true. We lipsynch.
**TAXI**   Very nicely done.
**SHRIMP**   Thank you. Now you know our nasty little secret. How about

you stop wrinkling the merchandise.

**TAXI**   How about you give me the straight dope on Mitzi Montenegro. If you wanna be around for your encore, pal.

**SHRIMP**   Since you put it that way, let me put it this way. And this way. And what about this way.

*(As Shrimp puts it various ways, Bop brings in Taxi's drink. It's foaming madly.)*

**TAXI**   You're a literal kid of guy, Mr. Bucket. Where's your brother, Doctor Gut?

*(Band plays ominous underscoring, Las Vegas big-band style.)*

**TAXI**   I wanna have words with him.

**SHRIMP**   My brother is a busy man, Mr. Taxi. He doesn't have time to play private eyes.

**BOP**   Your Ramos fizz, sir.

**TAXI**   Oh, no. I'm hip to this stuff.

**SHRIMP**   You make it hard on yourself, Mr. Taxi.

*(Bop saps Taxi. Taxi crumples.)*

**BOP**   Later for you, lightweight.

**SHRIMP**   *(To Bop.)* You young squid you. Let's blow this clam bar.

*(SHRIMP LOUIE reprise. Bop, Zoot, and Root join Shrimp.)*

### SHRIMP LOUIE, reprise

**SHRIMP**   I'm a burnin' burnin' hunk of Shrimp
**BOP, ZOOT** and **ROOT**   Shrimp Louie o Shrimp Louie
**SHRIMP**   I'm a burnin' burnin' hunk of Shrimp
**BOP, ZOOT** and **ROOT**
Shrimp Louie o Shrimp Louie
**SHRIMP**   Don't fuss with the dressin'
'Cause you know you ain't messin' with me
Of all the Louies which is the best
**BOP, ZOOT** and **ROOT**   Crab Louie?
**SHRIMP**   No way.
**BOP, ZOOT** and **ROOT**   St. Louie?
**SHRIMP**   Get real.
**BOP, ZOOT** and **ROOT**   Louie Louie?
**SHRIMP**   Even Louie Louie can't kick my bootie
**SHRIMP, BOP, ZOOT** and **ROOT**
Shrimp Louie
Shrimp Louie
Shrimp Louie to go
Shrimp Louie
**SHRIMP**   Eat it every day

**SHRIMP, BOP, ZOOT** and **ROOT**
    Shrimp Louie Louie Louie Louie Yeah!
    (*The Heartbreakers boogie on out, leaving the comatose Taxi on stage.*)

(*A blue spot on Taxi, face down and unconscious. The spot narrows to a pencil point, then extinguishes. When the house lights come up for intermission, Taxi is gone. But left behind is a chalk outline of his body on the floor.*)

END OF ACT ONE

# ACT TWO

*A bare stage. Taxi saunters out, jacket over his shoulder, cool as can be, and sings PRISONER OF GENRE.*

### PRISONER OF GENRE

**TAXI**    I take my coffee black
With a slug of rye or three
I call my mother – "Mac"
And you can make all my movies –"B"

I'm addicted to the style
And all my moves are noir
I'm a sucker for a smile
Across a crowded bar

I'm just a prisoner of genre, baby
I guess I've found my niche
I'm just a prisoner of genre, baby
A lonely captive of kitsch

I've surrendered to the slang

I make all my moves in raincoats
I got a roscoe in my pocket
If I thought I had a future
I'd run right out and hock it

I'm just a flat-out flake
I make out in smokey rooms
I'm dying for another take
And living for those zooms

I'm just a prisoner of genre, baby
I guess I've found my niche
I'm just a prisoner of genre, baby
A lonely captive of kitsch

J'adora my fedora

Tap City is my address
Where all the bulbs are bare

My haute cuisine is rice and beans
But I'll do it for the dare
(*Spoken:*) – plus expenses

I've been drugged and sapped
And slugged and slapped
Got neon on the brain
I risk my skin for just a fin
I'm a sucker for a dame

I'm just a prisoner of genre, baby
I'm so addicted to the style
So stamp me urgent and confidential
And slip me in your file

I'm just a prisoner of genre, baby
A prisoner, a prisoner – in style.
(*Sweet finish. Lights dissolve to:*)

(*In front of the Heartbreak. Taxi, out like, well, like the classic sapped hard-boiled gumshoe.*)
(*A reggae bass beat.*)
(*Taxi woozes to his feet.*)

**TAXI**  (*In the VO.*) I came to with a Mafiosa construction company slapping together a condo in my back brain. They were working overtime and pounding plenty o'nails. Two brothers, Guiseppe and Antoine. I clawed my way up through concentric spinning circles of trauma, dread, nausea, pain, and primary motor dysfunction. (*Staggers.*) I was dizzier than a dose of peroxide, and as feverish as a bottle of aspirin. My brain was pounding out a reggae back beat. Detective with eggcream all over his punim. C'mon, Taxi. Do something really tough – like get on your feet. You got a New York City driver's license. Prove you deserve it.
(*He swoons. Dolores, entering, catches him.*)

**DOLORES**  What's so macho about a New York City driver's license?
(*She props him back up.*)

**TAXI**  License to kill, sweetheart. License to maim.

**DOLORES**  Natty Taxi. Someone caught you looking uptown instead of down.

**TAXI**  Just as I had your shrimp-faced boss squirming like aquarium bait. Whoo. I feel like a short chunk of beef jerky. Chewed. I'm fading faster than a forged check.
(*Dolores straightens him by the lapels.*)

**DOLORES**  My dreams can't wait until tomorrow.

**TAXI**  Listen, as far as I'm concerned, your dreams can wait until Jimmy Hoffa shows up to claim his Social Security.

*(Reggae bass beat goes out. He starts off.)*

**DOLORES**  Where are you going?

**TAXI**  Home. I've had it. I've had it being pushed around on no sleep, and I've had it being conned by my own client. There are easier and cleaner ways to make a buck, and I'm gonna go find 'em. Right now.

**DOLORES**  Taxi, you can't leave me. Okay, what do you want?

**TAXI**  I want you to level with me. Who is Mitzi Montenegro?

**DOLORES**  She's just another ethnic dancer.

**TAXI**  Sure, sure, They all say that. Say, I caught the show tonight. Boffo charisma, mucho melisma.

**DOLORES**  What?

**TAXI**  You're a thrush. You may be an unreliable witness, but I dig the way you warble.

**DOLORES**  Taxi, I didn't do the show tonight.

**TAXI**  Don't kid me. I was this far away from you. I may have trouble picking a perp out of a lineup –

**DOLORES**  No way. I dropped one of Dr. Gut's brain bombers –

*(Ominous Underscoring.)*

**DOLORES**   – to pep myself up, and I was out before you could say Tito Puente.

**TAXI**  Either you've got schizoid amnesia, or the Bucket Brothers have a first-class female female-impersonator. Remember the blackout?

**DOLORES**  How could I? I told you –

**TAXI**  Onstage. Somebody tripped the breaker. I got up and whispered to you. You didn't whisper back.

**DOLORES**  Taxi, I'm telling you. It wasn't me.

**TAXI**  Mitzi Montenegro – what's she look like?

**DOLORES**  How should I know?

**TAXI**  Come clean, Con Leche. She's as familiar to you as a hangnail. Who is she?

**DOLORES**  My sister.

*(Taxi slaps her.)*

**DOLORES**  My sister!

*(Taxi slaps her again.)*

**DOLORES**  My sister!

*(Taxi slaps her again.)*

**DOLORES**  My sister! *(Slap.)* My sister! *(Slap.)* My sister!

**TAXI**  Not your daughter?

**DOLORES**  My sister!

*(She knocks him down with a right hook. He picks himself up.)*

**TAXI** I believe you. Don't hit me again. How long's she been gone?

**DOLORES** More than a month.

**TAXI** Was Mitzi the type to take a powder and not leave a forwarding address?

**DOLORES** Mitzi knew something wasn't on the level. She was just about to go to the authorities when she disappeared.

**TAXI** Cops?

**DOLORES** Health Department. She's my kid sister, Taxi.

**TAXI** Say no more. Where I come from, that counts for something. Don't worry, sweetheart. I'll find your dreams.

*(Dolores grabs him and kisses him three times.)*

**DOLORES** O, bueno! Mucho! Muchacho! Muchisimo!

**TAXI** *(In the VO.)* Her lips were a palpable lip batido –

**DOLORES** Don't do that in front of me, Taxi. Na khazan.

**TAXI** Qué tengo, Con Leche. Whatever you do, don't nod off. Get a cup of joe. Trust me.

**DOLORES** I'll take my bombers.

**TAXI** Don't you learn from experience? You're strung out like laundry. Fork 'em.

*(She hands him the vial Shrimp gave her.)*

**TAXI** Non-prescription speed only. Meet me in your room. I have to make a phone call.

**DOLORES** Bueno! Let's locate Mitzi, Tax! Undulate! Undulate!

*(She exits. He looks after her wistfully.)*

**TAXI** *(In the VO.)* I would have given a lot to undulate with Con Leche right about then, but time was short and talk is cheap. I had a hunch if I could find Mitzi, I'd clear up this caper like liniment on a charley horse. *(Beat.)* Well, they can't all be gems. To reorient myself, I did a quick mental hit and run.

*(Lizzy and Sally in a spot.)*

**SALLY** Her career didn't work out –

**LIZZY** – the way she'd planned.

*(Shrimp in a spot.)*

**SHRIMP** My brother left these for you, Miss Con Leche.

*(Dolores in a spot.)*

**DOLORES** I'm not dreaming the dreams I once had.

*(Root in a spot.)*

**ROOT** This is a sophisticated device. State of the art.

*(Zoot in a spot; holds up a three-fingered glove.)*

**ZOOT** Zere ees anozer one of zees. Have you zeen eet?

*(Shrimp in a spot.)*

**SHRIMP** Mitzi's in home appliances now. She's cool. Hey, Tax – You're beautiful, baby. Don't ever shave.

(*Bop in a spot.*)

**BOP** Comidas chinas y criollas! Mofungo!
(*All begin repeating their lines at once as the lights swim. A babble. Taxi cuts it off and everyone disappears.*)

**TAXI** (*In the VO.*) Those mental hit and runs were rough to take on no sleep. And I wasn't any closer to finding out if Dolores' dreams were being stolen, and if they were, why. But I wasn't born yesterday. I've heard enough ominous underscoring in my time to know that at the bottom of it all was Dr. Gut . . .
(*Ominous Underscoring.*)

**TAXI** Bucket. (*Pats pocket*). What? (*Pulls out his gat.*) Why had the Bop Op given me my gat back? It was time to recherchez the Heartbreak.
(*Goes to phone booth. Dials.*)

**TAXI** Bucket. Shrimp. Residence. Same to you. (*Dials.*) Bucket. Taxi. Taxi. I got something you want. Something you're looking for. Oh no? I wouldn't be too sure about that. Ask Professor Alors. Yeah, I'll hold.
(*Shrimp puts him on hold. Tinny Muzak comes out of the phone — SHRIMP LOUIE.*)

**TAXI** Gee, I oughta get this for the office.
(*Muzak stops. Taxi gets back on the line.*)

**TAXI** Surprised? What about this? Earlier tonight you smuggled a stiff into the Heartbreak. Isn't that the reverse of the house rules? My pleasure. You'll see me when you see me.
(*Taxi hangs up. The Heartbreak opens up and Taxi walks in.*)

**TAXI** (*In the VO.*) I took the shortest route to Con Leche's room.
(*Music. He travels. Enters Dolores' room.*)
(*Taxi holds the pill vial up to the light. He reads the Rx.*)

**TAXI** Take as needed for instant sleep. Catnap, one cap. Two caps: sleep soundly through sirens, heavy construction, marital discord, civil disorder, and decade's major cultural trends. For the Long Goodbye: scarf as many as fast as you can. Caution: do not ingest while vertical. (*In the VO.*) It did not seem like such a half-baked bad idea once I thought about it. I was dragging bun. I needed forty winks like a Chinese restaurant needs MSG. I could lie down on the job and do a little field research at the same time. The place to start putting the handcuffs on this sleep snatch was Con Leche's pillow. (*Investigates bed wiring.*) Kinky. (*Tries to open vial – can't.*) Detective-proof bottle. (*Gets it open. Still standing, he shakes out a pill and pulls out a pint.*)

**TAXI** (*In the VO.*) I crossed my palm with a logsawer, and tossed down a slug. Then a distant bell rang in the back of my cerebellum. Something about doctor's orders. Something about verticaallllllluuuuuuuu –
(*His eyes roll back in his head and he's out in a dead faint. The bed crackles and glows.*)

*(Huge arc of blue light.)*
*(Honk and wail from Blind Sax.)*
*(Weird greenish light up on Taxi, who is standing looking down at his sleeping self. Dream music, underscoring, and special effects.)*

**TAXI** *(In the VO.)* I was dreaming I had my own weekly series. The James Taxi show. Starring James Taxi. Beaucoup buckage. Endorsements. Fan mail. In the series, I'm the divorced father of three teenage private detectives. Two girls and a boy. It's a good premise. Comedy-suspense. I was just sitting down in my agent's office . . .
*(Lights swim. Music swims.)*

**TAXI** *(In the VO.)* – When suddenly there was a blinding jagged flash – nothing but late night snow on the small screen – purple and green afterburn on the backs of my eyelids like I'd had a flashcube go off in my face – cauterized cortex! My brain was being processed like Spam! *(Taxi dances back to the bed, jerking and twitching, a thousand volts of pure energy coursing through his body. He flops on the bed.)*
*(The lights stop swimming as Dolores enters. Taxi sits bolt upright.)*

**TAXI** I'll take the pigs with me!
*(Dolores slaps him.)*

**TAXI** *(Shakes out cobwebs.)* I gotta get a day job. What a night. What a head. Like a guacamole avocado.

**DOLORES** Taxi, what are you doing in my bed?

**TAXI** Sacrificing my body to detective science. I downed one of these.

**DOLORES** My pepsters from Doctor Gut.
*(Ominous Underscoring.)*

**TAXI** Yeah, these pepsters are first-class dozers, sweetcakes. Always read labels.

**DOLORES** Did you dance in your sleep?

**TAXI** Like a linebacker. Jètés somnambulés.

**DOLORES** Que pasa, Tax?

**TAXI** When my head hit the pillow, the Buckets siphoned off my dream faster than a vice cop on the pad.

**DOLORES** Why you?

**TAXI** Not me – you. They didn't expect anyone else to be using that futon.

**DOLORES** *(Outraged.)* Taxi! What do you take me for – a nun? Just because you don't have any social life –

**TAXI** Here's the scam – they've got Mitzi in the hotel somewhere, and she's doubling for you in the show. That wasn't you I saw out there tonight, it was your sister.

**DOLORES** My kid sister.

**TAXI** Your kid sister. And believe me, where I come from, that counts for something.

**DOLORES**  Taxi, why are they doing this to Mitzi?

**TAXI**  I don't know. But there's got to be major-league clammage, somewhere, in this dream snatch. Hotel do well?

**DOLORES**  Get real. This place doesn't do business on New Year's Eve.

**TAXI**  Go downstairs and stake out the lobby. If this jaspar from the Far East shows up, tip me. Jiggle the wiring.

**DOLORES**  I don't care what they say about you, Tax. I think you're jake.

**TAXI**  James. And just what do they say about me?

**DOLORES**  Oh hombre, por dios, no me hagas reir!
(*She exits.*)

**TAXI**  (*In the VO.*) I've always been a sucker for the enigmatic kind. I was overdue for a shrimp fry. I had something he wanted.
(*Traveling music. Taxi arrives at the Ice Bucket anteroom. Dry ice seeps. A rattan fan chair. Shrimp is practicing some moves with imaginary mike for Shrimp Louie.*)

**SHRIMP**  (*A capella.*) I'm a burnin' burnin' hunk of Shrimp I'm a burnin' burnin' hunk of Shrimp
Don't fuss with the dressin'
Cause you know you ain't messin' with me –

**TAXI**  Brushing up your act, Mr. Bucket?

**SHRIMP**  What's your professional opinion, Mr. Taxi?

**TAXI**  Get out of the business.

**SHRIMP**  I think I sound pretty good without the band. Shrimp Louie – a ca paella. Heh heh.

**TAXI**  I get the driftwood. You're one bad egg.

**SHRIMP**  Your use of the idiom is dazzling. Of course, you show folk. Life in the demi-monde. Sit down, sit down. Take the Huey Newton Chair.
(*Shrimp indicates the rattan fan chair. Taxi sits warily.*)

**SHRIMP**  Drink?

**TAXI**  Whiskey. Three fingers.

**SHRIMP**  (*Beat.*) Three fingers, eh? Chaser?

**TAXI**  Neat. No attitude.
(*Root appears and hands Taxi a drink.*)

**TAXI**  Swift. I like that it's not foaming. What's the call brand?

**ROOT**  Heart of Darkness. The White Man's Bourbon.
(*Root exits.*)

**TAXI**  Why does he get all the good lines?

**SHRIMP**  Affirmative action.

**TAXI**  Affirmative action. The Huey Newton Chair. You make the Heartbreak Hotel sound like a museum, Mr. Bucket.

**SHRIMP**  How perspicacious of you, Mr. Taxi. Yes, the Huey Newton

Chair is part of our American Icon collection. Huey endowed it.

**TAXI**  An endowed chair in a hotel?

**SHRIMP**  We're in a non-profit hotel. Huey was kind enough to leave us the chair.

**TAXI**  I'd like to take a gander at the rest of your collection.

**SHRIMP**  Not a chance. By appointment only. We're not a wax museum, Mr. Taxi.

**TAXI**  Oh? I thought maybe you were. What was that package you had delivered in the wee wee hours? A new exhibit?

**SHRMP**  A very old exhibit, Mr. Taxi. We'd sent it out for a little refurburation. Now, Mr. Taxi, I'm a busy guy. Belly up to the point.

**TAXI**  With pleasure. I decided to wink out in Con Leche's room. I popped a dubious dozer, and was out like a golfing doctor. While I was sawing my sheep, somebody lifted my dreams.

**SHRIMP**  Your – heh heh – dreams, Mr. Taxi? What would anyone want with your dreams? Dreams are so personal. Like underwear. You never have to worry about having your underwear snatched from the laundromat. They're too personal. They wouldn't fit. Dreams are the underwear of the mind, Mr. Taxi. Why take somebody else's? No deposit, no return. That does double for sordid, soiled, soggy, no starch, sewer-snooper dreams like yours – the grubby shorts of a truly short subject.

**TAXI**  If you were in my line of work, Mr. Bucket, you'd know there are plenty of creeps – right out there – who'll go for somebody else's boxers. But I'm not here to argue eschatology with you. I wasn't the intended. Nobody expected me to be on that futon. You were after Con Leche. You siphoned off my dreams because you thought they were hers. You're sucking up Con Leche's dreams like they were plankton. You've got her doped to the gills. Whatever you're using has a nasty side effect. It makes her dance in her sleep. She's no good in the act anymore, so you've got the supposedly missing Mitzi Montenegro doubling Dolores! You're an ethnic dancing junkie! Admit it! You're hooked!

**SHRIMP**  You're raving. How is such a thing possible?

**TAXI**  We may never know. But I intend to find out.

**SHRIMP**  If you'll excuse me, I've had enough of this bizarre conversation.

**TAXI**  Thanks for the gut bomb.

(*Ominous underscoring from Blind Sax.*)

**TAXI**  How do you do that?

**SHRIMP**  Aren't you forgetting something?

**TAXI**  Am I?

**SHRIMP**  You have something that belongs to me.

**TAXI** Oh, you mean – (*He pulls the three-fingered glove out of his pocket.*)

**TAXI** –a three-fingered glove?

(*Shrimp lunges for it, but Taxi pulls his gat. Shrimp puts his hands up. They sing a reprise of THREE-FINGERED GLOVE.*)

### THREE-FINGERED GLOVE, reprise

**TAXI** A three-fingered glove

**SHRIMP** Where did you find it

**TAXI** A three-fingered glove

**SHRIMP** What good can it do you

**TAXI** A three-fingered glove
Why don't you tell me

**SHRIMP** You're not a digital amputee . . .yet

**TAXI** Are you threatening me

**SHRIMP** Just you wait and see

**TAXI** Don't get tough with me

**SHRIMP** It was my Grandpa's
An heirloom you see
He lost a pinkie
It means bupkes to me

**TAXI** You can never ever really tell
I guess I'll have to put it away
And save it for a rainy day

**SHRIMP** and **TAXI**
You just wait and see!

(*Music out*)

**TAXI** I'll do that.

**SHRIMP** There's a reward.

**TAXI** How much?

**SHRIMP** Two C's.

**TAXI** Two G's.

**SHRIMP** Okay.

**TAXI** A G is worth more than a C, right?

**SHRIMP** Where I come from.

**TAXI** How do I know this is really yours? It may belong to some digitally challenged person.

**SHRIMP** I'll show you the mate.

**TAXI** Sealed deal.

**SHRIMP** Meet me in the laundry in ten. You drive a hard bargain, Mr. Taxi. I'm not used to negotiating at gunpoint. The security at this hotel is terrible. My apologies.

**TAXI**  Don't count your dim sum before it's steamed, Mr. Bucket.

**SHRIMP**  Don't press your duck, pal.

(*The lights blink conspicuously. Ominous underscoring. Lights restore to full and the underscoring phrase revs back up to speed and finishes.*)

**TAXI**  You oughta do something about your underscoring, it's death on wiring.

**SHRIMP**  A bientot, Mr. Taxi. A pleasure doing business with you. (*Shrimp fades.*)

**TAXI**  (*In the VO.*) I was in the vichyssoise no doubt about it. I had to make waves and fast. That power failure was a signal from Con Leche that the guest of honor was on his way.

(*He travels. Dolores is waiting in the lobby.*)

**TAXI**  Where is he?

**DOLORES**  (*Pointing.*) Incoming at nine o'clock.

(*Mr. Batsumashball enters. He is played by Root in dark glasses, turban, and sarong.*)

**MR. BATSUMASHBALL**  Sorry, so sorry, I am looking for Mr. and Mr. Bucket –

**DOLORES**  Oh yes, aren't you –

**MR. BATSUMASHBALL**  Yes, I am Mr. Batsumashball, from Nauru.

**DOLORES**  Right. Mr. Batsumashball, it was on the tip of my tongue.

(*Taxi slips up behind Mr. Batsumashball and sticks a gun in his ribs.*)

**MR. BATSUMASHBALL**  I knew it! I knew it! I knew America was a dangerous country! Take my traveler's checks! Take my Rolex! But please don't take my cocoanuts!

**TAXI**  I'll settle for your sarong. Take his chapeau.

**MR. BATSUMASHBALL**  Kinky American perverts.

(*The Band plays strip music, as Taxi takes off his clothes and puts on Mr. Batsumashball's sarong. He puts on Mr. Batsumashball's dark glasses and sandals, as Dolores holds the gun on him.*)

**TAXI**  Take a brain bomber, pal.

(*He stuffs one of the instant sleep capsules into Mr. Batsumashball's mouth – he's out on his feet instantly.*)

**TAXI**  Think of this as a hideous case of jet lag.

(*They stash him behind the palm. Dolores takes Mr. Batsumashball's turban and puts it on Taxi.*)

**DOLORES**  You look good. Your turban is crooked. Chicks dig turbans.

**TAXI**  I'll remember that.

(*She straightens it. They get tangled up.*)

**TAXI**  You got narrative structure, sister. You got plot points galore.

(*They're about to get into a heavy clinch when they hear voices.*)

**ROOT**  (*Offstage.*) I don't care how blasé you are, no one sleeps through the Big O.

(*Root and Bop enter.*)

**BOP**  Man, this scam is taking the scungilli outta my ramen.

(*Sees Dolores and Taxi.*)

**BOP**  (*To Dolores.*) I gotta question your taste in men. You the big noise from Nauru?

**TAXI**  I'm not Jackie O.

**BOP**  Jackie O got better shoulders, pal.

**ROOT**  The boss is waiting, Mr. Batsumashball.

**BOP**  Batsumashball?

**TAXI**  Walk this way.

(*They start to walk. Dolores tries to tag along but Bop stops her.*)

**BOP**  Not you, Miss Au Lait.

(*They fade as Taxi and Root travel.*)

**ROOT**  Is it true what they say about Nauru?

**TAXI**  Every word.

(*They arrive at The Ice Bucket. Lots of dry ice and neon tube gear.*)
(*Shrimp appears.*)

**SHRIMP**  Ah, our distinguished guest. Mr. Batsumashball, I presume.

**TAXI**  Mr. Shrimp, meet Mr. Batsumashball.

**SHRIMP**  Mr. Batsumashball. Delighted.

**TAXI**  Mr. Shrimp Bucket. So nice to be here.

**SHRIMP**  Cool your cuticles, Root. If you go down to the laundry, I think you just might locate that missing – item. And be sure to give our little friend a nice big tip for his trouble.

**ROOT**  No prob. (*Root exits.*)

**TAXI**  Ah, Mr. Shrimp. It is my understanding there are – Brothers Bucket.

**SHRIMP**  (*Chuckles.*) You're in for a treat. Allow me to introduce my distinguished brother. Doctor. Gut. Bucket.

(*Ominous Underscoring. The Huey Newton chair, which has been facing upstage, now swivels around. It is Gut. He is dressed like Huey Newton in the famous photograph: black beret, black leather jacket and pants, black boots. He has a black glove on one hand, a spear in one hand, and a machine gun in the other. Almost the spitting image of Huey – except that he's white and very overweight.*)

**GUT**  Welcome to our humble hotel, Mr. Batsumashball. Where we pursue our studies in American iconography and contemporary mythology.

**TAXI**  Your work is well known.

**GUT**  I certainly hope not. That would be – unfortunate.

(*Gut and Shrimp share an unpleasant laugh.*)

**GUT**  Perhaps we should proceed directly to the demonstration.
  (*Shrimp wheels out the Dream Device.*)

**GUT**  As you know, Mr. Batsumashball, we have only to perfect our delivery system to begin global operations.

**SHRIMP**  After that, it's clear scaling.

**GUT**  That's right, Shrimp.

**SHRIMP**  You got it, Gut.

**GUT**  Your world-wide electronics empire should solve all our problems.

**TAXI**  It should, shouldn't it?

**SHRIMP**  With a nice piece of change for you, Mr. Batsumashball.

**GUT**  This is the Dream Device, Mr. Batsumashball. A dream recorder and projector. It records on these discs –
  (*Shrimp holds up a shiny disc and inserts it.*)

**GUT**  – and projects a holographic image. The apparatus is a complete package. It transcribes the dreamer's dream, records it, and plays it back. We got some help on this from SONY.

**TAXI**  You should have come to me.

**GUT**  We've been working with a guinea pig. Stealing and recording her dreams. An exotic dancer.

**SHRIMP**  Please Brother Gut. An ethnic dancer. She's a narcoleptic. She's a dreamboat of a dreamer. Wanna see one?

**TAXI**  I didn't come all the way from Nauru to pick pineapple out of my belly button.
  (*Shrimp flicks a switch on the Dream Device.*)

**SHRIMP**  You won't believe the fidelity on this. The three-D is stunning. This is her favorite: "If I Was A Fool To Dream."
  (*Dolores appears in a spot.*)

### IF I WAS A FOOL TO DREAM

**DOLORES**  I'm in a bar, sweetheart
  Alone again, it's true
  I'll have a scotch to start
  A chaser for these blues

  I'll have another shot
  And wait for you to show
  Someone will ask me out
  I'll have to tell him no

  I'm in a state, sweetheart
  Alone, what else is new
  I'll have a scotch to start

My memories of you

If I could have you back
I'd change my foolish ways
If I could kiss your face
I'd never ever stray

Oh my darling so I'd say
Never leave me never go
Always take my breath away

(*Spoken:*)
I've kissed a lot of guys
They've asked me to be true
I've told a lot of lies
'Cause none of them were you

I'm in a sorry state
My heart is sad and blue
When I turn out the light
I'll dream a dream of you

I was a fool to dream
I was a fool to dream
I was a fool to dream
(*Spot on Dolores out.*)

(*Lights up on Taxi, Gut and Shrimp.*)
**TAXI**   She's so real.
**SHRIMP**   That hologram's patented. Our trademark: palpable image.
Wait'il you grok the Clam Room Show. It'll knock your sox off.
**GUT**   Now, Mr. Batsumashball. You're probably wondering why. Why
collect dreams?
**TAXI**   It had double-crossed my mind.
**GUT**   Why not cash? Precious gemoids? Negotiable securities and other
instruments of financial torture?
**TAXI**   Why not?
**SHRIMP**   Profit.
**GUT**   And power.
**TAXI**   How do you get profit and power from dreams? Mr. and Mr.
Bucket, I still don't smell those greenback dollahs.
**GUT**   You have an extraordinary command of the American idiom, Mr.
Batsumashball.

**SHRIMP**   The aboveboard legal side of the market is enormous, Mr. Batsumashball.

**GUT**   We'll be selling a modified version of this machine to psychoanalysts, therapists of every persuasion, and so on. And a home-use model – for the self-involved.

**SHRIMP**   Gonna be the biggest thing to ever hit Manhattan.

**TAXI**   You want me to perfect your long-range dream stealer –

**SHRIMP**   You'll get a share of the net.

**TAXI**   Gross, there's no such thing as net.

**SHRIMP**   Oh, you're sharp, Mr. B. Okay, gross.

**TAXI**   (*Snaps fingers.*) Dream piracy. On a global scale. The legal stuff for therapy will be chump change if you can pry open anyone's head in the world and extract their dreams like a gherkin.

**SHRIMP**   Go for it, Mr. B. Figure the angle.

**TAXI**   Gotta be cable. Mondo Video.

**GUT** and **SHRIMP**   Video Mondo!

**TAXI**   Thousands of new channels. They all need material. You tap into hot sources surreptitiously. Writers, artists, real DREAMERS. You suck out their dreams, like calamari, record 'em – and either screen the stuff raw, or put it into development.

**SHRIMP**   Now you're cooking with canned heat.

**TAXI**   Stealing dreams is much safer than stealing scripts.

**SHRIMP**   Hey, you can't copyright dreams.

**GUT**   Scripts for the insatiable maw of popular entertainment. The demand is endless, the supply anemic.

**SHRIMP**   And writers's block. You know how many writers out there got block? Many. Heads full of great plots and no way to get them out. It's like having a copper mine without a railroad.

**GUT**   We should capture all markets. Cable is just the beginning. Today, cable. Radio. Television. Hong Kong. After Hong-Kong – Hollywood. It's the great big banal American dream, Mr. Batsumashball: the conquest of Hollywood. The Heartbreak will replace Hollywood as the world-wide center of self delusion and primary source of pre-fabricated dreams. Brother Shrimp – If you please.
(*Shrimp wheels in a portable deep freeze: rhinestones and neon trim. Clouds of dry ice.*)

**GUT**   I'm sure you've heard all the classic American myths.

**SHRIMP**   Every kid knows 'em.

**GUT**   About this or that legendary artifact.

**SHRIMP**   It's a government secret. Some old lady has Custer's scalp in a hat box.

**TAXI**   The saucer people who live in the top of Mt. Shasta.

**SHRIMP**   Excellent, Mr. Batsumashball.

**GUT**   That particular myth is indigenous to California. My personal favorite is the poodle in the microwave.

**TAXI**   They put the poodle in the microwave to dry it off. And it blew up.

**SHRIMP**   I heard it was a wet cat.

**TAXI**   What's your position on Bigfoot?

**SHRIMP**   Bigfoot's one of the best.

**GUT**   Do you ever wonder how these Native American myths germinate?

**TAXI**   Every day.

**GUT**   Metastisizing into myths of Bunyanesque proportions? For one simple reason, Mr. Batsumashball – they're true.

**TAXI**   You got Bigfoot? I wanna see Bigfoot.

**GUT**   Perhaps this will convince you.

*(Shrimp opens the deep freeze.)*

**SHRIMP**   We keep our extra extra special stock in here.

*(Shrimp pulls out a hatbox, opens it and displays a mangy, moth-eaten blonde wig.)*

**TAXI**   Custer?

**SHRIMP**   Who else?

**TAXI**   Your mother, maybe.

**GUT**   A hard sell, eh, Mr. Batsumashball? Try this.

*(From the deep-freeze Shrimp extracts and brandishes a thin metal cylinder, three-feet long and shaped like a cigar.)*

**TAXI**   *(With reverence.)* Dillinger.

**GUT**   The one and only. According to popular mythology, Dillinger's – distinguishing anatomical peculiarity was detached after his demise and preserved. Pickled. In a jar.

**SHRIMP**   Smithsonian.

**TAXI**   I heard Walter Reed Hospital.

**GUT**   The value of this item only increases over the years as the stories grow more elaborate.

**TAXI**   Hard to exaggerate about something like that.

**SHRIMP**   One item that lives up to its billing.

**GUT**   And now, the piéce de resistance. Mr. Batsumashball, if you would be so kind.

*(Taxi goes into the deep freeze.)*

**TAXI**   Dillinger, I never bought. Jealous, I guess. But Bigfoot – I gotta hunch about Bigfoot. Oh, boy, Bigfoot!

*(He looks down into the deep freeze. WHEN YOU WISH UPON A STAR plays under.)*

**TAXI**   Uncle Walt.

*(Gut and Shrimp chuckle nastily.)*

**GUT**   Isn't he gorgeous?

**TAXI**   He looks better than he did on his last season. Those stories started just after Uncle Walt – after Uncle Walt – after he – went away.

**GUT**  They said he was terminal, so he had himself freeze-dried while he was still alive.

**SHRIMP**  Good career move.

**GUT**  Cryogenically preserved in a state of icy grace. In a tube in a tower of Sleeping Beauty's castle. Ready to return to us the day a cure is found.

**TAXI**  To create new and better Magic Kingdoms! The Second Coming!

**SHRIMP**  One of our better heists. And not easy. That Tinkerbell was a bitch.

**GUT**  Our interest in dreams and icons led us inevitably to Uncle Walt. The greatest purveyor of myth the world has ever known. Uncle Walt – what a dreamer. Once we've found a cure for what ails Uncle Walt –

**SHRIMP**  We'll bring him back to dream for the Bucket Brothers on an exclusive basis. He'll dream it our way.

**GUT**  Tickle those ivories! Palpitate those eighty-eights!
(*Gut and Shrimp sing NO MORE MAGIC KINGDOMS, anthem of incredible evil.*)

## NO MORE MAGIC KINGDOMS

**GUT**  No more Fred MacMurray
**SHRIMP**  No more Peter Pan
**GUT**  No more Pluto furry
**SHRIMP**  No more Pollyann –
**GUT**  – a!
**SHRIMP** and **GUT**
>  No more Cinderella
>  No more haunted house
>  No more Tinkerbells

>  No more Mickey Mouse

>  No more Magic Kingdoms
>  Uncle Walt's passé
>  He'll dream it our way, yeah

**GUT**  No more boring nature flicks
**SHRIMP**  No more prime-time swill
**GUT**  No more *Son of Flubber* tricks
**SHRIMP**  No more Hayley Mills
**SHRIMP** and **GUT**
>  No more Jiminy Cricket

> No more *Song of the South*
> Give me Wilson Pickett
> Instead of Donald's mouth

**SHRIMP**  Quack!
**GUT**  Quack!
**SHRIMP and GUT**
> Quack!

> No more Magic Kingdoms
> Uncle Walt's passé
> He'll dream it our way, yeah!

**SHRIMP**  We'll flip off the lid of Uncle Walt's id
> He'll french Sleeping Beauty adieu

**GUT**  They'll hump real fast then share a repast
> Of Thumper and Bambi ragout

**SHRIMP**  We'll bring back Annette in her sweater you bet
> To give us our afternoon thrill

**GUT**  If Daisy and Don can't get it on
> Snow White and the Seven Dwarves will

**SHRIMP and GUT**
> No more Magic Kingdoms
> Bucket Brothers rule
> We'll dream it our way yeah
> Oh yeah
> (*Big finish.*)

**TAXI**  That's some plan.
**SHRIMP**  A class scam. Worth billions.
**GUT**  That's conservative. With Uncle Wait under our thrall, the Bucket Brothers will rule the world of popular entertainment.
**SHRIMP**  So, Mr. B. Are you in, or are you in?
**TAXI**  Count me in. It may be repulsive, but it certainly sounds profitable.
**SHRIMP**  Terrific, Mr. B.
**TAXI**  I couldn't help but notice Uncle Walt's missing one of his cute little white three-fingered gloves.
> (*Music Sting.*)
**SHRIMP**  Lost in the laundry. So embarrassing. We always try to have Uncle Walt freshly pressed for visitors. Now, Mr. Batsumashball, what

about a little ethnic dancing to celebrate our new partnership? I'm sure the girls would be happy to oblige. Specialty of the house.

**TAXI** I'd like to see another sample.

(*A little miffed, Shrimp goes through a few discs.*)

**SHRIMP** Let's see. "IRS Chainsaw Massacre" – that's a revenge thing – "The Slattern of Soho" – that's one of mine. And look out, it is hot – let's see, here's a dud, "The ]ames Taxi Show" –

**TAXI** That sounds good.

**SHRIMP** No, it's a sit-com.

**TAXI** I heard it was comedy suspense.

(*Gut and Shrimp exchange glances.*)

**GUT** Where did you hear that, Mr. Batsumashball?

**TAXI** Word on the street.

**SHRIMP** Word travels fast to Nauru.

**GUT** Word on the street. I am continually dazzled by your grasp of the American idiom, Mr. Batsumashball. And come. Tell me. How is it you know so much about the Mt. Shasta saucer people and Bigfoot?

**TAXI** We keep in touch on Nauru. We have television.

(*Root and Blind Sax enter.*)

**ROOT** Taxi never showed. Boss.

**SHRIMP** What a surprise. So you heard his dream was comedy-suspense, did you, Mr. B.?

**TAXI** A real nail-biter.

(*Taxi is sweating. He pulls the three-fingered glove from his pocket, and mops his brow.*)

**GUT** I doubt that your high opinion of your own dream is shared by a significant portion of the viewing audience, Mr. Batsu-taxi.

(*Shrimp pulls a gun.*)

**SHRIMP** And unhand that glove.

(*Taxi takes off his dark glasses and turban, and hands Shrimp the glove.*)

**TAXI** (*In the VO.*) I had huevos rancheros all over my mugshot. I'd meant to grill Shrimp like a souvlaki. Instead, I'd skewered myself seven ways till Sunday. I'd always wanted my own weekly series, but comedy suspense, not sit-com. What the hell, you can't sneeze at residuals.

**SHRIMP** You're the only residual around here. You're a guy with no secrets, talk to yourself like that. Stay for dinner. Gracie's made extra.

**TAXI** I'd like to, but I left the top down on my convertible.

(*Gut twists Taxi's nipple.*)

**GUT** Manners, young man.

(*Shrimp relieves Taxi of his gun, and hands it to Blind Sax, who points it at the audience. Shrimp redirects him at Taxi.*)

**TAXI** You really think he should have that?

**SHRIMP** The NRA supports the constitutional right of blind people to bear arms.

(*Taxi glances into deep freeze.*)

**TAXI** Hey! What goes on here? There's no life support system hardware. Nothing to keep him hibernation fresh.

(*The Bucket Brothers grow very grim.*)

**TAXI** (*In the VO.*) The look on their faces told me I'd hit the bull's eye. It also told me I should have bitten my lips off.

**GUT** An unfortunate accident.

**SHRIMP** The support systems were unintentionally destroyed during the heist.

**TAXI** But that means now he's worth less than a frozen fish stick.

**GUT** We trust you can keep our little secret.

**TAXI** My lips are seals.

**GUT** I will miss our repartee, Mr. Taxi.

**SHRIMP** It was extra extra special.

**TAXI** I look forward to Uncle Walt's comeback.

(*Taxi moves for the exit. Root stops him.*)

**SHRIMP** He'll make his before you make yours.

(*Root grabs him.*)

**SHRIMP** You're such a fan of the maestro, perhaps you'd like to join him.

(*Root forces Taxi towards the freeze. Taxi elbows Root in stomach. The Band plays action-suspense underscoring. Taxi and Shrimp struggle for Shrimp's gun. Big fight stuff. Finally, Shrimp pistol-whips Taxi across the bridge of the nose. Taxi crumples to his knees. He passes a hand over his face and looks at the red stuff on his fingers.*)

**TAXI** God. Real blood. I hate that.

(*Reggae Bass Line.*)

**TAXI** (*In the VO.*) I was about to join Uncle Walt in the Deepest Freeze of all. My reggae headache was taking an encore. Days like this made me think I should have stayed in grad school. Then it hit me.

(*Flashback music. Shrimp is caught in a blinding spot.*)

**SHRIMP** Mitzi's in home appliances now. She's cool.

(*Music and spot out. Shrimp reels, rubs his eyes.*)

**SHRIMP** I haven't had a flashback like that since Tim Leary and I went barbecuing with Bobby. How do you do that?

**TAXI** How do you do the underscoring?

**SHRIMP** Trade secret.

**TAXI** Flukey ditto.

**SHRIMP** Enough shop talk. Hook him up.

(*Root pushes Taxi into the freezer and begins to attach him to some ominous-looking machinery.*)

**TAXI**  Mitzi's gotta be in the ice bucket. But where?

**SHRIMP**  You're the detective.

**TAXI**  Yes, yes I am. Over there. The walk-in cooler. Home appliances.

**SHRIMP**  How terribly perspicacious of you, Mr. Taxi.

(*Shrimp opens a closet. Mitzi is in a tube, played by Dolores in a shower cap.*)

**TAXI**  Is she in the same shape Uncle Walt is?

**GUT**  Her pulse is glacial, but rock steady. As long as we defrost properly, she'll be good as new.

(*Shrimp closes door on Mitzi.*)

**TAXI**  (*In the VO.*) It was all beginning to fall into place, like pecs and mams on a fortieth birthday. Mitzi on ice. The Bucket brothers' hologram fooled me, and I was ringside.

**SHRIMP**  I'm dying to hear the rest of this, but too much denouement always gives me gas. Which reminds me – (*To Root.*) Turn on the liquid nitro. A bientot, Mr. Taxi.

**GUT**  Bon soir, Mr. Batsumashball.

(*Root turns on the liquid nitro. It makes an evil hiss. Shrimp and Gut cackle madly. Taxi starts to quiver and shake and turn blue. The Band plays suspense music. Dolores bursts in, armed with a Dirty Harry-sized Magnum, followed by Lizzy and Sally, who are also armed with smaller pistols.*)

**DOLORES**  Hands up, Buckets. (*To Root.*) Nix the toxic waste, Rootie-tunes.

(*Root turns off the nitro. Gut points spear and machine-gun at Dolores. Shrimp aims Blind Sax at the Balkanettes.*)

**GUT**  Likewise, Miss Con Leche, let me urge you to do the same.

**SALLY**  Shrimp, your ass is filé gumbo now.

**SHRIMP**  Is this what they call a Mexican standoff?

**DOLORES**  I think I'm gonna ventilate you.

**SHRIMP**  A tough-talking woman with a Magnum always turns me on.

**DOLORES**  You are one sick Shrimp, you know that?

**SHRIMP**  Since you put it that way – let me put it this way. And this way. And what about this way?

(*As Shrimp puts it various ways, the Band plays some exciting kungfu fighting music and Root whirls and twirls and disarms Dolores, Lizzy and Sally in a series of astonishing lightning moves.*)

**DOLORES**  Oh! You! You! You Buckets, you!

**SHRIMP**  I promised you kung fu fighting. In you go. Join your flat-footed friend.

(*Root puts Dolores in the deep freeze with Taxi.*)

**DOLORES**  Sorry, Tax.

**TAXI**  I fell for it, too.

**SHRIMP**  Balkanettes, too. You don't want to dance ethnic, I'll find
somebody who does.

**SALLY**  Shrimp salad, I hope you deep-fat fry in fast-food hell for this.

**SHRIMP**  And after all I've done for you.

**LIZZY**  Bite mine!

(*Root stuffs the Balkanettes in the freezer. Dolores looks down.*)

**DOLORES**  Who's that?

**TAXI**  Uncle Walt.

**DOLORES**  My God.

**TAXI**  Mine too. (*To Shrimp.*) Let me put this other glove on him, will
you? He looks naked without it.

(*Shrimp tosses the glove to Taxi, who puts it on Uncle Walt.*)

**DOLORES**  You dream-sucking Buckets! Why are you putting the snatch
on my dreams? Why are you making me dance in my sleep?

**TAXI**  Allow me.

(*Music.*)

**SHRIMP**  Go ahead, Tax. I just love it when you detect.

**TAXI**  The whole enchilada?

**SHRIMP**  Be incisive. Relentless. We'll just wither.

**TAXI**  Everybody ready?

**BAND**  Hit it, Tax!

**TAXI**  Okay. But if I leave anything out, don't stop me – 'cause –

(*The Band segues into DOIN' THE DENOUEMENT.*)

## DOIN' THE DENOUEMENT

**TAXI**  I'm doin' the denouement
Red herring, McGuffin, Crazy Cat's paw
I'm doing the denouement
I'm runnin' the whole thing down

**ALL**  Denoue
Denoue
Denouement

**TAXI**  The Buckets invent the Dream Device
They put the snatch on poor Uncle Walt
Stash his technicolor ass on ice
Plan his final comeback from their secret vault

**GUT and SHRIMP**
We wanted to cure him not waste him
You gotta believe it's not our fault

We only meant to gently baste him
With crocodile tears and cryogenic salt

**TAXI** (*Spoken.*)
Tell it to the judge

**GIRLS** Shrimp is kinky for ethnic dancers
They hired Mitzi and sucked her dreams

**TAXI** Doped to the gills with Gut's enhancers
She somnambulated into their evil schemes

**ALL** He's doin' the denouement
Red herring, McGuffin, Crazy Cat's paw
He's doin' the denouement

**TAXI** I'm runnin' the whole thing down

**ALL** Denoue
Denoue
Denouement

**TAXI** They wear Mitzi out she starts to get wise
To keep her from blowin' the whistle
Put her tutus and tango shoes on ice
That's the preamble now here's the epistle
(*Spoken – to audience*)
You try to rhyme whistle – it's not that easy.

**SALLY** Thistle!
**SHRIMP** That's the meat, now here's the gristle?
**TAXI** Oh, please. (*Sings.*) Con Leche comes lookin' for Mitzi
**SHRIMP** We advertised for another thrush
**DOLORES** You couldn't call the Clam Room ritzy
**GUT** We slipped her a pill in her Chardonnay blush

**ALL** He's doin the denouement
Red herring, McGuffin, Crazy Cat's paw
He's doin' the denouement

**TAXI** I'm runnin' the whole thing down
(*The Band vamps.*)

**TAXI**  If you don't mind, I'll do the rest in prose. Rhymed exposition is murder.

**SHRIMP**  Put a Perry Mason on it, Tax, and let's wrap this tuna in nori –

**TAXI**  I always get suspicious when I see a stiff being carried into a fleabag hotel. In this case, it was a frozen stiff. Uncle Walt.

**GUT**  We'd sent him out to a specialist. But there was nothing to be done.

**TAXI**  The three-fingered glove belonged to Uncle Walt.

**SHRIMP**  That camembaert Professor Alors dropped it. I'll settle his hash later.

**TAXI**  No, he didn't. By the way, Professor Alors and Dr. Gut –

(*Ominous Underscoring.*)

**TAXI**  – are one and the same person.

(*All gasp.*)

**SHRIMP**  Don't be ridiculous.

**GUT**  You're hallucinating.

**TAXI**  (*To others.*) Ever seen them in the same room at the same time? Think about it.

**SHRIMP**  It's a theory.

**TAXI**  Once I figured out you were stealing Con Leche's dreams, I intercepted Mr. Batsumashball to find out why. And now I know.

**GUT**  Everybody wants to be in show business.

(*The Band surges up.*)

**TAXI**  (*Spoken.*) That's it! (*Sings.*)
I'm doin' the denouement
Red herring, McGuffin, Crazy Cat's paw
I'm doin' the denouement
I'm runnin' the whole thing down

**ALL**  Denoue
Denoue
Denouement

**SHRIMP**  Now that's private detection!

(*Big finish.*)

**GUT**  Where is Mr. Batsumashball?

**TAXI**  Stashed in the breakfast nook off the lobby.

**SHRIMP**  Sheer clam nectar, Tax. Hey, we're having some fun now. Okay! Enough denouement! Let's ice these turkeys! Liquid nitro and lots of it!

(*Root turns on the liquid nitro. Dry ice billows. The Bop Op bursts through the door, wearing a tatty Blackglama mink. He has a gun and he flashes a badge.*)

**BOP**  Special Agent – Lillian Hellman! You're now on ice, Buckets. (*To audience.*) The first time I met Dashiell Hammer, he arrested me for shoplifting costume jewelry at Lamston's. He was a Pinkerton, I was a

Pulitzer Prize winner. We laughed about it later – the little fox.

**TAXI** (*In the VO.*) Meanwhile, in another part of the forest, The Bop Op was undercover, stringing the Buckets along like a couple of sausages.

**DOLORES** When did you know the Bop Op was a cop?

**TAXI** Just now, when he flashed his badge.

**BOP** Drop 'em, Buckets.

> (*Root unties everyone, while Shrimp and Gut drop 'em. Bop turns Blind Sax and points him at the Buckets.*)

**BOP** Special Agent Lillian Hellman. Investigating the theft of Uncle Walt from Sleeping Beauty's castle. Your name is mud, Buckets. What else is in there with Uncle Walt?

**TAXI** This.

> (*He hands Bop the cylinder, Bop gets awe-struck and sensual.*)

**BOP** Dillinger. Do you know how long the Bureau's been after this? (*Takes it from Taxi and hefts it!*) What becomes a legend most.

**TAXI** I suspected you might be on our side.

**BOP** Special Agent Lillian Hellman. FBI and Copyright office.

**SHRIMP** Hey! You can't copyright dreams, I'm telling you.

**BOP** When did you start to catch on?

**TAXI** From jumpstreet, pal. You dropped the three-fingered glove. Not to mention the passkey and putting my piece back in my pocket.

**SHRIMP** Mink turncoat.

**BOP** And who says private dicks are slow?

**TAXI** I want my wallet and watch back, brown belle.

> (*Taxi gives him claim check. Bop gives Taxi his wallet and watch.*)

**DOLORES** Sure is complex.

**TAXI** If you're experiencing narrative motion sickness, don't let it get you down. It comes with the territory. By the time we close the covers on this one, you won't remember which ends are loose.

> (*Taxi takes a sad look at the thawing Uncle Walt.*)

**TAXI** He's starting to melt. How could you?

**SHRIMP** We didn't mean to break him.

**GUT** Obviously. His resale value in this condition is nil.

**SHRIMP** We even had to refreeze.

**TAXI** (*Aghast.*) You're never supposed to refreeze. (*Near tears.*) Poor Uncle Walt. No comeback now. Entertainment as we know it will never be the same.

**GUT** No more Magic Kingdoms, Mr. Taxi.

**TAXI** Lillian!

**BOP** Yeah, Nancy?

**TAXI** Put these perverts where the sun don't shine!

**BOP** You got it.

> (*He starts to herd off Root, Zoot, Shrimp and Gut.*)

**TAXI**  You don't look very worried.

**SHRIMP**  (*Laughs.*) Me? We have more lawyers than the District of Columbia. I'm about as worried as Standard Oil at tax time.

**TAXI**  Don't plagiarize my style, Bucket.

**SHRIMP**  Hey! You can't copyright style, I'm telling you.

**GUT**  We'll meet again, Mr. Taxi. In the sequel.

**SALLY**  Come catch our new act, Mr. Taxi.

**TAXI**  Wouldn't miss it.

(*Lizzy and Sally exit, singing NUEVO HUEVO.*)

**TAXI**  Thanks for your help, Lillian.

**BOP**  My pleasure, Nancy. Call me. We'll have lunch. (*Laughs girlishly.*) We'll leave you two flamingos alone.

(*Everyone exits.*)

**DOLORES**  Taxi! What about Mitzi?

**TAXI**  We'll come back for her tomorrow. One more night – she'll never know the difference.

**DOLORES**  Taxi, she's my kid sister.

**TAXI**  I know. And believe me – where I come from, that counts for something.

**DOLORES**  Listen, there are still a lot of things I don't understand.

**TAXI**  Don't sweat it. The genre teaches us to accept the inexplicable. It's a very metaphysical genre.

**DOLORES**  If you say so. Listen, Taxi. Thanks. No, seriously.

**TAXI**  All in a night's work.

**DOLORES**  I guess I've seen the last of you.

**TAXI**  In a pig's valise, sister.

**DOLORES**  I never thought you'd work that in.

**TAXI**  It came to me in a dream.

**DOLORES**  I like your style.

**TAXI**  Likewise, in spades.

**DOLORES**  May I call you Nancy James?

**TAXI**  I wish you would.

**DOLORES**  Besame mucho!

(*She grabs him and kisses him hard, bending him over in a tango swoon. In the middle of the kiss, he breaks off.*)

**TAXI**  (*In the VO.*) She had lips as sweet and full as ten pounds of sucre in a five-pound sack. They turned my spine to flan. I was diving head-first into a pool of passion-fruit punch, hoping I'd never have to come up for air.

(*Dolores drops him on the floor.*)

**DOLORES**  You gotta see somebody about that. I'm not spending the weekend with somebody who talks to himself in the past tense.

**TAXI**  Promise.

(*He picks himself up. They lock eyes and get steamy.*)

**DOLORES**   I don't care what they say about you. I think you're muy picante.

**TAXI**   What exactly do they say about me?

**DOLORES**   That you're fast as a claims settlement.

**TAXI**   Irony. I like that in a woman. You know, Con Leche, you're about as subtle as a pitcher of sangria.

**DOLORES**   Tell me more, big fella.

**TAXI**   You come on strong, like you're a double shot of tequila with a brew back. But you're really about as tough to take as a spring day.

**DOLORES**   Sweet. You hard-boiled guys have maple syrup in your veins.

**TAXI**   Don't stop now.

**DOLORES**   Taxi, you come on like a mouthful of razor blades, but you're really as hard-edged as a flour torfflla. You're as sweet as sopapilla.

**TAXI**   I've swapped similes with saps from Sunset to Sepulveda, but sister, you're something special.

(*Music.*)

**TAXI**   I like a gal who can spin a phrase.

**DOLORES**   I like a guy who can torture all day a figure of speech.

**TAXI**   Not to mention syntax.

(*They sing a reprise of IF I WAS A FOOL TO DREAM.*)


## IF I WAS A FOOL TO DREAM, reprise


**TAXI and DOLORES**

> I've been alone so long
> It doesn't matter why
> Others have come and gone
> I kissed them all goodbye
>
> 'Cause they weren't you, my dear
> Until you came my way
> I spent my nights alone
> And dreamed away my days
>
> I've been alone so long
> I couldn't speculate
> If I would recognize
> You as my lucky day
>
> I'm in a state, sweetheart

Of transcendental grace
I'll skip the scotch, instead
I'll kiss your silly face

If I was a fool to dream
Ah true love would come my way
Darling let me dream and never wake

Got a ballad to spare
It's bittersweet but true
Got a love I can share
A serenade for two

I've been a fool too long
It doesn't matter why
I'll be a fool for you
And kiss my blues goodbye
(*Sweet finish*)


**DOLORES**   You're like a day at the beach, big fella.
**TAXI**   Baby, by me that's okay.
   (*They lock eyes, get steamy, etc.*)
**TAXI**   Chaka chaka chaka cha.
   (*A sizzling kiss.*)
**DOLORES**   Let's blow this clam bar.
**TAXI**   Which way out of Dodge?
**DOLORES**   Scrape the gum off your shoes and walk this way.
   (*She starts off.*)
**TAXI**   Not a chance. Wait. I have something for you.
   (*He pulls the cylinder out of the deep freeze. She takes it from him.*)
**DOLORES**   Dillinger.
**TAXI**   It ain't Bigfoot.
   (*She sizes them both up.*)
**DOLORES**   I may need this. Let's go find out. Undulate, Taxi! Undulate!
   (*She undulates off.*)
**TAXI**   (*In the VO.*) It was time to give my faithful amanuensis "Legs"
   Lichtenstein a ring. Time to tell her to hold my calls, take in the mail,
   and put out the cat. Let's face it, it was time to undulate. I advise you
   to go home and do likewise. (*Beat.*) I wonder where you buy those cute
   little white three-fingered gloves?
   (*End Credits. Music up.*)
   (*Dolores and Company come back and sing a reprise of NEVER
   JUDGE A THRILLER.*)

# NEVER JUDGE A THRILLER, reprise

**DOLORES** and **GIRLS**
>I'm a thriller babe
>A serenade
>A killer babe
>I'm so glad you came
>You skimmed my pages sweetheart
>And followed my plot
>You found all the good parts
>'Cause I'm Hot Hot Hot

**COMPANY**
>Never judge a thriller by its cover, NO
>Never judge a thriller by its cover, NO
>
>I'm a best seller babe
>
>Read me straight through
>We'll give away the ending
>
>And make this old prose new
>
>Never judge a thriller by its cover NO
>Never judge a thriller by its cover NO
>Never judge a thriller by its cover NO
>
>Never, never, never, never, never
>Never, never, nooo
>
>Never, never, never, never, never
>Never, never, nooo

*(Repeat as needed.)*
*(Big finish.)*

### END OF PLAY

# IN PERPETUITY THROUGHOUT THE UNIVERSE
*This play is for Tzi Ma*


I used to stay up every night
I'd be so all alone
In my hand my trusty pen
I'd work it to the bone
Ghostwriter, writer, writer . . .

that's what they call me by name
Ghostwriter, for fortune and for fame

I been writin' down these old stories now
for eighteen years or so
People are startin' to call me a genius
I gotta tell 'em – no, no, no
A ghostwriter, writer
Tell me what do you have to do Ghostwriter, writer, writer, writer
To get your story through

*Garland Jeffries, Ghostwriter*


IN PERPETUITY THROUGHOUT THE UNIVERSE received its professional premiere on 10 May 1988, at Center Stage, Baltimore, Stan Wojewodski, Jr., Artistic Director, Peter W Culman, Managing Director. It was directed by Stan Wojewodski, Jr. The set design was by Christopher Barreca, the costume design was by Robert Wojewodski, the lighting design was by Stephen Strawbridge, the sound design was by Janet Kalas, the dramaturg was Rick Davis, and the stage manager was Meryl Lind Shaw. The cast was as follows:

| | |
|---|---|
| LYLE VIAL | Arthur Hanket |
| DENNIS WU | Tzi Ma |
| CHRISTINE PENDERECKI | Carolyn McCormick |
| MARIA MONTAGE | Jennifer Harmon |
| BUSTER | Laura Innes |
| MR. AMPERSAND QWERTY | Troy Evans |

This production was subsequently presented at the Hudson Guild Theater on 19 June 1988, Geoffrey Sherman, Producing Director.

## CHARACTERS

Dennis Wu
Christine Penderecki
Lyle Vial
Maria Montage
Buster
Mr. Ampersand Qwerty

*The actor who plays Dennis plays Tai-Tung Tranh.*

*The actor who plays Mr. Ampersand Qwerty plays Oscar Rang.*

*The actress who plays Buster plays Miss Petterson and Joculatrix.*

*The actress who plays Maria plays Claire Silver.*


## SCENE

The play takes place very late at night, in a series of offices and rooms in Manhattan.

# IN PERPETUITY THROUGHOUT THE UNIVERSE

## PART ONE

1. *Isolated in light: Tai-Tung Trahn. Thirtyish, chicly tailored businessman.*
   *Discovered with his back to the audience, curled in a ball. With an effortless leap, he jumps gracefully and lightly up on a table, and turns to the audience.*
   *He holds the backs of his hands up to the light, his fists clenched. He fans his fingers, first one hand, then the other. On the second he is wearing long, red-lacquered, Fu Manchu fingernails.*
   *He does a series of tai-chi moves, fanning his hands through the air. He turns his hands over.*
   *His palms begin to bleed. Profusely.*
   *Blackout, as*


2. *A reading lamp is turned on by Lyle.*
   *He tears open an envelope. He holds the letter up to the light and reads.*

LYLE   "This letter has been sent to you from Surinam for good luck. It has been around the world nine times. You will receive good luck six days after getting this letter. Providing you do not break the chain. This is NO JOKE." (*Making a note.*) No joke in caps. (*Reads.*) "Your good luck will also come to you through the mail. Send copies of this letter to people you think need good luck. Do not send money. Fate has no price. Do not keep this letter. It must leave your hand within 96 hours. An R.A.F. officer received $70,000 after he sent his letter out. Joe Elliot received $450,000, and lost it because he broke the chain. While in the Philippines, General Walsh broke the chain, and lost his life six days later. However, before his death, he did receive three quarters of a million dollars from a mysterious leper. Please send twenty copies of this letter to your friends and relations, and see what happens to you on the sixth day."
   (*Pause; Lyle turns the light off, as*)


3. *A room. Dennis turns on a lamp.*
   *Dennis and Christine, tossing unlit matches into a glass bowl.*

**DENNIS**   (*Tossing a match.*) Landlords.
**CHRISTINE**   Lawyers.
**DENNIS**   Bankers.
**CHRISTINE**   Real estate brokers.
**DENNIS**   Cab drivers.
**CHRISTINE**   Mimes.
**DENNIS**   Mimes?
**CHRISTINE**   You know. Mimes. (*She mimes.*)
**DENNIS**   Slowly for mimes. Chiropractors.
**CHRISTINE**   People who unwrap hard candies in the theatre.
**DENNIS**   Vanna White.
**CHRISTINE**   Madonna.
**DENNIS**   Garrison Keillor.
**CHRISTINE**   Mary Lou Retton.
**DENNIS**   Shirley MacLaine.
**CHRISTINE**   Andrew Lloyd Webber.
**DENNIS**   Doctor Ruth.
**CHRISTINE**   Pee Wee Herman.
**DENNIS**   Landlords.
**CHRISTINE**   We said that.
**DENNIS**   Worth repeating. Landlords.
**CHRISTINE**   Male gynecologists.
**DENNIS**   Immigration/naturalization clerks.
**CHRISTINE**   All petty bureaucrats, now and forever, world without end.
**DENNIS**   Amen.
   (*Dennis lights a match and tosses it into a bowl. The matches flare.*)
**CHRISTINE**   I love this list. This list is my favorite. People to kill after the revolution.
   (*They watch the flame.*)
**DENNIS**   Mimes.
   (*He smiles.*)
**CHRISTINE**   Always a promise for someone we hate.
   (*She turns the lamp off, as*)


**4.**   *Lyle turns on a light. He is alone. He opens a letter and reads.*

**LYLE**   "This chain comes to you from Venezuela. I myself forwarded it to you. But it is sent anonymously. Since this chain makes a tour of the world, you must make twenty copies of this letter and send it to your friends, relatives, and acquaintances. Send it anonymously. Do not put your name anywhere. In a few days, you will get a surprise. This is

true even if you are not superstitious."
(*Pause; Lyle turns the light off, as*)


**5.** *A light is turned on. Buster, Maria and Christine in the Montage Agency. Very late.*

**MARIA**  Your previous employers.
**CHRISTINE**  Brown and Scott.
**MARIA**  John Brown and Dred Scott.
**CHRISTINE**  Yes.
**MARIA**  Brown Do You Have A Restless Urge To Write Scott.
**CHRISTINE**  The original.
**MARIA**  The unsolicited of the world.
**CHRISTINE**  It was odious. Predatory.
**MARIA**  A complex and, for the client, financially exhausting fandango. Akin to dance lessons for lonely widows. Pyramid schemes. Door-to-door encyclopaedia sales in public housing projects where English is a second language.
**BUSTER**  Chain letters.
**MARIA**  The unsolicited of the world. I'm not scoffing. They paid the rent.
**CHRISTINE**  Self-delusion is always in season.
**MARIA**  A hardy perennial. What name?
**CHRISTINE**  Sorry?
**BUSTER**  Your nom de succor.
**CHRISTINE**  Ah. Albert Rutabaga.
(*Lights change.*
*A light comes on in The Brown and Scott Agency.*
*Chrstine moves to greet Oscar Rang, a shy man with a bow tie and a mss.*)
**OSCAR**  Jazzy. Zesty. Exuberant. It's a romance. But not a bodice ripper. Ballsier than a bodice ripper. More masculine. Sort of a thriller romance comedy adventure spy grand-guignol roman á clef love story. About a shy podiatrist and a gorgeous double agent with beautiful feet. Based on a true story.
**CHRISTINE**  A true story.
**OSCAR**  Loosely. Loosely based.
**CHRISTINE**  You're a podiatrist, Mr. Rang.
**OSCAR**  Yes. Yes, I am.
**CHRISTINE**  I've had several podiatrists.
**OSCAR**  Some specialties must just attract a more creative type person.
**CHRISTINE**  That must be it. Proctologists.

**OSCAR**  No. No, I wouldn't think so. No sense of humor.

**CHRISTINE**  You breached security, Mr. Rang.

**OSCAR**  I was in the neighborhood. I had an appointment with Albert. Mr. Rutabaga.

**CHRISTINE**  You rushed reception. You hurried down the hall. A loose cannon. There was no appointment. You never had one.

**OSCAR**  We've corresponded.

**CHRISTINE**  No.

**OSCAR**  Certainly. You're Mr. Rutabaga's assistant.

**CHRISTINE**  I am Mr. Rutabaga. Have been for 10 these many years. Brown and Scott's Rutabaga. For purposes of continuity. Client confidence. Many, many of our clients have been writing their first novels with Brown and Scott for many, many years. They'd never entrust their life's work to a new reader.

**OSCAR**  I see. You are – ?

**CHRISTINE**  Fourth-generation Rutabaga. Believe me, Mr. Rang, it makes no difference.

**OSCAR**  So you'll be editing my manuscript, Miss – ?

**CHRISTINE**  Christine Penderecki.

**OSCAR**  Penderecki.

**CHRISTINE**  Vetting. We like to call it vetting.

**OSCAR**  I know the term from Le Carré.

**CHRISTINE**  Sexier.

**OSCAR**  What's the first step? Vetting?

**CHRISTINE**  Vetting the manuscript is the second step. The first step is always money. For a series of escalating fees, Brown and Scott will edit your manuscript, and supervise an unlimited number of rewrites. This in no way obligates Brown and Scott to represent or otherwise promote said manuscript, but if they choose to do so, the usual onerous terms apply.

**OSCAR**  Gosh. Um, Brown and Scott represent a number of famous authors –

**CHRISTINE**  That's the hook.

**OSCAR**  Hook?

**CHRISTINE**  Yes, they do.

**OSCAR**  Chewy McTavish. Bingo Merkin. Mr. Ampersand Qwerty.

**CHRISTINE**  I don't think so.

**OSCAR**  He wrote *ZOG*.

**CHRISTINE**  Never heard of him.

**OSCAR**  *ZOG* is a great, great book.

**CHRISTINE**  Got by me.

**OSCAR**  Does Mr. Brown ever represent someone like me?

**CHRISTINE**  A podiatrist?

**OSCAR**  No, that's not what I – someone like me – unpublished, new –

**CHRISTINE**  Unsolicited?

**OSCAR**  Unsolicited. Does Mr. Brown ever represent unsolicited authors?

**CHRISTINE**  It's been known to happen.

**OSCAR**  Yes. Yes, it has.

**CHRISTINE**  Known to.

**OSCAR**  Chewy McTavish.

**CHRISTINE**  So the story goes.

**OSCAR**  They were hijacked together. A men's room in Morocco.

**CHRISTINE**  So the story goes.

**OSCAR**  Perhaps Mr. Brown will represent my novel. When it's finished.

**CHRISTINE**  You never can tell. After the sixth or so draft, he always takes a look.

**OSCAR**  Sixth or so? Oh, gee. Do you really think it might need that much work?

**CHRISTINE**  Brown and Scott like to say books are never written. They're rewritten.

**OSCAR**  How true. How true.

**CHRISTINE**  Very wise men, Brown and Scott. They also like to say the client never writes just one check.

**OSCAR**  Money is no object, Miss Penderecki. I'm in this for the duration.

**CHRISTINE**  That's swell, Mr. Rang. Leave a check with Phyllis on your way out.

**OSCAR**  Thank you, Miss Penderecki. Thank you so much. I look forward to working with you.

*(Oscar exits. Lights change.*
*Christine returns to The Montage Agency, and Buster and Maria.)*

**CHRISTINE**  No more mid-life crisis novels by housewives and businessmen. No more slim volumes of inspirational verse. No more Self-Help-How-To-Be-Your-Own-Best-Friend-Diet-Masturbation-And-Gardening Books. Why are we conducting this interview after midnight?

**MARIA**  No doubt Albert Rutabaga lives on after you.

**CHRISTINE**  No doubt.

*(Pause.)*

**MARIA**  I represent a handful of writers – no, let's call them *authors* – authors with intermittent literary cachet and *People* magazine profile. Their names appear semi-regularly in boldface in the better gossip columns.

**CHRISTINE**  The hook.

**MARIA**  Hook?

**CHRISTINE**   For the unsolicited of the world. The hook. The flashing lure. The glisten.

**MARIA**   The glisten. Yes.

**CHRISTINE**   The slender between-you-and-me illusory chance that super-agent Maria Montage herself will represent my first novel, negotiating over power lunch six-figure deals for spinoffs and sequels in all forms now known or hereafter invented in perpetuity throughout the universe.

(*Pause;*
*Maria moves to the window.*)

**MARIA**   I like the solace. The ambient hum. I like the preternatural hush of offices after business hours. The checkerboard of lit and unlit windows in the buildings across the airspace. We are tempted to speculate. We are tempted to discern patterns. Frame tales. Here a lonely cleaning lady. Here an after-hours word-processor, no doubt an aspiring something, a struggling artiste, word-processing not his chosen profession. Here a bankruptcy. An embezzlement. The consumption of a controlled substance. A dalliance between married members of the same sex. A woman in a fur bikini. And many, many lawyers. Of course. Four and twenty windows, and a lawyer's face in every one. This idle speculation, this discernment of shadows and fog, is what we do. What our writers do. After all.

(*Pause.She turns from window.*)

**MARIA**   I no longer deal with the unsolicited of the world. Unless they have their own publishing. Unless they are self-propelled. Those with a restless urge to write are on their own. No more nickle-dime rewrites. No more sniveling self-expression. Now all my clients pay up front in full for their delusions.

**CHRISTINE**   How can you give up unsolicited? Don't you have a condo in Carmel? Home in Majorca? Guatemalan maid?

**MARIA**   I have seen the light. My new clients deal in radical themes. Hold views mainstream publishers find – repugnant.

**CHRISTINE**   Ah. Vanity publishing.

**MARIA**   Who's to say? Their works sell well.

**BUSTER**   This is more than a market. It's a constituency.

**MARIA**   Part of my new roster. New look. New image for Montage. Along with my commercial – Buster, what's that quaint Yiddishism?

**BUSTER**   Schlockmeisters.

**MARIA**   Along with my schlockmeisters, I am collecting apostles of paranoia.

**BUSTER**   Conspiracy theorists.

**MARIA**   Of the left and right – but these days mostly right. Paranoia transcends politics. Becomes spiritual. All sorts of believers come to me. Translators of the arcane, the alchemical, the occult. And the odd billionaire whose slim volume of inspirational verse composed while ravaging a rain forest will be published on silk sheets and bound between the leather of an endangered species.

**CHRISTINE**  Magic.

**BUSTER**  Panic. Panic.

**MARIA**  The color of these true believers on the political spectrum does not interest me. Prose style is apolitical. And Montage sees the prose is polished.

**CHRISTINE**  That's the job.

**MARIA**  Yes.

**CHRISTINE**  Ghostwriter. Ghost writer.

**BUSTER**  Yes.

**MARIA**  A service. Rather more honest than the perpetual but expensive opiate paregoric you've been doling out to the ever-hopeful ever-pathetic at Brown and Scott.

*(Buster hands Christine a book.)*

**BUSTER**  Mr. Ampersand Qwerty.

**CHRISTINE**  I've heard the name.

**MARIA**  Mr. Ampersand Qwerty is one of the self-propelled. Mr. Ampersand Qwerty has no need of Random House.

*(Dennis appears in a light in another room.)*

**DENNIS**  He has Snowstorm. Snowstorm. The publishing arm of Aryan Universe.

**CHRISTINE**  Aryan Universe?

**DENNIS**  An organization dedicated to insuring white supremacy throughout the galaxy.

**CHRISTINE**  Do you believe in inter-galactic contact?

**DENNIS**  Did she tell you about Mr. Ampersand Qwerty?

**MARIA**  Mr. Ampersand Qwerty's works sell well. Precise figures are unobtainable. They do not appear on best-seller lists or in chain bookstores. Mr. Ampersand Qwerty's face has never graced the cover of a national publication printed on glossy stock. Nor are his books to be found in libraries. With the exception of smaller municipalities in the Great Basin-Plateau area.

**BUSTER**  High desert. Semi-arid.

**DENNIS**  Mr. Ampersand Qwerty is the author, so to speak, of several speculative books detailing a series of interlocking global conspiracies. A precise geography of hate. A visceral cartography of paranoia. Mr. Ampersand Qwerty's last book –

**BUSTER**  *ZOG*, which you have before you –

**CHRISTINE**  *ZOG* –

**DENNIS**  *ZOG* –

**BUSTER**  Not a biography of the late much-loved king of Albania –

**DENNIS**  *ZOG* is a white Christian supremacist acronym for Zionist Occupation Government.

**CHRISTINE**  Zionist Occupation Government.

**DENNIS**  The one you pay your taxes to. In Washington D.C.F.Y.I.

**CHRISTINE**  F.Y.I.

**DENNIS**  For your information.

**BUSTER**  *ZOG* did particularly well in the Great Basin-Plateau area.

**MARIA**  I'm going to put the office on a nocturnal schedule.

**CHRISTINE**  I'm sorry? Nocturnal? Evening hours?

**DENNIS**  She mean graveyard?

**BUSTER**  As opposed to diurnal.

**MARIA**  Midnight to dawn.

**CHRISTINE**  How unusual.

**BUSTER**  Some seasonal fluctuation. Keyed to sunrise.

**DENNIS**  I've lost my engagement book. My life is over anyway. What the fuck.

**MARIA**  I think it will put us more in touch with the paranoid impulses of the night.

**CHRISTINE**  It will me, I'm sure.

**MARIA**  I'm particularly interested in the universal ebb.

**CHRISTINE**  Ebb.

**MARIA**  Just before dawn. When the pulse – slumps.

**CHRISTINE**  I'm game.

**BUSTER**  Welcome to Montage, Miss Penderecki.

**CHRISTINE**  Ghostwriter. Who was Mr. Ampersand Qwerty's previous ghostwriter? For *ZOG?*

**DENNIS**  Lefkowitz.

**BUSTER**  Lefkowitz.

**MARIA**  Lefkowitz.

**CHRISTINE**  Lefkowitz. What happened to Lefkowitz?
  (*Dennis disappears.*)

**MARIA**  I don't know. We've lost touch.

**BUSTER**  We are awaiting Mr. Ampersand Qwerty's new material. As soon as he delivers it, you'll start writing.
  (*Christine gets up to leave.*)

**MARIA**  You know one of my staff.

**BUSTER**  Dennis Wu.

**CHRISTINE**  Yes.
  (*Pause. Maria smiles. Christine exits.*)

**MARIA**  Where is Lyle?

**BUSTER**  Vetting *Geronimo.*
  (*As Maria turns out the light,*)

**6.** *Lyle turns on a light. He is alone. He has an absolutely enormous manuscript before him.*

**LYLE** *Geronimo. (Beat.)* Part One. *(Pause. Lyle turns out the light, as)*


**7.** *The office. As always, very late. Dennis and Christine are playing the Chinese drinking game.*
*Dennis wins three rounds in a row.*

**DENNIS** Five. Ten. Drink. *(She drinks.)* Fifteen. Twenty. Drink. *(She drinks.)* Nothing. Five. *(She drinks.)*
**CHRISTINE** Fuck you, Wu.
**DENNIS** You'll get the hang of it.
*(Buster enters office, pushing a dim sum cart loaded with manuscripts.)*
**DENNIS** Love your dim sum cart.
*(Buster hands him three manuscripts.)*
**BUSTER** Dim sum du jour. Har gow. Shew my. Nor my gai.
**DENNIS** Three is a comic number in English. Why is that? Americans always tell jokes in three parts. A priest, a minister and a rabbi. A Jew, a Chinese, and an Italian on an iceberg. A talking dog in a bar always has three things to say: "roof," "roof," and "Dimaggio, maybe?" Weird custom.
**CHRISTINE** Tell a joke Chinese-style.
**DENNIS** Chinese-style?
*(Dennis tells an elaborate joke in Chinese. Long. With gestures. He finishes.)*
**CHRISTINE** I've heard that one.
**DENNIS** You should have stopped me.
**CHRISTINE** And I've heard it told better.
**DENNIS** You tell it.
**CHRISTINE** How's the punchline go again?
*(Dennis repeats punchline.*
*Christine repeats entire joke in Chinese, with gestures, verbatim, perfectly.*
*Beat. Dennis, stone-faced:)*
**DENNIS** You're just not a funny person.
**CHRISTINE** Fuck you, Wu.
*(Buster, in a light.)*
**BUSTER** I've been with Montage since the beginning. Before the beginning. My career as Maria's major-domo has been a real eye-opener. I now believe many things I didn't even know about before.

*(Christine and Buster exit. Dennis turns out the light, as)*

**8.** *Lyle turns on a light. He is alone, working, halfway through the gargantuan Geronimo mss.*

**LYLE** *(Sings.)* Oh, Lord, take me back I wanna ride in Geronimo's Cadillac.
*(Pause Lyle sighs, turns off light, as)*

**9.** *Dennis turns on an office light. Christine enters, with a copy of ZOG.*

**DENNIS** Check out *ZOG?*
**CHRISTINE** Dennis. Zionist Occupation Government. Is he serious?
**DENNIS** So serious.
**CHRISTINE** I thought this stuff went out of style. Years ago. Bad taste. Mouthful of ashes.
**DENNIS** It's like Dracula. You have to drive a stake through its heart. On the anti-Semitic spectrum, Mr. Ampersand Qwerty is a moderate. Compared to the Christian Identity folks. Who believe Jews are, you know. Of the devil.
**CHRISTINE** Offspring.
**DENNIS** Spawn.
**CHRISTINE** Dennis. How can you write this?
**DENNIS** I'm not writing it. I'm ghostwriting it.
*(Pause.)*
**DENNIS** Besides, Lefkowitz did *ZOG.* And he didn't flinch. This stuff is marginal in America. Maria's clients are marginal.
**CHRISTINE** I thought you said they were a constituency.
**DENNIS** A marginal constituency.
*(Pause.)*
**CHRISTINE** Dennis. Did you tell Maria I was looking for a job?
**DENNIS** No.
**CHRISTINE** Then why did Buster call me?
*(Buster in a light.)*
**BUSTER** Miss Penderecki.
**CHRISTINE** Yes?
**BUSTER** We understand Brown and Scott grow tiresome. We understand you shop around. We offer you surcease from unsolicited.
**CHRISTINE** Paradise.
**BUSTER** Are you interview receptive?
**CHRISTINE** Sorry?

**BUSTER**  When can you come in?

**CHRISTINE**  Sorry?

**BUSTER**  Tonight.

**CHRISTINE**  What time?

**BUSTER**  Late.

**CHRISTINE**  How late?

**BUSTER**  Very late.

**CHRISTINE**  How late is very late?

**BUSTER**  After midnight.

**CHRISTINE**  After midnight.

**BUSTER**  Before dawn.

**CHRISTINE**  Why?

**BUSTER**  It's a science project.

(*Pause.*)

**CHRISTINE**  You're joking.

**BUSTER**  Maria prefers.

**CHRISTINE**  Okay. Why not? Where?

**BUSTER**  At Montage. In the Flatiron. We're in the apex. Above the Tiger Balm Massage Parlor. It says "Never Closed – Always Open." In Korean neon.

**CHRISTINE**  Never closed – always open. I like that.

**BUSTER**  Redundant but not redundant. Never closed – always open. Korean neon koan.

(*Buster disappears.*)

**DENNIS**  Maria knows John Brown and Dred Scott. They have lunch.

**CHRISTINE**  She does. So then why did she ask me about them in my interview?

**DENNIS**  To see if you'd lie. To see if you'd tell the truth.

**CHRISTINE**  Never closed. Always open.

(*Christine picks up ZOG.*)

**CHRISTINE**  I can't wait to see Mr. Ampersand Qwerty's new manuscript. What vile conspiracy rears its godless head. I overheard two women in the ladies room discussing the low-frequency sound beam the Soviets are aiming at some city in the Midwest.

**DENNIS**  What's it do?

**CHRISTINE**  Makes everyone irritable. Depressed.

**DENNIS**  Why blame it on the Soviets? I'd be depressed if I lived in the Midwest.

**CHRISTINE**  A subliminal Russian rumble. Somewhere in South Dakota.

**DENNIS**  There are no cities in South Dakota.

**CHRISTINE**  It's a theory.

**DENNIS**  Everyone has a conspiracy theory.

**CHRISTINE**  I must take another look at *ZOG*. Take a look. Strange phrase. Take a look. Take. A. Look. (*Beat.*) Always a promise for someone we hate.
(*She turns out the lights as*)


**10.**  *Lyle turns on a light. He is alone, seemingly, with the enormous Geronimo mss.*

**LYLE**  Tony and Susan Geronimo. Charismatic pentacostalists. Listen to this. "Most nuns, and many priests, not to mention the vast majority of lay Catholics, are unaware of the Vatican conspiracy. They are unaware that the Vatican, the Red Whore of the Apocalypse, controls the global media, popular entertainment, and the worldwide trade in narcotics, arms, pornography, and white slavery. They are unaware that the Vatican's thrall extends over the Kremlin AND the White House."
(*Dennis appears.*)
**DENNIS**  China?
**LYLE**  Not a dent.
**DENNIS**  Superior culture tells.
**LYLE**  Listen to this. "The Vatican sponsored and controlled the Bolshevik Revolution, bankrolled the Nazi rise to power, and engineered the Holocaust."
**DENNIS**  That's a taste-free assertion.
**LYLE**  Unbelievable. And I mean that in the pre-lapsarian sense of the word.
**DENNIS**  Is it well-written?
**LYLE**  Shaky prose style.
**DENNIS**  That's why they come to Montage.
**LYLE**  That's why. This is my favorite. "It is a well-known fact that the Vatican assassinated Lincoln."
**DENNIS**  I heard that in Hong Kong.
**LYLE**  That's the sort of place you'd hear something like that. Jacket blurb: "Irrefutably proves the Pope is the anti-Christ – Satan's representative on Earth."
(*Lyle hands mss. to Dennis and disappears.*)
**DENNIS**  I can believe that. The guy wears a mumu.
(*Christine appears. Dennis fondles Geronimo.*)
**DENNIS**  I get a warm, warm feeling from this. Vast sinister networks.
**CHRISTINE**  Dennis, were you ever Lefkowitz?
**DENNIS**  I've perused the material. I was interim Lefkowitz. I was Lefkowitz for a week. I did the last chapter of *ZOG*. I love Papist

conspiracies.

(*Christine takes Geronimo mss. from him.*)

**CHRISTINE**   How many legions has the Pope?

**DENNIS**   Stalin.

**CHRISTINE**   Very good. Stalin.

**DENNIS**   Divisions. How many divisions has the Pope.

**CHRISTINE**   Legions is more romantic.

**DENNIS**   I wouldn't characterize Stalin as high romantic.

**CHRISTINE**   The hidden Stalin. The unknown Stalin. Stalin at home. A
side of the man we don't usually see. Do you believe in inter-galactic
contact?

**DENNIS**   Are you a resident alien?

(*They kiss, passionately. Maria enters. She watches for a moment.
Then:*)

**MARIA**   Christine. Dennis. Have you seen Lyle?

**DENNIS**   He was here.

**MARIA**   Has he brought in *Geronimo?*

**DENNIS**   Maria. Have you seen my book?

**CHRISTINE**   He left the manuscript.

**MARIA**   Give it me. No. What book?

**DENNIS**   My engagement book.

**MARIA**   No.

**DENNIS**   My life is over.

**MARIA**   Mine would be.

(*Maria exits with Geronimo mss.*)

**CHRISTINE**   Oy.

(*Lyle appears.*)

**LYLE**   The best part of the Geronimo program is the Geronimo
Foundation. The Geronimo Foundation buys babies. They intercept
unwed mothers on the abortion clinic doorstep, and pay them big
bucks to have the baby and give it to the Geronimos. Then the
Geronimos put it up for adoption.

**CHRISTINE**   Meanwhile bombing the clinic.

**LYLE**   You can't prove that. Although they may inadvertently contribute
to the climate of violence –

**CHRISTINE**   They'd never resort to violence itself.

**DENNIS**   Never.

**CHRISTINE**   Even to do the Lord's work.

**LYLE**   Well maybe the Lord's work.

**CHRISTINE**   What's the catch?

**LYLE**   The catch. Why should there be a catch?

**CHRISTINE**   There's always a catch.

**LYLE**   The catch is they never place the little suckers. That's the catch.

**CHRISTINE**  The babies.

**LYLE**  Right. They never put 'em up for adoption. They keep 'em. They put 'em in these baby camps. Fascist incubators. They raise 'em up to become storm troopers of the Lord.

**CHRISTINE**  Where is this baby camp?

**LYLE**  Somewhere in California.

**CHRISTINE**  Quite a conspiracy.

**LYLE**  Everyone has a conspiracy theory. How can you explain the world without a conspiracy theory?

*(Lyle disappears.)*

**CHRISTINE**  You and Lyle. You're both as paranoid as they are.

**DENNIS**  Everyone has a conspiracy theory.

**CHRISTINE**  I don't.

**DENNIS**  You should. How can you explain the world without a conspiracy theory?

**CHRISTINE**  I can't. I don't.

*(Pause.)*

**CHRISTINE**  How is your conspiracy theory different from their conspiracy theory?

**DENNIS**  They have guns. Machine guns. With silencers. Uzis.

**CHRISTINE**  Great names, though. Aryan Universe.

**DENNIS**  You have to admire the names.

**CHRISTINE**  Aryan Universe. Snowstorm. The Arm The Sword and The Handgun of the Lord.

**DENNIS**  Fortress America. Posse Comatose. The Church of Jesus Christ White Man.

**CHRISTINE**  Do you believe in inter-galactic contact?

**DENNIS**  Camaros of the Gods.

**CHRISTINE**  Camaros of the Gods.

**DENNIS**  No way.

**CHRISTINE**  I don't get you, Wu. You believe in fascist baby camps, but you don't believe in inter-galactic contact.

**DENNIS**  Oh, man.

**CHRISTINE**  We can still be friends.

**DENNIS**  Are we friends?

**CHRISTINE**  If we were, we could still be.

*(They kiss. Christine turns out light, as)*


**11.**  *Buster turns on a light. She is alone.*

**BUSTER**  I'm not a true believer, but you can convince me with facts. Tone of voice. Sincerity. I know when someone's telling the truth.

(*Pause.*)

BUSTER    I believe in automatic writing. I believe in out-of-body experiences. I believe anything and everything about Tibetan lamas, no questions asked. I believe Paul *is* dead. I believe in the white alligators in the sewers of New York who cause the steam to rise when they screw. I believe the assassination conspiracies. I know the CIA killed Kennedy, the FBI killed King, and the NYPD killed Malcolm X. I don't know about Bobby, but I have my theories. I believe the Jesuits killed John Paul I. I believe the Society of the Deadly Palm touched Bruce Lee in a certain way, and his blood sickened and he died three months later. Just touched him. Like this. Dennis also told me about the Chinese Mafia in Amsterdam who deal in diamonds and rhinocerous horn.

(*Pause.*)

BUSTER    I'm not sold on Maria's new clients. Yet. I don't believe the KGB is the root of all evil. But then again, who's to say? I certainly don't believe the Vatican is secretly financing abortion clinics and encouraging illegal immigration from non-white Catholic countries so that White America will be overwhelmed by large brown Catholic families. Some people do.

(*Pause.*)

BUSTER    I know AIDS is a CIA experiment they were running in Central Africa that got away from them. A mutated strain. Zaire. Haiti. New York. San Francisco.

(*Pause.*)

BUSTER    I believe in inter-galactic contact.
(*She turns the light off as*)


**12.**  *Lights come on in office.*
*Christine and Dennis are playing the Chinese drinking game. Lyle enters.*


LYLE    You got it, you got it, no doubt about it. Huddle and cling, huddle and cling. Which game is this?

DENNIS    Chinese drinking game.

LYLE    Who's winning?

CHRISTINE    He is.

LYLE    What are the rules?

CHRISTINE    He won't tell me. He says I'll pick it up as I go along.
(*Buster comes through with her dim sum cart, wearing a slouch hat.*)

BUSTER    Read 'em and weep. Fry your retinas on these.

CHRISTINE    Dash Hammett.

**BUSTER** Ray Chandler. My middle name is Noir.
**LYLE** What's your last name?
**BUSTER** Not a chance. Today's catch.
*(Buster hands Lyle a large stack of manuscripts.)*
**LYLE** Oh, for a short stack. My life is over.
**CHRISTINE** So's his.
**DENNIS** I've lost my engagement book.
**LYLE** I guess you won't be going out anymore.
**BUSTER** No more satin nights.
**LYLE** No more balmy dawns.
**BUSTER** That's all over now, baby blue.
**LYLE** No more controlled substances.
**BUSTER** No more wet sticky sex.
**LYLE** No more civilized conversation in boites.
**CHRISTINE** What's boites?
**BUSTER** A life of silence. A life of contemplation. A life of home
  entertainment. VCR – R.I.P.
**LYLE** Perhaps people will call.
**BUSTER** They'll assume he's died. Wonder what happened to old Dee
  Dub? Haven't heard from him he must be dead.
**LYLE** You're right. Speaking of dying. I was on the train coming down.
  Packed ass to forehead, as per usual. It's always rush hour on the IRT.
  Even after midnight. There was a woman standing in front of me. I was
  sitting. Attractive. Very attractive. Asian, Dennis, I don't mind telling
  you. Wearing very tight slacks. Lemon-colored slacks. Mid-twenties.
  Beautiful body. Beautiful. This luscious curve. Her belly. The inner
  thigh. There's something about that curve. Makes you ache. The way
  the belly curves, under. The tops of the legs. Ache. I had this urge. No.
  I was seized, yes, seized by desire. I'm sitting, she's standing, inches
  away. I can touch her crotch with my breath. I feel hot. Dazzled. I want
  to slide my hand in, ever so gently, my hand, slip it between her legs.
  Caress that curve. Slowly. In. Up. Obviously I didn't do it. I wouldn't
  be standing here telling you about it now. I'd be calling you from
  Riker's Island.
  *(Pause.)*
**LYLE** I have these moments. Runaway impulse. Stroke a stranger.
  Shoplift. Turn the wheel at 75 into the center divider. Late night
  moments of derangement. She would have screamed. Rightly so. She
  would have called for help. Called the police. I meant no harm. It was
  a tender impulse. A bad moment. I sat there, looking at that curve, stop
  after stop after stop, in a cold sweat. Aching to touch her. Shaking. I
  put my hands under my legs. I didn't trust myself. And my desire, by
  then, all tangled up with "My God, what are you doing? What are

you?" Finally, I got up and got off the train a stop early, careful not to brush against her. I would have done it. I had vertigo. I wanted. Wanted to go over. It became so clear to me. Transparent. All I had to do was slip my hand between her legs, caress this stranger for a moment, and my life would be over. My life as I know it. And I realized how you can throw your life away. Like that. In an instant. (*Silence.*)

**DENNIS**  This just happened?

**LYLE**  My life is a mystery to me.

(*Maria enters with a man in a bow tie.*)

**MARIA**  This is my staff. One of our most valued clients. Mr. Ampersand Qwerty, author of *ZOG*. Dennis Wu.

**DENNIS**  How you doin'?

**MR. AMPERSAND QWERTY**  Mainland, Taipei, or Hong Kong?

**DENNIS**  Staten Island.

**MR. AMPERSAND QWERTY**  Of course, of course.

**MARIA**  Lyle Vial.

**LYLE**  Like a pill bottle.

**MR. AMPERSAND QWERTY**  Lyle Vial. You know Biff Liff?

**MARIA**  And this is Christine Penderecki.

**MR. AMPERSAND QWERTY**  Charmed. Astonished. Where is Mr. Lefkowitz?

**MARIA**  Working at home today.

**MR. AMPERSAND QWERTY**  Rumor has it Mr. Lefkowitz is no longer with us.

**MARIA**  Us?

**MR. AMPERSAND QWERTY**  You. Montage.

**MARIA**  Not at all.

**MR. AMPERSAND QWERTY**  Word on the street. Deal with it.

(*Pause. Lyle slips out, unnoticed.*)

**MR. AMPERSAND QWERTY**  You'll see that he gets the new material.

**MARIA**  I'll hand deliver it.

(*Mr. Ampersand Qwerty gives Buster a thick file.*)

**MR. AMPERSAND QWERTY**  Lefkowitz did a super job on *ZOG*. Just stupendous. So long.

(*He starts out.*)

**BUSTER**  This way out, Mr. Ampersand Qwerty.

(*Buster shows Mr. Ampersand Qwerty out.*)

**CHRISTINE**  He doesn't know.

**MARIA**  Don't be ridiculous.

**CHRISTINE**  If he finds out.

**MARIA**  He won't. You'll study the file. You'll cop the style. As Dennis would say.

**DENNIS**  Very good, Maria. Way to speak American.

**MARIA**  Thank you. Where's Lyle?

**CHRISTINE**  Lefkowitz did *ZOG*.

**MARIA**  Most of it. All but the last chapter. Dennis did that.

**DENNIS**  I did it perfect, man. If he only knew.

**MARIA**  My little joke.

**CHRISTINE**  Why Lefkowitz?

**MARIA**  Mr. Ampersand Qwerty requested him.

**CHRISTINE**  Lefkowitz. Isn't Lefkowitz a Jewish name?

**MARIA**  Of course.

**CHRISTINE**  I don't understand.

**MARIA**  Something about a challenge. A provocation. A deep-seated belief in their superiority. He must be the best, he said. Who knows? Besides, you don't really think Mr. Ampersand Qwerty believes all that, do you?

(*Silence.*)

**CHRISTINE**  Why didn't he finish *ZOG?* Lefkowitz?

**MARIA**  Disappeared. Vanished without a trace. Nothing missing from his efficiency apartment. Every page in place. Very neat, Lefkowitz. One might say anal. We reported to the police. Sub rosa. 1 didn't see any point in telling the clients. I still don't.

(*As the lights go out in the office*)

**13.**  *A pool of light up on Lyle. He opens a letter and reads.*

**LYLE**  "Constantine Dat received the chain in 1959. He asked his secretary to make twenty copies and then forgot about it. A few days later, he lost his job. While berserkly searching for a revolver with which to slaughter his boss, his foreman, a co-worker who owed him twenty dollars, and another he suspected of sleeping with his wife, along with several relatively innocent bystanders, he found the chain in his upper right-hand desk drawer. The next day he sent it out to twenty friends and relatives he had intended to gun down in the street like dogs. Five days later he got an even better job and threw the revolver away. For No Reason Should This Chain Be Broken. Remember, send no money. It really, really works."

(*Lyle turns the light out as*)

**14.**  *Christine turns on a light in her room.*

**CHRISTINE**   It was just before dawn when I began vetting Mr. Ampersand Qwerty's material. The universal ebb. The time of night when you see things scuttle across the floor out of the corner of your eye. Mr. Ampersand Qwerty's manuscript concerned a conspiracy. Of course. Conspire. To breathe together. That would be my guess. (*She opens the file.*)

**CHRISTINE**   He began with a note to Lefkowitz.
(*Mr. Ampersand Qwerty appears in a light.*)

**MR. AMPERSAND QWERTY**   We think the pop-fic approach the right approach for this – campaign. The non-fiction novel. The novel as history. History, a novel. Reality/Fiction. America's ready for it. America's in the mood. A best-seller, Lefkowitz. (*Sings softly.*) Movin' on up, movin' on up. (*Breaks off.*) Begin with the following preface: Dear Reader. The imaginative and speculative inquiry. Fact or fiction. The boundaries blur. When the source is "deep." When a thoughtless footnote might mean the sudden death of an agent in a far-off cold country. Then the techniques of fiction serve the interests of truth. A paradox? Perhaps. The story I am about to tell you is full of paradoxes. Rest assured every word of this astonishing tale is true. Don't scoff. Turn the page. Be amazed.
(*Christine turns the page.*)

**MR. AMPERSAND QWERTY**   Here are the facts. Make it up, Lefkowitz, make it up. Don't forget to mention the Hmong. The mysterious deaths among the Hmong.
(*Mr. Ampersand Qwerty vanishes.*)

**CHRISTINE**   Mr. Ampersand Qwerty's file was a jumble of pamphlets, charts, wire-tap transcripts, immigration statistics, notes scribbled on cocktail napkins. Held together by a malignant certainty. This certainty promised and suggested a narrative. As I read, I began to feel a certain minor genre of pulp fiction might be successfully resuscitated for Mr. Ampersand Qwerty's ends. I started to sketch out an improbable plot. Using as my point of embarcation an alleged transcript of a purported interview.
(*Christine moves to a computer terminal and switches it on; it gives off a green glow. She begins to write.*
*Silence*
*Ghostly electric guitar in the far distance.*
*Claire Silver (Maria) appears.*)

**CLAIRE**   Following the debacle in Southeast Asia, with typical American naïveté, we welcomed the debris of Indochina into our country. We not only embrace our enemies after hostilities cease, we bare our necks and hand them swords. Boat people. Opportunists. Double agents. Triple agents. Parasites. Warlords and drug dealers.

Arms smugglers. With a big open-mouthed kiss we sucked the virus into our body politic. The analogy seems apt in this time of plague. (*Tai-Tung Tranh appears.*)

**TAI-TUNG TRANH**   Plagues and rumors of plagues.

**CLAIRE**   Thank you for seeing me, Mr. Tranh.

**TAI-TUNG TRANH**   It is brave of you to come, Mrs. Silver.

**CLAIRE**   Knowing what I know about you?

**TAI-TUNG TRANH**   If I were what you think I am. But I'm not.

**CLAIRE**   I know who you are.

**TAI-TUNG TRANH**   A merchant.

**CLAIRE**   A gangster.

(*Pause.*)

**TAI-TUNG TRANH**   Mrs. Claire Silver. A professional conspiracy theorist. Tracing the strands of the web back to the KGB spider. This bombing of a synagogue by a PLO splinter group in Brussels. This assassination of a Turkish consul and used car dealer in Los Angeles by Armenian terrorists. This heart attack of a Bulgarian dissident in London. You bring these incidents together. You make sense of them. You discern patterns. You seek a mastermind.

**CLAIRE**   Something like that. You've read my book?

**TAI-TUNG TRANH**   Your theories are well known. America is an amazing country. The most arcane professions of my homeland seem humdrum here. I come from a family of astrologers. In America, you have astrology in your morning paper. What is your theory about Tai-Tung Tranh?

**CLAIRE**   You are a former colonel in the Army of the Republic of Viet Nam.

**TAI-TUNG TRANH**   Mrs. Silver. Please. Take a close look. How old am I?

**CLAIRE**   I don't know. I've never been able to make out Asian ages.

**TAI-TUNG TRANH**   I am thirty-one. Too young, Mrs. Silver. Too young to have been a colonel. Even in the last days. When they were drafting twelve-year-old boys. No teenage colonels, Mrs. Silver. Your sources have made a basic mistake. They have confused me with my father. An understandable error. We all look alike. Fathers and sons, I mean. My father was a colonel in the ARVN. After the war – a redolent phrase, don't you think?

**CLAIRE**   After the war. Yes.

**TAI-TUNG TRANH**   After the war. After the war, my father – the Colonel—came to this country. He was forced to start from scratch. He took a job as a waiter. His fellow officers became cooks, bus drivers, postmen. His oldest friend, a neurosurgeon – a janitor at a private school. My uncles, a philosopher and a cellist, now own a small hand laundry in Greenwich Village. And so on. After the war, people of all classes risked life and limb to come to this country, where they were welcomed according to the time-honored American principles of refuge. Principles which make this beautiful country unique in the history of the world.

**CLAIRE**  Are you being ironic?

**TAI-TUNG TRANH**  Not at all.

**CLAIRE**  Good. You have no right.

**TAI-TUNG TRANH**  America transcends irony, Mrs. Silver. General Ky himself sold liquor in southern California. The doorman at your health club was a warlord in the Mekong Delta.

**CLAIRE**  You have been spying on me.

**TAI-TUNG TRANH**  A fairly notorious fellow. Do not forget him at Christmas time.

**CLAIRE**  Are you threatening me, Mr. Tranh?

**TAI-TUNG TRANH**  I am a merchant. I sell fish sauce and condiments. Do you care for Vietnamese cuisine?

**CLAIRE**  You are the oriental crime czar of a new Indo-Chinese Mafia which traffics in arms, narcotics, prostitution, and aliens.

**TAI-TUNG TRANH**  Asian crime czar. Orientals are rugs.

**CLAIRE**  You deny it?

**TAI-TUNG TRANH**  Mrs. Silver. In Saigon, we had servants. Do you understand? Now we are Americans. I sell fish sauce and condiments. You have crowned me the king of this imaginary criminal conspiracy. I am not your spider. The web is only in your mind.

**CLAIRE**  Hmong.

**TAI-TUNG TRANH**  Mung?

**CLAIRE**  Hmong.

**TAI-TUNG TRANH**  Mung is a bean, Mrs. Silver.

**CLAIRE**  Hmong is a people, Mr. Tranh, as you well know. Hill people from Laos.

**TAI-TUNG TRANH**  I know nothing of Laos.

**CLAIRE**  They worked for the CIA during the war.

**TAI-TUNG TRANH**  So did your doorman. They ran smack together.

**CLAIRE**  Now you are being offensive.

**TAI-TUNG TRANH**  Everyone knows the CIA ran heroin during the war. Air America. Claire Chenault. KMT warlords. The Shan states. Fortunes were made.

**CLAIRE**  Rubbish. Communist propaganda.

**TAI-TUNG TRANH**  You believe your conspiracies, and I'll believe mine.

**CLAIRE**  There have been a rash of mysterious deaths among the Hmong. I have reason to believe you know what is killing the Hmong.

**TAI-TUNG TRANH**   One of my favorite American things is the B movie. You sound like a B movie, Mrs. Silver. I have reason to believe. Rash of mysterious deaths. I know nothing of the Hmong.

**CLAIRE**   I believe you are instrumental in causing those deaths.

**TAI-TUNG TRANH**   Now you are being offensive.

(*He claps his hands. Miss Peterson (Buster) appears.*)

**TAI-TUNG TRANH**   Miss Peterson. Show Mrs. Silver out.

**CLAIRE**   I can find my own way. (*She exits.*)

**TAI-TUNG TRANH**   If you ever need fish sauce.

(*Mr. Ampersand Qwerty appears in a light.*)

**MR. AMPERSAND QWERTY**   So the only interview on record with Mr. Tai-Tung Tranh came to an end. But so did Claire Silver's investigation.

(*Mr. Ampersand Qwerty vanishes. Lights change. Sinister oriental movie music. Tai-Tung Tranh's manner transforms from prosperous Asian-American businessman to malevolent inscrutability. He strikes a series of Peking Opera poses.*)

**TAI-TUNG TRANH**   The white devil knows too much.

(*Miss Peterson has a pronounced Eastern European accent.*)

**MISS PETERSON**   You said it.

**TAI-TUNG TRANH**   She should never have mentioned the Hmong.

**MISS PETERSON**   Here is her file.

**TAI-TUNG TRANH**   Have you memorized it?

**MISS PETERSON**   At the Acolyte Academy we were taught to anticipate.

**TAI-TUNG TRANH**   You have the soul of a spy. I have read Mrs. Silver's chart. Her moon is in a malificent house.

**MISS PETERSON**   A pity.

**TAI-TUNG TRANH**   Take care of her.

**MISS PETERSON**   With pleasure.

(*Tai-Tung Tranh vanishes. Miss Peterson travels. Claire appears.*)

**CLAIRE**   What do you want?

**MISS PETERSON**   May I come in?

**CLAIRE**   If you insist.

**MISS PETERSON**   I have come to betray my yellow master.

**CLAIRE**   Come in. Sit down. Won't you make yourself comfortable?

**MISS PETERSON**   Thank you. You are so kind.

(*Miss Peterson removes her jacket.*)

**CLAIRE**   There is a sudden smell of jasmine in the air.

**MISS PETERSON**   I am ready to tell you everything I know. Here is your file. You may find it of interest. He knows everything about you. Your family history. Your radical youth. Your real name. Your links to crypto-Fascist and proto-Fascist groups. Your frequent trips to the

Great Basin-Plateau area. Your proclivities. Your liaison with a certain southern senator's wife. I've looked in your file. I've read deeply. I've exhausted you. I know everything. What you hate. What you dream. What you crave.

(*She strokes Claire's face.*)

**MISS PETERSON**    I know what you want.

(*Miss Peterson turns out the light, as*)

15. *Lights cross-fade up to Christine asleep in her room at the computer terminal.*

*Lyle appears.*

*The light in the room changes imperceptibly. A shadow fails across Christine. She awakens.*

**CHRISTINE**    (*Starting.*) Ridiculous. Lyle?

**LYLE**    I let myself in.

**CHRISTINE**    Lyle. How did you get in?

**LYLE**    I let myself in.

(*Lyle turns on a light.*)

**LYLE**    I got this letter. It's interesting. Let's hear it.

(*He unfolds a letter and reads.*)

**LYLE**    "The Doomsday Book, the great survey of Norman England, undertaken by William the Conqueror in 1085, contains the clue. Doomsday, so-called by the common folk because there was no appeal from its authority, was a record of what everyone and anyone owned, and what it was worth. The Doomsday Book records the existence of one female jester. A joculatrix. Her name is lost. This person, this joculatrix, is the inventor of the chain letter. Her original letter was first circulated among the barons, and lesser nobles, and later the monasteries. It was lost and presumed destroyed duriting the Cromwellian Ascendency, but was later discovered, some decades after the Restoration, in a box at the Drury Lane Theatre during a performance of Sheridan's *Duenna*. It is this original chain letter, the first chain letter in the history of the world, which is being sent to you now. Do not break the chain. It is over nine hundred years old. Make twenty copies of this letter and send it to friends and acquaintances."

**CHRISTINE**    God, I can't wait. I'm damp all over. Let's hear it. The world's first chain letter.

(*Lyle searches the envelope; it's empty.*)

**LYLE**    Not here. Nada. Ah, a note. "Being mailed to you under separate cover."

**CHRISTINE**    Jeez. What a tease.

**LYLE**  The world's first chain letter.

**CHRISTINE**  The world's first comedienne.

**LYLE**  Norman standup. A riot. Sheep jokes.

**CHRISTINE**  I want to be a joculatrix when I grow up.
   (*Pause.*)

**CHRISTINE**  I fell asleep over Mr. Ampersand Qwerty's manuscript.

**LYLE**  It's getting dark.

**CHRISTINE**  Nasty stuff. White nightmare.

**LYLE**  I'm looking forward to receiving the world's first chain letter.

**CHRISTINE**  Speaking of nightmare. Have you heard of the Hmong?
   The mysterious deaths among the Hmong?

**LYLE**  How did you know I'd know?

**CHRISTINE**  You always know this sort of thing.

**LYLE**  Stone Age mountain tribesmen. Hill people. Laos. Poppy farmers.
   Worked for the CIA during the war. After the war – after the war, the
   gratitude of a grateful nation. We get 'em out of Laos so the
   communists don't turn 'em into spring rolls. Bring 'em over, put 'em
   down in the middle of ex ex cee America. San Francisco, city by the
   bay. Culture clash to the max. Hunting wildlife in Golden Gate Park,
   barbequed squirrel in peanut sauce, hot and sour sparrow, eating the
   neighbor's cats and dogs. The Hmong didn't savvy supermarkets.
   (*Pause.*)

**LYLE**  The Hmong think they've been relocated to Hell. Noise, violence,
   crime. Rush hour on the Bay Bridge. The war seems peaceful by
   comparison. Cut off from their ancestors, no way to get back home
   from the land of the demons. Living in a nightmare world.
   (*Pause.*)

**LYLE**  The young men, twenty-five, thirty, start dying in their sleep. An
   epidemic. Healthy, no apparent causes. Just pop. Gone. Not a mark on
   'em. The Hmong think it's ghosts. Demons.

**CHRISTINE**  What do the doctors think it is?

**LYLE**  The doctors. The doctors think it's homesickness. Cultural
   dislocation. A broken heart. Could be. But why just the young men?
   Maybe it's Agent Orange. Maybe it's yellow rain. CIA, KGB. But no
   apparent organic cause. And why just the young men? The doctors call
   it Sudden Unexplained Nightmare Death Syndrome.
   (*Lyle smiles.*)

**LYLE**  The heart just stops in the middle of the night.
   (*He leaves. Christine goes to the computer terminal. The lights fade,
   leaving only the green glow of the monitor.
   Blackout.*)

**16.** *Dennis appears in a pool of light.*

**DENNIS**   Camaros of the Gods. Boss chariots. Visitors from outer space are the architects of certain ancient civilizations. Mayas. Incas. Egyptians. Easter Island. Atlantis. Even the Chinese. Note the absence of Greeks, Romans, Phoenecians, and Hebrews. Note the implication inherent in this cosmic scheme. These little brown people could not have built pyramids and great walls on their own, lacking as they did Western technology. Therefore, they must have had help from a superior culture. And since white people were still living in caves, it must have been white people from outer space. Who came down in their Camaros of the Gods, and spread benevolence and civilization. White people from outer space. There are no black people in Star Wars.
*(Pause.)*
**DENNIS**   Billy Dee Williams. Relax my hair. Is my hair relaxed?
*(Pause.)*
**DENNIS**   The great American yearning for the extra-terrestrial solution. What does it mean? Can it be as childish as it seems?
*(Pause.)*
**DENNIS**   I don't believe in inter-galactic contact. But I do believe in the international fascist underground.
*(Blackout, as)*


**17.** *Christine turns on a lamp. She is alone in her room. Before her, a stack of books: ratty paperbacks, library books with plastic covers, a great variety.*
*She reads the titles one by one.*

**CHRISTINE**   *Dr. Fu Manchu. President Dr. Fu Manchu. Emperor Dr. Fu Manchu. The Daughter of Dr. Fu Manchu. The Bride of Dr. Fu Manchu. The Shadow of Dr. Fu Manchu. The Drums of Dr. Fu Manchu. The Island of Dr. Fu Manchu. The Trail of Dr. Fu Manchu. The Insidious Dr. Fu Manchu. The Inscrutable Dr. Fu Manchu. The Wrath of Dr. Fu Manchu. The Mask of Dr. Fu Manchu. The Return of Dr. Fu Manchu.*
*(She turns off the lamp, as)*


**18.** *Mr. Ampersand Qwerty appears behind her. He turns on a lamp.*

**MR. AMPERSAND QWERTY**   White nightmare.

**CHRISTINE**   Pop literature. Comic books. Movies. Tabloids.

**MR. AMPERSAND QWERTY**   Symptomatic. They reflect a genuine message. An authentic impulse we ignore at our own risk. The drugstore rack –

**CHRISTINE**   The airport newsstand –

**MR. AMPERSAND QWERTY**   The supermarket checkout counter. Thermometers, on which we can read the temperature of our latest fever dreams.

**CHRISTINE**   White nightmare. Who chooses? What's available. The inventory of fantasy.

**MR. AMPERSAND QWERTY**   We do. Or rather, they do. We think the popular fiction approach the right approach for this – campaign. No one ever went broke overestimating the vulgarity of the American public.

**CHRISTINE**   H.L. Mencken.

**MR. AMPERSAND QWERTY**   Very good, Miss Penderecki. The non-fiction novel. The novel as history. History, a novel. I call it Apocalyptic Propaganda. Prophetic Jeremiad. Reality/Fiction.

**CHRISTINE**   Reality slash fiction.

**MR. AMPERSAND QWERTY**   Reality slash fiction. Precisely.

**CHRISTINE**   Polemic. Insinuation, innuendo, rumor, hearsay, prejudice. It's –

**MR. AMPERSAND QWERTY**   Yes –

**CHRISTINE**   Rather –

**MR. AMPERSAND QWERTY**   Absolutely –

**CHRISTINE**   Lurid.

**MR. AMPERSAND QWERTY**   No question.

**CHRISTINE**   Intemperate.

**MR. AMPERSAND QWERTY**   Not sober.

**CHRISTINE**   Inflammatory. Incendiary. Racist.

**MR. AMPERSAND QWERTY**   We want something which will ignite the imagination. The popular imagination.

**CHRISTINE**   *Yellow Emperor: The New Dr. Fu Manchu.*

**MR. AMPERSAND QWERTY**   Brilliant, Miss Penderecki. Brilliant. Genius stroke. We knew you were the ghostwriter for us.

**CHRISTINE**   A fairy tale. Czar of new Indo-Chinese Mafia. Murder, drugs, gun-running. It's a potboiler.

**MR. AMPERSAND QWERTY**   And how brilliant of you to rescue the Yellow Peril from the trash heap of fiction fashion. A coup.

**CHRISTINE**   It'll never fly.

**MR. AMPERSAND QWERTY**   America's ready for it. America's in the mood. This is our task. Snowstorm's task. To awaken America to this new danger. Before we vanish as a civilization.

**CHRISTINE**     Yellow peril. Asian domination of the world. A yellow emperor.

**MR. AMPERSAND QWERTY**     Don't scoff. Turn the page.

**CHRISTINE**     Sorry?

**MR. AMPERSAND QWERTY**     That's our motto. Snowstorm's motto. Don't scoff. Turn the page.

**CHRISTINE**     If this Tai-Tung Tranh person exists, so what? What's one more American Mafia? It's an accessory. Comes with every new immigrant group.

**MR. AMPERSAND QWERTY**     The hook.

**CHRISTINE**     Hook?

**MR. AMPERSAND QWERTY**     How we get the attention of White America. Give them crime. Sex. Miscegenation. Appeal to the deepest recesses of their little hearts. The assumptions they hold but don't acknowledge. That Americans have white skin and round eyes. Everyone else is – marginal. Everyone else is here on our sufferance. Everyone else has a hyphen. The tribal instinct, far from being obliterated, has reached its purest expression in this century.
(*Pause.*)

**MR. AMPERSAND QWERTY**     Don't scoff. Turn the page. There is another book. A serious study of global economics and demographics. Trends and projections. The economic aggression of Japan and the Four Tigers: Hong Kong, Singapore, Taiwan, Korea. The looming shadow of China. The sheer weight of billions and billions of people. Asian people.
(*Pause.*)

**MR. AMPERSAND QWERTY**     The color of America is changing, Miss Penderecki. By the turn of the century, you won't recognize any major American city. It won't be English as a second language. English will be the second language. Your children will have to learn Spanish or Chinese to get a job. Snowstorm does not intend to let America become a second-rate power and a Third World country.

**CHRISTINE**     America assimilates. Everyone wants to be American.

**MR. AMPERSAND QWERTY**     Too late. Too late. Too late. (*Pause. Mr. Ampersand Qwerty indicates Christine's stack of books.*)

**MR. AMPERSAND QWERTY**     *The Mask of Dr. Fu Manchu. The Diabolical Dr. Fu Manchu. The Claw of Dr. Fu Manchu.* To this day they sell well in the Great Basin-Plateau area. Curiously, after the war, the author of these books switched tactics. Dr. Fu Manchu became our ally, fighting the greater evil of communism.

**CHRISTINE**     You sound skeptical.

**MR. AMPERSAND QWERTY**     Fu Manchu as a hero did not prove popular with the American public.

**CHRISTINE**   Who is Tai-Tung Tranh? Really.

**MR. AMPERSAND QWERTY**   A merchant.

**CHRISTINE**   Fish sauce.

**MR. AMPERSAND QWERTY**   Hardly.

**CHRISTINE**   And this other book? The true story?

**MR. AMPERSAND QWERTY**   We shall slip it into the interstices of our story. Between the inter-racial sex scenes. When will you finish? Did you mention the Hmong? The mysterious deaths among the Hmong?

**CHRISTINE**   How did you know?

**MR. AMPERSAND QWERTY**   What?

**CHRISTINE**   I was the ghostwriter.

**MR. AMPERSAND QWERTY**   We chose you. We thought you might be receptive to new forms.

**CHRISTINE**   All forms now known or hereafter invented. In perpetuity throughout the universe.
(*Pause.*)

**MR. AMPERSAND QWERTY**   Contractual language. I never read contracts. My lawyers read them for me.

**CHRISTINE**   Wonderful phrase, isn't it? All forms now known or hereafter invented. In perpetuity throughout the universe. It's an attempt to buy a piece of the future. To protect oneself from the future.

**MR. AMPERSAND QWERTY**   The future is ours. If we protect ourselves.
(*Pause.*)

**CHRISTINE**   What happened to Lefkowitz?

**MR. AMPERSAND QWERTY**   He disappeared.

**CHRISTINE**   I know that.

**MR. AMPERSAND QWERTY**   So do we.
(*Mr. Ampersand Qwerty disappears. Christine turns out the light as*)

**18A.**   *Dennis turns on a light in another room. Christine moves to him. They undress each other. They make love.*
*The light gets very white, intense.*
*Sudden blackout.*

END PART ONE

# PART TWO

**19.** *Christine tums on a lamp. She is alone, in front of the word processor. She switches on the monitor. It casts a green glow.*

**CHRISTINE**   Just before dawn, I sat down to finish. I felt a queasy excitement. Illicit thrill. The Forbidden City. *Yellow Emperor: The New Dr. Fu Manchu.* I visualized the cover. A montage of faces. A handsome oriental gentleman. An attractive Caucasian woman. A flash of white breast. A ninja lurking in the background. I remembered my dream.
*(She begins writing. The green glow on her face intensifies, as the lights change. Chinese movie music, sinister, swells. Christine disappears.*
*Tai-Tung Tranh appears, as he did in the opening scene.*
*He uncurls his hands and tums the palms over. They are red and wet.*
*Miss Peterson appears. Kneels before Tai-Tung Tranh. Begins to wipe the blood off his hands.)*
**MISS PETERSON**   She bled profusely.
**TAI-TUNG TRANH**   She seemed – juiceless.
**MISS PETERSON**   She was the opposite of juiceless. She was – juicy.
**TAI-TUNG TRANH**   Succulent as bird-nest soup.
**MISS PETERSON**   Mmmmmmmm.
**TAI-TUNG TRANH**   You enjoyed.
**MISS PETERSON**   I enjoy my work. If I did not enjoy my work, I would do something else.
**TAI-TUNG TRANH**   Are you thinking of leaving me?
**MISS PETERSON**   Don't be paranoid.
**TAI-TUNG TRANH**   I would like that engraved on my cremation urn. "Don't be paranoid."
*(Miss Peterson finishes wiping Tai-Tung Tranh's hands.)*
**MISS PETERSON**   I think I missed a spot. *(Licks it off.)* Yumsters. *(Smiles and rises.)*
**TAI-TUNG TRANH**   You would do anything for me.
**MISS PETERSON**   Don't be paranoid.
**TAI-TUNG TRANH**   Bring me the Master Plan.
**MISS PETERSON**   You mean?
**TAI-TUNG TRANH**   Yes.
**MISS PETERSON**   The Doomsday Book.
**TAI-TUNG TRANH**   I hate it when you refer to the Master Plan as the

Doomsday Book. It is so melodramatic.

**MISS PETERSON**   I like melodrama. It keeps my interest at a fever pitch.

(*She presses a button. A huge leather-bound volume appears. Tai-Tung Tranh opens it.*)

**MISS PETERSON**   Shall I call the doctor?

**TAI-TUNG TRANH**   As I peruse the material. (*Miss Peterson opens a wallet-sized Watchman, and presses in a number. A light appears reflected on her face.*)

**MISS PETERSON**   Doctor. Put that away. You're wanted in the War Room.

(*She presses a button. The light goes out. Tai-Tung Tranh turns to the Master Plan.*)

**TAI-TUNG TRANH**   Ah, here is the heart of the matter. "The conflagration in Southeast Asia was the latest pearl in a string of carefully cultured stones that go back decades to the temporary defeat of Imperial Japan. There followed the victory of the so-called Communists in China, the Korean conflict, the French Indo-Chinese humiliation, and so on to the present day. The continued unrest in Cambodia, the openly capitalistic aspirations of Deng, the rumblings of rapprochement between Taipei and Beijing, the economic suzerainty of Japan and the Four Tigers, the Asian Diaspora in the West, all point to one thing. The colonization of America." Ah, Doctor. Come in.

(*Dr. Oscar Rang enters, and goes to Tai-Tung Tranh.*)

**TAI-TUNG TRANH**   I was just browsing in the Master Plan. We seem to be on schedule. 1997 is not so far away.

**OSCAR**   No. No, it's not. 1997 is just around the corner.

(*He kneels before Tai-Tung Tranh, and removes Tai-Tung Tranh's slippers. He massages Tai-Tung Tranh's feet.*)

**TAI-TUNG TRANH**   Where was I? "The colonization of America. Economic enthrallment." Ah. Ah. Ah. Yes. For an Occidental, your shiatsu is not bad.

**OSCAR**   Caucasian. Occidental is a college.

**TAI-TUNG TRANH**   Shut up. The master stroke of this scheme is the reversal of roles. Unlike the Mafia, who are essentially gangsters who dabble in business, we are businessmen who disguise ourselves as gangsters. Don't you think this is the master stroke? Miss Peterson?

**MISS PETERSON**   I think the master stroke of this scheme is its sheer unbelievability. It is paranoic.

(*Oscar holds up a bottle of nail polish.*)

**OSCAR**   Mandarin red?

**TAI-TUNG TRANH**   Of course, Doctor.

(*Oscar begins to paint Tai-Tung Tranh's toenails.*)

**TAI-TUNG TRANH**  We will use the heroin money to restructure the global economy. By 1997, America will be a dependent. A satellite. A colony. You missed a spot.

**MISS PETERSON**  I hate it when you talk business.

**TAI-TUNG TRANH**  What would you like me to talk?

**MISS PETERSON**  Pleasure.

**TAI-TUNG TRANH**  Stay there. Come no closer. Let me describe your Caucasian features. Let me speculate on your favorite positions. Let me hear those sounds you make in anticipation. The low, throaty ones.

**MISS PETERSON**  That's not fair. You know what I like.

**TAI-TUNG TRANH**  Not everything. Surely you have not told me everything.

**MISS PETERSON**  Don't be paranoid.

**TAI-TUNG TRANH**  I find you inscrutable, Miss Peterson.

**MISS PETERSON**  As soon as you're dry, I will show you a secret. (*She walks off, unbuttoning her blouse, and making low, throaty sounds. She turns and smiles. Music swells. She disappears. Oscar finishes painting Tai-Tung Tranh's nails.*)

**TAI-TUNG TRANH**  Now we have liquidated Claire Silver, the secret of the Hmong is safe.

**OSCAR**  Were the Hmong –

**TAI-TUNG TRANH**  Shut up. Don't interrupt. The Hmong are walking time bombs. The CIA used them as guinea pigs during the war. The Sudden Unexplained Nightmare Death Syndrome is the first manifestation of the plague the Hmong carry. We shall trigger an epidemic by means of a biochemical catalyst. At the same time conduct a disinformation campaign about its contagious qualities. The Americans will put the Hmong in concentration camps. Why not? It has happened before. They already hate the Hmong for their foreignness, their primitive ways, their *oriental* qualities.

**OSCAR**  Why do you want to martyr the Hmong?
(*He fans Tai-Tung Tranh's toenails with a small oriental hand fan.*)

**TAI-TUNG TRANH**  It will blossom into a vast American reaction against Asia and the Asians in this country. Japan and China will be forced to close ranks to protect their financial investments, their nationals, their vast holdings. Asian-Americans will be forced to realize there is no such thing. They will never be American, no matter how many generations forget their language and their culture. Many will die, but you occidentals know how cheap life is to us.

**OSCAR**  It's so complicated.

**TAI-TUNG TRANH**  You are a mere podiatrist. How could you hope to understand? Believe me, the end result will be the economic suzerainty of the Far East. The twenty-first century belongs to us.

*(He examines his nails.)*
**TAI-TUNG TRANH**   A particularly subtle shade of mandarin. I
commend your artistry. Now go away. I have something pressing. Miss
Peterson may have started without me.
*(Music. Lights change.*
*Oscar and Tai-Tung Tranh disappear.*
*Cross-fade to)*


**20.** *Christine at the terminal. Green glow.*
*She finishes.*
*She pushes a number of buttons, and the manuscript begins printing*
*out.*
*Slow light fade to*


**21.** *Lyle turns on a light. He is alone.*

**LYLE**   Two recent Japanese best sellers by Masami Uno assert Japan's
current economic problems – the surging yen, declining exports – are
the result of a conspiracy to "bash" Japan by international Jewish
capital. These books assert Jews form a secret nation within the United
States, where they control the major corporations: IBM, General
Motors, Ford, Chrysler, Standard Oil, Exxon, AT&T. Quote, America
is a Jewish nation, endquote. *(Beat.)* Mr. Uno describes himself as a
Christian fundamentalist. The titles of his books are *If You Can*
*Understand Judea You Can Understand the World,* and *If You Can*
*Understand Judea You Can Understand Japan. (Beat.)* Mr. Uno's
books have sold 700,000 copies. The first asserts the Jews caused the
Great Depression, and are plotting another for 1990. The second
asserts the scope of the Holocaust has been exaggerated. These books
are popular with businessmen, and well-read among Bank of Japan
officials. Other recent conspiracy best sellers in Japan include *The*
*Jewish Plan For Conquest of the World* and *How To Read the Hidden*
*Meaning of Jewish Protocol. The Secret of Jewish Power To Control*
*The World,* published in 1984, was written by Eisaburo Saito, a
member of Japan's upper house of parliament. *(Beat.)* You think I
make this stuff up? It's in *The New York Times.* I'll show you the
microfilm. *(Beat.)* Shichihei Yamamoto wrote a best-seller seventeen
years ago called *The Japanese and The Jews.* It sold three million
copies. Currently, there are 82 books in print in Japan with the word
"Jew" in the title. An ongoing fascination. Many books about Jews
circulate old legends, including a persistent theory the Japanese people

– or at least the Imperial family – are descended from the ten lost tribes of Israel. Some mention the historical persecution of the Jews and draw parallels with Japan, an island nation in a hostile world. Some promulgate the popular notion the Jews and Japanese were the principal victims of the Second World War. Some admiringly reccle bromides about Jewish financial acumen. One recent best seller is called *Make Money With Stocks Jews Aim At. (Beat.)* Here's the best part. Mr. Yamamoto's book, *The Japanese and The Jews*, was written under a pseudonym. Isaiah Ben Dasan.

*(Lyle turns out light, as)*


**22.** *Sound of printer. Lights up on*
   *Dennis and Christine doing one of their lists, tossing unlit matches into*
   *a glass bowl on each item.*
**DENNIS**   *Attack of the Puppet People.*
**CHRISTINE**   *Attack of the Crab Monsters.*
**DENNIS**   *Attack of the Fifty-foot Woman.*
**CHRISTINE**   *They Saved Hitler's Brain.*
**DENNIS**   *Mars Needs Women.*
**CHRISTINE**   *High School Confidential.*
**DENNIS**   *How To Stuff A Wild Bikini.*
**CHRISTINE**   *It's A Bikini World.*
**DENNIS**   *This Island Earth.*
**CHRISTINE**   *Panic in the Year Zero.*
**DENNIS**   *The Fearless Vampire Killers.*
**CHRISTINE**   No, that's a good movie.
**DENNIS**   Come on. *Bring Me the Head of Alfredo Garcia.*
**CHRISTINE**   *Faster, Pussycat, Kill! Kill!*
**DENNIS**   I don't think Russ Meyer should count.
**CHRISTINE**   A genius of the jump cut.
**DENNIS**   Yeah sure, he's an auteur. No way.
**CHRISTINE**   *Sex Kittens Go To College.*
**DENNIS**   If you say so. *The House That Dripped Blood.*
**CHRISTINE**   *I Wake Up Screaming.*
**DENNIS**   *I Am A Fugitive From A Chain Gang.*
**CHRISTINE**   *I, The Jury.*
**DENNIS**   *I Married A Communist.*
**CHRISTINE**   *I Was A Communist For the FBI.*
**DENNIS**   *I Walked With A Zombie.*
**CHRISTINE**   *I Died A Thousand Times.*
**DENNIS**   *I Spit On Your Grave.*
**CHRISTINE**   A great, great film. What about porn titles? I love porn

titles. They bespeak volumes about our subterranean selves.

**DENNIS**   They be speak?

**CHRISTINE**   *Back Door Santa. Wide World of Spurts. Pizza Boy – He Delivers. Lesbian Spies From Venus.*

**DENNIS**   You have to have seen these. You never saw *Lesbian Spies From Venus.*

**CHRISTINE**   I saw the ad. I saw the marquee. It's part of the zeitgeist.

**DENNIS**   Not on this list. *Yom Kippur Ninja Killers.*

**CHRISTINE**   No ninja, no kung fu.

**DENNIS**   Racist. How about those counterfeit documentaries like *Cannibal Holocaust?*

**CHRISTINE**   *Mondo Cane.*

**DENNIS**   Too mainstream.

**CHRISTINE**   Wait. This is a set. *Mondo Cane. Mondo Pazzo. Mondo Freudo.*

**DENNIS**   *Mondo Freudo?* Foul. You're kidding. I don't believe *Mondo Freudo* for a second.

**CHRISTINE**   You can look it up.

**DENNIS**   Casey Stengel.

**CHRISTINE**   Very good. I'd give a lot to see *Mondo Freudo* right now.
   (*Dennis lights a match and tosses it into the bowl; the matches flare.*)

**CHRISTINE**   I love this list. This list is my favorite.
   (*Christine turns off the lamp.*)


**23.**   *Dennis alone, in a light.*
   *Dennis tells the following joke in Chinese:*

**DENNIS**   *Ney gee ng gee do* Cock Robin *mei yup ying yip gai gee chin hoy geo mut murn? Kurn jal hey geu jo* Penis Rabinowitz!
   (*The only English words we hear are "Cock Robin" and "Penis Rabinowitz."*
   *Laughs uproariously.*
   *Then tells joke in English:*)

**DENNIS**   What was Cock Robin's name before he changed it to go into show business? Penis Rabinowitz.
   (*Stone-faced. Shrugs.*)

**DENNIS**   His agent made him change it. See here, big guy. Penis. Penis. Penis. It's just – too – *ethnic.*
   (*Pause.*)

**DENNIS**   Names, agents, aliases, circles of self-delusion. It's an excellent joke for Montage. It's a venue-specific joke.
   (*Pause.*)

**DENNIS**   Translation is an illusion.
(*Dennis turns out the light.*)


24. *Maria alone in a light. She wears a fur cap, fur coat, and sunglasses.*
*She goes to the window.*
*Pause;*
*Maria opens her coat. She is wearing a fur bikini.*

**MARIA**   Wild thing. You make my heart sing. You make everything.
Groovy. Wild thing. I think I love you. But I want to know for sure.
Come on and move me.
(*Pause. She growls.*)
**MARIA:**   Wild thing. You move me.
(*Pause. She closes her coat.*)
**MARIA:**   One never knows what to believe.
(*Pause. She turns out the light as*)


25. *Lyle turns on a light. He is alone. He opens a chain letter and reads.*

**LYLE**   "To the women in my life who know how to dream and create
their own reality. In about ten days you will be about ten thousand
dollars richer. Just send one dollar wrapped in a blank piece of paper to
the first name on this list. Strike that name and add your own. Then
send the letter to ten new prospects. At any one time there are only
four names on this list. Ten times ten times ten times ten equals ten
thousand dollars. WOMEN ONLY PLEASE." (*Makes note.*) Women
only please in caps. (*Reads.*) "Send the letter to women you know
personally. Send to those whom you would send good luck." (*Beat.*)
These people need a ghostwriter. (*Reads.*) "This is an entirely legal
letter. If you do not wish to participate, please return this letter to the
last name on this list. DO NOT BREAK THE CHAIN." (*Makes note.*)
Do not break the chain in caps. (*Reads.*) "Mail within forty-eight
hours. You will be surprised."
(*Beat.*)
Can you imagine? Ten thousand envelopes coming through my door?
Ten thousand little dollar bills dropping through my slot?
(*Sings.*) Hey, Mr. Postman, look and see, is that a letter in your bag for
me? Oh, Mr. Po-o-ost man, look and see, deliver de letter, de sooner de
better – (*Stops, looks at letter.*) "Women only. *Please.*"
(*He turns out the light, as*)

**26.** *Buster appears in a light.*

**BUSTER**   I believe in crystals, harmonics, and pyramid power. I believe in the prophecies of Nostradamus. I believe birds are messenger entities from the etheric plane. I believe in the G spot. I believe Idi Amin is living in Saudi Arabia, in a mansion with four wives and a bowling alley. I believe he practices every day. I believe he is a deadly serious bowler. I believe he bowls with fervor. I believe I have seen a picture of him in his bowling outfit. White shoes, grey slacks, pink ball embedded with gold glitter, black bowling shirt with "Idi" embroidered in white over the left shirt pocket. I believe he has made inquiries about joining the American pro tour.
*(Light fades out on Buster as sound of printer fades up.)*


**27.** *Dennis turns on a light. He is alone. Sound of printer fades.*

**DENNIS**   My life is a mystery to me.
*(Pause.)*
**DENNIS**   I've lost my engagement book. I've missed appointments. Lunches. Trysts. Late-night rendezvous at the Half Ass Cafe in Chinatown. Authentic Chinese slash American cuisine. Pastrami on rice. Corned beef on rice. Ham and eggs on rice. *(Beat.)* War, famine, revolution. The great displacements of peoples. The vast migrations of nations. The countless refugees. All part of a divine scheme. To create a greater diversity and higher quality of ethnic restaurants in New York City. God is a gourmet.
*(Pause.)*
**DENNIS**   I came to this country when I was twelve. In the airport, we heard Kennedy had just been assassinated. My father was afraid they might send us back. Kennedy opened the door to Asian immigration. Raised the quota. My father opened a restaurant in the suburbs. Served white-style Chinese food. Chow mein. He cooks. The customers call him Pop. I became an American. Ran with the brothers. My father said, *Do ng gere doe bin gor jee hii nee do.* You live like a stranger in this house.
*(Pause.)*
**DENNIS**   Wherever I go in the Chinese world, everyone knows I'm *mei kwok wah que:* An American. Tone of voice. Gestures. Way I walk. But in America, Americans ask me, what are you? What are you? You Japanese? You Chinese? What are you? *(Beat.)* I was an actor. I went to an audition. They wanted someone to play a Cambodian refugee. This refugee comes to America. Finds a new life. They said, what are

you? I said, American, what do you think? They said, no, what are you? Cambodian? No, Chinese. They said, we want a real Cambodian actor. I said, name two. Anyway, you can't tell the difference. I can't tell the difference. They said, the adviser on this project is Cambodian. He can tell. I said, Where is he? Let's see if he can tell. They said, you know, everyone wants to do this. I said, I don't. I left. I came to Montage. I became a ghostwriter.
(*Pause.*)

**DENNIS**   I don't know. I don't know what I feel like. Marginal. Sometimes I think in English. Sometimes I think in Chinese. I count in Chinese.
(*Pause.*)

**DENNIS**   Nowhere at home.
(*He turns the light out, as*)


**28.**  *Lyle is looking at the terminal screen. The green glow is the only light in the room.*
*Christine comes into the room. She starts.*

**CHRISTINE**   Lyle. Goddamit. How did you get in?

**LYLE**   I let myself in.

**CHRISTINE**   I need to finish printing out.

**LYLE**   You need to go to remedial narrative.

**CHRISTINE**   It appeals to the feverish imagination. To the fecund and fevered imagination.

**LYLE**   It boggles the mind what some people believe.

**CHRISTINE**   This is a future best seller.

**LYLE**   No doubt. William Martinex was arrested when he tried to buy two fifty-cent lottery tickets with a counterfeit ten-dollar bill. He became a government informer. He penetrated The Silent Brotherhood, and his revelations resulted in the arrest and conviction of twenty-three of its members on racketeering charges. Murder, bank robbery, extortion, arson. Psychiatrists say arsonists suffer from low self-esteem.

**CHRISTINE**   What does this have to do with *Yellow Emperor*?

**LYLE**   I don't know. Maybe nothing. The Silent Brotherhood has links with the Klan, the Aryan Nation, and other neo-Nazi groups. They belong to Christian Identity, a church which asserts that Jews are descended from Satan. The race of Cain. The Silent Brotherhood issued a manifesto, declaring war on the United States Government because it had been taken over by the Jews.

**CHRISTINE**   *ZOG.*

**LYLE**  Well, here's the best part. According to the Federal indictment, the members of the Brotherhood were acting out the plot of a privately published novel called *The Turner Diaries*. In the novel, a racist state is established in the Pacifiic Northwest through terrorism. (*Pause.*)

**CHRISTINE**  A novel. So Mr. Ampersand Qwerty missed the boat with *ZOG*.

**LYLE**  Certainly not the primary source. Not the soul and inspiration. I'm sure they have *ZOG* on their bookshelves. Background theory.

**CHRISTINE**  So that's why he turned to fiction. To fiction that calls itself fiction.

**LYLE**  Mr. Ampersand Qwerty thinks *Yellow Emperor* will be a real force for change. A sort of anti-*Uncle Tom's Cabin* for the eighties or nineties. Whenever the next big recession hits. He'll release it at just the right moment. When the breadlines are being blamed on the balance of trade and the new Sino-Nippon consortium.

**CHRISTINE**  Snowstorm.

**LYLE**  Snowstorm.

**CHRISTINE**  White nightmare. What should I do?

**LYLE**  Collect your check. If you don't ghost it, somebody else will. Guess what I got.

(*He pulls a large sheepskin page out of his coat and unfolds it.*)

**CHRISTINE**  The world's first chain letter.

**LYLE**  Got it in the mail today.

**CHRISTINE**  Postage due?

**LYLE**  It was postmarked Asunción.

**CHRISTINE**  Paraguay. Garden spot of the Southern Hemisphere.

**LYLE**  I hear the Bavarian cooking is muy bueno.

**CHRISTINE**  What's it say?

**LYLE**  Dunno.

**CHRISTINE**  What do you mean?

**LYLE**  It's in another language.

**CHRISTINE**  Norman.

**LYLE**  Norman English, Norman French, what is that, Middle English? Not Shakespeare, thank you very much.

**CHRISTINE**  What are you going to do?

**LYLE**  Get it translated.

(*Indicates monitor and Mr. Ampersand Qwerty's manuscript.*)

**CHRISTINE**  White nightmare.

**LYLE**  It's starting to get to me. *Geronimo.*

**CHRISTINE**  There's a sick thrill. Rings a primitive chord. Like looking at pictures of the death camps. You want to turn away. Avert your eyes. But you can't. It's not the pictures. It's not the images that make

you sick, and close your eyes. It's the thing in you. The pulse in you
that quickens. That thrills. You scare yourself. You close your eyes
and turn your head. You deny the feeling. You still your heart. You'd
like to have that moment back. That moment before you heard what
you heard. Saw what you saw. But there they are. Images. Anecdotes.
Half-remembered facts. Unfathomable statistics. I remember. I
remember the first time I had that feeling. I was a kid. I was in the
kitchen. The neighbor lady was telling my mother a story. Something
she'd heard. Or read. Someone she knew, I'm not sure. About a
woman. About what that woman did to her own child.
(*Pause.*)

**LYLE**  Don't tell me.

**CHRISTINE**  You can imagine.
(*Pause.*)

**LYLE**  No.

**CHRISTINE**  I had never imagined. A new world opened up before me.
A world I had never imagined.

**LYLE**  Never the same. After.

**CHRISTINE**  No. It's the same feeling, though. All these years later.
Reading his notes. Writing this story.
(*Pause.*)

**LYLE**  I get chain letters every day. General interest chain letters. Special
interest chain letters. Chain letters for blacks. Chain letters for women.
Chain letters for Native Americans. Chain letters involving money.
Chain letters involving photographs. Chain letters involving
videotapes. Chain letters in Spanish. Chain letters in Urdu. Chain
letters in Tagalog.
(*Lyle leaves.*
*Christine moves to the terminal and starts print-out again.*
*Lights fade to*)

**29.**  *A red room. Christine and Tai-Tung Tranh.*

**CHRISTINE**  Thank you for seeing me, Mr. Tranh.

**TAI-TUNG TRANH**  Not at all.

**CHRISTINE**  It's an ungodly hour.

**TAI-TUNG TRANH**  Yes.
(*Pause.*)

**CHRISTINE**  Sorry. You look like someone I know.

**TAI-TUNG TRANH**  It happens. How did you find me?

**CHRISTINE**  I have a friend.

**TAI-TUNG TRANH**  I see.

**CHRISTINE**  He made inquiries at the King Sun Care.

**TAI-TUNG TRANH**   Ah, the Half Ass. You would like the Half Ass. Too bad women are not welcome.

**CHRISTINE**   How Old World.

**TAI-TUNG TRANH**   Old World, New World, Third World. How can I help you, Miss Penderecki?

**CHRISTINE**   I wanted a fact.

**TAI-TUNG TRANH**   Yes?

**CHRISTINE**   You are familiar with Mr. Ampersand Qwerty?

**TAI-TUNG TRANH**   Yes.

**CHRISTINE**   He claims you are a crime czar.

**TAI-TUNG TRANH**   A kingpin. A kingpin of the oriental underworld.

**CHRISTINE**   Yes.

**TAI-TUNG TRANH**   I love old movies. Old American gangster movies. Al Capone. Bugsy Siegel. Dutch Schultz. Perhaps Mr. Ampersand Qwerty loves them too.

**CHRISTINE**   Is it true?

**TAI-TUNG TRANH**   I shall sue him for slander when his book is printed.

**CHRISTINE**   You know about his book.

**TAI-TUNG TRANH**   Oh, yes. I am well-informed. He wishes to foment anti-Asian sentiment in this country. Tie it to economic difficulties. As they occur. Not a new idea.

**CHRISTINE**   Does it worry you?

**TAI-TUNG TRANH**   I have the utmost faith in the essential decency of my new country.

**CHRISTINE**   Are you being ironic?

**TAI-TUNG TRANH**   Not at all. I am a merchant. This is the greatest country on Earth. I am quite happy to be here.

**CHRISTINE**   And the shift in economic power to the Orient?

**TAI-TUNG TRANH**   America assimilates. That is its genius. And you, Miss Penderecki, what do you do? What is your interest in Mr. Ampersand Qwerty's book?

**CHRISTINE**   I'm the ghostwriter.

**TAI-TUNG TRANH**   Ah. America is an amazing country, Miss Penderecki. In my homeland, we have no ghostwriters. Only ghosts.
(*Christine smiles and leaves.*
*Blackout.*)

**30.** *Buster, in a light.*

**BUSTER**   I believe D.B. Cooper is Idi Amin's bowling coach. I believe the body discovered in Brazil is not Josef Mengele, but Jimmy Hoffa. I

believe SONY stands for Standard Oil of New York. I believe MIT
stands for Made In Taiwan. I believe global economic collapse is
imminent. I believe in the legalization of heroin. I got a postcard from
Lefkowitz yesterday which assures me he is alive and well and living
in Asuncion. I don't believe that. I believe Lefkowitz is disappeared.
Has been disappeared.
(*Blackout, as*)

**31.** *Printer fades out.*
*Dennis turns on a light. Christine is there.*

**DENNIS**   Wars create refugees. Who come to New York and open ethnic
restaurants. It's a theory.
**CHRISTINE**   Sounds like NYPD to me.
**DENNIS**   NYPD? The boys in blue?
**CHRISTINE**   At last. A set of initials you don't know. New York
Provincial Disease. A fever state characterized by the hallucination that
New York is the center of the universe.
**DENNIS**   No way. No way New York is the center of the universe. Not
enough Chinese. Hong Kong is the center of the universe. But wait
until 1997. Try to hang on till then. Boom! 1997! Communists take
over Hong Kong, boom! We all come to New York. *Then* New York
will be *sang fun gor yu jal gair cheon sum!* The center of the fucking
universe.
(*Pause.*)
**DENNIS**   Let me read it.
**CHRISTINE**   Not yet.
**DENNIS**   *Yellow Emperor.*
**CHRISTINE**   *The New Dr. Fu Manchu.*
**DENNIS**   Modeled on anyone I know?
**CHRISTINE**   No.
**DENNIS**   I like to think I exert a powerful influence on all your waking
and sleeping moments.
**CHRISTINE**   It was all there. I just wrote it up.
**DENNIS**   You named it.
(*Pause.*)
**CHRISTINE**   You worked on ZOG.
**DENNIS**   That was different. That wasn't personal.
**CHRISTINE**   I could say the same.
(*Pause.*)
**DENNIS**   You know me.
(*Pause.*)
**CHRISTINE**   That's true. That disturbed me. Knowing you. Made it

more – forbidden. That's what it is, isn't it? If it's not personal, it's an abstraction. Someone else's problem. (*Beat.*) The limits of empathy.

**DENNIS** *ZOG.* Nobody believes that stuff. Not anymore. The Nazi geeks at the Institute For Historical Review. But this anti-Asian shit. It's everywhere. *The Times Magazine* cover. Threat from Japan. Blood red Rising sun. It's in the air. How we are putting America out of work. College quotas on Asian students. It's not our fault we're talented. Wake up and smell the coffee.

(*Pause.*)

**DENNIS** It's good to see the once-popular Yellow Peril coming back strong. I for one have missed it.

**CHRISTINE** Boat people. The Domino Theory. Domino, domino.

**DENNIS** Van Morrison.

**CHRISTINE** Very good.

**DENNIS** Don't call me yellow.

**CHRISTINE** Ochre. Umber. Off-peach.

**DENNIS** Tell the truth. Do I look yellow to you?

**CHRISTINE** I'd have to see more.

**DENNIS** Let me read it.

**CHRISTINE** Not yet.

**DENNIS** I'm anxious.

**CHRISTINE** So'm I.

**DENNIS** So my? That's Chinese for –

**CHRISTINE** Shut up.

(*They kiss.*
*They kiss again, more passionately.*
*Fades to black.*
*Cross sounds of printer coming up to*)


**32.** *Lyle turns on a light. He is alone.*


**LYLE** The Norman chain letter resists translation. Dennis says translation is an illusion. (*Beat.*) Everyone has a conspiracy theory. A woman handed me a pamphlet on the subway. Written by a retired engineer in New Jersey. According to him, the superpowers hired this Tokyo think tank to devise a scenario for limited nuclear. Should it come to that. This scenario envisions the incineration of Shanghai, Tokyo, Dusseldorf, and Manila. In other words, according to the author, forty million dead orientals. Orientals in quotes. He includes Dusseldorf as an oriental city because it's inhabited by Prussians and Turks. I know, I know. Here's the best part. This think tank is sponsored by our quote oriental friends in Jerusalem. End quote.

(*Beat.*) I don't know what it means. But this shit is everywhere when you look. (*Beat.*) Carlos has switched from the Palestinians to the Armenians. They blow up Turks. All over the world, even Dusseldorf. And he's financing his terrorist activities with smack. (*Beat.*) I begin to see a pattern. Make the connections. That's the scary part. (*Beat.*) A cab driver told me desertification is the result of a plot to manipulate the global weather. Starvation in the Third World is a consequence of this and other Western conspiracies, including contraception. Contraception, a double-bind genocidal plot. They buy it, their populations decline. They reject it, they have too many babies and starve. Heads we win, tails they lose. This cab driver was from Addis Ababa. (*Beat.*) I ponder *Geronimo*. America will never be seriously anti-Catholic. Or even anti-Semitic. Echoes of the Old World. This is the New World. We have another Other. Other others. Who bear no resemblance. Creatures from another planet. Unmistakable in their foreignness. Aliens. (*Beat.*) The Soviets have officially accused us of developing an ethnic bomb, a weapon which affects non-white populations exclusively. (*Beat.*) I know they are working on anti-matter bombs. Laser X-ray bombs. Stroke bombs, which induce cerebral accidents in mass populations. Microwave weapons. Brain bombs, which affect mental functions through long wavelength radiation of great intensity. The Soviets are aiming one right now at some city in South Dakota. I forget which one. We're not doing anything about it. We're monitoring the results. (*Beat.*) I think the human need for linear narrative, and narrative closure, coupled with our physiologically determined dualism which dictates our childishly Manichaean world-view – good guys, bad guys, Empire of Evil, Free World – plus our innate inability to tolerate the tensions of ambiguity, as a species, I mean, will bring on World War Three. We'll blow it up just to see how it ends.
(*Lyle turns off the light, as*)


33. *A light goes on in The Montage Agency.*
*Christine is sitting across from Maria, Mr. Ampersand Qwerty, and Buster.*


**BUSTER**  It's overdue.
**MARIA**  We are anxious. Anticipatory.
**MR. AMPERSAND QWERTY**  I've outlined your basic concept to Maria.
**MARIA**  Brilliant.
**MR. AMPERSAND QWERTY**  I'd go so far as to call it High Concept.

Wouldn't you?

**MARIA**  I would.

**BUSTER**  Bookstores across the Great Basin-Plateau Area clamor. They yearn. They back order.

**CHRISTINE**  Finishing touches. Loose ends.

**MARIA**  Please have a Xerox on my desk in the morning. I don't like the idea of just one copy. What if something happened?

**CHRISTINE**  What could happen?

**MR. AMPERSAND QWERTY**  I'd like my notes back. When you're done.

**CHRISTINE**  When did you tell her you knew?

**MR. AMPERSAND QWERTY**  She told me.

**MARIA**  We had to tell him. That something happened, has happened to Lefkowitz. That you were Lefkowitz now.

**CHRISTINE**  What did you tell him?

**MARIA**  We don't know.

**CHRISTINE**  You don't know what you told him?

**MARIA**  We told him we don't know what happened to him.

(*Pause.*)

**CHRISTINE**  What happened to Lefkowitz?

(*Pause.*)

**CHRISTINE**  Let me rephrase the question. What the fuck happened to Lefkowitz?

(*Pause.*)

**CHRISTINE**  He knows, Maria. He knew I was the ghostwriter from the beginning.

**MR. AMPERSAND QWERTY**  From the beginning? All right. Lefkowitz became fascinated by conspiracies. Working at Montage, you can imagine. A natural proclivity became an obsession. He began delving into the machinations of the world-wide heroin trade. An inexhaustible conspiracy. A life's work, unravelling. And who would believe the connections, the alliances, the depth of complicity?

**CHRISTINE**  Who indeed?

**MR. AMPERSAND QWERTY**  Any number of people could have disappeared him.

**CHRISTINE**  Disappeared him.

**MR. AMPERSAND QWERTY**  One of the newer verbs of the twentieth century. From the Spanish. Highly useful. Could have been anyone. KGB. CIA. ZOG.

**CHRISTINE**  One of his own? Wasn't Lefkowitz a trusted agent of the international Zionist-socialist-media-banking-homosexual conspiracy?

**MR. AMPERSAND QWERTY**  Don't scoff. Turn the page. I personally favor TTT as the agent of Lefkowitz' disappearance.

**CHRISTINE**   TTT?

**MR. AMPERSAND QWERTY**   Your friend, Mr. Tai-Tung Tranh.

**CHRISTINE**   You little devil. How did you know?

**MR. AMPERSAND QWERTY**   He called me himself. Wanted to know if you were my minion. I told him no, merely my ghost.

**CHRISTINE**   Local color. Background. Character detail.

**MR. AMPERSAND QWERTY**   That's what I told him.

**CHRISTINE**   He's quite obviously a merchant.

**MR. AMPERSAND QWERTY**   Indeed. He sells fish sauce and heroin. Wholesale.

(*Pause.*)

**CHRISTINE**   The manuscript and notes are in a metal box in the freezer compartment of my refrigerator. They're quite safe. I'll have a final draft on your desk Friday night.

(*Pause.*)

**MARIA**   Fine.

(*Christine gets up and exits.*)

**MARIA**   Buster.

(*Buster leaves the room.*)

**MARIA**   Do you know what happened to Lefkowitz?

**MR. AMPERSAND QWERTY**   Specifically? No.

**MARIA**   I don't believe you.

**MR. AMPERSAND QWERTY**   The truth exists independent of your beliefs.

(*Buster returns with a copy of the manuscript.*)

**BUSTER**   A good read. A page-turner from start to finish.

**MARIA**   The notes?

**BUSTER**   Couldn't get a copy of the notes.

**MR. AMPERSAND QWERTY**   It doesn't matter. I have copies of the notes. How soon?

**MARIA**   It's already proofed. Corrected galleys to you tomorrow night.

**MR. AMPERSAND QWERTY**   After that?

**MARIA**   Whenever you want. It's your publishing house.

**MR. AMPERSAND QWERTY**   Yes. Yes, it is. Isn't it?

(*Buster hands him the manuscript.*)

**MR. AMPERSAND QWERTY**   The fire next time. (*Beat.*) Snowstorm.

(*Blackout, as*)


**34.** *Dennis turns on a light. He is reading the finished manuscript.*

**DENNIS**   These people are aliens. Their agenda hasn't changed since the Crusades. The perennial A-list. Jews, blacks, infidels, gooks.

(*Christine comes into the room.*)

**CHRISTINE**  In perpetuity throughout the universe.

**DENNIS**  Aryan universe. Never closed, always open.

**CHRISTINE**  Aryan universe.

**DENNIS**  The dream of a pure white future. Snowstorm.

**CHRISTINE**  Star wars.

**DENNIS**  It's not a great idea to let white people have nukes.

**CHRISTINE**  We made 'em, we get to use 'em. Besides, you all invented gunpowder.

**DENNIS**  True. We started the whole thing.

**CHRISTINE**  Then what happened? No follow through.

**DENNIS**  We got distracted by fireworks. What can I tell you?

(*Dennis puts manuscript down.*)

**CHRISTINE**  He said America's in the mood.

**DENNIS**  He knows what he's talking about. When did he say that?

**CHRISTINE**  He paid me a visit. He knows I'm the ghostwriter.

**DENNIS**  He knows about Lefkowitz.

**CHRISTINE**  He knows everything. He was at the meeting.

**DENNIS**  When do you have to turn in the manuscript?

**CHRISTINE**  I told Maria Friday night. (*Beat.*) I saw Tai-Tung Tranh. He looks like you.

**DENNIS**  So?

**CHRISTINE**  He looks just like you. Everyone's starting to look alike. Mr. Ampersand Qwerty looks like a client from Brown and Scott. I think he's the same guy. He came there to check me out.

**DENNIS**  Don't be paranoid.

**CHRISTINE**  Little late for that.

**DENNIS**  What's he like? Tai-Tung Tranh?

**CHRISTINE**  A capitalist in a nice Italian suit. He believes in America.

**DENNIS**  Gotta be an immigrant. Lotta Vietnamese in Chinatown now.

**CHRISTINE**  Bother you?

**DENNIS**  No.

(*Lyle appears.*)

**CHRISTINE**  Lyle. Where did you come from?

**LYLE**  I let myself in. (*He sees the manuscript.*) Fini?

**CHRISTINE**  Si.

**LYLE**  The translation is giving me fits. It's not Norman. An obscure Gaelic dialect. Southern Manx. A dead language. They're running it through the computer now. Lends credence to the joculatrix theory. Once I get the computer translation, I'll do an adaptation. Something supple, clean, at once contemporary without being colloquial. Non-archaic. Translating from languages you don't know is not illusion, Dennis. It's art. Poetry.

(*He picks up the manuscript.*)

**LYLE**   Mr. Ampersand Qwerty is ecstatic. He loves it. *Yellow Emperor: The New Dr. Fu Manchu.* You did a brilliant piece of work for him.

**CHRISTINE**   He hasn't read it yet.

**LYLE**   They've all read it. Buster. Maria. I read it.

**CHRISTINE**   Where'd they get a copy?

**LYLE**   From you.

(*Pause.*)

**CHRISTINE**   Can you get it back for me?

**LYLE**   No. But I'll tell you where it is.

**CHRISTINE**   Lyle.

**LYLE**   It's your baby.

**CHRISTINE**   Right.

**LYLE**   Buster's desk. Bottom drawer. You can jimmy it with a bobby pin.

**DENNIS**   No telling how many copies there are. Or where.

**LYLE**   He's on the warpath. Smells blood and the best-seller list. He can't believe he wasted all that time on marginal fanatic fringe shit like *ZOG*.

**DENNIS**   America's ready for it.

**LYLE**   America's in the mood.

**DENNIS**   This book is a carrier. It spreads plague.

**LYLE**   I don't disagree with you.

(*Pause.*)

**LYLE**   I have to go turn in *Geronimo*, Part II. An illustrated history of the Illuminati. If I see any copies of *Yellow Emperor* lying around loose, I'll tuck 'em under my coat.

(*He leaves.*)

**DENNIS**   Snowstorm.

**CHRISTINE**   It's mine. I should deal with it.

(*Lyle comes back.*)

**LYLE**   Hear about Lefkowitz?

**CHRISTINE**   No.

**LYLE**   Found him chained to a pillar under the Manhattan Bridge. Off the coast of Chinatown. Positive identification from dental records.

(*Pause.*)

**LYLE**   Predictable.

**CHRISTINE**   How so?

**DENNIS**   He was doing a book on the scag trade.

**LYLE**   Some things are better left alone. Speaking of which, reading a fascinating new manuscript which scientifically proves that the body discovered in Brazil wasn't Mengele. It was Jimmy Hoffa.

**DENNIS**   Jimmy Hoffa hasn't been disappeared – he's just represented by William Morris.

**CHRISTINE**  Where's Mengele?

**LYLE**  Alive and well. Mengele will never die.

(*Lyle exits.*)

**CHRISTINE**  What's your position on D.B. Cooper?

**DENNIS**  Sounds like a list.

(*He gets the bowl and matches.*)

**CHRISTINE**  D.B. Cooper.

**DENNIS**  Jimmy Hoffa.

**CHRISTINE**  Robert Vesco.

**DENNIS**  Michael John Hand.

**CHRISTINE**  Carlos.

**DENNIS**  Abu Nidal.

**CHRISTINE**  Is this missing or most wanted?

**DENNIS**  What's the difference?

**CHRISTINE**  Martin Bormann.

**DENNIS**  Josef Mengele.

(*As Dennis and Christine sow their list, lights cross-fade up on The Montage Agency.*

*Lyle is jimmying open Buster's desk.*)

**CHRISTINE**  Ambrose Bierce.

**DENNIS**  Amelia Earhart.

**CHRISTINE**  King Pleasure.

**DENNIS**  Who's King Pleasure?

**CHRISTINE**  A great jazz singer. Disappeared one day in the fifties. Made a couple of fabulous records. Believed he was born on Saturn, or something. Believed he was a baby planet nucleus.

(*Lyle pulls open the drawer. It's empty.*)

**LYLE**  Nada.

**DENNIS**  Hart Crane.

**CHRISTINE**  Weldon Kees.

(*Christine tosses a lit match into the bowl; it flares.*

*An intense light erupts from the drawer, suddenly blinding Lyle. He shields his eyes.*)

**DENNIS**  I love this list. This list is my favorite.

(*Lights cross-fade to*)


**35.**  *Lyle in a tight pool of light. Twilight country sounds.*

**LYLE**  I've always had this sense of myself as a young aristocrat in the last days of Empire. A sense of waning. Walking through twilight. Dying light. Late summer. Rumours of trouble in the countryside.

Green trees dark against a pure cobalt sky. Soft air. An insect hum.
Fire on a distant mountain, burning through the night. Barbarian drums
in the distance. An oscillation. Tremor. Hazy and shimmering. Aura.
Seeing the aura. Hanging suspended. The unearthly quiet before the
quake. The last still seconds of calm before the cataclysm.
(*Beats of silence. A high-pitched hum, almost beyond hearing, growing
in intensity, snapping. The light gets very white, intensifies. A flash and
a horrendously loud slamming noise to black.*
*Then, the sound of a pennywhistle, as*)


36. *Light up on Joculatrix (Buster) dressed in bells and motley. She waves
the original chain letter.*

**JOCULATRIX**   This sheepskin comes to you from Whiffle-on-Trent. It
has been around the country seven times. It has even been to Ireland.
Make seven copies and send them to your friends and relations. If you
are short of sheep you may use leather. Do not break the chain.
Ethelrod the Alabaster broke the chain and became a leper, with
hideous, awful, hot and cold running sores. Thomas the Confessor
broke the chain and died three days later of blackwater fever. While in
the Holy Land, General Walsh broke the chain and lost his life. Or his
wife. One or the other. Sorry. I have these synaptic lapses. However,
before his death, or hers, he did receive a quantity of gold finger-bells
from a hydrophobic monk. Do not for any reason break the chain. This
letter will bring you good luck even if you are not superstitious. You
will be surprised.
(*Pause.*)
**JOCULATRIX**   I believe in the valley of the Hunzas in Asia, where men
live to be one hundred and five and father children, and women are
beautiful and happy. I believe Saint Brendan sailed his leather curragh
across the Western ocean and discovered a new world. It was cold,
boring, crawling with brown-skinned cannibals, so he said, this must
be Canada. I believe in Atlantis. Eh? I believe in the Seven Cities of
Gold. I believe in the Fountain of Youth. I believe this charm will
protect me from the fury of the Norsemen. Just kidding. I believe in
inter-galactic contact.
(*Blackout as*)


37. *A light is turned on by Dennis. Christine comes into the room with
several manuscripts.*

**CHRISTINE**   Two copies, and the corrected galleys.


226   Eric Overmyer

**DENNIS**  Lyle?

**CHRISTINE**  No sign Of Lyle. Just as well. He's been at Montage a long time. He likes it there. I wouldn't want to see him get fucked up on my account.

(*She goes into the other room.*)

**CHRISTINE**  (*Off.*) We'll cross our fingers. I've got the original notes. I think.

**DENNIS**  You think?

(*She re-enters with a metal box.*)

**CHRISTINE**  I think they're the original notes.

(*Dennis opens the box.*)

**DENNIS**  It's cold.

(*He opens it and takes out pages of notes and original printout.*)

**CHRISTINE**  I'm conflicted about this.

**DENNIS**  I'm not.

**CHRISTINE**  You come from an authoritarian, patriarchical tradition.

**DENNIS**  Love knows no frontiers.

**CHRISTINE**  Who said that?

**DENNIS**  Stalin.

**CHRISTINE**  See? I told you he was a romantic.

**DENNIS**  Now you know what to get me for my birthday.

**CHRISTINE**  What?

**DENNIS**  A document shredder.

(*He holds up the first page. She lights it.*)

**DENNIS**  *Yellow Emperor: The New Dr. Fu Manchu.*

(*He drops the flaming page into the bowl. He holds up a second page. She lights it.*

*The lights fade.*)

**CHRISTINE**  Always a promise for someone we hate.

(*The lights fade out as they add pages to the flames.*

*The only light is the burning manuscript.*

*Blackout.*)

## END OF PLAY

# THE HELIOTROPE BOUQUET
# BY SCOTT JOPLIN & LOUIS CHAUVIN
*This play is dedicated to Stan Wojewodski, Jr.*

THE HELIOTROPE BOUQUET BY SCOTT JOPLIN & LOUIS CHAUVIN was produced by Center Stage, Baltimore, Stan Wojewodski, Jr. Artistic Director, Peter Culman, Managing Director, in association with AT&T Onstage, in collaboration with La Jolla Playhouse, Des McAnuff, Artistic Director. It received its first performance on February 15, 1991, with the following cast:

| | |
|---|---|
| SPICE | Ellen Bethea |
| KEELER | L. Peter Callender |
| HANNAH | Linda Cavell |
| FELICITY | Denise Diggs |
| TRICK JOHN / DISAPPEARING SAM | Dion Graham |
| STARK | Wil Love |
| CHAUVIN | Victor Mack |
| SPANISH MARY / LOTTIE / BELLE | Essene R |
| JOPLIN | Monti Sharp |
| TURPIN | Jeffrery V. Thompson |
| JOY | Gina Torres |

| | |
|---|---|
| Stage Management | Julie Thompson |
| | James Mountcastle |
| Director | Stan Wojewodski, Jr. |
| Set Design | Christopher Barreca |
| Costume Design | Catherine Zuber |
| Lighting Design | Richard Pilbrow |
| Sound Design | Janet Kalas |
| Music Director | Dwight Andrews |
| Choreographer | Donald Byrd |
| Dramaturgs | Mona Heinz |
| | James Magruder |
| Recorded Pianist | William Ransom |

## SCENE

The play takes place in a Harlem rooming house, Christmas Eve, 1916, where Scott Joplin lives with his second wife, Lottie; in Dream New Orleans, c. 1900, in a sporting house called The House of Blue Light; in the Rosebud Cafe, St. Louis, 1905, and in Chicago, 1906, in an opium den known as The Sportin' Life.

The play should be performed without intermission.

## CHARACTERS

Joplin
Spanish Mary/Lottie/Belle
Hannah
Spice
Joy
Felicity
Trick John/Disappearing Sam
Turpin
Keeler
Chauvin
Stark

# THE HELIOTROPE BOUQUET
## BY SCOTT JOPLIN & LOUIS CHAVIN

**Part One:**
**JOPLIN'S DREAM**

> *Dream New Orleans. A sporting house called The House of Blue Light.*
> *A man is sleeping, lying across a piano. This is Joplin. On top of the piano is an electric Christmas tree.*
> *It is just before dawn. August. The light is soft and beautiful.*
> *The Women of the House enter. Joy, Felicity, Spice, Spanish Mary, and Hannah.*

**JOY**   Just before dawn.
**SPANISH MARY**   (*West Indian accent.*) Cool yet.
**HANNAH**   Before the day turns to fire.
   (*The air is filled with flashes of colored light, shooting stars.*)
**JOY**   Look! Shooting stars!
   (*The Women ooo & la.*)
**SPICE**   Lord. Shooting stars.
**FELICITY**   Oh, the air is full of colored light.
**JOY**   Nobody knows shooting stars, what they are.
**SPICE**   They say the earth is passing through the memory of an ancient world.
**SPANISH MARY**   Atlantis. Everybody knows that would be Atlantis.
**WOMEN**   (*Echoing.*) Atlantis.
**SPICE**   Was drowned.
**SPANISH MARY**   Was not drowned, was hurled into darkness.
**JOY**   That was Pompeii.
**HANNAH**   Pompeii the irredeemable.
**SPANISH MARY**   Atlantis. Hurled into darkness.
   (*The shooting stars vanish. The dark lightens. Dawn.*)
**FELICITY**   They're gone.
**JOY**   Melted by the sun.
**HANNAH**   Scared away by foolish talk.
**SPICE**   Like snow. Melted like snow.
**SPANISH MARY**   You never seen snow.
**SPICE**   I heard. I heard about snow.
**FELICITY**   Lord, it's cool now.
**SPICE**   For a moment.

**SPANISH MARY**   There's a lacy breeze.

**HANNAH**   Lacy breeze fluttering.

**SPICE**   Lacy breeze.

**JOY**   Spanish moss lacy in the live oak trees.

**FELICITY**   Fluttering.

**JOY**   Morning, morning, morning.

**FELICITY**   Morning in the House of Blue Light.

*(Sound of water, flowing over stone.)*

*(The Women wash themselves, pouring water from pitchers into small porcelain basins. For a moment just the sound of water, and dipping hands. Then: A customer, Trick John, stumbles in, piercing the perfect stillness.)*

**TRICK JOHN**   Sportin' house, take my money, make me sick. My head feels like a thunderstorm, hot 'n sore. Full of heat lightning, cracklin' from cloud to cloud. My eyes are plump as two parboiled peaches. My tongue's swoll up like it walked halfway to Egypt on its hands and feet.

*(The Women laugh.)*

**HANNAH**   What's the matter with you, Trick John, you should have been long gone –

**WOMEN**   *(Echoing one another.)* Long gone, long gone –

**HANNAH**   Long gone by now.

**TRICK JOHN**   Had a dream I couldn't crawl out of. Dreamed I went to my own funeral. Dreamed I looked down and there I was, laid out in a black suit and silk top hat, solid silver pocket watch tickin' away in my vest pocket, twenty dollar gold pieces on my eyes. And all the women were weeping.

*(The Women laugh.)*

**WOMEN**   Over you? My, my. Not you.

**TRICK JOHN**   Over me, yes yes, over me. Weeping and wailing, talking about what a sweet man I was. Just put that on my tombstone: He was a sweet man. That's why they called him Sugarcane.

**WOMEN**   *(Laughing.)* Sugarcane.

**FELICITY**   They don't call you Sugarcane, they call you Trick John.

*(Felicity goes to trick John, wraps herself around him.)*

**TRICK JOHN**   Don't you put your smell on me.

**FELICITY**   I've licked your eyes. I've stained your blood. You'll never wash my smell away. Sugarcane.

*(She kisses him deeply. He sighs.)*

**TRICK JOHN**   Oh, yes. Oh, my. Oh, God. Goodbye, baby, goodbye.

**SPANISH MARY**   Bye bye, now.

*(Trick John stumbles out. The Women laugh.)*

**WOMEN**   *(Echoing.)* Bye bye, now. Bye bye.

**HANNAH**   Morning. Morning, morning, morning.

**JOY**   Colors of the morning in the House of Blue Light.

**SPICE**   Magnolia breeze –

**FELICITY**   Ivory with a purple bruise, like the inside of my thigh –

**HANNAH**   Cotton taste in my mouth like old smoke swirling –

**JOY**   Tastes smokey red like whiskey, white like cigars –

**SPICE**   Sunlight piercing through a broken shutter slat –

**SPANISH MARY**   Dust sparks dancing in the tired air –

**FELICITY**   Silk chemise draped over the back of an ebony chair –

**HANNAH**   Cypress mist rising soft off the river –

**JOY**   Dew drop dripping down a sweet banana leaf –

**FELICITY**   Bowl of strawberries covered in cream –

**SPICE**   Handful of rhinestone rubies scattered across a blood-stained oriental rug –

**HANNAH**   Half a glass of bourbon under the bed –

**FELICITY**   Dollars dancing in the front parlor –

**HANNAH**   Sweet shuffle of money rubbing up against itself –

**FELICITY**   Money making money –

**SPANISH MARY**   Counting the money, money and love –

**JOY**   Damp sheets –

**HANNAH**   Musky shutters –

**SPANISH MARY**   Chasing the musk outdoors after a long night –

**HANNAH**   After a long night –

**JOY**   After a long night –

**FELICITY**   After a long night –

**SPANISH MARY**   After the blue ballet of money and love –

**WOMEN**   (*Echoing.*) All night, all night long –

**SPICE**   Blue light shining –

**HANNAH**   Cool, cool morning–

**JOY**   I feel so sweet, just to touch myself –

**HANNAH**   Be by myself –

**SPICE**   I feel so sweet –

**FELICITY**   So sweet –

**JOY**   Time for sleep. Sleep the day away.–

**WOMEN**   (*Echoing.*) Sleep the day, sleep the day, away.

(*The Women stretch and sigh. Joplin wakes with a start. The light changes.*)


*New York, 1916. Harlem rundown rooming house. The Women vanish, except for Spanish Mary, who throws on a robe, and becomes Joplin's wife, Lottie. Joplin painfully unclenches his hands.*

**JOPLIN**  Do my hands please, Lottie. Do my hands.

*(Lottie sighs, goes to him, takes his outstretched hand, kneads.)*

**LOTTIE**  Bad dreams, Joplin.

**JOPLIN**  Strange. I had strange dreams. All kind of strange and wonderful. New Orleans. The House of Blue Light.

**LOTTIE**  Oh, Joplin.

**JOPLIN**  You were there. Upstairs. With Trick John. No account, ne'er do well.

**LOTTIE**  That's enough.

**JOPLIN**  Dream every night of the House of Blue Light. This is what comes of keeping whores.

**LOTTIE**  And how are we to live, tell me that. Ragtime's over, Ragtime's gone, Ragtime's done.

**JOPLIN**  Six horses.

**LOTTIE**  Horses?

**JOPLIN**  In my dream. Six horses. Stamping in the black surf. Paper white hides, and moon-colored manes. Black water, black as coffee, and clear as a box of heaven. The water thick and hot as blood, and the surf burns them, burns and roils, foams white and surges up under their bellies, scalds their eyes. White paper hides, and eyes as big and pale and luminous as little moons.

*(Beat.)*

The deep draws them. The moon draws them. Lays down a sparkle on the water. They follow that sparkle, like children follow a stranger who's got sweets and money. The sea calls them. Calls us. Always. We have a longing for it.

*(Beat.)*

Then they drown. They choke, and they drown. Nostrils streaming black blood. The water will not let them go. And as the horses drown they have a memory of sunlight, and a longing for it, and for fields, and tall grass. A longing for dust in their mouths. For simple sweet rain instead of salty surf, and for sugar sky. Sugar sky. But they cannot catch their breath. The water will not give them up. They drown. The sea calls them, and they drown. They burn and they drown, longing for sunlight. Moon colored hooves, and white, white eyes.

*(He stops. Re-collects himself. Turns to Lottie.)*

**JOPLIN**  This was my dream. Six white horses drowning, burning and drowning in the coffee colored surf. And then the horses disappeared, and we came to the sportin' house. The House of Blue Light. You were there, but you weren't you, you were Spanish Mary.

**LOTTIE**  Hush, now, that's enough. Spanish Mary. That's enough. It's the sickness on you. The fever on you, God help us.

**JOPLIN**  Comes of keeping whores. That's why I dream of The House of

Blue Light, every night.

**LOTTIE**   How else are we to live? My God. Besides, this is not a sportin'
house. We just let rooms. Whores got to live somewhere, too.

**JOPLIN**   I am taken away from myself.

**LOTTIE**   I'll bring you coffee.

**JOPLIN**   Black as fever, please. And hot white milk with foam. Chicory.
That little lick of New Orleans. And beignets. Dusty white with sugar.
I need sweetness. I crave it. Sweetness in my mouth. Shoo the taste of
that vile dream away.

**LOTTIE**   I'll bring plums, too.

**JOPLIN**   Glossy black and purple.

**LOTTIE**   Sweet and cold.

*(Lottie goes. Joplin moves to the piano.)*

**JOPLIN**   Sweet and cold. Man needs sweetness. Sweetness belongs in a
man's mouth. Man should always have sweetness in his mouth.
*(He opens the bench, and brings forth a large manuscript, the
"Treemonisha" score.)*

**JOPLIN**   Still time. Still time. While there's still  time.
*(He sits at the piano. He hits a note. He writes. He hits another note.
He writes. Another. He writes. Another. Listens to the note fade away.
He puts the manuscript down. Gazes in silence a moment. Then a
dream of ragtime phrase plays, echoing in the ether. He listens, lost in
reverie.)*

**JOPLIN**   A dream of ragtime phrase. Oh I was young and easy when I
wrote that. Young and dumb. Thoughtless. Thought I'd live forever.
Play forever. Have strong hands forever. And the music would come.
Just come, and come, and come. Like a woman. In waves. Come like a
woman. Come upon me like heat, and come through me like lightning.
Music like heat lightning rolling across a sultry St. Louis summer
afternoon.

*(A burst of music. The lights change.)*

*St. Louis. The Rosebud Cafe. 1905.*
*Turpin, the proprietor, enters, trailed by the other piano
professors, Disappearing Sam and Keeler, and Spice, Joy Felicity
and Hannah.*

**TURPIN**   Cutting contest. Cutting contest. Make a mark, find a line. Tell
your business. Call on God and see if He's at home. See if He's at
home to you tonight.

**FELICITY**   And who are you when you're at home, Mr. Turpin?

**TURPIN**   This is my place. This bucket of blood is my home. So I guess you could say I'm God. At least hereabouts.

**FELICITY**   I could say that. But that don't make it true.

**TURPIN**   If I ain't God, I'll have to do until the real thing comes along.

(*Turpin gestures to the electric Christmas tree on the piano.*)

**TURPIN**   Voilá! Let there be light.

(*The tree lights up. Cheers from the crowd.*)

**TURPIN**   Told you. Told you I was God in this house.

**JOPLIN**   Wait, wait, you're confused. July ain't Christmas.

**TURPIN**   No, it ain't. But it ain't July, Joplin, it's Christmas time at the Rosebud Cafe, St. Louis Missouri, Nineteen Aught Five.

**JOPLIN**   Hot as Hades outside.

**TURPIN**   It's gonna snow like an orphan tonight. You're burning up, my friend. Sweating like a sick pig. Been messing with them poxy gals.

**JOPLIN**   No, I never.

(*The Women laugh.*)

**FELICITY**   Never touched them.

**JOY**   Never loved them.

**HANNAH**   Never came around.

**JOPLIN**   No, I never.

**HANNAH**   Could have sworn that was you.

**SPICE**   Could have sworn that was your sweet body inside mine.

**JOPLIN**   I'm a married man. Got a baby girl. Don't hold with the sportin' life, never have.

(*Belle appears.*)

**BELLE**   Joplin?

**JOPLIN**   Belle.

**SPICE**   Could have sworn that was you.

**HANNAH**   Could have sworn that was your sweet body inside mine.

**FELICITY**   I remember you.

**JOPLIN**   No.

**FELICITY**   Joplin, sure.

**SPICE**   Young piano professor.

**JOY**   Come upstairs, young piano professor.

**JOPLIN**   That was long ago. I was young.

**FELICITY**   You're still young. Come upstairs.

**JOPLIN**   No. Don't entice me.

(*The Women laugh.*)

**WOMEN**   (*Echoing.*) Entice me.

(*Joplin goes to Belle. They kiss.*)

**TURPIN**   Come on, come on. Now, let there be music! Cutting contest.

**DISAPPEARING SAM**   That right, cutting contest. Who the best?

**KEELER**   Cutting contest. Call on God, and see if He's at home. See if He's at home to you tonight.

**DISAPPEARING SAM**   Home to me, I'm the one.

*(Turpin brandishes a big gold medal.)*

**TURPIN**   I got a solid gold medal for the premier professor, for the finest purveyor of pianistic ledgermain. Solid gold, and nothing but.

**JOY**   Is it genuine?

**TURPIN**   You tell me.

*(He displays medal, hands it to Joy, who bites on it, considers.)*

**JOY**   Tastes genuine.

*(She hands it back to Turpin.)*

**TURPIN**   Tastes genuine, is genuine. Solid gold, and nothing but. Joplin, you go first.

**JOPLIN**   No, I can't. I wasn't there. I just heard about it later.

**TURPIN**   That's right. You were somewhere else that night. Somewheres else. Prob'ly with some poxy gal. 'Scuse me. I forgot. You don't hold with the sportin' life.

**JOPLIN**   Never have. I'm a married man. Got a baby girl. Belle

*(He looks around for Belle, who has disappeared. The Women laugh. Turpin points to Disappearing Sam.)*

**TURPIN**   Disappearing Sam, you're on.

**HANNAH**   Let me hear angels.

**SPICE**   Rapture me honey.

**JOY**   Send me to heaven.

**FELICITY**   Send me to hell.

*(The Women laugh. Disappearing Sam gestures to the piano. As he speaks, music plays. The Women ooo and la.)*

**DISAPPEARING SAM**   They call me Disappearing Sam because I am forever on the lam. Quicker than true love, slyer than a cobweb. My feet so fast they keep this dusty old world spinning 'round. I'm here, I'm there, and then I'm gone, darker than midnight and deeper than the dawn.

**FELICITY**   Disappearing Sam, uh, huh, – you know where the treasure's kept – Oh goodness, darling, Disappearing, stroke those ivory keys, please.

**DISAPPEARING SAM**   Don't blink or you might miss me. Don't think that you can kiss me, anymore than you can kiss your shadow's shadow. I'm a whirling dervish, a handful of quicksilver, a scrap of birdsong gone fluttering by. A moonbeam. A zephyr. And when I die, when I'm dead and gone, you'll feel this old world start to slow on down. Midnight won't ever be so deep, the dawn won't ring so rosy bright, and nothing will ever taste quite so sweet again.

*(Music finishes playing. The Women applaud.)*

**FELICITY**   Darling Disappearing, don't you go disappearin' yet.

*(She kisses him passionately.)*

**DISAPPEARING SAM**   Perhaps I'll stick around.

**HANNAH**   Wasn't that sweet?

**WOMEN**   (*Echoing.*) So sweet.

**FELICITY**   Wasn't that succulent?

**WOMEN**   (*Echoing.*) Mmmm, succulent.

**TURPIN**   Sweet, maybe – but not succulent.

**WOMEN**   (*Echoing.*) You're wrong, you're wrong, oh, you're so wrong.

**DISAPPEARING SAM**   You never heard playing like that before.

**WOMEN**   (*Echoing.*) That's right, that's right, that's right.

**TURPIN**   Just every day of my life. My sweet old mother plays better 'n that, and she got the shakes.

**DISAPPEARING SAM**   And you'll be a lucky man, you ever do again.

**HANNAH**   Too true.

**WOMEN**   (*Echoing.*) Too true, too true.

**TURPIN**   I'll take my chances. Keeler, you're on.

(*Keeler steps forward.*)

**KEELER**   Now I know why they call you Disappearing Sam. Your playing was so tender, so delicate, so truly heartfelt – I almost fell asleep. I almost drifted off to the land of dreamy dreams. A lovely lullaby of hummingbirds and lilac bushes. A touch of dewdrop and a minty lip.

(*Winks.*)

But I got something saltier for you, Ladies.

**HANNAH**   Ooh, I like salty.

**KEELER**   A diversion of my own devising. A concoction. A fascination. A ramdoozle. A fandango, and a slow tango.

**FELICITY**   Do tell, Keeler. Show us your two-hand magic.

**JOY**   Let us get a grip on what you do.

**KEELER**   Ladies and gentlemen. A confectionary delectation for the whole collected lacadation. For the entire assembled aggravation. Calculated to captivate. Guaranteed to give your very marrow a thrill.

**TURPIN**   Perhaps I should give you the gold medal for talking, just for talking.

**KEELER**   Stand aside. Prepare to be moved. Prepare to be raptured. Prepare to taste ambrosia on the lips of angels. Prepare to swoon from the sheer celestial vibrations of Saturn's rainbow rings. Y'all better find a soft place to land.

(*The Men and Women ooo, hoot, ahhh, and holler. Keeler tips his brim, acknowledging the accolades.*

**KEELER**   Yeah, you're right.

(*Keeler gestures to the piano, music plays.*)

**DISAPPEARING SAM**   Don't you hurt nobody, now.

**KEELER**   I got something that will make plain women pretty, and pretty women forever young. Take the ache from the back of a workin' man. Make vinegar taste like wine. Make raindrops shine like diamonds. Make a bee sting feel like a kiss, and bring tears to the boss's eyes. Turn cornbread into cobbler, and cobbler into Thanksgiving Day.

**JOY**   God, the man can play.

**FELICITY**   I'm stirred, I melt.

**SPICE**   Me, too.

**KEELER**   I don't have to talk. My playing talks sweeter than any man's melodies. Heavenly elixir. Sheer nectar. Pandemonium. I put my hands on a lonely out-of-tune rickety on-its-last-legs honkey-tonk piana and make it sound like an entire high-class top hat 'n tails sympathy orchestra. So listen, listen, listen.

**WOMEN**   (*Echoing.*) Oooo.

**HANNAH**   Now that I've heard heaven, stab me with dull scissors, and I'll die slow, but happy.

(*Music finishes playing with a flourish. Applause from the entire "lacadation." Except Turpin.*)

**TURPIN**   I was not taken off to heaven. I was not transported to distant shores. I did not hear no angels in the hallway.

**FELICITY**   That's because you're an insensitive man.

**JOY**   A brute.

**HANNAH**   A bully.

**SPICE**   And you cheat at cards.

**TURPIN**   I do the best I can.

**DISAPPEARING SAM**   You made up your mind beforehand, quit wastin' time, tell us who the winner is and let's go get drunk.

**TURPIN**   I don't know who the winner is, but I do know who the winners ain't.

**KEELER**   Do the best you can. I dare you. Won't be good enough. Not near good enough.

(*Turpin moves to the piano.*)

**TURPIN**   Talking won't get it.

**WOMEN**   (*Echoing.*) That's right, never does. Talking won't get it.

**TURPIN**   Talking won't get it, but playing will. Clear the cotton from out your ears and listen up.

(*Turpin gestures to the piano. Then he talks as the music plays.*)

**TURPIN**   A dream of ragtime rapture. Just a phrase. A taste. A lick. A breath. A breeze. A dream of ragtime rapture. Something to stir your heart and remind you of your life's best days, of the sweet moments, all the sweet moments, strung together like a handful of colored glass, and you can see down through 'em, each and every one, to the very last time you tasted wine, or stole a kiss, or felt the sun shine and the breeze blow, and thought some days, this ain't so bad, this life.

*(The Women prefer him clearly.)*

**HANNAH**  Oh, Turpin's got the touch.

**JOY**  I swan, make my head spin.

**SPICE**  Make my backbone rock and bend.

**FELICITY**  Oh, my.

**JOY**  Hot and sweet.

**HANNAH**  Sweet and cruel.

**FELICITY**  As homemade sin.

**JOY**  Now here's a man, I swan.

*(The music finishes.)*

**TURPIN**  Well, Keeler, it's clear, the ladies have their say. By popular acclaim, I give the medal to myself.

**DISAPPEARING SAM**  Cheat. Fixer. Con man. Dirty Dog. *(Howls.)* Ah oooo!

**KEELER**  They work for you, the poxy bitches. Who do you think you're fooling, who? Fool. You're not fit to play the parlor of the skeeziest, most scrofulous cathouse in town.

**TURPIN**  I scoff at your playing, Keeler. I cut you bad.

**KEELER**  Then scoff at this.

*(Keeler draws a pistol.)*

**TURPIN**  Lunatic.

**KEELER**  I pity you, fool.

*(Turpin draws a pistol. They fire at one another.)*

*(The Ladies scream.)*

*(Keeler falls, and Turpin runs out. Everyone leaves. A silent moment. A voice comes out of the shadows.)*

**CHAUVIN**  Wasn't that way at all.

*(Chavin steps out of the shadows, where he's been watching, and approaches Joplin.)*

**JOPLIN**  No.

**CHAUVIN**  You remembered it all wrong.

**JOPLIN**  Yes.

**CHAUVIN**  And you forgot me.

**JOPLIN**  Yes. No. I've never forgotten you.

**CHAUVIN**  Everyone's forgotten me.

**JOPLIN**  Not me. Not Joplin. I remember you every day of my life. Louis Chauvin.

**CHAUVIN**  Keeler died.

**JOPLIN**  That's right.

**CHAUVIN**  Turpin went to jail.

**JOPLIN**  That's right.

**CHAUVIN**  But that was later. And it wasn't about a cutting contest.

**JOPLIN**  No.

**CHAUVIN**   It was over a woman.

(*Joplin turns to see Belle standing on the edge of the light.*)

**JOPLIN**   Belle.

**CHAUVIN**   No, not Belle.

**JOPLIN**   My wife, Belle.

**CHAUVIN**   No, not Belle I said.

(*She disappears.*)

**CHAUVIN**   Some other, some poxy whore, some clapped-up bitch.

**JOPLIN**   The sportin' life. I warned you.

(*He looks back at Belle. She's gone.*)

**CHAUVIN**   All I knew, the sportin' life. Playing the parlor. Money and spunk. All kinds of spending going on upstairs. And look at you, Joplin. Nerves rotting away. Brain turning to gravy.

**JOPLIN**   Sins of my youth.

**CHAUVIN**   Lot of good it ever did you.

**JOPLIN**   What?

**CHAUVIN**   Worrying. Always worrying. One eye on tomorrow. Mr. Cautious Joplin. I won that contest.

**JOPLIN**   I remember.

(*Music. They all come back, Keeler, Turpin, Disappearing Sam, and the Women, except Belle. Chauvin steps back out of the light. As before: Joplin's memory, revised.*)

**TURPIN**   Cutting contest. Cutting contest.

**DISAPPEARING SAM**   That right. Who the best?

**KEELER**   Call on God and see if He's at home. See if He's at home to you tonight.

**DISAPPEARING SAM**   Home to me. I'm the one. A zephyr. A moonbeam. A scrap of birdsong gone fluttering by –

**KEELER**   A concoction, a delectation, a flash of fascination for the entire assembled aggravation, for the whole collected lacadation.

**TURPIN**   A handful of colored glass, remind you of your life's best moments, ain't so bad –

**DISAPPEARING SAM**   So listen –

**KEELER**   Listen –

**TURPIN**   Listen –

(*The Ladies prefer Turpin again.*)

**HANNAH**   Oh Turpin's got the touch.

**JOY**   I swan, make my head spin.

**SPICE**   Make my backbone rock and bend.

**FELICITY**   Oh, my.

**JOY**   Hot and sweet.

**HANNAH**   Sweet and cruel.

**FELICITY**   As homemade sin.

**JOY**  Now here's a man, I swan.

*(The music finishes. Turpin beams.)*

**TURPIN**  It's clear, the ladies have their say. By popular acclaim I give the medal to myself.

**DISAPPEARING SAM**  Cheat. Fixer. Con man.

*(Howls.)*

Ah ooooooooooooooo. Dirty Dog.

**KEELER**  They work for you, the poxy bitches. Who do you think you're foolin', who?

**TURPIN**  I cut you all bad.

*(Chauvin steps out of the shadows.)*

**CHAUVIN**  You ain't cut me.

**TURPIN**  Louis Chauvin.

*(The crowd murmurs his name.)*

**TURPIN**  The legendary Louis Chauvin. Where you been?

**CHAUVIN**  Waiting my turn.

**TURPIN**  We been saving it. It's your turn now. Take your turn. Do your best.

*(Chauvin nods, gestures at piano, music plays. The crowd is transfixed.)*

**CHAUVIN**  White moon drifting in a deep blue sky
Full moon Afternoon sky
What do they call that daytime moon
I wonder
God's one good eye
Maybe
Waking when it's dark
Playing piano til just before dawn
After it's all done
After it's all done
Juke joint gin mill honky tonk gut bucket tango palace
Sawdust and smoke
Coffee with a shot of rye
A woman slipping out of her dress
The back of her neck
All cool and sweet
Cold cold water on a sultry summer day
Deep sleep and no dreams
A ticket on the next train out of town
And enough money to get me
From here
To there

*(He finishes. A moment of silence, then cheers and applause. Turpin*

*hangs a gold medal around Chauvin's neck.*)

**TURPIN**  The winner, and always champion. As long as memory serves
– Louis Chauvin.

(*Cheers and applause.*)

**JOPLIN**  You were the piano wizard. You won the fair, too.

**DISAPPEARING SAM**  The World's Fair.

**KEELER**  The Great Exposition of Nineteen Aught Four. The World's
Greatest Cutting Contest. The World's Premier Piano Professors. From
the Four Corners of the Globe, from France and Abyssinia –

**ALL**  (*Echoing.*) France and Abyssinia –

**KEELER**  Connoisseurs of the Keyboards, from as far away as Budapest
and Madagascar –

**ALL**  (*Echoing.*) Talking about Budapest and Madagascar –

**KEELER**  Step up, step up, step up, step right up –

**CHAUVIN**  And be amazed.

(*Chauvin steps forward.*)

**CHAUVIN**  This is where I'm sposed to brag. Sposed to tell you how
brilliant like lightning flash in a bottle I am. How slick, how wicked
positively, how mellifluous, how sly, how absolutely splendid a man I
am. And I am. It's true. But why brag?

**HANNAH**  He is, it's true.

**SPICE**  Sweet and flash –

**JOY**  Brilliant and slick –

**FELICITY**  Mellifluous and salty.

**HANNAH**  No brag, no brag, just fact.

**SPICE**  Louis Chauvin. Funny looking man. Look like a frog fell in a
liquor barrel. But he could squeeze my heart like no man could.

**HANNAH**  I could hear him in my room, playing those rags. He'd take
my mind off what I was doing, take me away from myself.

**FELICITY**  He could make me enjoy it, even enjoy it.

**WOMEN**  (*Echoing.*) Enjoy it? You?

**JOY**  Not you.

**FELICITY**  It's true, even me.

**JOY**  Must have been in league with the devil then.

**WOMEN**  (*Echoing.*) Must have been.

(*The Women laugh.*)

**CHAUVIN**  This is where I'm sposed to tell you how I came to be a
natural genius. Untaught and unschooled, a child of nature. A primitive
artiste. An idiot savant. Music in my breath and God in my fingertips.
This is where I'm sposed to say I'm the seventh son of a seventh son.
Talk about mojo.

**MEN**  (*Echoing.*) Mojo –

**CHAUVIN**  And hoodoo –

**MEN**  (*Echoing.*) Hoodoo –

**CHAUVIN**  And Saint John the Conqueroo.

**ALL**  (*Echoing.*) Sweet Saint John the Conqueroo.

**CHAUVIN**  How a black cat scared my mama, when I was in her belly. How she took me to a gypsy woman when I was born.

**HANNAH**  And what did that gypsy woman say?

**CHAUVIN**  All kind of strange and wonderful.

**WOMEN**  (*Echoing.*) Strange and wonderful.

**CHAUVIN**  All kind of strange and wonderful.

**WOMEN**  (*Echoing.*) Strange and wonderful.

**JOY**  Is it true?

**HANNAH**  Is it true?

**FELICITY**  Is it true?

**CHAUVIN**  Is what true?

**JOY**  The black cat and the seventh son of a seventh son, and what the gypsy woman say.

**FELICITY**  Is it true?

**HANNAH**  Is it true?

**SPICE**  Is it true?

**JOY**  Is it true?

**CHAUVIN**  No, it ain't true. Just foolish talk. That's all.

**JOPLIN**  But it is true you could hear a song and play it back note for note. Just hear it once, and play it perfect. I know that's true. I saw you do that. More than once.

**CHAUVIN**  God blessed me, that's what's true. Not the Devil. God gave me an ear and a way to think in notes of music, like bits of colored glass. Like water flowing. Rings falling. Something dropping. Something hitting something else. That's what sound is. Keys on strings. Dropping like rain. Water on stone.
(*Pause.*)
It's a gift and cannot be explained, but that don't mean it's magic. Ain't magic.

**KEELER**  You played like magic. You cut us all. Then you went away. Disappeared.

**CHAUVIN**  Chicago.

**ALL**  (*Echoing.*) That's right, Chicago.

**TURPIN**  Heard you did the same thing there.

**CHAUVIN**  What'd you hear?

**TURPIN**  Heard you put everyone to shame.

**CHAUVIN**  Heard that, did you?

**TURPIN**  Yes, I did.

**ALL**  (*Echoing.*) That's right, that's right, Chicago, put everyone to shame.

**CHAUVIN**  Well, you heard wrong.
(*Beat.*)
I didn't do nothin' in Chicago but stay black and die.
(*Stunned silence. Everyone leaves but Joplin and Chauvin.*)
**JOPLIN**  You were too young to die.
**CHAUVIN**  Twenty-six and tired.
**JOPLIN**  The sportin' house life. I warned you.
**CHAUVIN**  And look at you, Joplin. Look at you now. Brain turnin' to cotton. Anyway, I didn't die of the sportin' house life. Never went upstairs too much myself. Never got poxed like you. Never too much afflicted with love. I stayed in the parlor. Played and drank. Drank some. Played some. Drank. Played. Keys on strings. Then something went wrong along my nerves. Got the shakes and tremors. Got the galloping screaming meemies. Lost the feel in my fingers. Couldn't find the keys no more. Could still hear the notes. But couldn't find the keys.
(*Pause.*)
**CHAUVIN**  Couldn't move my hands to play. But I could still hear melodies. Counterpoints. I could feel the bass line rubbing my heart.
(*Chauvin lets out a long anguished cry. A moment of silence follows. He smiles.*)
**CHAUVIN**  Couldn't do that either. Paralyzed. Couldn't talk, couldn't cry. Inside my useless body I still lived. And no one knew. No one knew. Far away. Trapped. Like I was trapped in a tunnel. Buried alive in my own body.
**JOPLIN**  That's a terrible way to die. Without music. Without hope.
**CHAUVIN**  Terrible.
(*He shrugs. Pause.*)
**JOPLIN**  You remember *The Heliotrope Bouquet*?
**CHAUVIN**  I do, do you?
**JOPLIN**  Of course. Every day of my life. John Stark –
**CHAUVIN**  Your white man –
**JOPLIN**  My publisher. Said it was sublime. The audible poetry of motion. His exact words.
**CHAUVIN**  The only piece of music mine was ever written down. I ought to thank you.
**JOPLIN**  You're welcome.
**CHAUVIN**  I never got my money.
**JOPLIN**  I didn't take it. John Stark said you couldn't be found.
**CHAUVIN**  I could have used that money, Joplin.
**JOPLIN**  Couldn't be found, no. John Stark said you could not be found.
(*John Stark appears.*)
**STARK**  Looked all over Chicago for you, Chauvin. The natural genius

of piano ragtime.

**CHAUVIN** Shoulda looked under my rock, Mr. Stark.

**STARK** Could not be found. Asked high and low. Louis Chauvin, you know him? Ragtime natural genius and co-author with the King of Ragtime, i.e. Scott Joplin, *The Heliotrope Bouquet*. A slow drag two-step. A piece of music which is the audible poetry of motion.

**CHAUVIN** What does that mean, Mr. Stark?

**STARK** Pure motion, pure energy, pure delight. Blake said, energy is delight. Delight is energy. Something like that. Something along those lines.

**JOPLIN** Thank you.

**STARK** Pure energy, pure delight.

**CHAUVIN** I guess I can rest easy, now.

**STARK** Yes, indeed, you'll be remembered.

**JOPLIN** If time is kind. If our children live, we'll all be remembered.

**STARK** We'll be remembered. We'll be remembered as if we were gods.

**CHAUVIN** If wishes were horses. If beggars could choose. If the river was whiskey, and I was a diving duck.

**STARK** Yes, indeed, Chauvin. If you live, your time will come.

**CHAUVIN** And if I don't?

**STARK** You'll be remembered.

**JOPLIN** Thanks to Mr. Stark.

**CHAUVIN** Thanks to you, Joplin.

(*Chauvin disappears.*)

**STARK** Praps he's sore I held his money all these years till I heard he passed away.

**JOPLIN** Always was a broody man.

**STARK** Held it in trust. Accumulated interest, compounded annual. Sorry I never could find him. And while I'm at it, while I'm here, as long as I'm in the neighborhood, let me publish your opera.

**JOPLIN** *Treemonisha.*

**STARK** *Treemonisha.*

(*He picks up the manuscript.*)

**STARK** This it here?

**JOPLIN** Yes sir, Mr. Stark.

**STARK** We'll cause a sensation. More than this single copy, I hope.

**JOPLIN** Yes, sir.

**STARK** Then I'll take this with me.

**JOPLIN** I'm not done.

**STARK** Doesn't matter.

**JOPLIN** Let me finish.

**STARK** Doesn't matter. Send the rest. What I'll do for you, Scott Joplin. Acclaim, success, and freedom from care. The crowned heads of

Europe meet the King of Ragtime. The toast of La Scala. The Great
Gilt Houses. A Chopin Joplin double bill. They'll be rocking on
their foundations with applause. Sipping champagne from the
chandeliers. A serious place in serious music history. The adoration
of multitudes. The respect of critics. A paragraph in the encyclopaedia.
Just what you deserve, at last. Nothing less. You'll be remembered.
(*Stark hands the manuscript back to Joplin.*)

**STARK**  When you finish. On second thought.

**JOPLIN**  Aren't you gonna – take it now. Please, Mr. Stark.

**STARK**  Thought I'd deserted you. Scott Joplin. Man I crowned King of
Ragtime. Man I made immortal. Telling people I turned my back.

**JOPLIN**  Never said that.

**STARK**  People exaggerate.

**JOPLIN**  Yes, they do.

**STARK**  I never cheated you. I always paid you your royalty. I always
paid you your due. I did my best.

**JOPLIN**  I know that, Mr. Stark. Won't you take this?
(*He tries to give the manuscript back to Stark, who demurs.*)

**STARK**  When you're done. Better hurry and finish. Ain't got much time.

**JOPLIN**  Who?

**STARK**  Time's running out. Never enough. Never as much as a person
thinks. Hurrying to the end. Everybody wants to go to heaven, but
nobody wants to die.

**JOPLIN**  Where did you hear that, Mr. Stark?
(*Stark starts to fade away.*)

**STARK**  Hope you have more than one. More than one copy of that work.
Of *Treemonisha*. Remember the one you lost. The ragtime opera you
lost.

**JOPLIN**  *The Guest of Honor.*

**STARK**  Lost in the mail, wasn't it? Destroyed in a rooming house fire?
Left in a bar on a drunken binge? Purloined from the Library of
Congress? Something like that. Something along those lines. Hope you
have more than one. More than one copy of that work. That
*Treemonisha*. Man can't stand to lose two life's works in one lifetime.

**JOPLIN**  That was in St. Louis. With Belle, sir. When the baby died.
(*Stark is gone, and Belle has appeared behind Joplin. She is holding
a bundle.*)

**BELLE**  Oh, Joplin.

**JOPLIN**  Belle. I'm so sorry.

**BELLE**  Coughed herself right out of this world and into the next. Poor
creature. Tiny thing. Never knew a word.

**JOPLIN**  I'm so sorry. If I could find my work. If I could just find my
work.

**BELLE**  What work? What are you talking about?

**JOPLIN**  *The Guest of Honor.* My opera. My ragtime opera. Mislaid. Misplaced. Where's it gone? Help me find it. If I could find that work, if I could just find that work, I could bring our baby back.

**BELLE**  Don't talk foolish.

**JOPLIN**  We could start over.

**BELLE**  I can't stay here.

**JOPLIN**  We'll go away to Chicago.

**BELLE**  You'll go.

*(Joplin grabs her.)*

**JOPLIN**  Don't go. Don't go. Don't go.

**BELLE**  I'm sore, Joplin. A walking bruise. A lame dog and a broken wheel. Singing never saved a soul. Singing never brought nobody back. Once you're dead you're done. I'm done, Joplin. Dead on my feet. I got no love for you or any man. Love died with my baby.

**JOPLIN** . Don't go. Don't go. Don't go.

*(He shakes her. She drops the bundle and screams.)*

**BELLE**  Joplin.

*(The bundle hits the floor and scatters: plums roll across the floor.)*

*(The lights change. Belle becomes Lottie, and stands before Joplin.)*

**LOTTIE**  Joplin. Look what you made me do.

*(She scurries about and picks up plums.)*

**LOTTIE**  They were perfect. And now they're bruised. Ruined. Just like life. Like getting old. You make me tired. Old man, you called me Belle again. Damn you.

**JOPLIN**  Sorry.

**LOTTIE**  Now sit.

**JOPLIN**  So sorry, Lottie. So sorry.

*(He sits at the piano. Lottie puts the plums in a bowl and sets them before him. Spice enters with coffee.)*

**JOPLIN**  Who's that?

**SPICE**  Spice, sir.

**LOTTIE**  Joplin. It's Spice. She's been here three months. You know who she is. Now hush.

*(Spice sets down the tray.)*

**SPICE**  Chicory coffee, Mr. Joplin, and hot milk.

**JOPLIN**  A little lick of New Orleans. Thank you, girl.

*(Spice turns to go.)*

**JOPLIN**  Girl?

**SPICE**  Yes, sir.

**JOPLIN**  You're not one of them fancy ladies?

**SPICE**  Sir?

**JOPLIN**  One of those filles des joi we got upstairs?

**LOTTIE**  Oh, Joplin.

**SPICE**  No, sir. I help Mrs. Joplin. Chores and such.

**LOTTIE**  That's enough.

**JOPLIN**  All right.

**LOTTIE**  Run along.

(*Spice approaches Joplin shyly.*)

**SPICE**  Sir, my mama said. I said I was working for you. I told her, she said. She said you were famous.

**JOPLIN**  Told you that.

**SPICE**  Yes, sir.

**JOPLIN**  I was famous long ago, child. When I was your age. When your mama was your age. And you were only one of a million things that might have happened.

(*Pause.*)

You could be my daughter. She'd be about your age. Prob'ly doing what you're doing. Fetch and serve. Scrub, cook, work for other folks. Most folks never taste what I have tasted.

**SPICE**  Sir. Play me? My mama said I should ask you. Could you play me something? Mr. Joplin? Please, sir, please?

**JOPLIN**  Can't play no more.

**SPICE**  My mama said I should ask you.

(*He waits. He spreads his hands several times over the keyboard, testing. He waits. Nothing comes. His hands hover over the keys. Waiting. Nothing comes. A long pause, poised over the keyboard. He gives up. Sags.*)

**JOPLIN**  Sorry, girl, can't play no more. Can't play a lick. Too old, too tired, too sick. Too sore. Been around the world and back. I was famous long ago. Most folks never taste what I have tasted. Now people forgot about me like I never been born. Gone, gone, gone. All that's gone. Done.

**LOTTIE**  Shoo now, Spice. Take coffee upstairs. The girls will be wanting some.

(*Spice scurries off. Joplin mutters.*)

**JOPLIN**  Whores in my house. Can't nothing good come of keeping whores.

**LOTTIE**  How are we to live? Tell me that. Now drink your coffee and take a rest.

(*She starts to go. Joplin notices the electric Christmas tree on the piano.*)

**JOPLIN**  What's that doing here?

**LOTTIE**  Oh, Joplin. It's Christmas Eve.

**JOPLIN**  Is it? I forgot.

**LOTTIE**  You'd forget your head, if you could. If it weren't screwed on.

**JOPLIN**  Thought maybe I was back in St. Louis. Before I knew you. Did I ever tell you about the Rosebud Cafe? And the cutting contest? Chauvin won.

**LOTTIE**  Did you ever not? Just every Christmas Eve.

**JOPLIN**  That tree reminds me –

**LOTTIE**  That's why we got it –

**JOPLIN/LOTTIE**  Of the Rosebud Cafe.

(*She goes.*)

**JOPLIN**  Oh, Belle. You disappeared. Never a word of you again. Wondering where you are. Wondering where you are, all these years. Miss you every day. Every day of my life. Wondering where you are. (*Chauvin appears behind him. Joplin senses his presence. Turns and sees Chauvin, who comes over to the piano. Joplin, watching Chauvin, puts his hands on the piano and begins to play – slowly at first, then, gradually, with transformed youthful energy – a beautiful rag. As Joplin plays, Chauvin watching, the lights fade to black. They come up on:*)


**Part Two:**
**CHAUVIN'S ROCK**


*Chicago, 1906, The Sportin' Life, an opium den. Chauvin is smoking an opium pipe.*

**CHAUVIN**  The Sportin' Life.

(*Music plays. Two couples, a Man and a Woman, and a Woman and a Woman, dance a slow sensual languid liguid tango.*)

**CHAUVIN**  The floor is satin
　　　　　　The ceiling's stars
　　　　　　The air is flashy with ribbons and pearls
　　　　　　Come on in
　　　　　　It's always Christmas in an opium den
　　　　　　This subtle smoke
　　　　　　Is the breath of God
　　　　　　Taste it
　　　　　　Come on in taste it
　　　　　　This subtle smoke
　　　　　　Is the breath of God
　　　　　　Taste it
　　　　　　Come on in taste it

This subtle smoke
The breath of God
(*Joplin appears.*)

**JOPLIN**  The Sportin' Life.

**CHAUVIN**  Yes, yes, yes, The Sportin' Life. That's the very name of this here place. The Sportin' Life.

**JOPLIN**  The one I warned you about. How can you stand it?

**CHAUVIN**  What a question. I can't stand it nowhere else. I'm raw. Like a baby got no skin. And daylight hurts my eyes. This place is soft. This place is easy. This place is full of places I have never been. Full of all kind of strange and wonderful. I float to China here and talk to dead Emperors. I been to Africa and back, to Ashanti and Ghana, Dahomey and Timbuktu. I been over to Peru to warn the Incas 'bout Pizarro. Thought he was their long lost white brother. Long lost white brother? I said, watch your neck, and save us all a trip to the New World.

**JOPLIN**  Did they listen?

**CHAUVIN**  Nah. Fools. These walls are sweaty with dreaming. I lick these walls and I dream other folks' dreams. I hear bells and chimes from heaven. Whistles and horns from hell. Angels and ancestors. And notes on the piano that are not there. That are not even there. This place is soft and easy and I can play here. And the rags flow through my fingers. And I don't have no need to write them down. I smoke my smoke, and I remember everything. And forget everything, too. Remember it all, and forget about it all, in the same breath.

**JOPLIN**  Ain't real. Ain't real. Won't last. Pour sunshine on this place, it'd curl up and die.

**CHAUVIN**  Don't tell me what's real. Ain't for you to say. Mr. Joplin. Mr. Cautious Joplin. Always with one eye on the future.

**JOPLIN**  I had a notion I could make my life shine.

**CHAUVIN**  Funny how things turn out.

**JOPLIN**  But I did. I took my gift and opened it.

**CHAUVIN**  For a time, maybe. But nothing lasts forever – wouldn't you say?

**JOPLIN**  Maybe. Some things last.

**CHAUVIN**  Last as long as a man can stay awake. Then they're gone. Life's a dream they say. An opium dream. What brings you here?

**JOPLIN**  Looking for you.

**CHAUVIN**  Why on earth?

**JOPLIN**  Know we got something to do together. Got to write together. Something fine. Want to get you published. Get you down on paper. So people will remember. So you will be remembered. Some things last.

**CHAUVIN**  Remembered for my association with the King of Ragtime?

**JOPLIN** Remembered for yourself. Your music.

**CHAUVIN** In amongst the dope fiends, the King of Ragtime. What brings you here?

**JOPLIN** Looking for you. I thought we might write something together. What's the matter? Can't you hear me through your subtle smoke?

**CHAUVIN** Somebody told me, came running in here one day, waving a piece of music and saying this guy's the King of Rag, the King of Ragtime. Not you, not Louis Chauvin, who can't even read his own name and I said do tell, who would that be, and he said, this here fella Joplin. And I looked up and there you were, large as life and twice as ugly. *Maple Leaf Rag.*

**JOPLIN** Grieves me you don't like it.

**CHAUVIN** But I do. Oh yes I do. My favorite. What brings you here?

**JOPLIN** My daughter died. My wife left me.

**CHAUVIN** Why didn't you say so? Life's a sorry poxy clapped-up bitch and a fading faulty memory. Come on in. This place here is as good a place as any to hide from her. The old whore. Life, I mean.

**JOPLIN** The feeling's on me. Stirring. Had the fever. Woke up in the middle of the night, staring at the ceiling. Had the fever urge to work. Start over. Start new. Make music. We'll write. I'll get what we do published.

**CHAUVIN** Like your famous. Like your world famous song, *Maple Leaf Rag.*

**JOPLIN** That's right. John Stark will pay us. Our creation.

**CHAUVIN** Mr. Stark. Your white man.

**JOPLIN** My publisher. That's the future, Chauvin. Got to have one eye on the future. Got to think about it before it happens.

**CHAUVIN** Far as I'm concerned, the day after tomorrow might as well be springtime on the moon.

*(Pause. Joplin's stymied. Chauvin considers. Then:)*

**CHAUVIN** I'm ready. Got a piece of music been rattling in my brain for days now like a lonely candy in a quart jar. Won't leave me alone at night.

*(Joplin looks. The denizens of the opium den are slumbering on the piano.)*

**JOPLIN** We need the piano.

**CHAUVIN** They're sleeping on the piano.

*(Chauvin gestures, and the electric Christmas tree lights up.)*

**JOPLIN** Is it Christmas?

**CHAUVIN** It's always Christmas in an opium den. Merry Christmas, Joplin. Want to hear my latest composition? *Christmas In An Opium Den Rag?*

**JOPLIN** I can't work here.

The Heliotrope Bouquet By Scott Joplin & Louis Chauvin  251

**CHAUVIN**  This is where I am. This is where I live. You staying and playing, or you praying and promenading?
(*Joplin considers. Looks at the Denizens.*)
**JOPLIN**  Let's play. But just us alone.
**CHAUVIN**  I can make them go away. It's my dream, not yours. My fever dream, my very own. You're not even here.
**JOPLIN**  I'm dreaming you. I'm dreaming you dreaming.
**CHAUVIN**  Are you sure? Maybe I'm dreaming you dreaming me dreaming.
**JOPLIN**  That's way too subtle for me.
**CHAUVIN**  We're dreaming each other dreaming each other.
**JOPLIN**  Then dream you make them go away.
**CHAUVIN**  All right. You say so. You're my guest. You're my dream.
(*Chauvin gestures to the Denizens.*)
**CHAUVIN**  Depart. Vanish. Perambulate. Leave this dream. Go console yourselves elsewhere. Dansez d'ici.
(*He waves his hands. An orchestral dance plays. The Denizens couple up, do a dreamy, macabre opium dance and disappear, leaving Joplin and Chauvin alone.*)
**CHAUVIN**  Never heard a rag like that, did you, Mr. King of the Ragtime Piano? *Christmas In An Opium Den Rag.*
**JOPLIN**  I always said you were the best. Everybody knew that. Wasn't me who crowned me King.
**CHAUVIN**  People forgot about me. Like I never been born.
**JOPLIN**  Let's make some music. Can you, are you able?
**CHAUVIN**  I'm fine. Fresh as the day my momma first laid eyes on me. Let's do it. Let's create.
(*Chauvin goes to the piano, sits. Silence. He listens. Then he plays, the middle section of "The Heliotrope Bouquet."*)
**CHAUVIN**  I hear the heliotrope. A heliotrope bouquet. Blossoms now in my brain. Hear it? Hear the flower open? Hear it root? Hear the way it buds and blossoms dying for the light. Listen.
(*Joplin listens as Chauvin plays. Then:*)
**JOPLIN**  I hear it.
(*Chauvin plays again.*)
**CHAUVIN**  Hear the way it's worn? Heliotrope flower, pinned in a young girl's curly black hair. All down her back. Bunches cut in bundles tossed down on a maple table. Stuck in a blue glass pitcher. Hear those flowers draw water as long as they can – sucking at life like a drowning man. Hear how the heliotrope bouquet wilts and dries, swoons and withers, curls up and blackens and dies. Hear how fast its beauty fades away?
(*He finishes. Turns to Joplin.*)

**CHAUVIN**  I feel better now. That ribbon's been winding through my dreams for days. Keeping me awake at night. That's my part. You do the rest. I'm not so good with endings. You're the man to tell me how it ends.

*(Chauvin gets up. Joplin takes his place at the piano.)*

**JOPLIN**  You don't leave me much.

*(He begins to play.)*

**JOPLIN**  Water and dirt, color, sap and pollen. Perfume. And a ripple of wind. Fields of heliotrope. Purple and white. The reappearance of spring. Come round again.

*(He plays. He stops.)*

**CHAUVIN**  That's a start. Now what comes after, what follows? State your intention. Your honor, sir, Mr. King of Ragtime Highness.

*(Joplin plays.)*

**JOPLIN**  Midsummer. Solstice. Full moon blossoms. Grows fat and full. Swells. Peaks. Pops. Comes. Gushes forth, life's sweet honey. Wax and wane. Wax and wane. Consummation. Culmination. Climax. Ripeness. And after ripeness, after ripeness – sweet resolution.

*(He plays. He stops. They both consider.)*

**CHAUVIN**  Sweet resolution. That's the difference between music and life.

*(Joplin plays the entire "Heliotrope Bouquet." Chauvin does a dreamy dance. Joplin finishes playing. Silence. The sound of one person applauding. John Stark appears.)*

**STARK**  The audible poetry of motion. Pure energy, pure delight. The only written remnant of the legendary Louis Chauvin left to the ages. The greatest ragtime player ever, who otherwise would have vanished from memory.

**JOPLIN**  From human memory.

**STARK**  From human memory. Still to be heard in the ether and the House of God.

**JOPLIN**  And in my head till my dying day.

**STARK**  Indeed. The Legendary Louis Chauvin, preserved here in my publication, *The Heliotrope Bouquet* by Scott Joplin and Louis Chauvin. This moment between two creative titans, this crossing of comets, this spark, this gossamer explosion, this fragile, wet, shimmering creation, this newborn dragonfly, this exquisite cry of an exotic bird hunted to extinction for its brilliant plumage – this sheer ephemera. I saved it. Preserved for posterity. Lightning positively captured in a bottle. The audible poetry of motion. Pure energy, pure delight. The only written remnant of Louis Chauvin. The legendary Louis Chauvin.

**CHAUVIN**  Sweet resolution. That's the difference between music and this life. I find my consolation in the piano and the pipe. Music's in the smoke, in the heliotrope.

**JOPLIN**   Still to be heard in the ether and the House of God. Chauvin's piano ringing ragtime in the House of God.

(*Belle appears.*)

**BELLE**   Wondering where you are.

**JOPLIN**   Belle.

**BELLE**   If the river were whiskey. If wishes were horses. If we didn't 4 have to die. If only life was sweet enough to want to live forever.

**CHAUVIN**   The House of God. Is that a Sportin' House?

**JOPLIN**   You're not as bitter as you pretend to be.

**CHAUVIN**   How would you know?

**BELLE**   Hear the way it's worn. Heliotrope flower pinned in a young girl's hair. Curly black hair all down her back. Before she knows what's coming. Before her life has passed her by.

(*Joplin goes to Belle. They dance, to a sweet waltz rag.*)

**JOPLIN**   I gave it up early. Wanted to make my life shine. And I did. I opened my gift.

**BELLE**   Oh you did, yes you did, Joplin.

(*Chauvin turns to Stark.*)

**CHAUVIN**   You never paid me a penny.

**STARK**   I didn't cheat you, Chauvin.

**CHAUVIN**   You never paid me my money.

**STARK**   I rescued you. I saved your work. Now people not yet born can trace your thoughts, follow the flight of your fingers across the keys, feel how your heart beat, how your breath went in and out as you made that song. I brought you back from the brink of oblivion.

**CHAUVIN**   You should have looked under my rock, Mr. Stark.

(*Chauvin glances at Belle, then Joplin. They stop dancing.*)

**CHAUVIN**   Don't believe in fate. Don't believe in God. Just luck. Bad luck, good luck. Bad luck, mostly, for most folks, most of the time. I was lucky for a little while. Then I wasn't.

**STARK**   The audible poetry of motion.

**CHAUVIN**   I'll never know. What's a published piece to me? Can't read.

**JOPLIN**   You'll die too young.

**CHAUVIN**   You'll live too long. Funny how things turn out. You're the one who'll fade away. Brain turnin' to cotton. Done in by the sportin' life. The one you always warned me about.

**JOPLIN**   I stopped going upstairs early. Wanted to make my life shine. And I did. One mistake. The past came back and ripped me up, ripped me open, like a rabid dog. Tore me up bad. Unforgiving.

**CHAUVIN**   Funny how things turn out. I ain't gonna dream about you any more, Joplin.

(*To Stark.*) Brought me back from oblivion, did you?

**STARK**   Did my best.

**CHAUVIN**   Wasn't enough. Whatever you did, wasn't enough. I died like a dog and lived worse. You should have looked here, under my rock. You owe me, Mister Stark. I ain't gonna dream about you anymore, neither.

(*Chauvin disappears. Stark starts to fade off, as the light changes.*)

**STARK**   So bitter. To be so sour, even beyond the grave. I did what I could. I treated you right.

**JOPLIN**   Never said you didn't.

**STARK**   People exaggerate.

**JOPLIN**   Yes, they do. My new opera – it's almost finished –

(*Joplin picks up the manuscript.*)

**STARK**   What's the hurry? Let me know when you're done. Drop me a line, Joplin. Take good care.

**JOPLIN**   Please, Mr. Stark. Why won't you take this?

(*The lights are fading back to Harlem, 1917. Joplin holds out the manuscript. He listens to Stark's voice fading away.*)

**STARK**   You'll get the respect that's due you at last. A serious place in serious music history. The adulation of multitudes. The crowned heads of Europe. A Joplin Chopin double bill. A paragraph in the encyclopaedia. An obituary in *The New York Times*. When you're finished. When you're done. Take your time. Let me know.

(*Stark fades away completely. Joplin is left clutching his opera score. Lottie approaches. He turns and looks at her. It takes him a moment to recognize her.*)

**JOPLIN**   Belle.

**LOTTIE**   Oh, Joplin. No, not Belle.

**JOPLIN**   She was here.

**LOTTIE**   This is Lottie. The second one. The one saved your sorry life, remember?

**JOPLIN**   Oh, Lottie, yes. Yes, my wife. My darling. Good soul.

**LOTTIE**   Thank you.

**JOPLIN**   Belle was here.

**LOTTIE**   Only in your dreams.

**JOPLIN**   And Chauvin.

**LOTTIE**   What did he want?

**JOPLIN**   Tell me I was right. Some things last. He heard what I said. He took it to heart. We wrote *The Heliotrope Bouquet* together.

**LOTTIE**   Oh, Joplin. That's my favorite. *The Heliotrope.*

**JOPLIN**   I know. He did the first part. I did the last.

**LOTTIE**   A sweet song. Sweet as twilight. Sweet as a Sea Island breeze. Sweet as my sweet youth, and my lost body.

**JOPLIN**  Some things last.

(*He stands motionless, lost in reverie. She leads him to the piano, and he sits. Then:*)

**JOPLIN**  Mr. Stark was here, too.

**LOTTIE**  Yes?

**JOPLIN**  Yes. He's going to publish my opera.

**LOTTIE**  *Treemonisha.*

**JOPLIN**  My masterpiece. Soon as I finish. Mr. Stark will publish it. I'll be redeemed. My little baby, I'll bring her back.

**LOTTIE**  Oh, Joplin. Mr. Stark turned his back on you years ago.

**JOPLIN**  I remember.

**LOTTIE**  Said he wouldn't publish that opera. Said no one would ever do that piece.

**JOPLIN**  Times were hard. The bloom was off the ragtime rose.

**LOTTIE**  Oh, Joplin. You always defended him.

**JOPLIN**  He always paid me my royalty. He always paid me my due.

(*Pause.*)

Ragtime's gone. Ragtime's over. Ragtime's done.

(*Pause.*)

I just have to finish. You'll see. I just have to finish. Still time. While there's still time.

(*Spice enters, with a wreath, ribbons, Christmas decorations.*)

**JOPLIN**  Who's that?

**SPICE**  Spice, sir.

**LOTTIE**  Oh, Joplin, you know who she is.

**JOPLIN**  Come here, child.

(*Spice goes to Joplin. He takes her hand.*)

**JOPLIN**  Pretty child. Where you been?

**SPICE**  Upstairs.

**JOPLIN**  I mean all these years.

**SPICE**  Sir?

**JOPLIN**  I been worried about you. Your mama told me you were dead.

(*Lottie becomes Belle. To Joplin, not to Spice, of course.*)

**BELLE**  She was dead, Joplin. Cold as snow, and all her color gone. But I found your score.

**JOPLIN**  *The Guest of Honor?*

**BELLE**  The one you lost.

**SPICE**  Sir?

**BELLE**  Brought it to Mr. Stark, which he published to great acclaim. And that's what brought our baby back to life. The sound of your songs sung reached heaven, and touched God's heart, and breathed breath back into our baby.

**JOPLIN**  I knew that would happen. I knew if I could find that lost score, my lost music.

**BELLE**  And now she's here. Same age she'd be as if she lived. A young woman. A grown woman. Pretty girl.

**JOPLIN**  I knew there was music to wake the dead.

(*Joplin holds her hand more tightly. She's frightened.*)

**SPICE**  Please, Mr. Joplin, sir.

(*Lottie moves to Joplin and Spice.*)

**LOTTIE**  Stop, now. You're scaring the poor child.

**JOPLIN**  No, I'm just so glad to see her after all this time.

(*To Spice.*)

You been a good girl?

**SPICE**  I do my best, sir.

**LOTTIE**  He's having a spell, child. Don't pay him no mind.

**JOPLIN**  Pretty child.

(*Lottie disengages Spice's hand from Joplin's.*)

**LOTTIE**  Run along now. The upstairs parlor needs a dust.

**SPICE**  Yes, ma'am.

(*She leaves.*)

**JOPLIN**  Such a pretty girl. Our daughter's beautiful.

**LOTTIE**  That's Spice, the serving girl. Oh, what's the use? Life's a sorry bitch and a fading memory.

**JOPLIN**  Belle.

(*He turns to where Belle was last standing. She's gone.*)

**LOTTIE**  Was she here again?

**JOPLIN**  Yes.

**LOTTIE**  Ghosts come and go. That's the advantage of being a ghost. You can do as you damn well please.

**JOPLIN**  I wrote that song in Chicago.

**LOTTIE**  I know.

**JOPLIN**  *Heliotrope.* With Chauvin. Tracked him down to an opium den. He died young.

**LOTTIE**  The good die young.

**JOPLIN**  He wasn't good.

**LOTTIE**  He was a good piano player.

**JOPLIN**  Yes, indeed. Your favorite.

**LOTTIE**  Never heard him play.

**JOPLIN**  No, the song. *Heliotrope.*

**LOTTIE**  Always.

**JOPLIN**  Did I write that song before I knew you, or after?

**LOTTIE**  Doesn't matter.

**JOPLIN**  I wrote it for you, whether I knew it or not. Whether I knew you or not.

**LOTTIE**  For me, or for Belle?

The Heliotrope Bouquet By Scott Joplin & Louis Chauvin  257

**JOPLIN**  For you, Lottie. Belle's dead. Belle's dead and gone. Done.

**LOTTIE**  Wish I could believe that.

**JOPLIN**  Long time gone. All these years. Wondering where, wondering where she is, where she went. Disappeared. Dear Lottie. My heart was broken before I knew you.

**LOTTIE**  Was it?

**JOPLIN**  Oh Lottie, yes.

**LOTTIE**  My heart was broken since I knew you, Joplin.

*(She turns on the electric Christmas tree. It lights up, Joplin is delighted, like a child. He claps his hands.)*

**JOPLIN**  Still time. Still time. While there's still time.

*(Joplin spreads out his score before him.)*

**JOPLIN**  If I were with my love, I would live forever.

*(He sits at the piano. Motionless. A new rag plays in the ether, all kind of strange and wonderful, unlike anything we've heard before.)*

*(Paralyzed, he listens as it plays, unable to write it down. The Tricks, Whores, and Professors of the Sportin' House of his youth appear, and do a slow, elegant dance in the dying light. As they dance, the light eventually fades to twilight. Everyone disappears.)*

*(Spice and Belle appear in a light. Joplin sees them, draws himself up, revived, becomes young again, puts his hands on the piano, and begins to play "The Heliotrope Bouquet." Spice and Belle disappear.)*

*(As Joplin plays, Chauvin appears, and approaches the piano. He leans on the piano and listens to Joplin play their composition. As the song finishes, the lights fade very slowly to black.)*

### END OF PLAY

# DARK RAPTURE
*for Ellen McElduff*


You never know what's out there, lurchin' in the dark rapture.

*Essene R*

Straight ahead and strive for tone.

*Benny Powell*


DARK RAPTURE was commissioned by The Empty Space Theatre, Seattle, Kurt Beattie Artistic Director. It received its first performance at The Empty Space May 6, 1992, with the following cast:

RAY .................................................................Peter Silbert
BABCOCK/NIZAM.................................................David Mong
JULIA .................................................................Katie Forgette
LEXINGTON/SCONES .......................................David Pichette
VEGAS / MATHIS/SCONES ...............................Robert Wright
TONY/DANNY/LOUNGE SINGER ...................Rex McDowell
RON/WAITER .....................................................Chris Shanahan
RENEE/WAITRESS.............................................Jessica Marlowe
MAX.....................................................................Sally Smythe

The production was designed by Peggy McDonald (set), Paul Chiming Louey (costumes), Michael Wellborn (lights), and David Pascal (sound). The production stage manager was Becky Barnett. It was directed by Kurt Beattie.


A revised version of DARK RAPTURE was presented by New York Stage and Film Compnay, Producing Directors Mark Linn-Baker, Max Mayer, and Leslie Urdang, at The Powerhouse Theatre at Vassar, Executive Director Dixie Sheridan, Producing Director Beth Fargis-Lancaster, July 15, 1992, with the following cast:

RAY.....................................................................David Strathairn
BABCOCK/NIZAM....................................................Dan Moran
JULIA....................................................Frances McDormand
LEXINGTON/MATHIS .....................................Jon Tenney
VEGAS/BARTENDER .....................................Larry Joshua
TONY/DANNY.......................................................Joseph Siravo
RON/WAITER/SCONES/LOUNGE SINGER ...Bruce MacVittie
RENEE / WAITRESS.............................................Marissa Chibas
MAX .....................................................................Ellen McElduff

The production was designed by Andy Jackness (set), Candice

Donnelly (costumes), Don Holder (lights), and Jeremy Grody (sound). The Production stage Manager was Elise-Ann Konstantin. The prodution was directed by Man Mayer.

The author wishes to thank Kurt Beattie and Bob Wright for their support, encouragement, and powers of persuasion, without which DARK RAPTURE would not have been written. And thanks also to Max Mayer and Leslie Urdang for the NYS&F Production, where the version of the play published here took shape under the most congenial of circumstances.

## CHARACTERS

Ray
Babcock
Julia
Lexington
Vegas
Tony
Ron
Renee
Max (Margaret)
Nizam
Mathis
Scones
Danny
Lounge Singer
Waiter (Cabo)
Bartender (Seattle)
Waitress (Key West)

The play requires 6 men and 3 women.
Ray, Julia and Max should not be doubled.
The other actors may be doubled in a number of ways:
The actor playing Babcock could also play Nizam.
The actor playing Lexington could play Mathis or Scones.
The actor playing Vegas could play Bartender (Seattle),and Scones or Mathis.
The actor playing Tony could play Danny and Lounge Singer.
The actor playing Ron could play Lounge Singer, Scones or Mathis & Waiter (Cabo).
The actress playing Renee should also play Waitress (Key West.)

# DARK RAPTURE

## Scene One

**Slide:** Northern California – A hillside.

> *Night. A great fire in the distance. Smoke. Gusting reddish light.*
> *Sirens. Howling wind. explosions.*
> *Ray appears, He's exhilirated, soaked in sweat & smeared with*
> *soot, grinning as he tries to catch his breath.*
> *Babcock appears out of the darkness. Ray senses his presence,*
> *turns, sees him & nods.*

**RAY** Quite a night.

**BABCOCK** Fuckin' A. Nothin' spookier 'n a night fire, man. Makes you feel so all alone. I remember. One time. Big Island. Lava flow. Big orange tongues a molten magma whatever creepin' down the hillside like some kinda hellacious glacier. Like some kinda red-hot tectonic taffy. Eerie fuckin' thing to be comin' at ya outa the fuckin' dark, I'm tellin' ya. Fry an egg on that air. That's how hot it was. Softboil one on the palm a your hand. Melt cars. Asphalt like butter. Houses'd just pop. Bang. Like paper bags. Like that.

> *(He cups his hands & slaps them together, making a popping*
> *sound.)*

**BABCOCK** Kablooee. Spontaneous combust. From the sheer fuckin' heat. Kablam. What can you do but grab the cat, count the kids, and say a prayer to St. Jude the lava runs outa geothermal juice 'fore it dessicates you 'n yours like so much delicatessan jerky. Just sit back 'n watch it comin' toward you. Like sheer fuckin' inevitability. Lurchin' outa the dark rapture.

> *(Pause. Ray looks at him, curious, then looks away. A series of*
> *explosions in the distance.)*

**BABCOCK** See what I mean? Poppin' those fancy houses. Like so many lightbulbs on blacktop.

**RAY** Eucalyptus.

**BABCOCK** Eucalyptus what? Trees?

**RAY** Those explosions. Eucalyptus. The resins. Flammable.

**BABCOCK** No shit. Eucalyptus trees. This is some night fire. Never seen nothin' like this. Whoosh.

**RAY** I have.

**BABCOCK** Bullshit. I mean. Hard to believe. All hell breakin' loose up there 'n flyin' around like pure fuckin' insanity. Full fledged firestorm. Half the goddamn city's up in flames.

**RAY** Cambodia.

**BABCOCK** Night fire?

**RAY** As a matter of fact.

**BABCOCK** I been Cambodia. Interesting place.

(*More explosions.*)

**BABCOCK** Fuck me.

**RAY** Exciting, isn't it?

**BABCOCK** Well, yeah. One word for it. Outa the ordinary.

**RAY** I mean, this is what we live for. Catastrophe. Chaos.

**BABCOCK** I know what you mean.

**RAY** Out of our control. This is what we really want. Deep down. This is where we get our stories. Surviving catastrophe. What do you think love is? What do you think romance is all about?

**BABCOCK** I always wondered.

**RAY** Ongoing twenty-four hour we never close home-made natural disaster. I mean, you can't always count on the occasional earthquake to come along just when you need a jolt of pure adrenaline to jump start your heart. What I'm saying is, we have a deep-seated need to manufacture our own inclement weather.

**BABCOCK** Hey. Into every life. A little rain must fall. Am I right?

**RAY** Right.

**BABCOCK** I was up north in Duckburg when Mt. St. Helens shot her wad. Never seen nothin' like that. A blizzard of dry grey ash. Fallin' and fallin', all night long. You never heard such a hush. Absolute silence. Seemed like the end of the world to me.

(*Pause. Babcock watches the fire rage.*)

**BABCOCK** Don't know what it is. Cataclysmic natural disasters just seem to follow me around.

**RAY** Used to set the jungle on fire all the time. Almost couldn't help it. No big deal.

**BABCOCK** Well, I guess natural catastrophes are pretty interesting. If you survive 'em. You got a house up there?

(*Ray looks up the hill into the dark.*)

**RAY** So far. Looks like.

**BABCOCK** Which one?

(*Ray points.*)

**BABCOCK** What the fuck you doin' down here, shootin' the shit with me?

**RAY** Came down to take a look. I wanted to get some distance. Get a vista. This. This is – spectacular.

**BABCOCK** Never know. Could get lucky. Wind might change. Could rain. Sometimes the fire jumps. Passes over for no particular reason, moves on to someone else. Like the Angel of Death. Could come through unscathed. Never know. On the other hand. Better grab the family snaps. Take what you need 'n leave the rest.

**RAY**    I'll do that. Quite a night.

**BABCOCK**    Fuckin' A.

**RAY**    Actually, the world seems very peaceful to me, tonight. Quiet.
*(Babcock extends his hand.)*

**BABCOCK**    Name's Babcock.
*(Ray hesitates a moment, then shakes Babcock's hand.)*

**RAY**    Pleased to meet you.

**BABCOCK**    Good luck up there.

**RAY**    Thanks.
*(Ray leaves. Babcock watches him go up the hill towards the fire and disappear into the night.)*

**BABCOCK**    Crazy fuck. Whoosh.
*(Babcock disappears.)*


## Scene Two

**Slide:** Cabo San Lucas. A hotel room.

> *Morning.*
> *Julia, half naked on the edge of the bed. Drinks from a bottle of tequila. Danny lies on the bed beside her, eyes closed, motionless.*

**JULIA**    Cabo. Tequila. White light. Blue and white light. Blue tiles, white curtains. Blue sky, blue sea. Hot white light. Scraps of white cotton clothing scattered across a blue bed. Straw flowers. Salt. Blue agave. Breeze.
*(She drinks. Holds out the bottle. Without opening his eyes or otherwise stirring, Danny reaches up with one hand, finds the bottle, takes it, drinks.)*

**JULIA**    I thought you were dead.

**DANNY**    Hmmmmm. Not yet. Couple more days of this.

**JULIA**    Think of something blue and white.

**DANNY**    You're drunk.

**JULIA**    Drinking all day. Drinking before dark. Drinking at dawn. This is a whole other world. This is a whole other way of life. I love this. I can see the attraction. I haven't done this since I was a kid. College. San Francisco. Used to hang out at this little laundromat on Potrero Hill. Get a bottle of gin and watch the dryer go round.

**DANNY**  Some fun.

**JULIA**  Some fun. It was, you know. It really was. Gimme.

*(She holds out her hand. He gives her the bottle. She drinks.)*

**JULIA**  It's gonna be hot today.

**DANNY**  It's hot everyday. That's what makes it Mexico.

**JULIA**  I'm starting to melt. Finally. Stress. Toxins. Melting away. I've been waiting for this. Heat and tequila. Doin' the trick.

*(She kisses him.)*

**JULIA**  And sex. Mustn't forget sex.

**DANNY**  No, no. I wouldn't.

*(They kiss.)*

**JULIA**  You could help me. Help me melt.

**DANNY**  Okay. Do my best. Give it a shot.

*(They kiss.)*

**JULIA**  It's gonna be hot. It's gonna be moist.

**DANNY**  Sticky. Hot and sticky.

**JULIA**  Juicy. Juicy, not sticky. We're gonna get wet. Very very very wet.

*(They kiss.)*

**JULIA**  We're gonna sweat. A lot. We're gonna slip 'n slide. We're gonna be damp all over.

**DANNY**  Promise?

**JULIA**  Cross my heart, hope to die.

*(They kiss.)*

**DANNY**  Julia.

**JULIA**  Danny.

*(She raises the bottle, looks at the worm.)*

**JULIA**  Dibs on the worm.

**DANNY**  All yours, baby.

**JULIA**  Oh, shit. We're outa salt. Oh, what, oh, what, oh what are we gonna do? Wait. Hold everything. I have an idea.

*(She leans over. Licks up his breastbone, licks the hollow of his neck. Smiles. Licks her lips.)*

**JULIA**  Salty.

*(She drinks.)*

**JULIA**  Ah. Not too shabby. Not too shabby at all.

*(He leans over. Licks up her breastbone. Licks the hollow of her neck.)*

**JULIA**  Ooo. Ah.

*(He licks the front of her neck. She closes her eyes, clutches his hair. He licks around the base of her neck, licks the back of her neck, behind her ears.)*

**JULIA**  Oh my god. Oh fuck.

*(He stops, pulls back, takes the bottle, licks his lips, drinks.)*

**JULIA**  Salty enough for you?

**DANNY**  Not nearly.

**JULIA**  I think you know what to do about that, cowboy.

**DANNY**  I think I do.

(*He takes a big swig, but doesn't swallow. They kiss. He opens his mouth. Tequila runs into her mouth, overflows, runs down her neck. They laugh. They fall back on the bed. They kiss.*)

## Scene Three

**Slide:** Northern California. The fire site.

> *Morning. Two men in suits, Vegas & Lexington, look over the charred landscape of ash & charcoal.*

**LEXINGTON**  X marks the spot.

**VEGAS**  Hard to tell.

**LEXINGTON**  There's the bend in the road. There's the ridge. Over there's where the big white Victorian was.

**VEGAS**  Sure?

**LEXINGTON**  Positive.

**VEGAS**  Kinda hard to get your bearings. In the absence of what was.

**LEXINGTON**  The white Victorian. Which was next to the craftsman bungalow. Which was next to the newish split-level with the leaky skylights.

**VEGAS**  How do you know they were leaky?

**LEXINGTON**  You ever heard a skylights don't leak? Can't be done. The limits of human ingenuity. We cannot keep skylights from leaking. We cannot cure the common cold. And we cannot make a good-tasting spermicidal jelly.

**VEGAS**  I grew up New York. You know? Always buildin' it up 'n tearin' it down. Once somethin' was gone I could never remember what it was before it wasn't. And once somethin' else went up in its place, forget about it. Walk by one day, everything's fine, like always, walk by the next day, hey, shit, it's gone, this wasn't here yesterday, what did this used to be, remember? Shit. I could never remember.

**LEXINGTON**  This is their house. The Gaines residence. Ray and Julia's. Where it was. Take my word for it.

**VEGAS**  We know where Julia is. So, where's Ray?

**LEXINGTON**  That's one question.

**VEGAS**  Think he's up here?

**LEXINGTON**  Possible. They're still digging 'em out. Bits and pieces.

**VEGAS**  Man, earthquake, flood, fire. The actuarials in this area are gettin' positively apocalyptic. What's next? Famine? I'm thinkin' about movin' somewhere safe.

**LEXINGTON**  Oh yeah? Somewhere safe? Where would that be? (*Pause. Vegas shrugs.*)

**VEGAS**  I'll let you know.

**LEXINGTON**  Radio says body count's twenty-eight. So far. Another fifty-three unaccounted for. Missing.

**VEGAS**  Including Ray.

**LEXINGTON**  Including Ray. Figure most a the so-called missing are just outa town.

**VEGAS**  Business.

**LEXINGTON**  Business. Yeah. But they're all on their way back home by now. Caught the late clips on CNN, holy cow, there goes the life's savings, the whole enchilada, up in flames, browned out in their bermudas, tossed 'n turned all night, grabbed the first flight out bright and early, throwin' back the bloody Marys and poppin' Prozac, already fillin' out claim forms, cryin' the blues over their BMW's. Couple of 'em are still stuck abroad somewhere, tryin' to get back from Paris. Prague. Constantinople. And some of 'em. Some of 'em are still blissfully unawares as to what's transpired to the old neighborhood. Yuppie scum. Fucked seven ways from Sunday and don't even know it yet. Took off for a long weekend, a little r 'n r, a little illicit extra-marital hanky panky. Bahamas. Rosarita Beach.

**VEGAS**  Cabo San Lucas.

**LEXINGTON**  Cabo San Lucas. Come home tan, laid, relaxed, got their lies and alibis all lined up like so many ducks, bang bang bang, are they in for a shock.

**VEGAS**  Could post-facto ruin your whole vacation. In retrospect. Cast a pall.

**LEXINGTON**  Doesn't do anything for my disposition. So maybe Julia is just tearin' off a piece on the side. Gets back from a little extra-marital fuckin' around, finds the house the husband the Mercedes, up in smoke. Let's hope she didn't lose anything didn't belong to her.

**VEGAS**  We know Ray didn't go to Cabo.

**LEXINGTON**  That we know.

**VEGAS**  Babcock had an extended conversation with him. (*Babcock appears.*)

**LEXINGTON**  Where? Here, at the house?

**BABCOCK**  Down there on the flat.

**LEXINGTON**  Fuck was he doin' down there?

**BABCOCK**  Who knows? Admirin' the view.

**LEXINGTON**  Sure it was him?

**BABCOCK**  Fit the description.

**LEXINGTON**  So you swap lies, trade recipes. Then.

**BABCOCK**  Then he goes back up the hill, see if the fire's gonna do his house. Guess it did, huh? He went in. He came back out. Carryin' a coupla suitcases.

**LEXINGTON**  Ah ha.

**BABCOCK**  Puts 'em down. Goes back in. Then this whole side a the hill goes up. Whoosh. Then I don't see him no more. Then I don't see nothin' no more, on account a the smoke. Then I go home. Call you guys, tell you to come up, maybe we got a problem.

**LEXINGTON**  So what'd you talk about? You and Ray?

**BABCOCK**  Natural disasters. Catastrophe theory. Chaos. Cambodia.

**LEXINGTON**  Cambodia.

**BABCOCK**  Cambodia. Jungle fires versus conflagrations in a semi-wooded urban setting.

(*Lexington sighs, turns to Vegas.*)

**LEXINGTON**  So Ray could be up here. Somewhere. Amongst the rubble. Last seen.

**VEGAS**  Crispy critter.

**LEXINGTON**  It's possible.

**VEGAS**  Likely, even.

**LEXINGTON**  Awful convenient.

**VEGAS**  He didn't know.

**LEXINGTON**  Opportunity. Window of.

**VEGAS**  He wasn't in on it. Assuming there's something to be in on.

**LEXINGTON**  You know how many people go missing every year? Never come back from that fifteen minute jaunt around the corner? Go to the market for a quart a milk and vanish into thin? Take the main chance and disappear? Walk away and don't look back?

**VEGAS**  I dunno. How many?

**LEXINGTON**  Many. I dunno. A lot. I read. A million.

**VEGAS**  A million a year?

**LEXINGTON**  Yeah. Something like that. A million. Roughly. More or less.

**VEGAS**  I'd say less. I mean, a million a year. Pretty soon that'd add up to nobody left to mind the fuckin' store.

**LEXINGTON**  Factor in babies.

**VEGAS**  Factor in dead people.

**LEXINGTON**  Okay, a lot. Less than a million. Go missing. Take off. Change their names.

**BABCOCK**  Guys dodgin' child support.

**LEXINGTON**  Not just. Not only.

**VEGAS**  I been tempted. Start over.

**LEXINGTON**   Yeah, sure. Who hasn't? A clean slate. Which takes how long you figure before it gets completely fucked up again like your old life?

**VEGAS**   Not long.

**LEXINGTON**   Not long indeed.

**VEGAS**   Because, like the man said, wherever you go, there you are.

**LEXINGTON**   Right. So we wait a few days, see if they find Ray Gaines amongst the rubble. They don't, we wait for him to fuck up his brand new last best chance.

**VEGAS**   Which he would be bound to do.

**LEXINGTON**   I feel certain of it.

**VEGAS**   He didn't know. He had no idea this was his main chance. The door swings open. Hallelujah. He didn't know.

**LEXINGTON**   Maybe he suspected. Maybe the hairs on the back a his neck stood up.

**VEGAS**   That happen to you?

**LEXINGTON**   Yeah. Happen to you?

**VEGAS**   Yeah. Definitely. Alla time.

**LEXINGTON**   Babcock. Happen to you?

**BABCOCK**   Never.

**LEXINGTON**   How come you're still alive?

**BABCOCK**   Just lucky, I guess.

**LEXINGTON**   What about the merry maybe widow?

**VEGAS**   Julia? Maybe.

**LEXINGTON**   Maybe she'll come back from Cabo.

**VEGAS**   If she didn't, that would be a big big clue.

**LEXINGTON**   Maybe at this moment, the hairs on the back of her neck are standing up.

**VEGAS**   I wouldn't be surprised. What I hear, everything else was.
(*They laugh.*)

**LEXINGTON**   Wonder if Ray knew about that? His wife and Danny. The stuntman.

**VEGAS**   Hey. Modern marriage.

**LEXINGTON**   Babcock. Ever been to Cabo?

**BABCOCK**   Baja? Sure. Tuna fishing.

**LEXINGTON**   Bring me back a can.
(*Babcock nods, leaves.*)

**VEGAS**   Cabo. Wonder she's still there.

**LEXINGTON**   See how she takes the news when she gets back.

**VEGAS**   If she gets back.

**LEXINGTON**   Like you say. That would be a big big clue.
(*It starts to rain.*)

**VEGAS**   Startin' to rain. Shit.

**LEXINGTON**  Let's get the hell outa here before the whole hillside slides into the Bay.

**VEGAS**  Life's little mysteries.

(*They go. The sound of the rain intensifies.*)


### Scene Four

**Slide:** Los Angeles. A used car lot.

> *Night. Vapor lights. Wet pavement gleams. Plastic pennants. Two young men, Tony and Ron, stand smoking cigarettes. A middle-aged salesman, Nizam, approaches them, all smiles.*

**NIZAM**  How can I help you?

**TONY**  Looks like you had some rain.

**NIZAM**  Yeah. Cloudburst. Didn't last long.

**RON**  Could use it up north.

**NIZAM**  I heard. Terrible, terrible. What a tragedy.

**TONY**  They know, was it arson?

**NIZAM**  I don't know. I don't know. Do they know? Has it been on the news? I don't think they know yet.

**RON**  Had to be arson.

**TONY**  Why?

**RON**  So big.

**NIZAM**  Not necessarily. The drought's been worse up north than here, even. Terrible.

**TONY**  Really.

**NIZAM**  Oh, my, yes. Awful. Whole municipalities running out of water.

**RON**  We're not from around here.

**NIZAM**  Desalinization plants. That's what they're building up north. That's the future. If I were your age. That's what I'd get into.

**TONY**  Desalinization.

**NIZAM**  Yes. A gold mine.

**RON**  Sounds exciting.

**TONY**  Like the Middle East. Right?

**NIZAM**  I don't know.

**TONY**  Kuwait. Didn't the Iraqis?

**NIZAM**  Yes, I think so.

**RON**  Pumped oil into their desalinization plant.

**TONY**  Fucked up their drinking water.

**NIZAM**  I seem to recall that.

**TONY**  You look like you're from the Middle East.

**NIZAM**  Los Angeles.

**RON**  We're from Detroit.

**TONY**  The Motor City.

**RON**  Why we're here. Wheels.

**NIZAM**  So. You are thinking about buying a car?

**RON**  Oh, we're gonna buy us a car.

**TONY**  Why we're here. Tony –

**NIZAM**  Pleased to meet you.

**RON**  Ron –

  (*They shake.*)

**NIZAM**  I am Nizam.

**TONY**  Nizam. Sounds Middle Eastern.

**RON**  Tony, give the man a break. He already told you.

**NIZAM**  Yes. I am American.

**TONY**  Yeah. Just asking. You know. Roots. Background. Ethnic
  heritage. Which chip of the glorious mosaic. Sounds Middle Eastern.
  Nizam. You know, like Tony, that's Italian or something.

**RON**  You're not Italian.

**TONY**  My point. Like in Detroit, a lotta people from the Middle East.
  You know. Chaldeans. Lebanese.

**NIZAM**  I am American.

**TONY**  I understand that. Just wondering about your name. Nizam. What
  kind of name is Nizam? That's all.

**NIZAM**  I don't know. What kind of car are you thinking about?

**RON**  Good shape. Good mileage. Oil tight. Never been in a bad wreck.
  Odometer hasn't turned over.

**TONY**  In short. The impossible dream, huh?

**NIZAM**  Not at all. We have a number of vehicles that fit that description.
  May I show them to you?
  (*He starts off. Ron follows. Tony doesn't move. Nizam & Ron stop,
  look at Tony.*)

**RON**  You comin'?

**TONY**  Don't think so.

**RON**  What's the problem?

**TONY**  Let's go somewhere else.

**RON**  Long as we're here.

**TONY**  I don't like the vibe.

**NIZAM**  I thought you were interested in buying a car.

**RON**  We are.

**NIZAM**  I did not mean to insult you. Please accept my apologies.

**TONY**  I was only making conversation.

**NIZAM**  My fault. I am sensitive about my name.

**TONY**  No, I was bein' nosey. None of my business.

**NIZAM**   Okay. No problem. Okay?

**TONY**   Okay.

**NIZAM**   Good.

*(He starts off again. Tony doesn't budge. Nizam stops.)*

**TONY**   I'd still like to know. I mean. Let's establish a little trust here. This is a fraught situation. Used cars. I like you call 'em used cars, by the way. Not pre-owned or some such bullshit.

**NIZAM**   Well. There is no need for such subterfuge, is there?

*(Pause.)*

**NIZAM**   People have stereotypes. I'm sure you understand.

**TONY**   They make assumptions.

**NIZAM**   Exactly so.

**RON**   People are prejudiced.

**NIZAM**   Undoubtedly I am oversensitive –

**TONY**   No, no, not at all. Ron and me, we know what you mean. We get that all the time. Wise guys. Goombahs. Guidos. Greaseballs. Guinea fucks.

**NIZAM**   I thought you said you were not Italian.

**TONY**   My point. What is it people call us?

**RON**   When they find out our ethnic point of origin?

**TONY**   Exactly.

**RON**   Rug merchants.

**TONY**   Rug merchants. You ever heard that one, Nizam?

**NIZAM**   No. What is that? Lebanese?

**TONY**   I'm surprised you never heard that, Nizam. A person of your particular ethnicity.

**NIZAM**   I'm not an Arab. I told you.

**TONY**   I didn't say you were a rag head. Towel head. Camel jockey. Nizam. Nizam. I don't know. Sounds Turkish to me. What do you think, Ron?

**RON**   Nizam? Turkish. Definitely.

**NIZAM**   I don't understand. I thought you were interested in buying a car.

**TONY**   Oh, we're gonna buy us a car.

*(Pause.)*

**NIZAM**   Who are you?

**RON**   Just a couple of rug merchants from Detroit.

**TONY**   You never heard that one, Nizam? Rug merchants. Armenians.

*(Pause.)*

**NIZAM**   I don't have a quarrel with you, my friends.

*(Pause.)*

**NIZAM**   Stupid, really. I always meant to change it. George. I like George. My parents.

(*Pause.*)

**NIZAM**  I always wanted an American name. I was born here. L.A. East Hollywood. Western and Santa Monica. An Armenian neighborhood. (*Pause. Smiles.*)

**NIZAM**  Please, my friends. I'm sorry. I should have just told you. Let us go look at some cars. Yes?

(*He takes a step toward the lot. Tony draws a gun. Nizam stops.*)

**NIZAM**  Please. I have a family.

**TONY**  Give me your wallet.

**NIZAM**  Tell your friend not to shoot me.

**RON**  He has a mind of his own. Better do as he says.

(*Nizam hands Tony his wallet.*)

**TONY**  Kneel.

(*Nizam kneels.*)

**NIZAM**  There's money in the office safe. You can have that.

**TONY**  Speaking of prejudice. How do you feel about rug merchants? Deep down.

**NIZAM**  I would never use that term.

**TONY**  Armenian Holocaust?

**NIZAM**  Terrible.

**TONY**  Did it or did it not occur?

**NIZAM**  I don't know. Ancient history. Probably.

**TONY**  Probably?

**NIZAM**  I had nothing to do with that. I am an American. I was born in Los Angeles.

**TONY**  You keep saying that. Like it made a difference. The Turkish government says the Armenian Holocaust never happened. The Turkish government says although it never happened, even so, the Armenians brought whatever didn't ever happen on themselves. A few people died. Unfortunate. Wartime. The odd atrocity. Can't be helped. Regrettable. But nothin' like the more than one and a half million Armenian dead. Is that your position? In the ballpark?

**NIZAM**  I am an American citizen. I know nothing about that issue.

**TONY**  That issue? That issue?

(*Tony has been looking through Nizam's wallet. Now he pulls out a card.*)

**TONY**  I would think the Honorary Turkish Vice-Consul to the City of Los Angeles would tend to agree with his government on that issue.

**NIZAM**  An honorary position. Ceremonial. Not political. I just help people. You know. Visa problems. Translators.

**TONY**  Okay.

(*He puts the gun away.*)

**TONY**  You can get up now.

(*Nizam gets up, slowly. Pause.*)

**RON**   Sorry.

(*Tony hands Nizam his wallet.*)

**NIZAM**   Thank you.

**RON**   You speak Turkish?

**NIZAM**   No.

**RON**   Too bad. Your parents, right? Mine, too. They never spoke Armenian at home. Never wanted us to learn, wanted us to be American.

(*Nizam doesn't answer. Pause.*)

**RON**   East Hollywood. I got cousins, East Hollywood.

(*Pause.*)

**RON**   My Dad. My Dad always said. The terrible thing was. We were brothers. Us and the Turks. We lived together. He'd get real quiet. His eyes would get very big and dark. Whole thing really tore him up.

(*Pause.*)

**TONY**   So. About this car.

**NIZAM**   You still want to see a car?

**TONY**   Why we're here. Wheels.

**NIZAM**   I think you should go now. Get the fuck out.

(*Pause.*)

**RON**   C'mon, Tony. Man's upset. Can't blame him. Little outa line.

**TONY**   Wait wait wait. What is your feeling about this? Now that we're not chatting at gunpoint. Speak freely. Nizam. I'd really like to know.

**NIZAM**   About what? The Armenian Question?

**TONY**   Yeah. The Armenian Question. That issue. That ancient history.

**NIZAM**   All that happened a long time ago. Nineteen, what?

**TONY**   Fifteen, sixteen, seventeen, eighteen, nineteen –

**NIZAM**   A long time ago. Before I was born. Before my father was born. In Turkey. It doesn't matter to me.

**TONY**   It matters to us.

**NIZAM**   I understand.

**TONY**   But did it happen? Do you believe it happened? That's what I want to know.

**NIZAM**   I'm sure something terrible happened. Terrible things happened. I'm sorry.

**TONY**   I'm not looking for an apology.

**NIZAM**   Okay.

**TONY**   I'm looking for acknowledgement. That's all. Admission of guilt. What the Germans did to the Gypsies and the Jews. What the Japanese did to the Chinese and the Koreans. What the Americans did to the blacks and the Indians. The truth of what happened. That what happened happened.

**NIZAM**  I understand. I know how you feel.

**TONY**  Do you.

**NIZAM**  You think some great injury was done your grandparents. Great-grandparents. By mine. You want retribution. Like the blacks. Reparations for slavery. But the slaves are all dead. And so are the slave owners. The living don't know. Who did what to who. So long ago. It has nothing to do with us. We weren't there.
(*Pause.*)

**TONY**  History is a living wound.

**NIZAM**  Listen. I don't know what my great-grandparents did to yours. Probably nothing. I haven't done anything to you. I won't pay reparations. Not to you. Not to the blacks. I didn't own any slaves. I didn't kill any Armenians. I don't know anyone who did.
(*Pause.*)

**TONY**  That sound like an unequivocal admission of historical culpability to you?
(*Pause.*)

**RON**  No.

**TONY**  Me either.
(*Tony pulls his gun and fires, shooting Nizam in the throat. Nizam falls, flops, lies still. Tony stands, looking at the body. Blood begins to spread over the pavement.*)

**RON**  C'mon. Let's go pick out a car.
(*Ron walks off. Tony puts his gun away, walks over & spits on Nizam & walks off.*)


### Scene Five

**Slide:** Seattle/Cabo San Lucas.

> *Late afternoon. Simultaneously.*
> *A chic espresso bar in Seattle. Deserted. Rain. A steady downpour. Ray sits, nursing a capuccino & looking out at the rain. And:*
> *An open-air thatched-roof bar/restaurant in Cabo San Lucas. Sun. Sounds of birds. Danny & Julia are eating, drinking cans of Tecate.*

**RAY**  This is it, huh? Famous Seattle rain. Like this all the time?

**BARTENDER**  What's your name?

**RAY**  Ray.

**BARTENDER**  Where you from, Ray?

**RAY**  California.

**BARTENDER**  Ever been here before?

**RAY**  Never.

**BARTENDER**  You know that expression? Put it where the sun don't shine? They were talkin' about Seattle.

**RAY**  Relax. I'm not up here to drive up the real estate market, congest traffic, keep the salmon from spawning, or otherwise Californicate Seattle. Really.

**BARTENDER**  You know, we have a lot of expressions here. California stop. California driver. California consciousness.

**RAY**  Hey. I come in peace. Honest.

**BARTENDER**  I'll be the judge of that. So what brings you to paradise? If not to fuck it up?

**RAY**  Vacation. Thought I'd get outa town 'til my local NPR station finishes its annual pledge drive.

**BARTENDER**  God, I hate that. Yak yak yak. I'd subscribe already if they'd just shut the fuck up. 'Nother capuccino?

**RAY**  Why not?

*(Bartender moves off. Julia sighs & stretches.)*

**JULIA**  Nice. I love it here.

**DANNY**  Yeah. I'm not used to dining al fresco en Mexico. How do you keep the birds from shitting in your enchiladas?

**JULIA**  Hunker over your plate.

**DANNY**  Then they shit in your hair.

**JULIA**  Life is choices, babe. I could just stay here forever.

**DANNY**  You'd get so bored in a week.

**JULIA**  We haven't even done everything on our wish list yet.

*(They kiss. Bartender brings Ray another capuccino.)*

**BARTENDER**  *(Re: rain.)* Picked a great weekend.

**RAY**  I thought you said it was like this all the time.

**BARTENDER**  Promise me you won't move here. I'll slip you a copy of the secret sunshine schedule.

**RAY**  Secret sunshine schedule.

**BARTENDER**  Kinda like the Farmer's Almanac. Closely guarded secret. Gotta be a native to get one.

**RAY**  Like you.

**BARTENDER**  Fuck, no, I'm from Cleveland.

*(He moves off. Danny and Julia break their kiss.)*

**JULIA**  You've just given me several new ideas for this afternoon's siesta.

**DANNY**  I was wondering.

**JULIA**  What?

**DANNY**  About your husband.

**JULIA**  Oh, shit.

**DANNY**  Sorry.

**JULIA**  Last thing I want to talk about.

**DANNY**  Forget it.

**JULIA**  What?

**DANNY**  Just. What does he think?

**JULIA**  I don't know.

**DANNY**  No phone calls, no letters.

**JULIA**  There aren't any phones. The Mexican mail. That's why we're here. Cabo. That special magic.

**DANNY**  What does he think you're doing?

**JULIA**  He trusts me.

**DANNY**  That's good.

**JULIA**  He's a trusting soul.

**DANNY**  Just wondering.

**JULIA**  Why?

**DANNY**  I don't have a clear picture of him, that's all. Ray. El Rey. Ex-Ray. El Ray-o ex.

**JULIA**  Nice guy.

**DANNY**  Trusts you.

**JULIA**  Yeah.

**DANNY**  What is it he does? You told me, I forgot.

**JULIA**  What does he do or what does he wanna do?

**DANNY**  Both.

**JULIA**  He teaches an extension course at State. He wants to be a writer.

**DANNY**  Really.

**JULIA**  Screenwriter.

**DANNY**  Really. How unusual.

**JULIA**  He does some word processing for a big law firm downtown.

**DANNY**  Any good?

**JULIA**  Dynamite. Dynamite word processor.

**DANNY**  Screenwriter.

**JULIA**  I don't know. Okay. Maybe. Has promise. I can't tell. I'm not objective. Mostly he lives off my trust fund.

**DANNY**  And wants to be in show business. Like you.

**JULIA**  Like me. The difference is –

**DANNY**  Yes?

**JULIA**  I'll do it. I will. No question.

**DANNY**  I'm sure. I have no doubts.

*(Pause.)*

**DANNY**  Would you hire him? Write your first film? Give him a shot?

**JULIA**  No.

**DANNY**  That's cold. Your own wife the producer. Can't catch a break.

**JULIA**  I don't believe in nepotism.

**DANNY**  You'd hire me. I'd do your stunts.

**JULIA**  I'd hire you to body double the leading man. The nude scenes. Get your buns on film. Make you famous.

**DANNY**  I started as a focus puller. I could pull your focus.

**JULIA**  Anytime. Please. Please pull my focus. Please.

**DANNY**  Anytime.

(*They kiss. A woman, Renee, comes into the espresso bar. Sits near Ray. Catches his eye. Smiles.*)

**RENEE**  Wet enough for you?

**RAY**  Must say that a lot here. Must be one of the favorite local sayings. Like the one about moss growing on your north side.

**RENEE**  I wouldn't know. I'm from Tampa.

**RAY**  Spanish moss.

**RENEE**  Kudzu.

**RAY**  All that sunshine and kudzu started to get to you, didn't it?

**RENEE**  I needed a break. A change.

**RAY**  I know what you mean. Too much of a good thing can drive a man insane.

**RENEE**  Woman, too.

(*Bartender comes over. Renee peruses the menu.*)

**BARTENDER**  Hey. Local Seattle joke. How much is a Scandanavian haircut? Four dollars. A dollar a side. Guess you have to be a native to appreciate the contours of that particular joke. What'll you have?

**RENEE**  What's a decaf doppio mocha macchiato?

**BARTENDER**  Specialty of the house. Absolutely delicious.

**RENEE**  Absolutely not. Cafe con leche, please.

**BARTENDER**  Hey, Spanish is the loving tongue. Latte. Unleaded or regular?

**RENEE**  Regular. No question. Leaded. Extra lead.

**BARTENDER**  Maximum butter fat?

**RENEE**  With a spoon.

**BARTENDER**  Alright.

(*Bartender moves off. Babcock enters the Cabo cafe, sits, watches Danny & Julia neck.*)

**RENEE**  I've never seen so many espresso bars. Per capita.

**RAY**  Crazy for caffeine. Whole town's wired for sound.

**RENEE**  I guess that's one way to cope with the rain.

**RAY**  I can think of others.

**RENEE**  Me, too.

(*Danny and Julia break their kiss.*)

**DANNY**  Gonna have to spend more time in L.A.

**JULIA**  I already am.

**DANNY**  I spend a lot of time in L.A. I live there.

**JULIA**  I noticed.

*(Pause.)*

**DANNY**  Does he know?

**JULIA**  No.

**DANNY**  He doesn't know what you do in L.A.?

**JULIA**  He knows I'm putting together a deal. He doesn't know what I do. Who I do.

*(She kisses him. Babcock looks around for a waiter. Waiter approaches.)*

**WAITER**  Si, senor.

**BABCOCK**  Tecate, por favor.

**WAITER**  Si, senor.

*(Waiter follows Babcock's gaze. Danny & Julia, getting hot & heavy.)*

**WAITER**  No hay problema. Estan casados.

**BABCOCK**  Si. Pero no uno con la otra.

*(Waiter walks off. Danny & Julia get up and leave. Bartender brings Renee's latte.)*

**BARTENDER**  There you go. A big steaming cup of high-octane, cholesterol-rich, artery-clogging, keep-you-up-all-night-staring-at-the-ceiling-grinding-your-teeth heaven. Enjoy.

*(He leaves.)*

**RENEE**  Cheers.

**RAY**  Salud.

*(They clink cups. They drink. A long look.)*

**RENEE**  My name's Renee Valenzuela.

**RAY**  Spanish.

**RENEE**  Cuban, actually.

*(A pause. She looks at him, expectantly. He decides.)*

**RAY**  Ray. Ray Avila.

**RENEE**  Avila. Sounds Cuban.

**RAY**  Czech. Neruda. Neruda was a Czech name.

**RENEE**  Who's Neruda?

**RAY**  A poet.

**RENEE**  A Czech poet.

**RAY**  A Spanish poet. Chilean, actually.

**RENEE**  Oh.

*(She smiles.)*

**RENEE**  Ray. So, Ray. Tell me about yourself.

*(He smiles.)*

## Scene Six

**Slide:** San Francisco. Law offices of Mathis & Scones.

*Morning. Julia, dressed in a sober suit, sits across from Mathis, who opens a briefcase and extracts a stack of papers.*

**MATHIS**   I'm sorry this has taken so long, Mrs. Gaines. My apologies. Profuse.

**JULIA**   That's quite alright, Mr. Mathis.

**MATHIS**   We appreciate your patience. We are inundated at the moment. The fire. You can imagine. A veritable tsunami of claims. And the percentage of fraudulent claims. Distressingly high.

**JULIA**   Really.

**MATHIS**   Shocking. People exploiting their personal calamity for remuneration. Imagine. We're seeing some preposterous inflations.

**JULIA**   Really.

**MATHIS**   Oh, my, yes. Very creative. Stupid, some of them. Demonstrably false. I mean, would you put in a claim for a painting which is already hanging in at least one major museum? Please. That's why your claim is such a pleasure – well, not a pleasure, of course –

**JULIA**   It's alright. I know what you mean.

**MATHIS**   But straightforward. Honest. Well-documented.

**JULIA**   Yes. Well. I never imagined. You take precautions, but you never imagine. Funny. There were things in the safe deposit box that surprised me. Some silly mementos of our honeymoon. Seashells. I didn't think Ray was so. I don't know. Sentimental. And then there were things missing. Things I expected to find. Photo album. His passport. His lucky Buddha. He never travelled without his lucky Buddha. For a crazy moment I thought, maybe he isn't dead. Maybe he's just gone somewhere. He'll come back.
*(Pause.)*

**MATHIS**   Where would he go?

**JULIA**   I don't know.
*(Pause.)*

**JULIA**   I suppose they were just lying around the house somewhere. Lost in the fire.
*(The door opens. Scones enters, with a folder.)*

**MATHIS**   Ah. Here he is.

**SCONES**   Julia.

**JULIA**   Mr. Scones.

**SCONES**   How are you?

**JULIA**   Holding up. Quite a shock.

**SCONES**  I should imagine.

(*Pause.*)

**JULIA**  I was in Cabo. I came down to breakfast. Saw the paper. The
headlines. Two days old. And then I couldn't get a seat on a plane
back. And then when I got home. And saw the house. Where the house
had been. You just can't imagine. You can't conceive of this
magnitude of misfortune. Always to others. Never to me.

(*Pause.*)

**JULIA**  And then when they found the body. What was left of the body.
His wedding ring, melted from the heat of the fire. Fused with bone.
Not even enough for an urn. Some bone dust, some fragments, the
melted ring. All it amounted to in the end was a small ornamental box.
Carved. Hardwood. I held it in my hand. I shook it. It rattled and
shushed.

(*Pause.*)

**MATHIS**  I understand the service was quite elegant.

**JULIA**  Lovely. All his friends. His favorite Bach.

**SCONES**  It was beautiful.

**JULIA**  Very nice of you to come.

**SCONES**  We thought the firm should be represented. And I knew Ray
slightly. Mutual friends. The Aragons. We played racquetball once or
twice.

(*Scones opens his folder. Takes out two checks, and some papers,
glances at them briefly and passes them across to Julia.*)

**SCONES**  The first is for the house, the second is the life insurance
payment. Accidental death. Totaling, less our fees and expenses, one
point one million dollars. Please sign at the red x's and initial within
the circles.

(*Julia signs.*)

**MATHIS**  Will you be rebuilding?

**JULIA**  No. I'm selling the property. Moving to Los Angeles. I have
business interests there.

**SCONES**  Starting over. Starting a new life.

**MATHIS**  It's best. It's the best thing.

**JULIA**  Yes.

**SCONES**  Well. If there's anything further we can do. Please don't
hesitate to call.

**JULIA**  Thank you. Mr. Scones. Mr. Mathis.

(*Julia pockets the checks. Stands.*)

**JULIA**  Goodbye, gentlemen. I'm sure I'll never see either of you ever
again.

(*She leaves.*)

## Scene Seven

Slide: Seattle. A hotel room.

*Evening. The sound of a constant, steady rain drumming against the window. Renee is in bed.*

**RENEE** My great-grandfather worked in the cigar factories in Ybor City. The Cuban quarter of Tampa. With Jose Marti himself. Then when Marti went back to Cuba to fight for independence, my great-grandfather followed him. So there was this link with Tampa and my family that goes way back. So when my parents left Cuba after Castro, they moved to Tampa instead of Miami, because of what my Dad heard from his grandfather.

*(Ray appears in the doorway from the bathroom, wearing only a towel & brushing his teeth.)*

**RENEE** My great-grandfather never touched a tobacco leaf in his life. He didn't even smoke. He was a reader. He read out loud while they worked. Rolling cigars. Newspapers. Pamphlets. Socialist tracts. Revolutionary stuff. Fairy tales. Novels by Balzac. The workers demanded a reader. And the owners paid. They thought it would improve productivity. The owners didn't care. It was all in Spanish. And the Cubans were all going back to Cuba as soon as they could. Didn't have anything to do with Ybor City. With America.

*(Pause.)*

**RENEE** My dad was a big man. Big hands. He never talked politics. Which was unusual. I mean, my uncles. Whenever they started, Castro this, Castro that, he'd just sit and stare. Like he was a million miles away. Back in Cuba, maybe.

*(Pause.)*

**RENEE** I came home from college one spring to check on him. My mom had died the year before. It was late. Ten o'clock. He was sitting at the table in his undershirt. It was hot already. He was sweating. He was eating yucca, drinking rum. I could smell the garlic from the street. Through the screen door.

*(Pause.)*

**RENEE** I like yucca. Reminds me of my dad. So there he was. Eating yucca, drinking rum, watching TV. The local news. Haitians, boat people, down in Miami. Complaining about the preferential treatment for Cuban refugees. And my dad's kinda drunk. And he starts in on what I call the Cuban catechism. The catalogue of sorrows and betrayals. Marti. Batista. Castro. Exile in America. Bahia de Cochinos. Bay of Pigs. And I asked him. Were you in the Bay of Pigs? I'd never asked him that before. And he said no. He was in the second wave. Which never happened. Stuck in Miami. Waiting to go in. Attack Havana. Take back the casinos. And then he started talking about Kennedy. The betrayal. He promised them. He sold them out. He made a deal with the Communists. I never heard my father like that. So bitter. From the heart. Hate from the heart.

*(Pause.)*

**RENEE**   And then he said, I never told anyone this. Not even your mother. And I said, Popi you can tell me. And he said, I know who killed him.

*(Pause.)*

**RAY**   Kennedy.

**RENEE**   Kennedy.

*(Pause.)*

**RAY**   So. Did he tell you?

**RENEE**   Yeah. He made me swear first. Which I did. On my mother's memory.

*(Pause.)*

**RAY**   You're not gonna tell me?

*(She smiles and shrugs.)*

**RAY**   You know who killed Kennedy? And you're not gonna tell me?

**RENEE**   I swore.

**RAY**   Well, that's an interesting story, Renee. A little frustrating.

*(Pause.)*

**RAY**   It lacks an ending. It's a bit of a tease, if you know what I mean.

*(Pause.)*

**RAY**   You know the answer to the greatest mystery of the Twentieth Century, and you're not gonna tell me? Renee. I thought we had a nice time. Didn't we have a nice time?

**RENEE**   Yummy. Better than fried yucca.

**RAY**   That good? So, tell me.

*(Pause.)*

**RENEE**   He's dead now. Popi. I guess it doesn't matter.

*(Pause.)*

**RENEE**   He did.

**RAY**   Who?

**RENEE**   My father. My father killed Kennedy.

**RAY**   Your father.

**RENEE**   Was the second gunman on the grassy knoll.

**RAY**   He told you that.

**RENEE**   Yeah. That's what he said. The second gunman. The grassy knoll. They started calling it that later. He didn't know it was the grassy knoll then. He was just there. He fired the second shot. The one that killed him. The one that blew his head apart.

**RAY**  What else did he tell you?

**RENEE**  Nothing.

**RAY**  No details? No context? No plot?

**RENEE**  No.

**RAY**  Other Cuban exiles?

**RENEE**  I assume.

**RAY**  Who he was working for?

**RENEE**  Oh. CIA. Obviously. Goes without saying.

**RAY**  Oh, sure. Well. It'd better. If you know what's good for you. Wait. Your father told you he killed Kennedy. You believed him?

**RENEE**  Wild, isn't it? I mean, my Daddy killed the President? Popi? But then I started to think about it. I mean, somebody had to do it. I mean, it had to be somebody. Somebody did do it. And why shouldn't that somebody have a family and a daughter? Why shouldn't that somebody be my father? Yeah. I believe he did. No question. He never lied to me. Not once in my whole life.

**RAY**  But. How do you feel about it? Daddy killed the president?

**RENEE**  He was my father.

(*Pause.*)

**RENEE**  So, you see. If my great-grandfather hadn't gone into exile in Tampa with Jose Marti, maybe we wouldn't've come back to this country, and my father wouldn't've killed Kennedy. You can just never tell where a thing gets started, can you?

(*Ray nods, goes back into bathroom to rinse out his mouth. Renee reaches over, turns out the light. Ray re-enters the room in the dark. Gets into bed.*)

**RAY**  What about Oswald?

**RENEE**  He didn't say.

**RAY**  Renee –

**RENEE**  He didn't say. I forgot to ask.

(*Pause. Ray turns the light on. Looks at her.*)

**RENEE**  I wasn't thinking clearly.

(*He turns the light out. Pause.*)

**RAY**  I'm in bed with a woman whose father killed Kennedy. Told her he killed Kennedy. What am I supposed to feel? I'm not clear what I'm supposed to feel.

**RENEE**  Feel this.

(*Pause.*)

**RAY**  That feels nice.

**RENEE**  Oh. Yes.

(*The sound of Ray & Renee rolling off the bed & hitting the floor. Pause.*)

**RAY** Don't stop.

**RENEE** I can't see a fuckin' thing. Oh. There we go.

**RAY** Right.

(*They continue in the dark.*)


## Scene Eight.

**Slide:** Santa Barbara. A greenhouse.

> *Afternoon. Rows and rows of orchids. Julia is waiting. She paces a*
> *little. Sighs. Footsteps on wooden boards. She gets very still. They*
> *come nearer. Nearer. She tenses, almost holding her breath.*
> *Babcock appears. She relaxes. Glances at him briefly, then looks*
> *away. He stands and watches her until she looks back at him. She*
> *frowns.*

**JULIA** I know you.

**BABCOCK** Doubt it.

> (*He walks off. Distracted, Julia takes a pack of cigarettes out of her*
> *purse, extracts one, and lights up. Takes a drag. A smoke alarm bleats.*
> *She jumps.*)

**JULIA** Jesus.

> (*She grinds out the cigarette under her heel. The alarm stops.*
> *Lexington and Vegas appear behind her. Sensing their presence, she*
> *turns, sees them, starts again.*)

**JULIA** Oh. Mr. Lexington. Mr. Vegas. You frightened me.

**VEGAS** Us?

**JULIA** You.

**LEXINGTON** Shouldn't smoke in here.

**JULIA** Forgot where I was. You're late.

**VEGAS** God, it's sexy in here. So sexy. Must be the heat, huh? So damp.
Sultry. All this perfume. Hothouse, huh? These flowers are. They're
obscene. Orchids. Look like sex. Like female genitalia. Don't they?
Julia?

**JULIA** Yeah. That's what they look like. Pussies.

**LEXINGTON** So. How ya doin', Julia?

**JULIA** I've been better.

**VEGAS** Did we express our condolences?

**JULIA** No.

**LEXINGTON** Forgive us. We've been remiss.

**JULIA** Thank you.

**VEGAS** The loss of your husband. A hard thing.

**JULIA** Yes.

**LEXINGTON** You were close.

**JULIA** We were married.

**LEXINGTON** Leaves us with a problem, though. Apparently.

**JULIA** The money.

**VEGAS** Isn't that always the problem? These situations?

**JULIA** Bad luck.

*(Pause.)*

**JULIA** I don't know what to do.

**LEXINGTON** This is a problem.

**VEGAS** Maybe we can help.

**LEXINGTON** Tell us where the money is.

**JULIA** What do you mean? You know where the money is. It's gone.

**VEGAS** Not gone. Missing.

**JULIA** It was in the house. It burned up in the fucking fire.

**VEGAS** That fire was somethin', you know? I personally know eight
mid to high level dealers, down dudes, lost homes in that fire. Those
guys. Pounds of money. Acres of cash. Big burlap bags of swag in the
basement. Enough loose scratch up there to put a dent in the national
debt. So much cigarette ash. Tragic.

**LEXINGTON** We too have our financial anxieties. You may not realize.
Cash flow. Payroll.

**VEGAS** Not taxes, thank God.

**LEXINGTON** No. Not taxes. We don't pay taxes. We do pay tribute.
Contrary to what you may think we are not at the top of the fuckin'
food chain. Far from it. Plus, the precedent. Heinous. We can't just let
this go. We can't just chalk it up to a so-called act of God and write it
off. We'd be outa business in a week.

*(Pause.)*

**LEXINGTON** What I wanna know is. Why was our money in your
house? Isn't this the crux? The very essence of the matter? Why we're
havin' this little chat? *(Inhales.)* Perfume. Sheer perfume.

**VEGAS** Nectar.

**LEXINGTON** Pleasant surroundings. An unexpected perk.

**VEGAS** I never been to Santa Barbara before. Nice. Doesn't Reagan live
around here somewhere?

**LEXINGTON** Still. I'd like to get back to L.A. before dark.

**JULIA** The paperwork wasn't in place.

**LEXINGTON** You're kidding.

**JULIA** I've been constructing a plausible scenario. Hong Kong investors.
Capital flight. Large amounts of insecure cash seeking fiduciary
sanctuary. Until everything was in place I couldn't deposit that much
unlaundered money without risking exposure. Putting our arrangement

in jeopardy.

**LEXINGTON**  Everything was in place. You assured us. Partner.

**JULIA**  Last minute offshore snafu.

**VEGAS**  Somebody's brother-in-law in the Caymans needed help with his daughter's orthodonture.

**JULIA**  Something like that. I was set to make the initial deposit first thing that morning. The day after the fire. Bad luck.

**LEXINGTON**  The day after the fire.

**JULIA**  Yes.

**LEXINGTON**  You were in Cabo. With Danny.

(*Pause.*)

**LEXINGTON**  How were you supposed to make the fuckin' deposit from Cabo?

**JULIA**  Ray.

**VEGAS**  I told you.

**LEXINGTON**  No, you didn't. Don't start with me.

**JULIA**  Per my instructions. Pre-arrangements.

**VEGAS**  You wouldn't want to share those pre-arrangements with us.

**JULIA**  Our deal was, the details are my affair.

**VEGAS**  So to speak.

**LEXINGTON**  Our deal was, the money washes through the Caymans' account, less your split. No sign of it, last time I looked. Not a red fucking cent.

(*Pause.*)

**VEGAS**  Ray.

**JULIA**  He didn't know. He trusted me.

**LEXINGTON**  He trusted you? He trusted you? You're in Cabo, fucking some stunt man. Oh, by the way, honey, while I'm in Baja, boffing my boyfriend, could you please run this seven million dollars in small unmarked bills down to this crooked banker friend of mine. He's gonna launder 'em for me at the local fluff 'n fold. Don't ask any questions, I'll explain the whole thing when I get back.

**JULIA**  The parcel was sealed. He had no idea.

**VEGAS**  A trusting soul, this Ray.

**JULIA**  Yes.

(*Pause.*)

**JULIA**  How did you know? About Cabo? About me and Danny?

(*They shrug.*)

**JULIA**  That guy who walked through here. I have seen him before. In a cafe in Cabo.

**VEGAS**  Fuckin' Babcock, huh? 'Bout as inconspicuous as a tarantula on a slice of angel food cake.

**LEXINGTON**  That's good. You make that up?

**VEGAS** Raymond Chandler.

**LEXINGTON** I don't know him. Sounds like a smart cookie. Could he maybe replace Babcock.

**VEGAS** He's dead.

**LEXINGTON** Too bad. Sounds like the kinda guy with whom you could go to the track. Entertaining. So. Julia. To return to the crux.

**JULIA** I'll pay you back.

**LEXINGTON** Goes without saying.

**VEGAS** But how?

**LEXINGTON** You don't have our investment. Without which you don't have your production company. And our arrangement is. What's the word? Moot.

**VEGAS** Too bad. We were looking forward. A long-term arrangement. Convenient and profitable for both parties. A little glamour. Could rub off, who knows. Maybe you win an Oscar. Thank us, your acceptance speech. My good friends, colleagues.

**LEXINGTON** I told you.

**VEGAS** Don't start with me.

**LEXINGTON** This is what we get for wantin' to be in show business. Succumbing to the lure.

**VEGAS** You know what they say. A propos show business. Be careful who you get in bed with. You lie down with whores, don't be surprised you get up with clap. Or somethin' worse. Somethin' terminal. (*Pause.*)

**JULIA** What can I do?

**LEXINGTON** I wonder what really happened. I see several scenarios. Yours.

**VEGAS** Unforeseen offshore snafu. Fire. Money and husband, burned to a fare thee well. Double whammy. What's a grief stricken widow to do?

**JULIA** Yes.

**LEXINGTON** Or. The money wasn't in the house.

**JULIA** What do you mean?

**LEXINGTON** Maybe you took the cash to Cabo with you. Pretty nice nest egg. Screw show business. Spend the rest a your life fuckin' Danny under the coconut palms. Then the fire. The perfect out. Stash the dough in Mexico. Come back, blow smoke up our nose, cry some crocodile tears at the funeral. Perfect. Takes balls.

**JULIA** No.

**LEXINGTON** Or. Here's an interesting one. Ray took the money.

**JULIA** Ray is dead.

**LEXINGTON** So you say. Ray took the money. Peeked in the package. Biggest fire a the century. The door swings open. The main chance.

Hallelujah. He thinks, fuck the pre-arrangements. Take the money and run. Sorry, honey. Doesn't mean I don't love you. But let's face it. Seven million dollars is seven million dollars.

**VEGAS**  Res ipsa loquitor.

**LEXINGTON**  Fuck's that?

**VEGAS**  Thing speaks for itself.

**LEXINGTON**  No shit.

**VEGAS**  Cheer up, Julia. Maybe he'll drop you a postcard from Belize.

**JULIA**  They found his body.

**VEGAS**  They found a body. Not even. Bits and pieces. Bits and pieces.

**JULIA**  I told you. The money was at the house. Ray was to take the money to the banker as soon as everything was in place. I left town. I went to Cabo. To distance myself. To provide deniability.

**VEGAS**  To get laid.

**JULIA**  That was lagniappe,

**LEXINGTON**  Fuck's lagniappe?

**JULIA**  A little something extra. A little something on the side. As we say in New Orleans.

**VEGAS**  You from New Orleans?

**JULIA**  Originally.

**VEGAS**  Never been to New Orleans.

**JULIA**  You should go. So. When I got home, everything was fucked up. Ray was dead, the money was gone. End of story.

**VEGAS**  Not quite.

(*Pause.*)

**LEXINGTON**  She's cool. Gotta hand it to her. Ice water veins.

**VEGAS**  Why we got in bed with her. In the first place.

**LEXINGTON**  I'm gonna call you Ice Water from now on. Instead a partner. We know a few things, too.

**JULIA**  I'm sure you do.

**LEXINGTON**  How many things we know?

**VEGAS**  At least three. Probably more.

**LEXINGTON**  We know your banker.

**JULIA**  Oh? Who would that be?

**LEXINGTON**  Mr. Souza. Chinese-Portuguese guy from Macao. Am I warm, Ice Water?

**JULIA**  Lukewarm.

**LEXINGTON**  We had a chat with Mr. Souza. He said he was expecting an initial deposit in the neighborhood a five million dollars.

**VEGAS**  We said seven.

**LEXINGTON**  He said five. Said you told him to expect five. He seemed quite certain on this particular point. This was a discrepancy.

**VEGAS**  A two million dollar discrepancy. If I remember the arithmetic the nuns taught me.

**LEXINGTON**   A nice segue. Brings us to the second thing we know. We know you're in bed with someone else.

**VEGAS**   Coupla rug merchants of our acquaintance.

**JULIA**   Rug merchants?

**VEGAS**   Standard ethnic epithet. Armenians.

**LEXINGTON**   Ron 'n Tony. Crack 'n smack.

**VEGAS**   You're a girl got a lotta guys. Popular. Lined up around the block. In bed with so many partners, must get confusing. James. Danny. Me 'n Lex. Mr. Souza. The rug merchants. Anybody else? Hope you use prophylactics. Cause you're fuckin' a lot of people. (*Pause.*)

**LEXINGTON**   How much?

**JULIA**   Three hundred percent. Guaranteed.

**VEGAS**   Dream on.

**JULIA**   They promised me a quick return on my investment. I needed more money for a bankable star. Foreign pre-sale.

**LEXINGTON**   I mean, how much you invest with our friends Ron 'n Tony?

**JULIA**   Two million. I held five back. To deposit with Mr. Souza.

**VEGAS**   Sure.

**JULIA**   I swear.

**LEXINGTON**   Don't swear, Ice Water. Tell me somethin'. This windfall profit a three hundred percent. You planning to share that with us? Partner?

**JULIA**   Fuck, no. I was planning to put it all back in the movie.

**LEXINGTON**   I like your balls. I have to admire your balls.

**VEGAS**   Heard from Ron 'n Tony?

**JULIA**   Not lately.

**LEXINGTON**   Took a powder, didn't they? So to speak. Tell you what they been up to recently. Blew away some used car dealer.

**VEGAS**   Dumb fucks.

**JULIA**   Why?

**LEXINGTON**   He sold them a lemon. Who knows? Some Armenian thing. Militant bullshit. Used the money you gave 'em to finance their pathetic operation.

**JULIA**   Fuck.
(*Pause.*)

**JULIA**   You know where they are.

**VEGAS**   That's the third thing. Third thing we know. You thinkin' what I'm thinkin'?

**LEXINGTON**   Recoverable. Part of it, anyway. Still leaves us short five, and change.

**VEGAS**   Which maybe you stashed in Cabo. Insurance. Case the deal
with Ron 'n Tony went south. Which it appears to have done in a
hurry.
**JULIA**   Ray is dead. The money was in the house. The five million. It
burned. Ron and Tony ripped me off for the other two. That's the
reality.
**LEXINGTON**   So you say.
**VEGAS**   Not one of the things we know. For a fact.
**LEXINGTON**   What's that word? Lagniappe?
**JULIA**   Lagniappe.
**LEXINGTON**   We got a lagniappe for you. Partner.
(*Pause.*)
**LEXINGTON**   Ever been to Key West?
(*She looks back and forth between them, wondering.*)


## Scene Nine

**Slide:** Key West. The Smudgy Cockatiel.

> *Sunset. The veranda of a Victorian gingerbread hotel. Potted
> palms, flowers, Japanese lanterns. A breeze. A Combo plays. A
> Lounge Singer sings "Jamaica Farewell." He finishes. The very
> slightest smattering of applause from the few people sitting on the
> porch, including Ray, who is with an attractive woman, Max.*

**LOUNGE SINGER**   Thank you. Thank you. I'm gonna take a short
break now for sex on the beach.
(*Rimshot.*)
**LOUNGE SINGER**   That's a drink. With rum. Safe sex on the beach is
without the rum.
(*Rimshot.*)
**LOUNGE SINGER**   Sorta like a Virgin Mary. Shirley Temple. Nancy
Reagan. Tipper Gore. Hello? You all come in the same car?
(*Rimshot.*)
**LOUNGE SINGER**   Like they say, not a dry seat in the house. But
seriously. Ladies and germs. We'll be back after a brief pause for some
serious altitude adjustment. In the meantime, let's have a big hand for
the band. They're Doing The Best They Can. That's the name of the
band, not necessarily the opinion of the management. C'mon, give it
up. Give it up for They're Doing The Best They Can. Yeah. Alright.
Yahoo. Oh, boy.
(*He exits into the lobby.*)

**RAY** They're good. They're really pretty good. They're not that good.

**MAX** (*Southern accent.*) Let's have another mai-tai, they'll get better again.

(*She holds up two fingers & signals a Waitress.*)

**WAITRESS** Mas mai-tais?

**MAX** Por favor. So. Ray –

**RAY** Max.

**MAX** That's my name. Don't wear it out.

**RAY** How'd you ever get a name like Max? I like women with men's names. Max. Sam. Michael. Turns me on.

**MAX** Whatever floats your boat, sugar. Now, listen. There's some parts of your story I don't quite understand.

**RAY** Like what?

**MAX** Your house burned down.

**RAY** Right.

**MAX** While your wife was in Cabo San Lucas.

**RAY** Right.

**MAX** With her boyfriend. The stunt man. Screwin' her brains out.

**RAY** We don't know that.

**MAX** We can imagine. Listen, you don't go to a foreign country to commit adultery and then not commit it, if you know what I mean.

**RAY** You're probably right.

**MAX** Okay. She's in Mexico. Screwin' her brains out. And in general, your domestic situation sucks. Is that a fair summation?

**RAY** Close enough.

**MAX** So this fire comes along. The window of opportunity opens and you dive through it, and disappear. Here's my question. Why?

**RAY** What do you mean?

**MAX** Your wife's actin' like a crazed mink, why not just call a lawyer? Get a divorce.

**RAY** That wouldn't've changed anything. Don't you see? Married, divorced, dead. Bing, bing, bing. Same old conveyor belt. Same old station stop on the same old commuter train everyone else is on. Didn't you ever want to start over? Burn off your old life? Make a clean break? Go somewhere you don't know anyone and no one knows you? Where nobody has any assumptions about who you are? That fire. I saw that fire and I felt – blessed. Ecstatic. Free. Everything I owned. Papers. Photos. Family heirlooms. All my personal possessions. Gone. Up in flames. Like shedding an old skin. All that baggage. That history. That old life that didn't work. That I'd fucked up from day one. Melted away. I saw myself floating up from the flames like the phoenix. I could walk away from all that. Spit out the ashes. Reinvent myself.

(*Pause.*)

**RAY**  So I bugged out. Got on a plane to someplace I'd never been before. Cool my heels and think about how to do this. How to disappear. How to reincarnate.

**MAX**  Seems extreme. But I understand the impulse. I've been there once or twice myself. Light out for the territory and don't look back. It's very American.

**RAY**  Huckleberry Finn.

**MAX**  So you go to Seattle. Somewhere you don't know a living soul. You get lucky, first thing. Find yourself a Cuban-American princess from Tampa who claims her Daddy killed Kennedy. Don't walk away, Renee.

**RAY**  Pretty weird, I admit.

**MAX**  Even weirder, a few days later you pick up a copy of the *Chronicle* at an outa town newspaper stand. There's your name, a picture of the grieving widow. They've identified your remains. Found a body. Whose?

**RAY**  A looter, maybe. Somebody who was in the wrong place at the wrong time. Who knows? Unlucky for him. Lucky for me. Makes me not missing. Makes me dead.

**MAX**  So now you're deceased. You roll clear across the country to start your new life. Rollin' on the bias to the end of the line. Until you can't roll any further. Like a cue ball rollin' on a downhill slant toward the corner pocket of a table on the tilt. A straight shot. Like you're on a wire. A track. And you drop plop in the pocket here in Key West. With all the rest of us left over, burnt out, semi-retired, freelance drug dealers, gun runners, dope smugglers, sponge divers, snook fishermen, con artists, right-wing Cuban terrorists, beatnik hippie homosexuals, assorted social misfits, full-time professional beach combers, conchs, shrimpers, suckers and spies.

**RAY**  Don't forget drunks.

**MAX**  Drunk is redundant in Key West, darlin'.

**RAY**  Happy to be here.

**MAX**  Happy you're here. This is the place, baby. The original on the lam, in a jam, made in the shade, don't ask too many questions, place. You know, they used to deliberately set the lights in the channels to lure ships onto the reef. Then they'd go out and salvage the wrecks. Console the survivors. Chuck 'em under the chin. Give 'em some hot coffee, dry drawers, and a ticket on the next train outa town. Wreckin' was the major industry. Cigars and shrimp a distant second. By the way. What's your last name? Did you say?

**RAY**  Which one? My old one, or my new one?

**MAX**  Either.

*(Pause.)*

**MAX**  Pretty tall tale, Ray.

**RAY**  You don't believe me?

**MAX**  I have my doubts. I admit. A little skeptical around the edges.

**RAY**  What'd I leave out?

**MAX**  For starters, you say you want to burn off your old life and disappear down the rabbit hole, but you don't do anything about your appearance. Grow a mustache. Dye your hair. You don't even change your first name. And as soon as you get to town, launch your new life, you take up with some strange woman, tell her the whole crazy scheme.

**RAY**  I felt I could trust you.

**MAX**  Jury's still out.

*(Pause. Ray smiles.)*

**RAY**  It's a screenplay,

**MAX**  Thought so. Thought you made it up.

**RAY**  I wanted to try it out on you. Crack a bottle of champagne over my story, and see if it would make it past the reef to open water. My real name's Ray Avila, not Raymond Gaines. I'm not married. I'm not dead. I don't live in the Bay Area. My house did not burn down.

**MAX**  Thanks a lot. How'm I 'sposed to trust you now? First thing, before we've even slept together, you tell me a whopper.

**RAY**  Pretty entertaining, though.

**MAX**  Mildly entertaining.

**RAY**  More than mildly.

**MAX**  Needs work.

**RAY**  I admit.

**MAX**  How's it turn out?

**RAY**  I don't know yet.

**MAX**  Some story. Got a title?

**RAY**  Dark Rapture. As in, you never know.

**MAX**  You never know, what?

**RAY**  You never know what's out there, lurchin' in the dark rapture.

**MAX**  I'm not familiar with that particular saying.

**RAY**  Cambodia. Used to say that in Cambodia. Seemed appropriate. You never did know. And the rapture was very dark. Very dark indeed.

*(Pause.)*

**RAY**  They used helicopters in Southeast Asia. You may have heard. And some of these pilots. Show boats. Liked to clip the tops of the trees. Fly as low as possible over the rice paddies. Churn the surf. The real macho hot shots would bomb down these dirt roads, nothin' more than tracks through the jungle, six or so feet off the ground, strafing everything in sight, blowing up water buffalos, having a great time. So what the VC'd do, Khmer Rouge, Pather Lao, whatever, they'd string a wire across the road, or a rope, between the trees. First thing in the morning, here comes hot shot, hell bent for leather, whompa whompa whompa, twing. Hits that wire, clips his rotors, goes up in a fire ball. Whoosh. Which event I always thought was the war in a nutshell. All it took to even the playing field, bridge the gap in technology, bring down a multi-million dollar machine, was a piece of wire strung across the road.

*(Pause.)*

**MAX** You were a helicopter pilot?

**RAY** Door gunner. Strafing those villes. I was the guy, after interrogation at five hundred feet, used to kick the prisoners out the door.

*(Pause.)*

**RAY** Kidding. I'm kidding.

*(Pause.)*

**RAY** I was a door gunner on a Huey. But I never kicked anyone into the ether.

*(The Combo starts in on "Margaritaville.")*

**MAX** C'mon. Let's go dance barefoot on the beach.

*(Max pulls Ray out of his seat & onto the dance floor.)*

**RAY** I lit up an elephant once. A thousand rounds. Dissolved in a big pink cloud.

**MAX** Liar. You are some liar. Ray.

**RAY** I went to college with a pathological liar. A liar of Pinocchio proportions. Certifiable. World-class liar. He'd make up the most outrageous stories. Scary part was, he seemed to believe them. Everything he said. Every last lie. I thought he should be institutionalized. Instead, he grew up to be a presidential speechwriter. He's in Washington working for the current administration, as we speak. It's true, I swear.

*(Max takes Ray by the hand and leads him toward the beach. The Combo & Lounge Singer continue with "Margaritaville." Babcock appears on the veranda. Slow fade to black.)*

## END ACT ONE

# ACT TWO

## Scene Ten

**Slide:** Key West. The Smudgy Cockatiel.

*Sunset. Ray and Max are the only customers. The veranda is otherwise deserted. The light is hallucinatory, strange, violet and pearl-colored. A stiff breeze is blowing.*

**RAY**   God, the light's strange. Looks bruised.
**MAX**   Hurricane light. All purple and mother-of-pearl.
**RAY**   I shoulda gone to the Bahamas yesterday, like I planned.
**MAX**   Ever wonder why, in the movies, they like to have wild, passionate, out of control sex standing up against a wall? Preferably in public?
**RAY**   Often. Every waking moment.
**MAX**   I mean, this is completely mythological. Some weird Hollywood idea of a good time. Our eyes meet. We kiss. Suddenly we're chewing each other's lips off. We're knocking furniture over in a mad dash to get to the nearest wall. You slam me, bam, up against the wall, I hike up my skirt, wrap my legs around your waist, rip rip rip, my blouse, your shirt, my panties, your pants, fabric fabric fabric, buttons buttons buttons, pop pop pop, you're magically hard as a rock, I'm miraculously pre-lubricated, we maneuver everything just so, I slip you in, ooo eee ah, a perfect fit, we have an immediate volcanic simultaneous orgasm without benefit of protracted foreplay, or formal introduction, all in an impossible, uncomfortable, positively painful position while you throw your back out, and I scrape every last inch of skin off my shoulder blades. Which is exactly what you would expect to result from having wild, out-of-control, wake the entire neighborhood, bump-and-grind, howl at the moon sex, up against a stucco wall. I mean, why don't they just lie down? Get horizontal like the rest of us.
**RAY**   I don't know. Looks better for the camera.
**MAX**   I guess. But, you ever try that for real? Doesn't work. Angles are all wrong. I mean, where's the attraction? You always end up on the floor anyway. Gravity dictates.
**RAY**   What do you think? I guess it's too late to leave town. Maybe we should have.
**MAX**   Poor Ray. You were just passing through weren't you? Then you

met me.

**RAY**   Yeah. Blew my itinerary.

**MAX**   We'll just hang tight. Weather the storm. I like hurricanes. We'll be okay. Where's the waitress? I want another mai-tai.

**RAY**   Battening down the hotel hatches. Hurricane shutters. Hurricane lamps.

**MAX**   We'll get drunk and watch the palm trees bend over parallel to the ground. Always exciting.

**RAY**   This is my first hurricane.

**MAX**   They're fun. Scary as shit.

**RAY**   At this point, I don't think we have any choice.

(*Pause.*)

**MAX**   Ray. You know, I was looking for. Well. I was basically going through your drawers. Snooping around. I wanted to read your script. I didn't find it.

**RAY**   Script's not in my drawers.

**MAX**   I found some other stuff. Passport. With your picture. Some other stuff says you're you. Sorry. I like you. I'm a suspicious bitch. I wanted to make sure. I mean, you are some liar. We know that's true.

**RAY**   Should I ask you for your ID?

**MAX**   I'd be hard pressed to prove everything I've told you. I tend to exaggerate a little. Embroider around the edges. Most of it's more or less factual. I found the clipping. About the fire. How they found this fella's body. Gaines? About his wife. A picture of the grieving widow.

(*Pause.*)

**RAY**   Research. Where I got the idea.

**MAX**   I thought you made that story up.

**RAY**   I did. Most of it. Clipping was just a point of departure.

**MAX**   I apologize for going through your things.

**RAY**   Don't worry about it. Script's in the closet. I'll dig it out. If you really wanna read it.

**MAX**   In the suitcases?

**RAY**   You go through those, too?

**MAX**   Course not. They were locked. I didn't have the moxie to try and jimmy 'em.

**RAY**   Nothin' in 'em but scripts. Papers. Contracts. Bullshit. My life is about little scraps of paper.

**MAX**   Efficiency experts say you should only handle a piece of paper no more than one time. It's in your hand, then it's outa your life.

**RAY**   Interesting.

**MAX**   Before I was a drug dealer, I was an efficiency expert. And before I was an efficiency expert, I was an exotic dancer. Princess Totempole. I had a black wig, and a pair of trained ravens, who would pluck the scarves off my body, one by one.

**RAY**   Trained ravens.

**MAX**   Tristan and Isolde. They were very talented. And then
when Tristan and Isode got too old to pluck, I put away the black wig
and started performing under the stage name of Miss Cherry Bounce.

**RAY**   Miss Cherry Bounce.

**MAX**   After the drink. Cherry bounce.

**RAY**   I'm not familiar with that particular drink.

**MAX**   It's a southern concoction. Cherries marinated in vodka and pure
grain alcohol. Packs a punch. The highlight of my act as Miss Cherry
Bounce was an interpretive dance to the theme from *Perry Mason*.
(*She scats some bars, mimes a few moves. Sexy and very dramatic.*)

**MAX**   It was wildly popular.

**RAY**   I'll bet.

(*Babcock strolls onto the veranda, sits at the next table.*)

**BABCOCK**   Hey.

**MAX**   Hello.

**BABCOCK**   I know you.

**RAY**   I don't think so. Sorry. Can't think where.

**BABCOCK**   Ever spend time in the Bay Area?

**RAY**   Not to speak of.

**BABCOCK**   Well. Who knows? It'll come to me. Mind if I join you?

**MAX**   Hey. Lifeboat party. More the merrier.

(*Babcock pulls up a chair at their table.*)

**BABCOCK**   I'm Babcock.

**RAY**   Ray Avila. And this is Max.

**BABCOCK**   Max. Pleased to meet you.

**MAX**   Ditto, I'm sure.

**BABCOCK**   Max. What is that short for? Maxine?

**MAX**   Margaret.

**BABCOCK**   Margaret. Really. I like that.

(*Babcock looks around for the Waitress.*)

**BABCOCK**   Kinda slow. Who do you have to know to get a drink in this
stellar establishment?

**MAX**   They're all inside, getting ready for Hurricane Lazlo.

**BABCOCK**   Lazlo? This is a Hungarian hurricane?

**RAY**   I'll go to the bar. What do you want?

**MAX**   Mai-tai.

**BABCOCK**   Cuba libre.

**RAY**   Right back.

(*Ray exits into the hotel.*)

**BABCOCK**   Remember when hurricanes had women's names? I'm
nostalgic for that era. Hurricane Annabella. First hurricane of the

season. Never been in a hurricane myself. Bound to happen.

**MAX** How so?

**BABCOCK** Cataclysmic natural disasters just seem to follow me around. Been in earthquakes, bad ones. Eruptions. Floods. Tidal waves. Typhoons. Blizzards. Big big fires. Read about the recent Bay Area blaze?

**MAX** Yeah. As a matter of fact.

**BABCOCK** I witnessed that up close. Chaos. Sheer chaos.

**MAX** Really. You live there?

**BABCOCK** No. Lucky for me. Just visiting. I know Ray from somewhere. Tell me. You know, was he ever in the service? Southeast Asia?

**MAX** Not that I know of.

**BABCOCK** I thought maybe. Cambodia. Probably not. Long time ago. So. Max. What it is you do?

**MAX** A little of this, a little of that. Like everyone in Key West. In the summer we live off the fish. In the winter we live off the Yankees.

**BABCOCK** I know what you mean. A little of this, a little of that. Me, too.

(*Pause. They trade smiles.*)

**BABCOCK** What line a work is Ray in?

**MAX** Screenwriter.

**BABCOCK** Really. How unusual. Must be exciting.

**MAX** You don't sound like a Yankee.

**BABCOCK** What do I sound like?

**MAX** I don't know. Can't quite place it.

**BABCOCK** Maybe I'll go see can I help Ray with the drinks. Back in a flash.

**MAX** 'Kay.

(*Babcock exits into the hotel. The light darkens. The wind comes up. The rain starts.*)


### Scene Eleven

**Slide:** Key West. The Smudgy Cockatiel.

*Morning. The veranda. Babcock is smoking a cigarette. Lexington, Vegas, and Julia come out of the hotel.*

**VEGAS** Which way's Cuba?

**BABCOCK** That way.

**VEGAS** See it from here?

**BABCOCK**  Ninety miles. Look at that surf. Killer surf.

**VEGAS**  What was it like?

**BABCOCK**  Exciting. No other word for it.

**VEGAS**  Sorry we missed it. Stuck in Miami. They closed the airport. I never been in a hurricane. One a my unfulfilled aspirations. This place held up pretty good.

**BABCOCK**  Hey. These old buildings. They knew whereof. Built for the weather. You know? Not like this new condo shit. Windows fall out when somebody slams the door. Plus. We were lucky. A mile from here there's nothin' standing. Looks like Hirofuckingshima. Palm fronds all over the place.

**LEXINGTON**  You through?

(*Pause.*)

**BABCOCK**  Don't know how he coulda got off the island.

**LEXINGTON**  By boat. Would be my guess. This being an island and all.

**BABCOCK**  Maybe he had time to get up to the next Key before the hurricane hit. Be foolish to try.

**VEGAS**  Plus, the desk clerk. Said he had a coupla heavy suitcases. Which are nowhere to be found.

**LEXINGTON**  Ray comes outa the men's room. Spots Babcock in the bar, talking to this Max girl. He runs upstairs. Grabs his suitcases. Down the back stairs. Runs down to the dock. Persuades some Bahamian fisherman take him up the next Key. With a hurricane comin'? You buy that?

**VEGAS**  Maybe he didn't grab the suitcases. Maybe she did. The girlfriend.

**LEXINGTON**  Max.

**VEGAS**  Ray sees Babcock, figures the jig is up. Goes out the rear exit. Clothes on his back. Gives him a fighting chance. While Babcock is out lookin' for him in the middle of Hurricane fuckin' Lazlo, Max grabs the bags. Buries 'em in her back yard.

**LEXINGTON**  Permutations. Fuckin' permutations are drivin' me batshit.

**BABCOCK**  I'll go toss her place.

**LEXINGTON**  Not yet.

**JULIA**  Wasn't Ray.

**LEXINGTON**  Then who? Wasn't Ray, then who?

**JULIA**  Ray is dead.

**LEXINGTON**  Goin' by the name of Ray Avila.

**JULIA**  If it is Ray, and he did take the money, why would he call himself Ray Avila? Avila's a Spanish name.

**BABCOCK**  Cuban, actually.

**VEGAS** Life's little mysteries.

**BABCOCK** She told me he was a screenwriter.

**JULIA** Who isn't?

**LEXINGTON** Wasn't your husband, then who?

**VEGAS** Fits the description.

**LEXINGTON** We describe him, everybody says, yeah, sounds like the guy. What more do you want? What else do we have to go on? In the absence of a fuckin' photograph.

(*Julia gives him a look.*)

**LEXINGTON** I know, I know. Don't tell me. The fire.

**VEGAS** Awful convenient.

**JULIA** Ray was average. When you describe Ray, you describe a lot of guys.

**VEGAS** If Babcock had seen him, we'd know.

**LEXINGTON** Yeah. We'd know was it the same guy he talked to the night of the fire.

**BABCOCK** Missed him by that much. Hey. Know what I think? I think this guy, whoever he is, Ray Avila, Ray Gaines, just ran outa luck. If the fire didn't get him, the hurricane did. The snook are feedin' on him as we speak.

**LEXINGTON** Babcock. Ever been to Tampa?

**BABCOCK** Sure. Alla time. Excellent Cuban food.

**LEXINGTON** Bring me back a plate a ropa vieja.

(*Babcock puts out his cigarette, exits into the hotel. Julia looks at Lexington.*)

**JULIA** What's in Tampa?

**LEXINGTON** Busch Gardens.

(*Pause.*)

**JULIA** What now? May I ask?

**LEXINGTON** We'll hang out. Eat some conch fritters. Go talk to Miss Max. See if she has any fresh dug holes in her back yard. It'll be fun. Treasure hunt. Then we'll go down the end of Duvall Street. Watch the sunset. Look for the famous flash a green.

**VEGAS** Get Jimmy Buffet's autograph.

**LEXINGTON** Tomorrow we'll go back Miami. Drop a dime on our friends in the rug racket.

(*He looks at Julia.*)

**LEXINGTON** Okay with you? Partner?

**JULIA** You weren't gonna call me that.

(*The Waitress comes out on to the veranda.*)

**WAITRESS** What'll it be?

**VEGAS** Mai-tais all around.

**WAITRESS** You got it.

(*She exits into the hotel. Vegas looks at Julia.*)

**VEGAS**   Are we having fun yet? Julia?

(*Julia looks at him, gets up, goes into the hotel.*)

**VEGAS**   What's in Tampa?

**LEXINGTON**   Calls to Ray Avila from a pay phone in Ybor City to here at the Smudgy Cockatiel on a regular basis. Desk clerk said it was always the same woman.

**VEGAS**   Not much to go on.

**LEXINGTON**   How'd he get off the island? Guy's good.

**VEGAS**   Not that good. Maybe Babcock's right. Maybe he didn't. Maybe he's fish food.

**LEXINGTON**   Fuckin' Babcock. Had him between his thumb and forefinger.

**VEGAS**   Yeah. We have to do something about that.

(*Pause.*)

**VEGAS**   Missed him by that much. You buy that?

**LEXINGTON**   No.

**VEGAS**   Me either.

**LEXINGTON**   Said he got a tip.

**VEGAS**   Yeah. But instead a meeting us in Miami as per our instructions, he goes on ahead, gets here first, spooks him.

**LEXINGTON**   Fuckin' Babcock. What's he up to?

**VEGAS**   He's got the hook in. Deep. Playin' this Avila guy like a bone fish, givin' him lotsa line, lettin' him run, hopin' he'll run to the money. Babcock won't reel him in 'til he's sure, one way or the other. Is this guy really Ray Gaines, where's the money.

**LEXINGTON**   Babcock, Babcock, Babcock. Scammin' us all the way. Problem is, so much loose cash floatin' around, nobody's inclined to share.

**VEGAS**   Isn't that always the problem, these situations? Chum's in the water.

**LEXINGTON**   Fuck's chum?

**VEGAS**   You know. Blood. Guts. Gets 'em excited.

**LEXINGTON**   Feeding frenzy.

**VEGAS**   Exactly.

(*Lexington stands.*)

**LEXINGTON**   Let's go talk to Miss Max.

**VEGAS**   What about the mai-tais?

**LEXINGTON**   Fuck the mai-tais.

(*Lexington exits into the hotel, passing the Waitress on her way out with a tray of four mai-tais.*)

**WAITRESS**   Where'd everybody go?

**VEGAS**   Somethin' came up.

(*He lays a fifty on her tray.*)
**VEGAS**    Put those in a go cup for me, will ya, darlin'?
**WAITRESS**    No problem.
   (*She follows him in.*)


### Scene Twelve

**Slide:** Tampa.

>  *Night. A half-darkened kitchen. Babcock is sitting at a formica table in his undershirt, eating yucca and drinking beer. He's sweating, mopping his brow with a paper towel. He hears the front door lock turn, and stops eating. Listens intently. Footsteps move through the next room and stop just outside.*

**BABCOCK**    Renee? Mi hija?
   (*Pause. Ron and Tony come into the kitchen.*)
**BABCOCK**    Oh, boy.
**TONY**    What smells?
**BABCOCK**    Garlic and lemon.
**TONY**    What're you eating? Garlic soup?
**BABCOCK**    Yucca.
**TONY**    Fuck's yucca?
**BABCOCK**    It's good. It's a tuber. Want some?
**TONY**    No, thanks.
**BABCOCK**    Lexington and Vegas are looking for you.
**TONY**    They found us.
**RON**    Why we're here.
**TONY**    Help you out.
**BABCOCK**    How so?
**TONY**    We cut a deal. This your house?
**BABCOCK**    No.
**TONY**    You look pretty much to home.
**BABCOCK**    I know the person owns this place. Stay here I'm in town.
**RON**    Renee?
**BABCOCK**    Yeah. What kinda deal?
**TONY**    Lexington and Vegas. Had we known.
**RON**    Never. We're not crazy.
**TONY**    We figured this Hollywood producer. This Julia Gaines girl. Song and dance about Hong Kong investors. She wants to get into wholesale product. Okay. Rip her off. Who's she gonna tell?
**RON**    Her agent?

**TONY**  She gonna tell her agent a coupla dealers ripped me off, do somethin' about it? I don't think so.

**RON**  Turns out these Hong Kong investors turn out to be Lexington and Vegas. Oh, shit.

**TONY**  Holy shit. Luckily, she backs us up on this.

**BABCOCK**  Julia.

**TONY**  Right. That we had no idea. In the dark. We came this close. Lexington and Vegas are not guys to fuck around with. I like your house.

**BABCOCK**  I told you. Not mine.

**TONY**  Still. Nice.

**RON**  Also luckily, we still had most of the dough.

**TONY**  Kills me. But. What can you do? Who's Renee?

**BABCOCK**  My daughter.

**TONY**  She around?

**BABCOCK**  No. She's outa town. Why I'm staying here.

**TONY**  But when we came in. You thought it might be her.

**BABCOCK**  I didn't know. Who else had a key?

**TONY**  Us, actually.

**BABCOCK**  So you pay the money back. Most of it.

**TONY**  Yeah. Kills me. We had a sweet sweet deal lined up.

**RON**  Arms for Armenia.

**BABCOCK**  Catchy.

**TONY**  First-class ordnance. State of the art anti-personnel devices.

**RON**  A little something for the old country.

**TONY**  These Azerbaijani fucks. Turks by another name. And, let's face it. A Christian island in a Muslim sea. All those people are Turks. One kind or another. So the kin folk could use some help. But. What can you do?

**RON**  We'll promote something else.

**TONY**  We paid back what we had. Said they'd forgive the rest. Clear our tab. On condition we pitch in.

**BABCOCK**  Help me find Ray.

**TONY**  General idea.

**RON**  Got any hunches?

**BABCOCK**  What'd they turn up at the girlfriend's?

**TONY**  Max?

**BABCOCK**  I take it not the money.

**TONY**  Not the money nor Ray nor this Max girl neither. She was outa there so fast she forgot to turn her Mr. Coffee off. Melted the element.

**RON**  Any idea where we should look next?

**BABCOCK**  I think maybe he went to New Orleans.

**TONY**  The Crescent City.

**RON**   What makes you think that?

**BABCOCK**   Maybe you should check it out.

**RON**   Maybe we will.

**TONY**   Why don't you tag along?

**BABCOCK**   I'll join you there. Leave word. Gotta touch base with Lexington and Vegas.

**TONY**   Let's go now. Their idea.

**BABCOCK**   Mind if I call 'em?

**RON**   Feel free.

(*Pause.*)

**BABCOCK**   Now?

**TONY**   Why not?

**BABCOCK**   Middle of the fuckin' night for Christ's sake. Next plane's tomorrow morning.

**TONY**   We'll drive.

**BABCOCK**   You serious?

**RON**   It'll be fun. Watchin' the sun come up on The Redneck Riviera. Beautiful.

**TONY**   C'mon. Throw some stuff in a bag. Let's go.

**BABCOCK**   Okay. Sure.

(*Babcock pushes back from the table. As he gets up he picks up his plate of yucca and his beer bottle and takes a step towards the sink. Moving suddenly, he hurls his plate in Ron's face and breaks the bottle across Tony's. He tries for the door. Tony tackles him, puts a gun to his head, and a knee in his back.*)

**TONY**   Stop. Stop now. Just stop. I don't wanna have to whack you in your daughter's house.

(*Babcock lies still.*)

**RON**   You okay? Got blood all over.

**TONY**   You can drive me to the emergency room later. Toss the rest of the house.

(*Ron exits. Tony stands.*)

**TONY**   Stay down. Don't do anything stupid.

(*He finds a cloth, holds it to the side of his head.*)

**TONY**   Babcock. What kind a name is Babcock?

**BABCOCK**   I don't know.

**TONY**   When'd you change it?

**BABCOCK**   I never changed it. Not like some.

**TONY**   So what is Babcock? Alias?

**BABCOCK**   Nom de guerre.

**TONY**   Fuck's that mean? Who are you when you're at home?

**BABCOCK**   Chibas. Jose Marti Chibas Valenzuela.

**TONY**   That's a mouthful. A Cubano mouthful.

**BABCOCK** Chinga tu madre.

**TONY** Now, I know what that means.

(*Ron enters the room, carrying something wrapped in soft black cloth. He puts it on the table.*)

**RON** Look at this.

(*Tony unwraps the bundle. Inside is a high-powered sharpshooting rifle, in pieces, immaculately kept. He holds it up to the light.*)

**TONY** Well well well. What do you hunt, Chibas? Deer?

**BABCOCK** Javalinas.

**RON** Fuck's a javalina?

**BABCOCK** Wild pigs.

(*Tony examines the rifle.*)

**TONY** A real collector's item. Circa 1960. Cherry. You don't use this much.

**BABCOCK** Once or twice.

**TONY** A real museum piece.

(*Pause. He looks at Ron.*)

**TONY** Put it back. Leave her something to remember her Daddy by.

(*Ron shrugs. Wraps up the rifle, exits.*)

**TONY** Go ahead. Get up.

**BABCOCK** gets up.

**TONY** Let's go for a drive.

(*Babcock gets up.*)

**TONY** See how far we get.

(*Babcock exits. Tony follows him. As he leaves the room, he turns off the kitchen light, leaving it in darkness.*)


## Scene Thirteen

**Slide:** New Orleans. The Napoleon House.

*Afternoon. Ray and Renee are sitting at a table, drinking Pimm's Cups. The door is open to the sidewalk. Light and air are streaming in.*

**RAY** Everywhere I go has peaked. Hawaii. Key West. Greenwich Village. Puerto Vallarta. Katmandu. You should have seen it back when. Before it got popular. Before the tourists slash criminals slash developers ruined it. It was something in the old days. Boy. Things ain't what they used to be. Too bad. Shoulda seen it. Shoulda been there. Mexico. Tahiti. Bali. Big Sur. Whole fuckin' world's past its prime. But. But I like it here. You do? You like this? This is nothing.

Shoulda seen it before it got ruined. Before it got fucked up. Say that about New Orleans, too. Crime. Kids on bicycles with automatic weapons. Can't go out after dark. Too many tourists. Too much graft. You should been here back in the days it really was The City That Care Forgot. By which I suspect a lotta people mean, before black folks got the vote. The Planet of New Orleans. Been in decline since the Civil War. So to say New Orleans is past its prime is really beside the point.

**RENEE**   Your wife was from New Orleans?

**RAY**   Originally.

**RENEE**   You're divorced?

**RAY**   She's deceased.

**RENEE**   Sorry.

**RAY**   Yeah. I like it here. I like you can sit on the east bank of the Mississippi, and watch the sun come up over the West Bank. Place is surreal. I like the decay. I like the humidity. I like the way the sewers back up when it rains. I like the above-ground cemeteries, the dripping walls, the hurricanes, the whole below-sea level soggy underfoot suck your sneakers off swamp thang program. Everything damp. Decadent. Rotten. Basically, I like New Orleans because it looks and smells and tastes like a tropical cathouse.

**RENEE**   I have something to tell you.

**RAY**   You're married.

**RENEE**   No.

**RAY**   You're gay.

**RENEE**   I don't think so. I lied to you. About my father. About Popi.

**RAY**   He didn't kill Kennedy.

**RENEE**   No. I mean, as far as I know, he did.

**RAY**   That's a relief. I was just glueing my belief system back together. My world view.

**RENEE**   He's not dead. My dad. I lied about that. But I swore on my mother's memory I'd never tell. And I felt bad about breaking my word. But I had to tell someone. What I told you. About Popi. After all these years. And I felt I could trust you.

**RAY**   People feel that way. I don't know why.
   (*Pause.*)

**RENEE**   What're we gonna do here?

**RAY**   Go to Mother's. Get a shrimp po'boy. Drive out St. Claude Avenue to the lower Ninth Ward, take a look at Fats Domino's house. Take a nap. Ruin our livers. All kinds of excitement.

**RENEE**   That sounds good. Especially the part about the nap.

**RAY**   Renee. Thanks for meeting me here. Bringing my things.

**RENE**   No problem. C'mon, let's go. I'm starving.

*(She picks up her purse and strolls out. He downs his drink, and follows.)*


### Scene Fourteen

**Slide:** New Orleans. A hotel room.

*Night. Ray is sitting on the bed, his shoes off. Lexington is smoking a cigarette. Vegas is scrutinizing Ray's passport.*

**LEXINGTON** Well?
*(Vegas shakes his head.)*
**VEGAS** Good. Professional. Expensive. Kosher? I don't think so.
*(He tosses it to Ray.)*
**VEGAS** How much you pay for it?
**LEXINGTON** Who are you?
**RAY** That's me.
**VEGAS** That's your picture. But your passport's forged. How come you have a forged passport, pal?
**RAY** That's my passport.
**LEXINGTON** What's your real name?
**RAY** It's right there.
**LEXINGTON** Ray Avila? I don't think so. I think you're Raymond Gaines. Married to Julia Gaines.
**RAY** I'm divorced.
**LEXINGTON** I'm not surprised. You being deceased and all. Hell on the home life.
**VEGAS** Where's the money?
**RAY** I don't have any money. Wish I did.
**VEGAS** Let's say you're Ray Gaines. Not Ray Avila. Let's say Ray Avila doesn't exist. Let's say you stole our money. Which we want back.
**RAY** No. Sorry.
**LEXINGTON** Five million.
**RAY** Wouldn't that be nice?
**VEGAS** Your wife's parcel. You were supposed to take to Mr. Souza?
**RAY** Sorry. Name's Avila. These other people. Ray and Julia Gaines. Souza. I don't know them.
**LEXINGTON** Where are the suitcases?
**RAY** Suitcases.
**VEGAS** You check into a hotel, you got suitcases. Where are they?

**RAY**  You got the wrong guy.

**VEGAS**  I don't think so. I think you're Ray Gaines alright. Why didn't you change your first name, Ray, while you were at it?

**RAY**  I give up. Too much trouble?

**VEGAS**  No. No, this is trouble. What you got now.

**LEXINGTON**  If he is Gaines, whose body did they find in the rubble?

**VEGAS**  The meter reader, who knows? Life's little mysteries.

*(The key turns in the lock.)*

**LEXINGTON**  One a which we're about to clear up.

*(The door opens, Renee enters carrying a large white paper sack. Starts when she sees Lexington and Vegas.)*

**LEXINGTON**  Who the fuck're you?

**RENEE**  Who're you?

**RAY**  This is my friend, Renee.

**VEGAS**  What's in the bag, Renee?

**RENEE**  Muffulettas. Want one?

**VEGAS**  Fuck's a muffuletta?

**RENEE**  Sandwich. Olive spread and cold cuts.

**VEGAS**  Sounds horrible.

**RENEE**  Suit yourself.

*(She sits on the bed next to Ray, unwraps the sandwiches, gives one to Ray.)*

**RAY**  You mind?

**VEGAS**  Be my guest. I personally would not choose something called a muffuletta for my last meal.

**RENEE**  What does he mean by that? Ray?

**RAY**  A joke. Relieve the tension.

**RENEE**  I wasn't tense.

**VEGAS**  We are.

**RENEE**  Ray, who are these payasos? They're scaring me.

**RAY**  They think I'm somebody else. They think I have something of theirs I don't have.

**RENEE**  What?

**LEXINGTON**  Five million dollars. Less incidental expenses. Incurred galavanting all over the country.

**RENEE**  No way. No way he has five million dollars.

**VEGAS**  How would you know? Renee.

**RENEE**  I don't. I don't know.

**VEGAS**  I hope you don't.

*(A key turns in the lock.)*

**VEGAS**  That must be the goombahs now.

**LEXINGTON**  About time.

*(The door opens, Ron and Tony enter. Tony is carrying two heavy*

*suitcases.)*
**RON**   Look what we found.
*(Tony sets the suitcases down.)*
**TONY**   We persuaded the manager to open the office vault.
**RON**   He didn't wanna do it, but we appealed to his pain threshold.
**LEXINGTON**   Where's Julia?
**RON**   In the hall.
**LEXINGTON**   Ask her to come in.
*(Ron opens the door, steps into the hall. Everybody waits. In a moment, Julia steps into the room. She sees Ray, stares. Ron comes in behind her, closes the door. Everybody waits.)*
**LEXINGTON**   I believe you two. May have met.
**JULIA**   No.
*(Pause.)*
**JULIA**   No. Never.
**RAY**   Mrs. Gaines. I take it.
**JULIA**   This is not my husband. This is not my Ray. Ray Gaines. Not at all.
**VEGAS**   You sure?
**JULIA**   Don't be stupid.
**LEXINGTON**   Who the fuck are you?
**RAY**   Avila. Ray Avila.
**TONY**   Avila. What kinda name is Avila? Spanish?
**RAY**   Czech, actually.
**TONY**   Sounds Spanish to me. Cuban.
**RON**   You got Cubans on the brain.
**LEXINGTON**   Ice Water. What're you saying?
**JULIA**   I'm saying I don't know who this man is. I've never seen him before. My husband is dead. He died in the fire. I wish you'd quit torturing me.
*(Lexington turns to Tony.)*
**LEXINGTON**   What're you waiting for? A papal dispensation? Open 'em.
**TONY**   Alright. Alright. Don't get your boxers in a wad.
*(Tony picks the locks on the first suitcase. Ron picks the locks on the second suitcase. Tony pops the locks on his suitcase.)*
**TONY**   Voilá.
*(The suitcase is full of scripts.)*
**TONY**   What the fuck?
**RAY**   Spec scripts.
*(Pause. Julia starts to laugh, hysterically.)*
**JULIA**   Spec scripts. Jesus. That's hilarious. Spec scripts. Hee hee. Spec scripts. Whoo. Whoo. Hysterical. You caught yourself a screenwriter.

A felonious screenwriter. Congratulations,
*(Julia's laughter subsides. She stops laughing, wipes tears from her eyes. Looks at Lexington and Vegas, who aren't laughing.)*
**JULIA**   I'm sorry. Inside joke. Spec scripts. Hoo hoo.
*(Ron pops the locks on the second suitcase. He turns it over, scattering the contents. It's full of papers.)*
**LEXINGTON**   Maybe we shoulda held onto Babcock. ID this bird.
**TONY**   Shoulda thought a that before we went to Tampa.
*(Lexington looks at Ron and Tony.)*
**LEXINGTON**   Go on. Get the fuck outa Dodge. We're square.
**TONY**   Can I get it in writing?
**VEGAS**   Hey. Up to this moment, contrary to all expectation, you been a coupla very lucky white boys. Don't fuck up your undeserved good fortune.
**TONY**   You say so. See you around.
**RON**   Ciao.
*(They leave. Lexington fixes on Ray. He draws a gun, points it first at Ray, then holds it to Julia's temple.)*
**LEXINGTON**   Lie to me, Ice Water. Tell me he's not your husband.
**JULIA**   No. This man is not my husband.
*(Lexington cocks the gun. Points it at Ray.)*
**LEXINGTON**   You don't care? You don't care if I waste this asshole?
**JULIA**   Be my guest. For all I know, he stole the money. Murdered Ray. Left his body to burn. In fact, do him. Go ahead. Do him. I want you to. Just in case.
*(Pause. Lexington considers. Vegas touches his arm.)*
**VEGAS**   Lex. Give it up. The money's gone. It's history. It's in the video stores.
*(Pause. Lexington wavers.)*
**VEGAS**   What'll we do with these loose ends? We can't do 'em here.
*(Pause. Lexington looks them over.)*
**JULIA**   Who're you talking about?
**LEXINGTON**   All a you. All three a you.
**JULIA**   Please.
**LEXINGTON**   Don't beg, Ice Water. Ruin my image.
*(Pause.)*
**JULIA**   I think we should resurrect our original arrangement.
*(Pause. Lexington lowers the gun.)*
**LEXINGTON**   You're kidding.
**JULIA**   You got most of the two million back from Ron and Tony. I told you I'd pay back the rest.
*(Pause.)*
**VEGAS**   Whaddya think? Wanna get back in bed with her?

**LEXINGTON**  She's got balls.

**VEGAS**  Why we got in bed with her in the first place. Honest mistake. Over ambitious. Took a gamble. Didn't pan out. Wasn't a bad deal. We still need a reliable fluff 'n fold on a regular basis.

**JULIA**  I'll throw in the money from Ray's life insurance policy. As a token of good faith.

**VEGAS**  How much you get from that deal?

**JULIA**  Five hundred K.

**VEGAS**  That all? You got burned, babe. So? Whaddya think?

**LEXINGTON**  I don't know. Ice Water. Still got a burning desire to make movies?

**JULIA**  Of course.

**LEXINGTON**  We participate from dollar one a the gross.

**JULIA**  I basically have no problem with that.

**LEXINGTON**  First, you pay us back the seven million you owe us.

**JULIA**  Five. You got two back already.

**LEXINGTON**  Seven. The original five plus two for vigorish and sheer fuckin' aggravation.

**JULIA**  What choice do I have?

**LEXINGTON**  None.

**JULIA**  Sounds wonderful to me.
    (*Pause.*)

**JULIA**  I keep the life insurance money.

**LEXINGTON**  They just get bigger 'n bigger, don't they? What do you do, sprinkle testosterone on your Lucky Charms?

**JULIA**  I need to buy a house.

**VEGAS**  Five hundred K in L.A.? That's a teardown, babe. A fixer-upper in the Valley. You can't buy anything for five hundred K in L.A. –

**LEXINGTON**  Hey. Hey. Hey. You through? Wait downstairs. Partner.
    (*Julia leaves.*)

**VEGAS**  So whaddya think?

**LEXINGTON**  I still think she took the five million in the first place, stashed it in a coconut in Cabo. What the hell. We get some proof? We can always do her later.

**VEGAS**  See how her first picture turns out. Whack her for sheer aesthetic reasons.

**LEXINGTON**  Good idea. Furthermore, I feel I should do these two on general principles. Leading us on a wild fucking coast-to-coast goose chase.

**VEGAS**  Lex –

**LEXINGTON**  Why do you have a forged passport, pal?

**VEGAS**  Lex. Lotsa people got forged passports. Including us. Come on. Let's go talk to our new partner. I got an idea I wanna pitch her. For a western. Come on. Let it go. These people are tourists.

**LEXINGTON**   Okay, okay. Fuck. Can't do you here, anyway. Let's get outa here. Fuck.

(*They leave. Pause. Renee looks at Ray.*)

**RENEE**   Who are you?

**RAY**   Raymond Avila.

**RENEE**   Did you take their money?

**RAY**   No.

**RENEE**   Who was that woman?

**RAY**   I don't know. Never saw her before.

**RENEE**   Then what was that all about?

**RAY**   Mistake. They mistook me. They thought I was somebody else.

**RENEE**   Some mistake. That man was talking about killing us. We came this close to being murdered.

**RAY**   I know. I know.

(*Pause.*)

**RAY**   Renee. You didn't tell anyone you were meeting me here, did you?

**RENEE**   No.

(*Pause.*)

**RENEE**   Just my dad.

(*Pause.*)

**RENEE**   He wouldn't tell anyone. I trust him.

**RAY**   You trusted me, too. Shows you what a judge of character you are.

(*Pause.*)

**RENEE**   Who would he tell? He doesn't have anything to do with these people. These gangsters.

(*Pause.*)

**RAY**   How did you happen to pick Seattle for a vacation? Did you say?

**RENEE**   Far away from Tampa as I could get.

(*Pause.*)

**RENEE**   As much as I like you, Ray, I don't wanna be here if they change their minds and come back.

**RAY**   Neither do I.

**RENEE**   I think I better go home now. Call Popi.

(*She gets up, goes into the bathroom. Ray takes a bite of his muffuletta.*)


### Scene Fifteen


**Slide:** Los Angeles.


*Danny's apartment. He is shiftless, lounging on the floor watching a video, eating popcorn. Doorbell rings. He gets up, goes to the door, opens it. Julia steps in.*

**DANNY**   Hey.
**JULIA**   Hey, yourself.
   (*He gives her a kiss.*)
**DANNY**   Glad to see you. Sight for sore eyes. Come in. You look beat.
**JULIA**   Rough trip.
   (*She comes in, sets her bag down.*)
**DANNY**   Make your deal?
**JULIA**   Yeah. Yeah, I did. I think so. I think it's all coming together. At last.
**DANNY**   That calls for a celebration. Let me pop a bottle of Dom.
   (*He goes in the other room. Julia collapses for a moment. Danny returns with a bottle of Dom Perignon and glasses.* )
**DANNY**   You okay?
**JULIA**   Just jet-lagged. I'll be alright in a minute.
**DANNY**   So, tell me about your trip. How was New York?
**JULIA**   Oh, you know. New York.
   (*He pops the cork.*)
**DANNY**   Yeah. Goin' to hell in a handbasket. New York, New York. Sound so nice, they had to name it twice. Tell me what street compares to Mott Street in July. I'll tell you what street compares to Mott Street in July. Last time I was in New York they were havin' a garbage strike in the middle of the summer. Mott Street was pretty fuckin' ripe. Incomparable. I haven't been back since. What a place. The city so cold it wouldn't give God a break.
   (*He fills the glasses, hands her one.*)
**DANNY**   Here's to your deal.
**JULIA**   Yeah. Thanks.
   (*They clink glasses. Drink.*)
**DANNY**   This is what you wanted. The show business.
**JULIA**   Lucky me. I'm so lucky. We're all so lucky. Just a lot of lucky so-and-so's.
**DANNY**   Yeah. I guess we are. Comparatively.
   (*She drains her glass, puts it down.*)
**JULIA**   Still want to pull my focus?
**DANNY**   Sure. All night long.
**JULIA**   Let's go, cowboy. I'm in a mood.
   (*She walks off. Danny finishes his drink, picks up the bottle, and follows.*)

# Scene Sixteen

**Slide:** Becquia, St. Vincent. The Frangipani Hotel.

*Afternoon. The patio. Lots of breeze and tropical light. Ray is
lounging in a robe and sandals, talking to someone in the pool.*

**RAY**   What do you wanna do? We could take the boat over to St. Vincent
this afternoon. Walk around Kingstown. Go up to Round Hill. Look at
the view. Buy fresh bread from the prisoners. Speaking of bread, we
could go to the botanical gardens. Oldest botanical gardens in the
Western Hemisphere. They have the original breadfruit tree there. The
one Captain Bligh brought from Tahiti to the New World to feed the
slaves. The original Captain Bligh. No kidding. Not the original
breadfruit tree. The original breadfruit tree's daughter.
*(Max comes on, out of the pool, wrapping a robe around her.)*

**MAX**   Whatever you want.
*(She gives him a kiss. Sits next to him.)*

**MAX**   All this high life. I'm getting too old for it.

**RAY**   I love this place. The Frangipani. The flamboyant trees. The star
apples. Up on Mt. Pleasant, all those inbred white people eating
mangos. Descendants of buccaneers. And over on the other side of the
island, the mulatto whalers. Harpoons and open boats. I mean, there's
this whole color caste thing on this tiny island. Five thousand people.
Fascinating. I was talking to the Prime Minister in the bar last night at
jump up.

**MAX**   His family owns the Frangipani.

**RAY**   I know. Still. To be chatting with the Prime Minister of St. Vincent
over a couple of cuba libres. You know he takes the boat back and
forth to St. Vincent everyday? Talks to Parliament. Comes back to
Becquia in the evening, hangs out at the bar. Now that's my idea of a
country. A hundred thousand people. Size a country should be. We
could sail down to Petit St. Vincent tomorrow.

**MAX**   Sure. Why not?

**RAY**   Stay there a coupla days. Sail down to Mustique. Spend the winter
in Grenada.

**MAX**   Why not? We got time. We're retired. We're rich.
*(They kiss.)*

**MAX**   We're so lucky, aren't we?

**RAY**   We are. Lucky.
*(Pause.)*

**RAY**   You could've gone anywhere. The window was wide open.

**MAX**   I thought about it. After you left, and that guy went to look for you and never came back, there I was, sitting on the veranda of the Smudgy Cockatiel, all by myself, drinking a mai-tai, hurricane comin', thinking, oh boy oh boy, is this strange. I went upstairs, got your suitcases, took them to my sister's on the other side of the island. Waited there a few days. Snuck back to my house, which they'd totally trashed. They even dug up the yard. At that point, I didn't know what to do.

**RAY** Did you ever pop the locks?

**MAX** Never did. I really wanted to be able to say with conviction, at gunpoint if necessary, that I had no idea what was in your bags. The way you took off, and the way they trashed my house, I figured it had to be money or dope. And I honestly didn't know if you were dead or alive. So when that car pulled up in front of the house in the middle of the night, I started to wish I had crawled through that window, while I had the chance, and disappeared. I was so glad to see you get out of that car, and not some bad guy with blood in his eye. Some heavy with a hard on. Ray.

**RAY** I didn't really think you'd be there. Driving across the causeway. Over the ocean, through the Keys. Full moon. I kept thinking. She's gone. And so's the money. I never expected to see you again.

**MAX** Takes two to tango, like the song says. I like you, Ray. You've definitely captured my interest. And maybe someday you'll tell me who you really are.

**RAY** Maybe.

(*They kiss.*)

**MAX** Your wife?

**RAY** My widow.

**MAX** Saved your life.

**RAY** Hers, too. She had no choice. They would have done everyone. Had she tapped me.

**MAX** Still.

**RAY** Still. Always was cool. I thought she might lose it when she walked through the door and saw me. Took her by surprise, no question. A bad bad moment. Teetering on the brink.

**MAX** I'm not cool. I'm hot.

**RAY** Why I like you.

(*They kiss.*)

**MAX** She know you took the money?

**RAY** She'll never know. Not for certain.

(*Pause.*)

**RAY** I can't even remember who I used to be.

**MAX** Neither can I. From here on in we can make it up as we go along.

(*They kiss again.*)

**MAX** Tell me something. Ray. That guy they found in your house? The body? Your ultimate out? Did you kill him?

**RAY** No. Swear.

**MAX** I believe you.

*(Pause. Babcock enters, sits near them. They stare at one another for a moment.)*

**MAX** Oh, shit.

**BABCOCK** Coincidence. Really. This time. No kidding. You're Ray Gaines, right? Or is it Avila?

**RAY** Avila. Ray Avila.

**BABCOCK** Have it your way. And you're Max, I recall correctly. Short for Margaret.

**MAX** That's right.

**RAY** Babcock, wasn't it?

**BABCOCK** I don't remember.

*(Pause.)*

**RAY** I thought you were dead.

**BABCOCK** Look who's talking. I made a deal with the guys they sent. The goombahs. We got to shootin' the shit. Passin' the time. They were takin' me out to the Atchafalaya Basin to become part of nature's rich gumbo. Turns out I'm connected. Certain arms merchants. I had some money stashed offshore. A little somethin' for my old age. A rainy day. We made a trade. Money. Weapons. I agreed to leave the country. Change my name. Cease and desist. They agreed not to kill me. Worked out well for everyone.

*(He offers his hand.)*

**BABCOCK** Chibas. Jose Marti Chibas Valenzuela.

*(Ray stares at him.)*

**RAY** Valenzuela. Sounds Cuban.

**BABCOCK** As a matter of fact.

**RAY** We have to be going now. Don't take offense when I say I hope we never meet again.

**BABCOCK** Good luck. Watch your back. You never know what's out there, lurchin' in the dark rapture.

*(They look at each other a moment. Ray nods.)*

**RAY** No. That's right. You never do.

**BABCOCK** Thought so. Thought that was you. Lit up that ville pretty good. Whoosh.

**RAY** Quite a night.

**BABCOCK** Fuckin' A. Nothin' spookier than a night fire, huh? Makes you feel so all alone.

**RAY** Yeah.

*(Max takes Ray's arm.)*

**MAX**  Senor Chibas. Have a wonderful new life.

**BABCOCK**  You too, mi hija. You, too. Vaya con dios. Hey, Ray.
Straight ahead, and strive for tone.

**RAY**  I'll do that.

*(Ray and Max leave. Babcock leans back in his chair. Sips his drink.
Renee comes on. Gives Babcock a long kiss on the mouth.)*

**RENEE**  Jose. Mi hijo.

**BABCOCK**  Renee. Mi hija. Want a drink?

*(She sits in the chair beside him.)*

**RENEE**  Who were you talking to?

**BABCOCK**  Tourists.

**RENEE**  Popi? How long are we going to stay here? I'm bored. Can we
go to Mustique? See if Mick Jagger's hangin' out? We could call him.
He's in the book, you know. He's *listed.*

**BABCOCK**  Thought we'd leave in the morning. Go down to Grenada.
Spend some time. Look around. See what we see.

**RENEE**  Whatever you want, mi amor. Whatever you want.

*(The lights slow fade to black. The bird and sea sounds intensify.)*


### END OF PLAY